The Shadow of Unfairness

The Shadow of Unfairness

A Plebeian Theory of Liberal Democracy

JEFFREY EDWARD GREEN

OXFORD
UNIVERSITY PRESS

OXFORD

UNIVERSITY PRESS

Oxford University Press is a department of the University of Oxford. It furthers
the University's objective of excellence in research, scholarship, and education
by publishing worldwide. Oxford is a registered trade mark of Oxford University
Press in the UK and certain other countries.

Published in the United States of America by Oxford University Press
198 Madison Avenue, New York, NY 10016, United States of America.

© Oxford University Press 2016

Library of congress Cataloging-in-Publication Data
Names: Green, Jeffrey E. (Jeffrey Edward), author.
Title: The shadow of unfairness : a plebeian theory of liberal democracy / Jeffrey Edward Green.
Description: New York, NY: Oxford University Press, 2016. | Includes bibliographical references and index.
Identifiers: LCCN 2015043794 (print) | LCCN 2016005457 (ebook) |
ISBN 978–0–19–021590–3 (hardcover: alk. paper) | ISBN 978–0–19–021591–0 (E-book) |
ISBN 978–0–19–061136–1 (E-book) | ISBN 978–0–19–060067–9 (Online Component)
Subjects: LCSH: Representative government and representation. | Democracy. |
Social status—Political aspects. | Political participation—Economic aspects.
Classification: LCC JF1051.G743 2016 (print) | LCC JF1051 (ebook) | DDC 321.8—dc23
LC record available at http://lccn.loc.gov/2015043794

1 3 5 7 9 8 6 4 2
Printed by Sheridan Books, Inc., United States of America

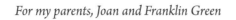

For my parents, Joan and Franklin Green

CONTENTS

PREFACE

In our time it is the mark of philosophical discourse to speak in impersonal terms, divorced from the vagaries of personal biography, and the book you hold here will obey this stricture. At the same time, where can philosophical inspiration come from if not the conditions of one's own personal life? Moreover, no one reads philosophy merely to get at the desubjectivized truth of the matter—as if philosophy were pure logic unalloyed with any trace of authorial expressivity. Rather, in encountering philosophy we expect to have our eyes opened through engagement with a singular mind and all the originality, creativity, uniqueness, and no doubt proclivity to error this implies. For some, the melding of the personal and impersonal is a reason to be suspicious of philosophy. For those drawn to philosophy, however, it is perhaps what instills philosophy with its strength and beauty. Either way, philosophizing—at present at least—involves a particular person aiming to speak and argue in an impersonal way.

One way to resolve this tension between the personal and impersonal is to believe that both poles are in fact ultimately the same. Hobbes, for instance, states in the introduction to his magisterial *Leviathan* that the underlying method of his philosophy is "*Nosce teipsum, Read thy self*" which teaches that "whosoever looketh into himself, and considereth what he doth, when he does *think, opine, reason, hope, feare, &c*, and upon what grounds; he shall thereby read and know, what are the thoughts, and Passions of all other men, upon the like occasions."[1] Emerson says something similar when he proclaims, "To believe your own thought, to believe that what is true for you in your private heart is true for all men—that is genius. Speak your latent conviction, and it shall be the universal sense; for the inmost in due time becomes the outmost."[2]

A different way to reconcile the impersonal idiom of philosophy with the particularity of the person who philosophizes is to see this particularity as residing exclusively in what today would be described as "academic research": the study of the world and the reading of books. When Machiavelli briefly discusses his biography in his prefatory letter to *The Prince*, he presents the two main personal assets he brings to his political philosophy as "a long experience with contemporary affairs [*una lunga esperienzia delle cose moderne*]" and "a continual reading of the ancients [*una continua lezione delle antique*]."[3] The preface to Machiavelli's other masterpiece, *The Discourses on Livy*, likewise points to his deep study of history as the single most important personal element informing and legitimating his authorial voice.[4]

We have, then, at least two different kinds of reading: the internal reading of oneself, on the assumption that one's inner truth will be recognized as true by others, in the manner of Hobbes; and the external reading of the world and texts, following Machiavelli. Both are ways the personal biography of the author might be brought into harmony with the impersonal pursuit of philosophical truth. The reflections I put forward in this book have been shaped by both forms of reading. But if my external reading is obvious and reveals itself on virtually every page that follows, the internal reading that also has guided this book remains hidden and, so, is something I feel compelled to confess and acknowledge in this preface.

What, then, is the content of my reading of myself? It is nothing other than my sense of being a plebeian: that is, someone who, despite living in a liberal-democratic regime espousing free and equal citizenship, knows himself to be merely an ordinary citizen with a political voice dramatically diminished compared to the powerful few who are not ordinary; someone, moreover, who at forty-two years feels his political ordinariness ossifying into a state of permanence; someone who, crucially, recognizes that the differentiation of the ordinary from the exceptional cannot be explained entirely in terms of ambition or merit, but also stems at least in part from other factors, above all wealth, that make it impossible to understand it as fully fair; and thus someone who experiences his political ordinariness not with blandness as a matter of indifference, but rather problematically as an enduring source of concern. What will come ultimately from my translation of this personal experience of being a plebeian into an impersonal philosophy of plebeianism remains to be seen, but at this moment I can at least repeat the words of Nietzsche, written in his own preface to one of his *Untimely Meditations*: "I have made an effort to describe a feeling which has tortured me often enough; I revenge myself in making it public."[5]

The venture of this book is that my own plebeianism is not particular to me or to the American and Swedish polities of which I am citizen, but is a fundamental and inescapable feature of any liberal-democratic regime. Of course, if I am right, what is universal is not the plebeian identity itself—since the very idea implies that there always will be some who escape its confines—but the Few-Many distinction as a permanent feature of political reality. Coming to grips with this distinction—insisting on its enduring presence in liberal democracy over and against willful blindness to it and, even more, trying to show how it might be enlisted for progressive ends—is the ambition of what I write here.

The Shadow of Unfairness
and the Logic of Plebeianism

There is strong shadow where there is much light.
—Goethe, *Götz von Berlichingen*

1.1 The Idea of the Shadow of Unfairness

The purpose of this book is to understand the meaning of liberal democracy and, in particular, the key moral ideal informing it: the ideal of free and equal citizenship. The book is guided by the twin goals of intellectual honesty (the desire to understand liberal democracy as it really is, with regard to both its possibilities and limits) and progressive purpose (the desire to contribute to the ongoing process, in operation at least since the rebirth of democracy at the end of the eighteenth century, whereby democratic principles and practices are continually revamped in light of ever-evolving conceptions of social justice). It is guided, moreover, by the belief that these two goals are mutually reinforcing: that, in particular, an honest account of what can and does go on in liberal democracies would only lend precision and force to a progressive spirit—and that, from the other side, one of the central roles of a progressive mindset is to provide a penetrating and sober assessment of reality.

The fundamental idea informing this book is the idea of the *shadow of unfairness*, by which I mean the inescapable sense citizens in any imaginable liberal democracy will have that its arrangements, however just, are not wholly so—or, more precisely, the sense that no matter how much the ideal of free and equal citizenship might inform the institutions and practices of a well-functioning liberal-democratic state, this ideal does not, and can never, fully describe political life in even the most advanced and enlightened liberal democracy. The shadow of unfairness does not therefore refer to gross and correctible forms of injustice such as those relating to corruption, the arbitrary infringement of civil liberties, an authoritarian overreach of executive power, or a clearly exploitative maldistribution of resources—though it is possible, and indeed likely, that better attunement to the shadow of unfairness would only lessen the toleration for these and other solvable problems. What the shadow of unfairness does refer to is the circumstance that even the most progressive, well-ordered liberal-democratic regime will not be able to satisfactorily realize a civic life that might be said to be truly free and equal in the fullest sense. To refer to the shadow of unfairness as inescapable does not mean that all citizens necessarily will feel it, but that in any conceivable liberal-democratic regime at least some significant portion will and that those who do experience it will be right in doing so.

The shadow of unfairness is most clearly perceived, by way of contrast, when juxtaposed to the long-standing liberal-democratic wish not only that liberal-democratic institutions (e.g., universal suffrage, competitive elections, political offices formally open to all, and basic rights like those of speech, assembly, thought, and religious conscience) reflect the idea of free and equal citizenship, but that—more than this—the citizens destined to live within liberal-democratic regimes might be made to *feel themselves as free and equal* in their political relations. That is to say, the prevalent view among the chief expositors of the liberal-democratic project is that citizens in liberal democracies either do already, or in the future could be made to, experience themselves as fully free and equal members of their polities, irrespective of the inequalities stemming from socioeconomic status and the possession of formal political office. For John Rawls, perhaps the most influential recent philosopher of liberal democracy, the meaning of a well-ordered liberal-democratic regime is not just that its institutions are organized on the abstract premise that citizens are free and equal, but that it actually generates and reinforces in the citizenry their sense of being free and equal members of their political community. A just liberal-democratic regime is, for Rawls, one consisting of "social institutions within which human beings may . . . become fully cooperating members of a society of free and equal citizens."[1] For the leading German political philosopher Jürgen Habermas as well, liberal democracy is conceived not just institutionally, but experientially: as the "promise of a self-organising community of free and equal citizens."[2] Likewise, with Martha Nussbaum, "the idea of the citizen as a free and dignified human being" is no mere presupposition, but the very quality of life within a just liberal-democratic order.[3] For Ronald Dworkin, too, liberal democracy is not simply the institutions that differentiate it from authoritarian and non-democratic regimes, but the capacity of these institutions to generate a feeling among the citizenry that they live in a society that "respects each individual's status as a free and equal member of the community."[4] In affirming free and equal citizenship as something citizens in a just liberal-democratic polity are actually supposed to *feel*, these preeminent liberal-democratic philosophers are only elaborating the ideology of the founding documents of the liberal-democratic experiment, which themselves include the experiential expectation that citizens in a liberal democracy might come to understand themselves to be free and equal in their civic relations.[5]

It is just this unadulterated feeling of free and equal citizenship that the shadow of unfairness deems as a false expectation of political life within any conceivable liberal-democratic regime. However admirable the principle of free and equal citizenship in its abstraction, however remarkable the achievements at the institutional level that have been realized as a result of the commitment to this principle, however much these institutions may provide ordinary citizens with *some* experiential sense of being free and equal, and however much ongoing and future reforms (such as efforts to reduce the effects of socioeconomic status on opportunities for education and political engagement) might further enhance the scope and depth of this feeling, the fact remains that no ordinary citizen in a liberal democracy, either today or in a more enlightened future, can be expected to feel fully free and equal. The structure of the liberal-democratic regime will not allow it. This is what the shadow of unfairness indicates and announces.

Now what underlies the shadow of unfairness? What prevents the full feeling of free and equal citizenship? Three elements seem most significant. First, the shadow of unfairness inheres in the fact that the logic of collective action divides liberal democracies, as well as political organizations within them, between leaders and rank-and-file and that, further, the demographic conditions of mass societies produce millions more citizens than there are positions for active political leadership. This means that ordinary citizens in even the most progressive liberal-democratic regime understand themselves as being at a distance from power, neither holding great authority *nor expecting to in the future*—a phenomenon I describe as *remove* and discuss further in Chapter 2. And it also means that ordinary citizens understand themselves as being able to influence events only insofar as they can affix themselves to a larger mass of like-minded others— a phenomenon I designate as *manyness* and also elaborate in the second chapter. If all citizens were subjected to these same constraints, their effects would be minimized at least in the sense of not disturbing the feeling of free and equal citizenship. But because these constraints are not evenly distributed, because there are always some who escape them (i.e., who are near, or hope to be near, the centers of power and whose individual judgments can directly impact the fate of their regimes in an unmediated, highly articulate fashion), both *remove* and *manyness* cannot help but generate in the ordinary citizen at least a glimmer, at least a *shadow*, of a sense of unfairness.

To be sure, in a well-functioning liberal-democratic state, those who are active leaders in politics are supposed to make decisions and enact policies that serve the underlying interests, preferences, and values of the broader, less-participatory electorate. But the shadow of unfairness also arises from a second source: the problem that the essential questions of *whether* and *to what extent* and *by what measure* liberal-democratic states actually represent their citizenries as free and equal citizens will remain impossible to determine with full confidence. We lack today, and have always lacked so far, clear metrics by which ordinary citizens might gauge how well they are being represented in the present moment or make comparative judgments about the relative representivity of any two moments in political time. The problem is not simply that the question of how to assess representation remains mired in endless debates, often of such complexity that it is impossible to expect ordinary citizens to follow them. Even more problematic is the likelihood that this seemingly interminable contentiousness was foreordained by the question itself: that representation—a polity that successfully respects the choices and needs of its citizens—is in a variety of ways an unverifiable proposition whose precise mechanics will never be satisfactorily uncovered such that there might be a wide consensus about just what they are. Insofar as we do not possess an established criterion for measuring the impact of public opinion on policy, insofar as even the most confident defenders of representation almost never affirm it as total or unambiguous, insofar as ordinary citizens lack opinions on a great many issues and thus cannot be represented in these domains, insofar as government helps form the very public opinion that would hold power accountable and responsive, and insofar as the highest echelons of leadership obviously have the discretion to disregard public opinion even when it does seem clear—for all these reasons it makes sense to acknowledge representation as something too hazy ever to be established with full confidence.[6] The point is not to deny representation in its entirety, but only the outlandish overconfidence sometimes voiced by political scientists when they make claims like, "There exists about a one-to-one translation of preferences into policy" or, "From this review of our knowledge a two-word conclusion emerges: 'Representation works.'"[7] The shadow of unfairness stems from the suspicion that representation, however difficult to refute in any absolute sense, is likewise just as impossible to unequivocally affirm. The opacity of representation means that ordinary citizens cannot see their leaders merely as public servants, but must also understand them as holders of an immense, disproportionate power beyond the scope of full accountability. And this, too, carries with it an ineradicable trace of unfairness.

Third, the shadow of unfairness results from the inescapable incursion of socioeconomic inequality into civic spaces, a phenomenon I describe as *plutocracy* and elaborate in Chapter 2. An underlying aspiration of liberal democracy is that one's socioeconomic status should not impact one's capacity as a citizen to participate in politics or one's ability as a child to develop one's faculties and then compete for opportunities and honors within a polity's social life. But as I more fully explain in the next chapter, a liberal-democratic society always will be constrained in how much it can do to achieve such ambitions, due to both the family (which ensures that the arbitrary conditions of a child's birth partially affect chances for "success" in life) and the institution of private property (which cannot help but give the wealthy on average greater opportunities for political access, influence, and participation than the less wealthy). Put in more concrete terms, the shadow of unfairness with regard to this plutocratic circumstance reminds us that in even the most progressive liberal-democratic states, similarly talented and motivated children from different socioeconomic backgrounds do *not* grow up with roughly equal prospects of career achievement—and, likewise, similarly talented and motivated citizens from different socioeconomic backgrounds do *not* enjoy roughly equal prospects of holding office and influencing elections. To be sure, there is always something that a society can do to lessen such effects— and accordingly there is a sizable difference between the educational and political systems of the more egalitarian liberal-democratic countries and the less egalitarian. But insofar as some meaningful degree of plutocracy nonetheless will always characterize the civic life of any liberal-democratic regime, even the most enlightened and advanced, here too we find another key source contributing to the shadow of unfairness.

These three elements—the differentiation within political life between a select cadre of leaders and a great many with no expectation (let alone possession) of formal political power, the profound unverifiability besetting determinations of representation, and the plutocratic incursion of socioeconomic status into the spheres of educational and political opportunity—constitute the most fundamental elements of the shadow of unfairness. To be clear, these are not necessarily the only nor the worst problems a liberal democracy might face. There are often other important sources of unfairness within any given society. But whereas more familiar and more severe problems—such as corruption, legalized discrimination against racial minorities and women, religious persecution, and destitution—are in principle solvable, the shadow of unfairness is a permanent mar on liberal-democratic regimes' capacity to fully realize the norms of free and equal citizenship. The shadow of unfairness, then, is part of the very nature of liberal democracy. It therefore ought to be integrated into the definitional understanding of liberal democracy, not just in the name of honesty and truth, but also because—as this book aims to establish—confronting the shadow of unfairness can refine and embolden the progressive spirit already at work within our liberal democracies, rather than quell or quench it.

But the dominant trend in the political culture clearly is to remain blind to the shadow of unfairness. Instead of acknowledging the inherent limits of the liberal-democratic project, much more prevalent are those perspectives espousing a basic *sunniness* regarding the ultimate perfection or perfectibility of the liberal-democratic regime. Such sunniness can be seen, for example, whenever it is suggested—however impossibly—that the world's most advanced liberal-democratic states have achieved the full realization of the liberal-democratic idea.[8] It can be seen, furthermore, whenever it is imagined that liberal democracies *have no nature*—that is, no limiting set of parameters—because their institutions enable an ongoing and permanent process of experimentation, redefinition, and improvement regarding the realization of free and equal civic relations.[9] Most commonly, however, it is found in the expectation that the obstacles to free and equal citizenship are in principle fully surmountable. Most philosophers of the liberal-democratic project, for instance, are well aware that no historical or extant regime has adequately prevented the arbitrary effects of socioeconomic status from interfering with equality of opportunity in the educational and political realms. They would not deny the findings of cross-national studies that have concluded that "the political advantage of those citizens more advantaged in socioeconomic terms is found in all nations"— or that "no democratic nation lives up to the ideal of participatory equality."[10] But rather than confront this plutocratic circumstance as an inevitable problem that will shadow even the most progressive liberal-democratic regime, the posture of leading liberal-democratic thinkers is to imagine that well-chosen future reforms in election law and education can make it so that socioeconomic status will not unfairly impact one's capacity as a citizen to participate in politics or one's ability as a child to develop one's faculties and compete for opportunities in a polity's civil society. Rawls is but the paradigmatic instance of a much broader trend (which I analyze in greater detail in Chapter 2), when he upholds, as a legitimate expectation of a future, properly ordered liberal-democratic state, that "all citizens, whatever their economic or social position, must be sufficiently equal in the sense that all have a fair opportunity to hold public office and to affect the outcome of elections"—or when he likewise imagines a liberal-democratic regime that will have a plutocracy-free educational system: "Those who have the same level of talent and ability and the same willingness to use these gifts should have the same prospects of success regardless of their social class of origin, the class into which they are born and develop until the age of reason. In all parts of society there are to be roughly the same prospects of culture and achievement for those similarly endowed."[11] The sunniness of the philosophers in this respect only mirrors the sunniness of the founding proclamations of the liberal-democratic idea, in which one likewise finds statements regarding the ultimate perfectibility of equal civic opportunity. The Declaration of the Rights of Man and the Citizen (1789), for instance, asserts, "All citizens, being equal in the eyes of the law, are equally eligible to all dignities and to all public positions and occupations, according to their abilities, and without distinction except that of their virtues and talents" (Article 6). More recently, the United Nations Universal Declaration of Human Rights (1948) upholds the promise of an educational system based entirely on merit (Article 26: "Technical and professional education shall be made generally available and higher education shall be equally accessible to all on the basis of merit") and a political system in which "everyone has the right of equal access to public service in his country" (Article 21).

Without wishing to interfere with the progressivism sustained by this pervasive sunniness, the polemical premise guiding this book and its central notion of the *shadow of unfairness* is that such sunniness nonetheless is excessive and objectionable on numerous grounds. It *blinds* us to the real nature of the liberal-democratic regime, which as such must involve limits and not just indefinite future possibilities for revision. It *evaporates* all progressive energies not focused on the asymptotic desire to approximate conditions of free and equal citizenship, *desiccating* any effort to make the future understanding and pursuit of democracy different from that of the present. And, as I discuss in Chapter 4, in its false suggestion that the life of the ordinary democratic citizen might somehow go on in the *eternal daytime of good conscience*, it fails to consider that in politics, as in any celestial body, there is no light without dark, no day without night: that ordinary citizens, like the Machiavellian Prince, will need to "learn how not to be good" (or, as I describe it, engage in various forms of *principled vulgarity*) if they are to effectively pursue a better liberal-democratic future in a world that will never fully respect them as free and equal citizens. Against these threats of a hyperbolic sunniness in democratic theory, the shadow of unfairness offers some hope of protection. It shades the glare of unreal expectations, disclosing more clearly the true features of ordinary citizenship in any conceivable liberal-democratic regime. If its dogged focus on inescapable unfairness admittedly darkens the sky of democratic theory, it is but a partial darkening which, like an enveloping atmosphere, enables the growth and development of new ideas in democratic thought: above all, the idea that the purpose of liberal-democratic progressivism is not only to make the future more free and equal in its civic relations, but to acknowledge and address the unfairness that always will have been part of any specific moment in a liberal democracy's development. And in insisting that ordinary citizens living beneath the shadow of unfairness must themselves become darker in order to operate effectively within its constraints, the shadow of unfairness helps extend the tradition of political modernism—the tradition which understands the tragic truth that political ethics is an autonomous sphere irreducible to ethics as such—to the purview of ordinary citizens. In all of these respects, the shadow of unfairness in no way means to call into question liberal democracy's status as a uniquely moral form of political regime, whose development and improvement is perhaps synonymous with the pursuit of justice itself. Like any shadow, the shadow of unfairness is itself produced only in relation to light—which in this case means simply that the shadow of unfairness is not at all a rejection of idealism in liberal-democratic theory, but simply a call to pursue ideals from a perspective of greater honesty and perspicacity regarding the actual nature of the liberal-democratic project.

1.2 Theorizing Beneath the Shadow of Unfairness: The Idea of Plebeianism

The challenge to political philosophy posed by the idea of the shadow of unfairness is to conceptualize liberal democracy in a way that understands that liberal democracy's status as the best regime in history, even if true, does not make it pure, perfect, or perfectible. It is the challenge to theorize the meaning of liberal democracy in a way that respects the fact that even if ordinary citizens fated to live within liberal-democratic polities have more political liberties than inhabitants of other states, this does not mean that they are thereby fully free and equal vis-à-vis fellow citizens more advantaged with regard to wealth, renown, and possession of official political power. It is the challenge, furthermore, to recognize that the genuinely superior moral aspirations of the liberal-democratic project do not preclude ordinary citizens committed to pursuing this project from sometimes having to transact in ethically ambiguous though politically necessary transgressions of established norms of civility. In other words, the challenge posed by the shadow of unfairness is the challenge not to let the real achievements of the liberal-democratic regime lead to an unreal assessment of its nature, nor allow a legitimate attachment to the principles of free and equal citizenship to hinder an ever deeper understanding of how to bring these principles to bear upon a political world that will always to some degree elude them. To go further in the development of liberal democracy we must go backward—in the sense of beginning to acknowledge permanent limits to the idea itself. If Tocqueville in the early nineteenth century, inspired by the high idealism surrounding the birth of the liberal-democratic project, called for "a new political science for a world wholly new," the shadow of unfairness, whose permanent cast has only become more apparent in the two centuries since Tocqueville, suggests the need, rather, for "a new political science for a world only partially new"—a world that has been and will continue to be transformed and rendered more just by the rigorous demands of free and equal citizenship, but that cannot— and will never—entirely escape the feudal past in which lineage and wealth make their impact felt on civic relations.

It is with these challenges in mind that this book makes its central claim: that *liberal democracy is best conceived as plebeian democracy*—or, that plebeianism, an idea almost unprecedented in political thought, has the potential to specify both the limits and possibilities of the liberal-democratic regime in a manner superior to the more familiar accounts of liberal democracy centered on the expectation of the ultimate *full realization* and *pure experience* of free and equal civic relations.[12] In making the case for a plebeian theory of liberal democracy, the book defends four overarching ideas.

First, plebeianism insists on the disappointing but true circumstance that within liberal democracy *ordinary citizenship is second-class citizenship*. That is to say, over and against the idea that individuals in contemporary liberal democracies simply are free and equal citizens, plebeianism asserts, as a descriptive matter, that in fact there are numerous second-class, or plebeian, aspects to the structure of ordinary political life—above all the structures that I have already mentioned and will detail in greater depth in Chapter 2: *remove, manyness*, and *plutocracy*. These structures, and their permanence, comprise the main elements of the shadow of unfairness and are key reasons why the expectation that citizens in a well-ordered liberal-democratic regime might understand themselves to be fully free and equal is misguided. However empowered and respected ordinary citizens might feel in a just liberal-democratic state, they will also, understandably and inescapably, feel at least a modicum of *indignation* at the second-class, plebeian features of their political existence.

Plebeianism's second main idea relates to its proposals for how liberal democracy might be improved within a context where the shadow of unfairness is recognized as permanent. This is the idea of *reasonable envy* against the most advantaged members of society, in particular the superrich.[13] In contrast with the widespread reluctance in contemporary liberal-democratic theory and practice to identify, let alone uniquely burden, the superrich, reasonable envy is the notion that there are good liberal-democratic reasons for singling out the economically most advantaged citizens for special regulatory treatment—and that, furthermore, there are some circumstances in which such burdening is appropriate even if it has negative or neutral material impact on the rest of society. As Chapter 3 more fully explains, there are at least three grounds for a liberal-democratic society to devote special regulatory attention to its richest citizens: a *heuristic* interest in making use of the expectations of the superrich to help clarify complex and contested judgments about whether a system of inequalities is in fact mutually advantageous and consistent with agreed-upon principles of distributive justice; a *protective* interest in guarding against threats to civic liberty posed by the superrich; and a *redressive* interest in imposing public burdens on the most advantaged class—the class that has benefitted the most within a society that is not fully fair—which might serve to acknowledge and in small part remediate the shadow of unfairness itself. Together, these three bases for regulating the most advantaged class ought to make it clear that even though it calls for the reintroduction of the Few-Many distinction, plebeianism in no way condones oligarchy. What separates a plebeian republic from a merely oligarchic one is that with plebeianism the differentiation between the Few and the Many is meant to problematize, regulate, and contest—and not simply instantiate—the superior power of the superrich.

The third main component of plebeianism reflects the fact that what the shadow of unfairness darkens is not simply the full moral integrity of the liberal-democratic polity, but also to a certain extent the full moral integrity of ordinary citizens committed to seeking progressive plebeian goals within such a regime. That is, over and against the familiar aspiration that citizens in a well-ordered liberal-democratic society might operate entirely on the basis of an ethics of civility—that is, an ethics suitable to how free and equal citizens would address each other in deliberating together about what laws and policies best realize the common good—plebeianism stands for the idea that everyday citizens devoted to furthering the project of liberal democracy must also engage in what I refer to as *principled vulgarity*. Such vulgarity takes numerous forms which I analyze in Chapter 4, including the vulgarity of *classism* (insisting on the Few-Many distinction), *arbitrariness* (the impossibility of defining the cutoff between the Few and the Many in a wholly convincing manner), *non-deliberative discourse* (the disruptive or not fully articulate forms of communication that characterize ordinary citizens' efforts to be heard before powerholders), and some element of *rancor* (the indignation, ingratitude, and elements of envy that inform plebeian political psychology beneath the shadow of unfairness). I call these vulgar because, in violating norms of civility, they are bases on which advocates of plebeian reforms will be made to feel guilty by espousers of more traditional conceptions of liberal democracy. Yet I also call them principled because, as this book aims to make clear, they are nonetheless justifiable on liberal-democratic grounds and, indeed, essential to the pursuit of a more progressive liberal-democratic regime beneath the shadow of unfairness. Learning to endure the plebeian bad conscience—that is, to accept that the commitment to plebeian goals cannot be altogether exalted or guiltless, but will involve morally ambiguous undertakings—is an essential task for a plebeian theory of liberal democracy and a key part of what political maturity entails from the plebeian point of view. The idea of principled vulgarity also promises to democratize a perspective hitherto restricted to elite powerholders. After all, the concept of politically necessary yet morally ambiguous action is not unfamiliar within the history of political thought, but those who have embraced it so far have tended to apply it to the ethical purview of political leaders who, in the considered opinion of certain political philosophers like Machiavelli, need to be able in certain circumstances to deceive, steal, and kill in order to properly execute their responsibilities to the state. Plebeianism, with its concept of principled vulgarity, aims to appropriate the spirit, though not the letter, of this Machiavellian teaching for popular ends, delineating what transgressive behaviors might be required by ordinary, second-class citizens should they take up the position of engaged advocates for plebeian aims and policies.

The fourth aspect of a plebeian theory of liberal democracy follows from a problem generated by the first three: that politics is unlikely to be a source of happiness for the ordinary, second-class citizen, but rather will involve stresses and strains stemming from a civic life darkened by the shadow of unfairness. The understanding of oneself as a second-class citizen, the recognition that socioeconomic inequality will forever infect civic relations, and the various forms of vulgarity required by plebeian political advocacy—all make political life a source of discontent for the plebeian. This circumstance points to a psychopolitical need that has been surprisingly unaddressed within the study of democracy: the need for ordinary, second-class citizens to find *solace* in the face of the shadow of unfairness, *not* so as to finally relinquish their political energies and commitments, but only to prevent the discontent likely to characterize their political lives from extending beyond politics and unduly undermining their overall capacity for well-being and peace of mind. One can imagine, of course, various ways of finding solace in a context of political disappointment and this book does not claim to provide an all-encompassing solution to the problem. But in addition to raising the need for solace itself, the theory of plebeian democracy I defend rehabilitates an appreciation, common among ancient philosophers of egalitarianism, for how egalitarian ideas and practices might actually contribute to the periodic transcendence of political concerns and, in so doing, provide a uniquely democratic kind of solace in the face of political frustrations. This dynamic whereby egalitarianism does not motivate, as it usually does, political concerns and projects—but, on the contrary, inspires behaviors beyond the confines of law, governance, and civic life—is what I describe in Chapter 5 as *extrapoliticism*. The idea of extrapoliticism may strike the reader as strange. Yet, as I aim to establish, extrapoliticism is both as old as democratic thought itself and, regardless of its provenance, compelling in its logic. Numerous egalitarian commitments have a double potential, functioning as a grounds for democratic government and as an extrapolitical vehicle for transcending the political as such. The belief in human equality, for example, most commonly drives efforts to democratize institutions, but if one thought that all human lives were equally desirable—the beggar and the billionaire, the outcast and the president—one would be unable to operate politically because basic political notions like benefit and harm, or justice and injustice, would lose their meaning. Drawing on ancient theorists of egalitarianism attuned to its extrapolitical potential, the argument in Chapter 5 shows how numerous other egalitarian commitments—including free speech, solidarity, and self-sufficiency—are susceptible to a similar double function-ing. Because egalitarianism can inspire both political action and the transcen-dence of the political, democratic theory has resources for exploring both how liberal-democratic regimes might be progressively reformed and how politi-cally marginalized citizens fated to live within them might attain a uniquely egalitarian form of solace in the face of their polities' inevitable shortcomings. Combining an abiding concern with public affairs with a solace borne from the temporary transcendence of the political requires a delicate balance, but plebeianism insists that such a task is possible (since both elements stem from an underlying egalitarianism) as well as desirable (since the plebeian is after all faced with a double desire: to improve and to cope with a politics always darkened by the shadow of unfairness).

These four elements of plebeianism—a second-class *identity*, an *ideal* of regu-lating the most advantaged, an *ethics* of vulgar political discursivity, and a psy-chopolitical *need* for solace—define what is at stake in the book's main claim that *liberal democracy is best conceived and pursued as plebeian democracy*: a project which aims not to undermine liberal democracy, or the central ideal of free and equal citizenship upon which it rests, but only to clarify the limits of these com-mitments and to show how an understanding of such limits might further, rather than detract from, what can be achieved.

The four chapters that follow take up each of these elements, respectively. In advance of that discussion, what remains in this chapter is to further clarify the meaning of a plebeian theory of democracy by illuminating four of its over-arching features: its commitment to developing, not abandoning, the liberal-democratic regime (1.3); its reliance on the plebeians of ancient Rome as an instructive analogue for ordinary, second-class citizens today (1.4); the sense in which it might be considered a contribution to democratic realism (1.5); and its incorporation of my earlier work in democratic theory, *The Eyes of the People* (1.6).

1.3 Why Plebeianism Aims to Develop,
not Abandon, Liberal Democracy

It will be asked why it is appropriate to continue to work within a liberal-dem-ocratic paradigm in the face of the shadow of unfairness. If liberal democracy will always be darkened by some element of unfairness, is this not reason to jettison it in favor of more radical alternatives? This challenge is important because it is a reminder that as much as this book will be resisted by an anti-progressive unwillingness to find the shadow of unfairness a real and permanent mar on liberal democracy, it also will be criticized by those committed to a more fundamental transformation of the liberal-democratic regime and, perhaps, the institutions of private property and the family upon which this regime rests.

In defending a concept of plebeianism intended to develop, rather than abandon, liberal democracy, I am encouraged, first of all, by the dominance of this form of polity in the world today. Not only have liberal democracies spread across a good deal of the globe over the last two centuries, but they are widely seen as being morally superior relative to all other extant forms of government. The logic of plebeianism is to consider how an already embraced political regime might be led to make its ideas and institutions even more just.

Such an approach would not be possible, of course, if liberal democracy were a static entity. But one of the remarkable features of the liberal-democratic project has been its capacity for internal critique and ongoing progressive development. Most notably, norms of inclusion with regard to gender, race, and class have been dramatically expanded since the emergence of liberal democracy at the beginning of the nineteenth century. This record of continual evolution ought to give political thinkers and activists confidence that the liberal-democratic ideal of free and equal citizenship is a potent vehicle for future political change. Plebeianism is precisely an attempt to rely on this ideal to disclose problems (the shadow of unfairness) and partial solutions (the identification and regulation of the most advantaged class) hitherto mostly absent from the theory and practice of liberal democracy.

Skepticism regarding both the desirability and possibility of more radical alternatives purporting to cancel the shadow of unfairness is another motivation for my decision to work within a liberal-democratic paradigm. Do radicals really want to get rid of private property and the family? If not, then some degree of the distortion these bring to civic equality—and, with it, the shadow of unfairness—will continue to operate within any post–liberal-democratic society. And if radicals were to favor the abolition of the family and private property, the revolutionary society they created would still likely contain a political hierarchy—with a ruling elite making not-fully-persuasive claims to representation—again suggesting, albeit in a different way, that the shadow of unfairness darkening contemporary liberal democracy would continue to darken more radical politics as well.[14]

Beyond concerns about the capacity of radical schemes to cancel the shadow of unfairness, there is also the problem that too often radicalism remains much less clear about the new society it would inaugurate than the evils of the old society it would abolish. This issue is perhaps especially relevant today, when even those sympathetic to the radical left lament the difficulty of formulating compelling alternatives to market-based, liberal-democratic regimes[15]—an aphasia reflected in the fact that one of the most important instances of radical leftism in the twenty-first century, the Occupy Movement of 2011–2012, was notoriously reticent about its programmatic agenda. If a usual response to this problem is the abstract call to reject "false necessity" and restore faith in new and untried possibilities as such, it seems another, more concrete, no less worthy alternative would be to deploy a revitalized political imagination toward advancing a liberal-democratic tradition that already has some track record of emancipatory change.[16]

Finally, it is hardly obvious that plebeianism, because it aims to extend a well-entrenched paradigm, is necessarily less committed to fundamental change than schemes that would scrap the political system wholesale. The plebeian insistence that no wealthy or powerful person can understand his or her advantages as fully legitimate—and that the most advantaged need to be identified and regulated as a class—represents a significant intensification of liberal-democratic progressivism. Moreover, the radicalness of political ideas should not be judged independently from their likelihood of being implemented. Because plebeianism rests on prevailing liberal-democratic norms of free and equal citizenship, because it focuses on the incremental extension of liberal democracy to include the regulation of the most advantaged class, it has potentially wider appeal than philosophies outside the liberal-democratic fold. At the same time, accepting the fundamental notion animating plebeianism—the constitutive unfairness of liberal-democratic regimes—has the capacity to powerfully alter the practice of liberal democracy, not only by introducing a new dimension to democratization (the imposition of regulatory burdens on the most powerful, i.e., those who have prospered the most within conditions that are not fully fair), but by reinvigorating too-often-dormant efforts to do what can be done to make liberal democracies relatively more fair (through, for example, reducing the plutocratic elements of their educational and political systems). For these reasons, radicals who wish to go further should ask themselves whether plebeian ideas and ambitions are nonetheless a path they would still need to traverse on the way to attempting something more transformative.

My purpose, however, is not to discredit more aggressive efforts to reform political society, but only to defend the viability of a plebeian philosophy aimed at seeking solutions through the further development of liberal-democratic ideas and practices. The polemical target of plebeianism is not political radicalism but the hyperbolic sunniness that denies the shadow of unfairness, conceives of liberal democracy as a perfect or perfectible regime, and thereby prevents an honest and progressive development of liberal-democratic ideas and practices. Still, because the notion of the shadow of unfairness might suggest a fundamental delegitimation of liberal democracy, it is important to clarify the logic for persisting within a liberal-democratic framework.

1.4 Why Analogize with the Roman Plebs?

Plebeianism is not a widely used notion in political philosophy. It is more a neologism than a retrieved idea from a forgotten past. Why, then, employ it as the master-concept to summarize the overall significance of the book's main claims?

On the *connotative level*, the notion of plebeianism is useful because it suggests an uncomfortable, ambiguous ethical mood: like words such as "common," "mean," "average," or "base," *plebeian* indicates something that is popular but still somehow unappealing. Such a connotation coheres well with the central ambition of this book, which is to compel those committed to the project of liberal democracy to recognize that they will always have to wrestle with the uneasy fact of an inevitable shadow of unfairness darkening even the most advanced liberal-democratic states.[17]

A further reason for my use of the concept of plebeianism is that, on the *socioeconomic level*, it suggests a class-based differentiation between the Few (who are not plebeians) and the Many (who are)—and it is a core feature of my argument to say that democratic theory would benefit from the reintroduction of the Few-Many distinction vis-à-vis the prevailing *ideology of undifferentiated free and equal citizenship* as the right way to make sense of civic relations in a liberal-democratic polity.

But perhaps most important, on the *historical level*, I rely on the master-concept plebeianism to summarize the main elements of the theory I defend because these elements were all more or less reflected in the institutions and practices that informed the life of the *plebeians* in the late Roman Republic, especially in the century prior to its end around 44 BCE.[18] That is to say, each of the four aspects of plebeianism I introduced in Section 1.2 find some analogue in the plebeian republic of ancient Rome. First of all, as a form of civic identity, *plebeian* in late republican Rome designated a form of citizenship that was at once ordinary and yet second class. Plebeians were distinguished from first-class citizens (i.e., the Senatorial and Equestrian classes) who alone possessed the right to hold high office (the so-called *ius honorum*), whose votes were counted more in legislative assemblies, and who usually possessed great wealth. Although plebeians could vote and enjoyed civil equality (in the sense that their persons and property were protected on the same terms as all other citizens), they necessarily understood themselves as second-class citizens whose political lives did not afford the same opportunities for empowerment as those of the elite first-class citizens.[19] In many respects, then, Roman plebeians had their political experience constrained by conditions of remove, manyness, and plutocracy. Second, Rome's plebeian brand of republicanism implies ideals of political progressivism distinct from any simple oligarchy because the differentiation of civic classes did not merely serve the aggrandizement of the elites, but involved various institutions that imposed special economic and political *burdens* upon them: the *contio*, where political leaders sometimes had to appear in public under conditions they did not control, contested by rivals and a hostile crowd; the *tribunes of the plebs*, who, elected by the plebeians, could bring charges against powerful Romans, employ their right of veto (*intercessio*) to interfere with the designs of high magistrates, and also provide a jurisdiction in which ordinary citizens might appeal any alleged mistreatment at the hands of state officials (*provocatio*); and, perhaps most important, *euergetistic social norms*, according to which wealthy Romans, especially those with political ambition, were expected personally to fund numerous activities, including festivities, the construction of public monuments, and even at times the costs of the magistracies they held.[20] In other words, the most advantaged in Rome were not just elevated, but regulated and constrained, by differentiated citizenship. Third, with respect to civic ethics, many have attributed to the Roman plebs a form of political expressivity unconfined to prevailing contemporary norms of civil discourse. Specifically, due both to the lack of genuine contexts for deliberative discourse (i.e., the *mass* structure of plebeian power) and to the class consciousness of the plebs (their acute and ongoing suspicion of non-plebeian elites), the plebeians were led to numerous vulgar practices and attitudes: for example, the disruption of reasoned debate, a persistent challenging of the sanctity of private property, general indignation, and a desire to punish the most advantaged in ways sometimes disproportionate to their actual guilt.[21] And fourth, with regard to the psychopolitical need for solace, the Roman plebeians' attraction to Epicureanism—a philosophy which, among other potential functions, enabled the temporary transcendence of political cares through sublimating egalitarian ideas and practices in a nonpolitical direction—is a suggestion, which I pursue in Chapter 5, that at least some Roman plebeians recognized the importance of combining an abiding commitment to politics with the solace borne from periodically adopting an extrapolitical mentality.[22]

That the historical situation of the plebs of the late Roman Republic mirrors in certain respects my own contemporary, liberal-democratic rendering of plebeianism to refer to a second-class civic identity, a project of regulating the most advantaged, an ethics of principled vulgarity, and a need for solace ought not be seen as merely incidental to my argument or simply as a curiosity. Rather, throughout the chapters that follow I repeatedly rely on the Roman plebs as an *historical analogue* that helps to illuminate with greater precision the meaning plebeianism might have today. To be sure, plebeianism is intended first and foremost as a present-oriented approach to liberal democracy, not as a defense of ancient Roman republicanism which, even at its most progressive, did not attain the level of free and equal citizenship achieved by present-day regimes committed to universal suffrage, the idea of universal human dignity, gender equality, the absolute ban on slavery, the formal rejection of hereditary power, and social welfare policies securing basic well-being and opportunity to all citizens regardless of their socioeconomic condition. Clearly, then, I do not at all mean to say that contemporary citizenship, in both its possibilities and limitations, is exactly like that of the Roman plebs, since there are crucial differences. But if this is the case, why invoke the analogy at all? Why not defend my understanding of present-day ordinary citizenship in its own, unmediated terms without appeal to ancient politics?

Beyond the humanistic desire to make past ideas and practices relevant to the present, and beyond the aesthetic desire to lend a certain unity to disparate reflections—since it is after all a primary purpose of philosophy to comprehend phenomena with an eye toward the whole, or at least to provide an integrative account rather than a disaggregated collection of discrete facts[23]—it seems that analogical reasoning is especially important to the study of democracy, particularly as it pertains to the lived experience of ordinary citizens. I submit we are always analogizing with regard to citizenship and politics: the vastness, complexity, and multiplicity of institutions and practices that comprise political life require for their intelligibility simplifying metaphorical constructs. For example, much depends on whether the state is likened to a human body (as among medieval writers invoking the idea of the *body politic* such as John of Salisbury and Christine de Pizan), to a family (Filmer), to a church (as in medieval and early modern Caesaropapism), to a group of friends allied against some external enemy (Schmitt), or to a system of voluntary cooperation for material advantage (Rawls)—even though it is rarely only a literal designation that is at stake.[24] Within the specific realm of citizenship the relevance of analogy is clear, as the very word for citizen as the term arose in the West—*polites* or *civis*—has direct etymological connection to the word for *polis* or *city*. Accordingly, *civitas* means simultaneously the abstract idea or condition of being a citizen (i.e., citizenship) and the concrete collection of citizens in a state—in particular, initially at least, in a *city*.[25] This etymology is important because it suggests how our notion of citizenship is already caught up in an iconography of local, small-scale, face-to-face exchanges where deliberative, inclusionary, and relatively egalitarian modes of decision-making are enabled. The prevalence of this implicit likening of citizenship to the kind of activities practiced in comparatively intimate groupings like parliaments, town meetings, and public squares can be found in the frequency with which citizenship is imagined as citizens collectively enacting laws in a legislative assembly,[26] in the tendency for parliamentarians to understand themselves as the most popular branch of government if not the People themselves, and in the degree to which the suffrage is invested with extra-electoral, legislative significance.[27] Further, it is not just the etymology of the term *citizenship* but the highly moralized connotations surrounding the idea that indicate the notion's implicit reference to an idealized understanding of politics centered on pure relations of freedom and equality. Pocock, for example, recognizes that the word *citizenship* is more than a descriptive term but already an enunciation of an ideal: "There is not merely a 'classical' ideal of citizenship articulating what citizenship is; 'citizenship' is itself a 'classical ideal,' one of the fundamental values that we claim is inherent in our 'civilization' and its 'tradition.' "[28] To the extent this is so, the mere use of the word *citizen* to characterize an individual's political status is itself a metaphor for the underlying moral integrity of the polity that individual inhabits.

Insofar as our language about citizenship is already metaphorical, the question that should be asked is *which* analogy ought to be drawn. Against the prevalent democratic imaginary—which likens mass democracies to cities, the life of the citizen to the task of legislation, and both to a perfected account of what politics ideally should be, so that the most immediate connotation of citizenship is still the idealized Aristotelian notion of "holding office and giving judgments"[29]— plebeianism relies on the addended, chastened term *"plebeian* citizenship" so as not to forget the mass dimension of political life, the detachment of ordinary citizens from the most concentrated centers of power and decision-making, and the inevitable intrusion of socioeconomic inequality into political and educational institutions.

But even if I am right that our understanding of citizenship already relies heavily and inescapably on implicit analogies, the further question should be asked: why *this* analogy with the Roman plebs and not some other? If the point is to stress the less-than-ideal account of contemporary civic life, why not liken the ordinary citizen (or the conception of citizens in their collective capacity) to the pre-liberation status of women (as Aristotle did[30]), or to a child (as Locke suggested[31]), or to an oracle (something which must be consulted and to a certain extent obeyed, but lacks firm control and is subject to manipulation), or to a foreigner (e.g., the metic in ancient Athens)? Without dismissing the potential value of these alternate constructs, I think the analogy to the Roman plebeians is most apt. Plebeian is already a conception of citizenship. It departs in only a limited and precise way from the reigning idea of undifferentiated free and equal citizenship: at Rome, the second-class status of plebeians inhered in the fact that whereas they enjoyed civil equality (the full protection of their persons and property before the law), their political rights made them second class (they could not run for high office and their votes were counted less than those of the more advantaged citizens in the Equestrian and Senatorial orders). Thus, while other constructs analogize with respect to figures beyond politics, plebeianism relies on a thoroughly political metaphor to model a kind of citizenship that is simultaneously robust but second class.

But still, even if we are always analogizing in our understanding of citizenship and even if the plebeian analogy is appropriate relative to other possibilities, why not let the analogy only inspire but not directly inform a theory of contemporary liberal democracy? Why not let the figure of the Roman plebs play only a background role, instead of drawing out the comparison through repeated invocation of ancient Roman politics? One advantage of explicit analogizing with the past is that it offers an alternative form of normative theorizing that may overcome some of the challenges associated with more common modes of humanistic political analysis, whether analytic or historical. Specifically, analogical reasoning can maneuver between the abstraction of purely analytic modes of thought (which sometimes are accused of being too decontextualized to be rendered practicable) and the mere empiricism of purely historical modes of investigation that, in their factual concreteness, lack an obvious normative dimension (and, thus, sometimes are accused of being without relevance to the concerns of the present). Unlike strictly analytic theory, an analogic approach such as the one I pursue here can defend its ideals—in this case, the ideal of identifying and regulating the most advantaged class—not just by showing that they *should* be realized (that they accord with certain principles and commitments we ought to have), but that they *have been realized* (that other times and places have managed to achieve them to some meaningfully greater degree than our own).[32] And unlike strictly historical approaches, the analogical normative theorizing I employ, though guided by the highest standards of fidelity to fact, makes no claim for a comprehensive understanding of the historical time and place it invokes. Rather its engagement with the past is unabashedly shaped by the problems facing the present. While such an approach might frustrate the historian's insistence on avoiding anachronism, it also has the benefit of vivifying the past by making it something not just to know but to use—something that might be the possession not merely of historians and other experts but the broader citizenry more generally.[33]

For these reasons, then, this book explicitly and continually insists upon the similitude of citizenship in contemporary liberal-democratic states to the situation of the Roman plebs. In doing this it is guided by the idea, well expressed by de Baecque, that "to choose the right metaphors, describe them, clarify the tale, is to propose an interpretation of history, a way of thinking, a way of knowing."[34] And in its desire to have this similitude impact the future practice of liberal democracy, the book is close to the perspective of Rancière when he writes that "politics occurs wherever a community with the capacity to argue and make metaphors is likely . . . to crop up."[35] And yet it would be a profound misunderstanding of the purpose of this book were it to be conceived only as an analogy—only as an effort to show certain resemblances between the structures, possibilities, and limitations informing ordinary citizenship in late republican

Rome and those informing present-day liberal democracies. The central arguments I defend—that ordinary citizenship today is experienced in relation to specific second-class structures (remove, manyness, and plutocracy), that the pursuit of free and equal citizenship would be better realized if joined with a newfound willingness of liberal-democratic societies to identify and regulate the most advantaged as a class, that ordinary citizens attentive to the limitations and possibilities of contemporary liberal democracy will need to engage in various vulgar modes of political discursivity, and that politics so conceived generates a hitherto neglected need for solace—are not "like" or "similar to" what I take to be the foundation of a progressive concern for the future of liberal democracy, but rather precisely *are* this foundation. That I rely on analogy ought not reduce my project to an exercise in analogy. The ultimate purpose of analogical normative theorizing, at least as I practice it here, is to serve the larger goal of illuminating the reality of our political situation in the here and now.

1.5 Plebeianism as Democratic Realism

In making the overarching claim that *liberal democracy is best understood and pursued as plebeian democracy,* this book operates on numerous levels. It emphasizes the second-class aspects of ordinary citizenship in contemporary liberal democracy. It justifies the progressive project of regulating the most advantaged class. It recognizes that a morally ambiguous ethics of principled vulgarity sometimes will inform ordinary citizens' political advocacy for plebeian ends. And it addresses the issue of how everyday citizens are supposed to cope with their likely political discontent. The rest of the book explains these claims in greater detail, but here at the outset it is worthwhile to reflect on an underlying value that informs all of them and that makes it so their pursuit can be conceived as a single, unified project rather than an amalgamation of discrete ends: this is the value of *reality*. The premise of plebeianism is that prevailing accounts of liberal democracy today suffer from *unreality* insofar as they take the ordinary citizen to be (or potentially become) fully free and equal vis-à-vis citizens with significantly greater amounts of wealth, fame, and political influence; insofar as they assume progressive liberal-democratic reform might dispense with a notion of the most favored class; and insofar as they suppose ordinary civic life in a so-called well-ordered liberal-democratic state might be free of moral dilemmas and other psychological challenges. Overcoming these various forms of unrealism is a chief value of a plebeian contribution to the study and practice of liberal democracy.

But in invoking reality as an orienting norm of this project, I clearly do not mean to appeal to the normal rendering of democratic realism as an approach to democracy opposed to idealism, since plebeianism is fundamentally an effort to reform liberal democracy in light of the moral ideal of free and equal citizenship (and in "light" of the shadow of unfairness cast by the very commitment to this ideal). This means that plebeianism must be sharply differentiated from more familiar forms of democratic realism which do in fact stand for the attenuation of moral idealism in democracy, such as descriptivism (the pursuit of a theoretical understanding of democracy based not on moral considerations, but only factual features defining states that call themselves democracies);[36] minimalism (not just the thinning down of the moral meaning of democracy in the face of the impossibility or undesirability of more robust moral notions, but the interpretation of democracy in terms of principles and practices that, because they are only definitive of a basic threshold, do not lend themselves to future progressivism);[37] or other forms of objection to excessive moralism in politics as being ineffectual or dangerous.[38] When Connolly calls Schumpeter "a 'father' of American realist theories of democracy"—and when Posner, building off of Schumpeter, describes his own recent contribution to democratic theory in terms of "realism"—we find examples of democratic realism in these usual, anti-idealistic forms.[39]

This conventional understanding of democratic realism will strike many as limited and misguided, above all for its tendency toward complacency.[40] But this conception of realism as the opposite of idealism is not the only way to understand realism, nor is it the kind of realism informing the plebeian theory I defend in this book. There is an alternate tradition of realism for which realism stands opposed not to idealism per se, but to *illusion*.[41] It is something like this kind of realism that informs T. S. Eliot when he pronounces, "Human kind cannot bear very much reality" and, more recently, Lacanian-inspired political theorists when they write about the difficulty of a society coming to terms with the Real.[42] Framed in the language of democratic theory, this alternate conception of realism aims to combat three kinds of illusions: the illusion of a false ideal, the illusion due to inattention to implementation, and the illusion of perfection.

First, there is the illusion of a false ideal (rather than idealism as such)— where the ideal is false because it denies basic features of *actual existence* understood to be unalterable. The ideal that citizens be free from work of all kinds, for example, might be said to be unreal because it denies the actuality of scarcity and the necessity of labor that have always been a part of human society and for which there is no apparent remedy. Within the study of democracy, E. E. Schattschneider's classic text, *The Semisovereign People: A Realist's View of Democracy* (1960), likewise might be considered realist in this respect, since it did not aim to undercut idealistic approaches to the study of democracy, but only sought to challenge what Schattschneider felt were faulty ideals—like the ideal that the pluralistic competition for power might be sufficient to render that competition fair and equal, or the ideal that the electorate in a mass democracy might possess an omnipotent authority.[43] Schattschneider's injection of sobriety was not meant to cancel or oppose idealism, as Schattschneider himself was engaged in an act of morally infused social criticism and believed that democracy itself was social-critical.[44]

Second, there is illusion in the sense of inattention to the institutions and practices needed to *realize* or *implement* the ideal, insofar as such implementation involves requirements irreducible to the simple abstract agreement about the ideal itself. It makes a palpable difference to the reality of the ideal of universal peace, for example, whether such peace is to proceed via pacifism and nonviolence or through a federation of well-armed polities prepared to use force. Something like a realist insistence on implementation can be gleaned from recent, influential philosophical defenses of political realism, like those of Bernard Williams or Raymond Geuss, for whom realism is less the diminishment of normative theory than the insistence that normative analysis is illusory if it does not emerge out of a prior, historically situated engagement with actual institutions and motivations. Yet, unlike them, the illusion to which I mean to object is not moral apriorism (the desire to have politics live up to some prior, transhistorical moral aspiration) but ideals which do not, by themselves, sufficiently acknowledge which institutions are required to either realize them or respond to the fact that they are not fully realizable.[45]

Third, realism conceived as opposed to illusion (rather than to idealism) stands for the recognition that, given the *imperfection* of the world, any commitment to ideals often will generate on the characterological level various forms of ethically ambiguous behavior such as the drive to struggle against opponents or the susceptibility to disgruntlement. Elements of this form of realism can be seen, for example, among so-called "Christian realists" of the last century like Reinhold Niebuhr who define realism in part in terms of the "inevitability and necessity of social struggle" even on behalf of right[46] as well as among contemporary secular thinkers who have appropriated this insight with respect to liberal democracy.[47] By imperfection, then, I mean something different from what is contemplated under the heading of "nonideal theory," at least as this notion usually is employed to refer to exceptional obligations that arise in a context of gross and correctible injustice.[48] Instead, with imperfection I mean to indicate the way the ordinary commitment to certain political ideals—even in relatively well-ordered states not hampered by severe forms of injustice—is nonetheless constrained by lingering shortcomings regarding the full implementation of those ideals, so as to generate both the need for polemical forms of political advocacy that in certain cases may violate norms of civility as well as a political psychology strained by frustration, disappointment, and the temptation to despair.

Now these three aspects of democratic realism—conceived as the commitment that allegiance to a particular democratic ideal not blind us to what is *actual*, nor ignore the requirements of *implementation* when these are not entirely continuous with the ideal itself, nor lead us to overlook the *imperfections* infecting and informing the concrete advocacy of the ideal by ordinary individuals—roughly correspond to the main elements of the plebeian theory of liberal democracy I defend in this book. Consider, in this regard, the following three points of connection.

Actuality: Plebeianism takes a double stand on the idea of actuality, affirming both the abstract point that such a thing exists (i.e., there really are permanent and inescapable social structures conditioning the practice of liberal democracy) and the concrete point that our account of actuality ought to include an appreciation for how ordinary civic life is shaped by the specific structures of *remove, manyness,* and *plutocracy.* To the skeptic who refuses to acknowledge the very notion of actuality, a theory of plebeianism can respond by providing strong empirical, analytic, and commonsense-based evidence suggesting why certain features of the liberal-democratic regime (e.g., the disproportionate political and educational opportunities enjoyed by the rich) ought to be seen as permanent, not contingent, elements of its nature—and by pointing out how the skeptic's premise of a nature-less liberal-democratic regime, utterly unconditioned by actuality and thus open to infinite reform and reinvention, serves (however unwittingly) the ideological function of making liberal democracy seem perfectible and thus perfectly just in its long-term potential. But, in fact, such skepticism toward actuality is highly anomalous in political philosophy. Most leading perspectives within contemporary political philosophy operate, however implicitly, with some notion of the actual. Specifically, the idea that political ideals must be constrained by a conception of social structures understood to be permanent can be found even among highly idealistic paradigms of liberal-democratic justice—whether those of Rawls, Dworkin, Nussbaum, or luck egalitarians—who all end up affirming some version of what Rawls calls the "circumstances of justice": basic facts about our reality that any ideal account of justice has to respect and incorporate. Typically, these include such realities as scarcity, the inescapable pluralism of metaphysical worldviews, and the fact that, despite diversity, there are some basic goods (like wealth and income, welfare, or capabilities) that all individuals are presupposed to want to maximize.[49] Without an appeal to such circumstances, ideal theories would suffer from unreality in the sense of lacking a currency of justice (an objective good to be distributed) or in the sense of being too unconstrained in their ambitions (e.g., without scarcity, justice might stand for the ideal, but unrealistic, aim of making all individuals free from work and worry). Plebeianism builds upon this already existing, though often unacknowledged, conception of actuality informing contemporary theories of liberal-democratic justice, arguing that in addition to the more familiar "circumstances of justice," liberal democrats should recognize plebeian phenomenological structures (remove, manyness, and plutocracy) as no less foundational conditions informing any effort to realize free and equal citizenship.

Implementation: Plebeianism is also realist in the sense that it recognizes that the implementation of moral ideals is an autonomous domain of justice irreducible to an abstract understanding of the ideals themselves. Specifically, while a plebeian approach to liberal democracy accepts, like all perspectives within liberal-democratic thought, the propriety of free and equal citizenship as the abstract moral ideal informing the conception of justice in a liberal-democratic state, it nonetheless argues that the effort to realize this ideal—and confront the intractable ways in which this ideal cannot be fully achieved—requires, paradoxically, the differentiation between the Few and the Many. Now, as with plebeianism's concern with actuality, plebeianism's recognition of implementation as an essential aspect of social justice irreducible to the formulation and justification of the principles being implemented is hardly novel, but rather only a more explicit and intense development of trends already at play in contemporary liberal-democratic thought. Critics, like Geuss, who accuse highly idealistic models of justice of having no independent notion of implementation—so that implementation means simply applying in the world a philosophically derived model of justice—overstate their case if they forget the way such models do sometimes rely, however minimally, on an irreducible conception of implementation.[50] The Rawlsian system, for example, presents the account of social justice to be implemented by legislators in terms not entirely identical to the account of social justice that is initially formulated and justified in abstract form.[51] Dworkin, too, understands that his central distributive ideal—that individuals are to have equal opportunities "to design a life according to their own values" and that this is achieved "when their wealth and other resources depend on the value and costs of their choices, but not on their luck, including their genetic luck in parents and talents"—is an "ideal [that] cannot be realized perfectly," a circumstance which leads Dworkin to develop an approach to the implementation of social justice slightly distinct from the ideal of social justice itself.[52] Similarly, certain luck egalitarians recognize that because their animating ideal commitment—that inequalities should be a product of morally deserved circumstances like choices rather than morally undeserved factors like luck—may not be possible to fully implement (since sometimes it is difficult in analyzing given situations to separate out the role of choice from that of luck), it may be appropriate to implement luck egalitarianism with institutions that do not themselves directly aim to altogether neutralize morally

arbitrary elements of an economic distribution.[53] Building off of these existing ways in which contemporary models of justice understand implementation as an irreducible feature of the commitment to free and equal citizenship
(so that implementation is not simply realizing the plan, but adjusting it to
some degree), the plebeian theory I defend stresses that the *most advantaged*
have a special role to play in the implementation of free and equal citizenship: i.e., that the commitment to realizing what can be achieved in the way
of free and equal citizenship counterintuitively requires some differentiation
between the Few and the Many.

Imperfection: Finally, the realism of plebeianism inheres in the degree to
which it recognizes how worldly imperfection makes it so that the commitment to the political ideal of free and equal citizenship cannot be an altogether
exalted enterprise, but involves various ethical challenges. On the one hand,
these challenges stem from the problem that plebeian advocacy for liberal-
democratic ideals requires commitments not entirely consistent with the ideals
themselves. Specifically, if the ideal of free and equal citizenship would seem to
support a public life characterized by an ethic of civility, the concrete advocacy
for free and equal citizenship beneath the shadow of unfairness implicates the
ordinary citizen in various standpoints—classism, arbitrariness, non-deliberative discourse, indignation, ingratitude, and envy—not entirely consistent with
civil modes of public discourse. On the other hand, the ethical challenges of
plebeianism arise from the discontent a plebeian is likely to experience as a
result of living in a polity insufficiently characterized by relations of free and
equal citizenship. Addressing the psychopolitical unhappiness of plebeian citizenship—and raising the question of how ordinary, second-class citizens are
supposed to cope in the face of it—are key tasks for a plebeian philosophy of
politics.

Together, both elements, the fraught ethics of plebeian advocacy and the
problem of plebeian discontent, reflect a realist appreciation for the ethical
challenges generated by imperfection. Here, too, plebeianism only radicalizes a
realism already at play within conventional approaches to liberal democracy centered on the ultimate full realizability of free and equal citizenship. It is commonplace within these approaches to recognize exceptional circumstances in which
a polemical—rather than strictly civil—form of political advocacy is required,
whether in the form of doing battle against those who deny the very postulate
of free and equal citizenship, or in the form of non-deliberative political protests
aimed at correcting gross injustice.[54] But for plebeianism the ethical challenges
of political advocacy—and of political life more generally—are omnipresent,
not episodic, since plebeianism is grounded on a permanent frustration with the
inability of all contemporary liberal democratic states, even the most advanced
and progressive, to satisfactorily institutionalize free and equal citizenship and,

specifically, to satisfactorily provide citizens with the opportunity to engage each other as free and equal cohabitants of the public realm.

Plebeianism, then, injects realism into the study and pursuit of liberal democracy not because it abandons or attenuates moral idealism in politics, but because it insists that such idealism must attend—with greater awareness than is commonly the case—to the conditions of actuality, implementation, and imperfection. Critics, to be sure, will object that the idea of realism is indeterminate. It is, ironically, one of the most metaphysical and speculative notions in political philosophy and not infrequently has been interpreted in an overly broad fashion.[55] In the pages that follow, I endeavor to reduce the risk of indeterminacy by focusing less on abstract features of realism than on specific, substantive advances that would make the conceptualization and pursuit of liberal democracy less prone to illusion going forward. Realism itself becomes unreal if it is reduced to a philosophy of methodology.[56] But an even more fundamental response to skepticism vis-à-vis the idea of realism is to at once acknowledge the genuine difficulties with the term but at the same time insist that such difficulties are the necessary price of wrestling with a vital notion. However complex and contested, reality is an essential idea for any responsible political theory. A political theory out of touch with reality would be *immature* (an argument I pursue in greater depth in Chapter 4). Even more problematic than specifying just what reality means is the flight from reality that not uncommonly occurs in democratic theory: specifically, the illusory and excessive sunniness which denies the shadow of unfairness and thereby obscures the real nature of liberal democracy and the conditions under which it can be most effectively pursued.[57]

1.6   Bread and Circuses Revisited

The conventional understanding of plebeianism is summed up by Juvenal's famous denunciation of the Roman plebs for sacrificing their political liberty for two meager hopes: bread and circuses.[58] In defending plebeianism as an important philosophy for contemporary democratic life, I redeploy and reverse Juvenal's satire of the plebs. Read metaphorically and progressively (and also in conjunction with certain historical facts about the Roman plebs Juvenal does not consider), the notion of "bread and circuses" is transformed so that it means: in a world where full democratic participation and equality cannot be sufficiently realized, popular empowerment can no longer merely mean attempts at self-legislation but should be pursued within two supplemental dimensions—on the one hand, *the ocular realm of appearances* (not just circuses and games, but a vigilant patrolling of leaders so that their projects and their persons fall beneath the critical glare of public surveillance), and on the other hand, the *economic realm* (not just free bread for citizens, and not just welfare for the needy, but various economic burdens placed on the most advantaged members of society as a form of redress for their never-fully-deserved and never-fully-innocuous good fortune). Read in this fashion, "bread and circuses" names not only a regrettable condition (the intractability of the Few-Many distinction in economic and political life and, so, the failure to achieve full-fledged democracy), but also a progressive approach for working within it. And it is the ambition of this book to defend the contemporary relevance of plebeianism on both counts: arguing, first, that in key respects liberal democracy today is plebeian in character and, second, that the acknowledgment and acceptance of our plebeianism can effectively stimulate and shape progressive energies.

This redeployment and normative reversal of Juvenal's quip also provides a framework for clarifying how this book coheres with my earlier work, *The Eyes of the People: Democracy in an Age of Spectatorship* (2010). Generally speaking, *The Shadow of Unfairness* concerns the economic, or "bread," side of plebeianism, whereas the earlier project confronts the ocular, or "circus," aspect. While it is true that *The Eyes of the People* does not explicitly present itself as a theory of plebeianism, it nonetheless operates within a plebeian framework insofar as it takes seriously the difference between ordinary and elite forms of political identity and upholds as a progressive, democratic ambition the regulation of the Few (i.e., having political leaders appear in public under conditions they do not control). Moreover, the term that *The Eyes of the People* does employ to summarize the theory it defends—plebiscitarianism—is etymologically linked to plebeianism. In retrospect, it may have been better to have relied on the concept of plebeianism from the start, especially since the plebiscitarian tradition *The Eyes of the People* recovers, as represented both in figures like Max Weber (a defender of it) and more recent democratic theorists (who invoke *plebiscitary* as a term of abuse), does not understand the People in a democracy to be in possession of a full-fledged "*scitum*" or decision-making power, but rather makes use of the idea of plebiscitarianism to refer precisely to a political landscape where the People is deeply constrained in its opportunities for making substantive choices about laws and policies.[59] However, since plebiscitarianism had been used as a concept by Weber—and since I aimed to rehabilitate the influence and importance of his and other like-minded thinkers' ideas about democracy—I operated with this notion, despite the counter-literal usage it enjoys. In any case, my defense of a plebiscitary account of politics in *The Eyes of the People* should be seen as part of a larger defense of plebeianism. The central phenomenon analyzed in *The Eyes of the People*—the fact that most citizens most of the time are but spectators of political life rather than decision-makers—is a key element, but not the entirety, of the plebeian relation to politics. The contribution of this book, then, should be conceived as a further elaboration of plebeian politics to include circumstances, problems, and hitherto underemphasized normative aspirations that, even if they go beyond spectatorship, still share the same foundational concern of *The Eyes of the People*: how to realize the empowerment of ordinary citizens, in the fraught condition of their everydayness, within a mass liberal-democratic regime.

Why Ordinary Citizenship Is Second-Class Citizenship

I see it feelingly.

—Shakespeare, *King Lear*

2.1 The Idea of Inescapable Structures Conditioning Civic Experience

One of the central meanings of the shadow of unfairness, and the plebeian theory of democracy it inspires, is that ordinary citizens within any conceivable liberal democracy cannot be expected to understand themselves simply as free and equal co-participants in a shared political life, because their experience of politics necessarily will be shaped by certain *second-class civic structures.* Of these structures, three seem most significant and comprise the focus of this chapter. First, there is the structure of *remove,* by which I mean ordinary citizens' realization, once a certain age is reached, that not only do they not hold high office or great power but that they never will. Second, the structure of *manyness* refers to the circumstance that whatever empowerment ordinary citizens can realize within a given liberal democracy is almost certain to require affixing themselves to a much larger mass of like-minded others (e.g., a majority, special-interest group, or protest movement). This means that the empowerment of the ordinary citizen involves less expressivity or opportunity for discretionary judgment than the empowerment of the select few who, unconfined by manyness, can have their decisions more directly impact the fate of their polity. Finally, the structure of *plutocracy,* in the specific sense I shall employ the term, indicates ordinary citizens' awareness that, despite the best efforts of their states to neutralize the effects of socioeconomic status on opportunities for civic engagement, their economic resources are not irrelevant to their political voice but in fact at least somewhat determinative, on average, of the amplitude and volume of that voice, the frequency of its exercise, and its likelihood of securing a meaningful audience. Plutocracy also indicates citizens' expectation that their socioeconomic status is not irrelevant to their children's educational opportunities. Taken together, these second-class structures condition ordinary civic life in even the most progressive and well-ordered liberal-democratic states. They are not, in principle at least, a function of now-discredited forms of exclusion, such as those based on race, gender, or formal property requirements, but rather constitute the primary ways civic life in *any* liberal-democratic regime will be darkened by the shadow of unfairness.

To speak of "inescapable" structures conditioning everyday political experience—to invoke the idea of necessity with regard to the liberal-democratic regime—might seem highly objectionable, given that all institutions are revisable and reformable at least *in potentia*. In response to this challenge it is important to specify that I do not question the capacity of social reform and revolution to remake fundamental aspects of the political world. All I mean to assert is that any particular regime—such as the regime I analyze in this book, *liberal democracy grounded on private property and the family*—has a distinct nature and, as such, is not open to limitless alteration or reform. Moreover, in invoking the idea of inescapable limits conditioning the practice of liberal democracy, the plebeian theory I defend is not putting forward an altogether eccentric notion, but only contributing to the pre-existing and well-established—if often implicit—conception of limits already at play in contemporary political thought. As I discussed in the last chapter, it is common for even the most idealistic of contemporary liberal-democratic philosophers to assume certain structures as absolutely fixed and unchangeable aspects of a political reality upon which normative reasoning must build. Thus, underlying conditions like scarcity, diversity, and a minimal notion of the good (e.g., that wealth and income are things, *ceteris paribus*, that individuals want more rather than less of) are taken to be immutable elements of political reality. What ought to be in question, therefore, is not whether it is permissible to speak of unchanging aspects of political reality, but the precise understanding of just what this reality is. That is, one should aim to provide a defensible account of reality, not dispense with the notion. Plebeianism contributes to this goal, arguing that the inescapable structures conditioning our politics are not exhausted by scarcity, diversity, and the desirability of economic resources, but include, additionally, the second-class structures of *remove, manyness,* and *plutocracy* that inevitably will inform the ordinary experience of citizenship.

To call into question the very idea of inescapable limits conditioning the practice of liberal democracy would, in effect, deny the existence of reality itself—or at least drain the force out of reality by reducing it only to what exists today on the assumption that an entirely different kind of reality might be possible tomorrow. Such an inability to confront reality in its genuine potency is the signature of political immaturity, aspects of which I diagnose in Chapter 4. Of course, it becomes impossible to appeal to a notion of reality if that notion is reduced to the absurd meaning of what is absolutely without exception the case in all circumstances. In both social science and political philosophy alike, we must operate with a notion of reality that defines rather what is *permanently prevalent within a given arrangement*, where it is understood both that there will be exceptions to the prevailing trend and that there is always the possibility of jettisoning the underlying arrangement in favor of an alternative system. Aristotle's otherwise elliptical concept of nature—"among us, some things are by nature even though they are changeable"—is in fact a helpful way of conceptualizing the kind of realities philosophically infused social science ought to disclose: realities that define what for the most part occurs within a given framework, but which might be changed if that framework were to be replaced by another.[1] Liberal democracy, then, is not merely a regime that provides arguably unprecedented resources for ongoing political and social change (i.e., the use of lawmaking to continually revise the terms and conditions of public life), but is itself subject to a set of limiting parameters that define its nature. A responsible and mature democratic theory, therefore, should provide not only an account of *what is now* (the specific laws and policies defining a particular liberal-democratic polity's specific commitments), nor only an account of *what should be* (how those laws and policies might be changed to more fully realize a standard of justice), but an account of *what always will have been* (the limiting parameters that arise from the anatomy of the liberal-democratic regime itself).

2.2 The Phenomenological Aspect of Second-Class Citizenship

What makes remove, manyness, and plutocracy specifically plebeian structures is not simply the *classist* reason that they refer to what is typical of ordinary civic experience as opposed to elite modes of political engagement, nor merely the *pejorative-connotative* reason that they suggest why everyday political life is likely to be experienced as something disappointing and inferior and thus potentially productive of at least a modicum of indignation from those fated to endure it, but the *historical* reason that they clearly recall aspects of the political lives of the Roman plebs. A plebeian, in the political-economic sense that emerged in the last century of the Roman Republic, was a citizen who was not a member of the two aristocratic classes—the Senatorial and Equestrian orders—and so was merely an ordinary citizen, usually lacking high levels of wealth, political power, and notoriety. For the Roman plebeian, remove was a legalized feature of political experience. While plebeians could vote in assemblies for laws and leaders (albeit in a way that diluted their votes relative to the aristocratic elite), they were ineligible to run for high office.[2] The plebeians' situation was thus one in which they not only did not serve as the leading magistrates, but could not expect to do so in the future. With regard to manyness, the constraint on the nature of political expression available to the Roman plebeians is revealed perhaps most starkly in the non-deliberative character of the Roman assemblies, which enabled plebeians to vote, but usually only in a binary yes-no response to a question put before them.[3] Because ordinary citizens could not rise to speak for or against a particular law being considered for ratification, there was simply no scope for the individuality of the plebeian, as a unique decision-maker aiming to contribute on the basis of his particular judgment, to shine forth. This circumstance, along with the other main vehicles of plebeian empowerment— such as shouting down leaders as they appeared on the public stage and threatening unruly protest of various kinds—meant that a plebeian could only impact politics if his single perspective was joined to a larger mass of like-minded others. Finally, the plebeian also experienced plutocracy, since by the late Republic especially, one's designation as a plebeian was largely, if not primarily, a function of lower socioeconomic status, as opposed to indicating an ethnic or otherwise hereditary identity.[4] Entrance into the lower of the two aristocratic classes, the Equestrian order, required great wealth (400,000 sesterces). And admittance into the Senatorial order, in addition to depending on the attainment of high office (e.g., consul, praetor, or aedile), also had wealth as at least an informal prerequisite. A plebeian, then, experienced himself to be such in no small measure because of his middling or meager economic resources. Horace aptly described this plutocratic circumstance when, referring to the 400,000 sesterces qualification for acceptance into the Equestrian order, he quipped, "You have intelligence, have breeding, have eloquence and honor, but if you are six or seven thousand sesterces short of the four hundred thousand, you shall be a plebeian."[5] Thus, the remove, manyness, and plutocracy conditioning civic life in today's liberal democracies resemble in important respects the ordinary experience of citizenship in ancient Rome and other similarly constituted regimes.

Of course, analogy cuts both ways: the disclosure of likenesses between two entities that are not in fact the same necessarily also implies the further thought of how these two similar things nonetheless remain different—indeed, different in the very domain within which their similarity resides. And it is precisely this simultaneous act of likening and differentiating that enables an analogy's illuminating function. Thus, in arguing that second-class, plebeian civic structures persist within contemporary liberal democracy, it is also important to acknowledge the clear discontinuities between the civic cultures of ancient Rome and present-day liberal democracy—not merely so as to recognize limits to the plebeian analogy, but to better understand its meaning. Specifically, in attending to the plebeian aspects of the contemporary experience of democracy, I do not mean to say that the *principles* of liberal democracy dictate that there should be two classes of citizens—one first class and the other second class—as it seems clear that the reigning ideology is precisely one of undifferentiated free and equal citizenship.[6] Nor do I mean to say that the *formal institutions* of contemporary liberal democracy differentiate citizens on the basis of social class, as these institutions—universal suffrage, competitive mass parties, parliaments and magistracies for which any citizen may compete in an election—do not discriminate, officially at least, on the basis of class, race, gender, or any kind of aristocratic criteria.[7] But politics is not only a function of the principles and formal institutions constituting a particular regime. It is also fundamentally about the *experiences* of actual individuals living within the regime. Any full understanding of ordinary citizenship within liberal democracy ought to include, then, not just the abstract ideals and values that we expect politics to realize, and not just the officially constituted bodies and organizations that are depended on to do this work of realization, but the *phenomenological bearing* of ordinary citizens to their polity. And it is precisely in relation to this experiential, phenomenological aspect of civic life that the second-class, plebeian civic structures operate today. Unlike in ancient Rome, remove, manyness, and plutocracy define neither the principles nor the formal institutions of liberal democracy, but they do inform the way ordinary citizens within a liberal democracy experience these principles and institutions and thus are vital to a full understanding of the meaning of the liberal-democratic project.

In its account, then, of remove, manyness, and plutocracy as permanent civic structures, plebeianism aims to contribute to the phenomenology of ordinary political life in contemporary liberal democracy. At its best, such a phenomenology overcomes the unreality of a merely abstract or formal analysis by insisting on comprehending liberal democracy, not simply in the manner of an outside observer looking in on democracy from without (what one of the great founders of the phenomenological method, Edmund Husserl, criticized as the naïve or natural attitude, or "die natürliche Einstellung"[8]), but in terms of the involved, first-person perspective, whereby the meaning of democracy is inseparable from the way that meaning is disclosed to undetached participants in democratic life.

It must be stressed that in calling for and in part supplying phenomenological examination of contemporary liberal democracy, a plebeian theory of democracy such as I defend in this book is not seeking an empirical account of political behavior, which conceives of political analysis either in terms of knowledge about the specific and contingent beliefs, attitudes, and practices of citizens in a certain regime at a given time, or in terms of the scientific understanding of how and why these beliefs, attitudes, and practices change from one time period to another. Not only does empirical analysis of this type tend to be grounded in the "natural attitude" (as civic behavior is treated as independent from and external to the position of the social-scientific observer), but it usually confronts the surface-level facts of political life—for example, the distribution of preferences and behaviors within a mass electorate, the specific mechanisms by which political opinion in a given case is informed and exerts its influence, the asymmetries of information within a particular political body, and, on the basis of these, causal models that predict how preferences, behaviors, and information interrelate—rather than the underlying structures determining the shape of political experience as such. Accordingly, numerous influential purveyors of the phenomenological method have differentiated phenomenology from empiricism, with Husserl juxtaposing phenomenology to the study of mere facts,[9] Heidegger distinguishing phenomenological analysis of the underlying structures of human existence (the *existenzialien*) from the specific existential (*existenzielle*) choices of concrete individuals,[10] and more recent students of phenomenology distinguishing it sharply from behavioralism.[11] Indeed, one feature of phenomenological analysis is that it brings to light structures which often remain unobserved precisely because they are more the conditions of experience than specific experiences themselves. As Heidegger argues, the object of phenomenology is "something that proximally and for the most part does *not* show itself at all: it is something that lies *hidden*, in contrast to that which proximally and for the most part does show itself; but at the same time it is something that belongs to what must show itself, and it belongs to it so essentially as to constitute its meaning and its ground."[12]

As a way to understand the difference between principles, institutions, and phenomenological experiences, consider the example of voting. A principle-based approach considers the right to vote in periodic elections as a key aspect of what free and equal citizenship requires. An institutional approach seeks to realize that principle through evaluating alternative voting structures, addressing such questions as membership (at what age should citizens vote), how to count votes (e.g., proportional or first-past-the-post), and the frequency of elections—all with an eye toward finding the concrete set of electoral laws that best serves citizens' status as free and equal. Empirical-behavioralist approaches concern themselves with actual election results, providing statistical analyses of turnout, levels of partisanship, and the like. Phenomenological analysis, by contrast, would approach voting as a lived experience, uncovering the basic structures of the act of voting. Some of these structures—like intentionality (the making of a decision)—accord well with the other forms of analysis, while other structures—for example, the ordinary elector's *reactivity* to a pre-selected, often binary set of possible choices, the *relation of hierarchy* constituted by the vote (insofar as voting legitimates which extraordinary individuals will possess vast, asymmetrical power), and *rarity* (insofar as part of the phenomenon of voting is its exceptional nature[13])—problematize the ease with which voting can be explained within normal (i.e., principle-based and institutional) understandings of liberal democracy.

Because the general object of normative analysis has tended to be institutions (presidential versus parliamentary systems, deliberative versus aggregative procedures, etc.) and principles (teleology versus deontology, liberal egalitarianism versus libertarianism, etc.)—not *experiences*—the phenomenology of liberal democracy remains relatively unexplored. The great political phenomenologists to date have tended to focus on the elite experience of politics (as in Arendt's theatrical conception of political life as the experience of self-revelation and the performance of deeds and speeches on the public stage) or on political phenomena that are not strictly democratic (as in Schmitt's definition of political experience in terms of the friend-enemy distinction). When an attempt has been made to analyze the phenomenology of ordinary political life in a liberal democracy, the usual bias has been to treat the citizen in the exceptional mode of decision-making and, in any case, without attention to the fundamental differences between ordinary and extraordinary modes of political existence.[14] A plebeian theory of democracy aims to correct this imbalance and provide phenomenological analysis of ordinary civic life in contemporary liberal democracy.

By phenomenology, then, I mean nothing other than an approach to political life that insists upon the actual experience ordinary citizens have in relation to politics. Its findings are not diametrically opposed to principles and institutions, but it modifies these insofar as these institutions and principles either admit of no experience or are experienced in ways discontinuous with their intended purpose. In the present context, the value of phenomenological analysis is not that it suggests a wholesale methodology for doing political theory, but rather that it can perform the more targeted task of exposing and correcting some of the *unreality* that accrues when liberal democracy is too easily associated with the simple norm of free and equal citizenship. This norm may characterize the *principles* on which liberal-democratic states are grounded (as revealed, for example, in founding documents and widely shared political attitudes) and it might inform the *formal institutions* constituting liberal-democratic regimes (e.g., universal suffrage and universal eligibility for office-holding and party membership), but it does not adequately describe the ordinary liberal-democratic citizen's *lived experience* of political life.

All of this is of course merely prefatory to the most vital question: what, after all, is the phenomenological structure of everyday democratic life? In what follows, I elaborate the three phenomenological structures that I have already introduced: remove (2.3), manyness (2.4), and plutocracy (2.5). These three structures not only disclose aspects of ordinary liberal-democratic reality largely hidden by the prevailing emphasis on the principles and formal institutions of free and equal citizenship, but demonstrate how the phenomenon of democratic life is in certain respects in conflict with these principles and institutions. Given this divergence, these three structures point toward a reinterpretation of the fundamental liberal-democratic commitment to universal human dignity, which I pursue in Section 2.6. There I argue that as much as liberal democracy meaningfully instantiates a politics respectful of human dignity, the phenomenological structures of remove, manyness, and plutocracy mean that liberal-democratic politics also offend ordinary citizens' dignity to some degree. Accordingly, these phenomenological structures reveal at least some modicum of *indignation* as an inevitable and appropriate plebeian bearing toward the liberal-democratic political world.

2.3 Remove

Just as the Roman plebs not only did not hold office but understood that office-holding was permanently foreclosed (since such positions were restricted to members of the aristocratic orders), so do today's everyday citizens experience politics in a way that takes it for granted that they will never have political careers. Phenomenologically speaking, especially once the period of early adulthood has passed, a citizen who has not attained wealth, fame, or some other special credential has no realistic expectation that he or she will serve in, let alone seek, a position of political leadership. I call this bearing to politics *remove*: the ordinary citizen's perceived sense of occupying the periphery of power—of lacking the notoriety, influence, and wealth that would make it possible to operate in politics as an *individual* whose decisions have a direct bearing on political events—and at the same time knowing that there are others who do not face this same lack.

Remove is not remoteness. Governmental authority today is close, if not omnipresent, due to both its scope and the new technologies with which it accesses citizens and is accessed by them. Rather, remove refers to the fact that one does not possess or expect to possess the highest powers, that there are others besides oneself who possess these powers, and that accordingly one's bearing toward great power includes some combination of deference, acquiescence, complaisance, humility, detachment, frustration, and perhaps critique or resistance. This bearing, with all the middlingness, mediocrity, and commonness it implies, is definitive of the ordinary experience of political life.

Remove is inscribed in the demographic conditions of mass societies (in which only a few thousand are formally empowered in a society of millions, if not billions), in the distribution of wealth (even relatively egalitarian societies like Nordic countries have a richest class vastly more wealthy than the average citizen[15]), and in the fact, *pace* Warhol, that fame is not evenly distributed but one of the scarcest commodities in the world. It is inscribed, too, in the circumstance that while it is possible to be wealthy but not politically powerful or famous (an infant who has inherited a large fortune), or famous but not powerful or rich (a notorious criminal in jail for life), or politically influential but not famous or rich (Nancy Reagan's astrologist), it is an obvious feature of our world that wealth, fame, and political influence are mutually supportive of each other and that, further, at a certain amount of intensity each dimension must of necessity overflow into the other fields. (I pursue this idea of the *fluidity of power* in Section 2.5). Another crucial source of remove is the electoral structure of politics within contemporary mass liberal democracies. Indeed, remove is part of the very logic of elections, which pick only a very small fraction of citizens to serve as leaders in prominent public offices. That electoral institutions generate remove was obvious to a long, premodern tradition of thinking about politics, which continually recognized the *aristocratic* aspect of electoral modes of leadership selection compared to other alternatives, like sortition.[16] If the primary emphasis within this line of thought was that elections tended to favor the wealthy and well-born, underlying this was recognition of the related fact that elections exclude most citizens from the fullest forms of active political life.

Remove is such an obvious feature of political life—such a clear and defining aspect of ordinary political experience within contemporary liberal democracies—that it would be unworthy of serious scholarly attention were it not ignored, opposed, or otherwise marginalized by leading paradigms of democratic thought. When deliberative democrats, for example, argue about how citizens are to address each other when discussing and deciding public business—whether, for example, they should be altogether barred from introducing religious doctrines in such contexts—they presuppose a proximity to power (i.e., a flattening of the difference between ordinary and exceptional modes of citizenship), which, were it true, would override and cancel remove. To the fastidiousness with which deliberative democrats debate the ethics that ought to guide advocacy on the public stage, a plebeian democrat might respond, at least with respect to ordinary citizens, by repeating Golda Meir's quip: "Don't be so humble: you're not that great." Likewise, when political analysis centers, as so much of it does, on the vote—the rare exception within the political calendar when a relative closeness to power is achieved (i.e., when ordinary politics is itself suspended)—then here too the basic structure of remove remains largely unobserved. Or, when liberal democracy is analyzed in comparison to authoritarian regimes—with diminished civil liberties and often no political rights—the phenomenon of remove becomes difficult to keep in view. And the libertarian critique of the state, with its call for a much more minimal regulatory governmental apparatus, implicitly de-emphasizes remove, since the experience of being on the periphery of power is lessened to the extent the scope of that power is itself diminished.[17]

Blindness toward remove is perhaps most starkly reflected by leading liberal-democratic theorists of justice who, because their focus is largely limited to the principles and institutions required by a just liberal-democratic society (at the expense of the *experiential* issue of how these principles and institutions would be felt by ordinary citizens in a well-ordered regime), often fail to recognize remove as an essential feature of ordinary civic life. Rawls, for example, who likens the different roles citizens play in politics to various positions on a baseball team, denies that the scarcity of political space (the existence of a few high offices in a polity of millions) is itself a mark against equal political liberty. He argues:

> Players in a game do not protest against there being different positions, such as that of batter, pitcher, catcher, and the like, nor to there being various privileges and powers specified by the rules. Nor do citizens of a country object to there being different offices of government such as that of president, senator, governor, judge, and so on, each with its special rights and duties. It is not differences of this kind that are normally thought of as inequalities, but differences in the resulting distribution established by a practice, or made possible by it, of the things men strive to attain or avoid.[18]

Such a perspective is hardly idiosyncratic to Rawls, as other influential liberal-democratic philosophers have followed him in refusing to see the differential between those with and those without formal decision-making authority as a source of inequality and hierarchy.[19] Part of what grounds this sanguinity, no doubt, is the belief that such a division of labor is inescapable in a mass liberal-democratic regime. But regardless of its inevitability, such a division ought to be appreciated for generating the condition of remove as the standard experience of politics for most citizens. Ordinary citizens come to experience their lack of political office as constant and invariable. Given this phenomenological circumstance, the metaphor of the game is highly misleading. The game suggests an ongoing process characterized by a fluctuation of positions, whereas in truth civic roles become ossified in the face of the semi-permanence regarding who is powerful, rich, famous, and merely ordinary. The game suggests the chance to play again, whereas politics involves the unrepeatable singularity of a human life. The game suggests that everyone prospectively has roughly equal prospects of holding a position of prominence, whereas citizens approach politics from unequal starting points due in part to the impact of socioeconomic status on political opportunity (a problem I confront in the discussion of plutocracy in Section 2.5).

Against these various forms of blindness toward remove, plebeianism emphasizes it as an important and inescapable feature of ordinary civic life in a liberal democracy. In making this claim, I do not mean to understate the significance of the difference between legally mandated remove from politics (such as existed in ancient Rome) and the kind of remove that arises primarily from informal, non-juridical structures conditioning political life within a mass society. After all, if inaccessibility to high office in the former case is something like a truly permanent condition, within the latter it is not legally foreclosed as there is always the technical *possibility* of holding great power.[20] It would be a mistake to deny the reality of this difference, or even that it has experiential consequences: above all the experience in the latter case of being afforded an abstract and official respect from the constitutional system in which one lives. But we fail to account for the reality of the ordinary citizen's situation if we leave matters there. The crucial point about remove within the contemporary context is that it refers not to abstract possibilities but to highly likely, near certain, probabilities. The difference between possibility and probability has not been sufficiently attended to with regard to its impact on the phenomenology of ordinary citizenship in contemporary mass democracy. While possibilities cannot be denied, they also cannot be *experienced* unless they also are joined with a sufficiently high level of probability. It is possible that an asteroid will soon hit the earth, that I will find a large bag of money tomorrow, that next summer will be the coldest by far on record. Yet these are mere possibilities, of very low likelihoods, such that if I plan my behavior in expectation of them, I will do things that are almost certain to be irresponsible and unwise. That modern citizens live in countries where it is possible to hold high office is a genuine achievement in the history of politics, but it does not cancel the fact that the probability of holding these offices is so low as to be of negligible impact on the way ordinary citizens experience their actual political lives.

Once we think in terms of probabilities, the question of remove becomes a function of age, as the balance between possibility and probability shifts further toward the latter as one enters adulthood and grows older. The older one is, the lower the probability of escaping a situation of political ordinariness. This fact is realized, however implicitly, in the degree to which egalitarian political systems are celebrated, not for equalizing the socioeconomic and political opportunities of their living adult members, but rather for aiming to equalize the opportunities of the *children* of their living adult members.[21] And it is often said in praise of a country with egalitarian values that it does not matter who one's parents are, that anyone can have a child who grows up to become rich, famous, or politically powerful. All of this is of real value and ought never be underestimated as an achievement, given the long history of legalized exclusion and formalized aristocracy within politics. But we do a disservice to the description of political reality if we fail to recognize that these ideals bypass the living and actual experience of most adults: the experience of not only not being exceptionally powerful, but of not expecting to be. In this respect plebeianism is a doctrine of political maturity in the very literal sense of referring to an outlook of a mature, ordinary adult, with a firm sense of probabilities, rather than of a young child with a livelier sense of possibility. I return to this notion of political maturity, and its special relevance to plebeian ethics, in Chapter 4 (Section 4.4).

2.4 Manyness

Everyday citizens are not of course entirely bereft of effective political power. Their lack of high office and other positions of prominence does not render them servile or oppressed or altogether silenced. They can vote, protest, speak out, and participate in voluntary organizations like parties and public interest organizations. But these typical modes of popular empowerment usually can function only if the ordinary citizen who relies on them is able to have his or her political objective shared by a much larger aggregate of like-minded others. So even if the ordinary experience of liberal democracy is not without some sense of potency, this potency only arises through the power of a sizable group or organization of which the ordinary citizen is a part. Such a requirement restricts the meaning of political autonomy for the ordinary citizen, leaving little in the way of *individual judgment, decision-making, and recognition on a public stage*. A plebeian theory of democracy thematizes this phenomenological structure conditioning ordinary civic life as *manyness*. Manyness does not mean that ordinary citizens have no power, but only that that power is mediated by membership in a larger mass (e.g., electorate, public opinion, protest movement) which not only is itself highly limited in its expressivity (usually bound to binary pronouncements) but mostly neutralizes the opportunity of its individual members to achieve the self-disclosure, discretionary decision-making, and fame of political elites with far more robust opportunities for political action.

Conceptually, manyness can be seen as a middle position between two categories of political experience that Hannah Arendt juxtaposed: *togetherness* (the genuinely political and liberating condition in which equal yet distinct beings are able to speak and perform deeds before each other, have their individuality shine forth, and thus distinguish themselves) and *sameness* (the condition, typical of mass institutions like a labor force within a factory or an army, where even though a large number of individuals are simultaneously present they remain silent and passive, prone to mere behavior rather than genuine action).[22]

Manyness shares with togetherness the engagement of political activity, but also reflects the fact that such activity neither enables nor requires individuals' discretionary judgment, let alone the revelation of individual identities through action and speech on a public stage. An example of manyness, as Arendt herself implies, would be trade unionism, in which a group of politically active laborers seeks to realize its interests in society without achieving individual self-disclosure or the spontaneity and unpredictability of action in its pure sense.[23] More generally, Arendt reflects on the phenomenon of manyness, even if she does not use the explicit term, when she refers to a diminished form of political action that no longer reveals individual subjectivities but rather is reduced to mere partisanship: "Without the self-disclosure of the agent in the act, action loses its specific character and becomes one form of achievement among others. It is then indeed no less than a means to an end than making is a means to produce an object. This happens whenever human togetherness is lost, that is, when people are only for or against other people, as for instance in modern warfare, where men go into action and use means of violence in order to achieve certain objectives for their own side and against the enemy."[24] Manyness, then, does not mean that the ordinary citizen does not make decisions, but only that such decisions typically involve no more discernment than the judgment of with which side, among a limited selection of options, to ally oneself.

One reason I describe manyness as a *plebeian* structure is that it is particularly well exemplified by the Roman plebs of the late Republic. Manyness constrained the empowerment of the Roman plebs in at least four distinct ways. First of all, with regard to the assemblies—whether the *comitia centuriata* (where plebeians along with all other citizens voted for powerful magistrates like consuls and praetors, enacted some legislation, and also voted as jurors in capital cases), the *comitia tributa* (the main legislative organ in the late Republic as well as the site of numerous trials), or the *concilium plebis* (where plebeians alone voted on binding laws, or *plebiscites*, for the Republic and elected their tribunes)—plebeians' expressivity was limited to up-down votes on the matter at hand.[25] That is to say, plebeians could neither convene the meetings (this was the prerogative of magistrates and tribunes), nor directly determine the agenda (this too was done by magistrates and tribunes), nor speak within them, nor introduce amendments, nor otherwise distinguish themselves individually. Second, with respect to the *contio*, the informal assembly where magistrates would address an amassed crowd about public business and impending votes in the formal assemblies and courts, popular empowerment was no less shaped and constrained by manyness. It was not just that the *contiones* did not officially decide any matter, as these were only occasions for political elites to disseminate information, publicize their agendas, and occasionally debate rivals.[26] Even more significant is that the right to address the public was almost entirely restricted to magistrates and other members of the senatorial elite.[27] The *contio* thus reflected what Morstein-Marx has well described as a "hierarchical speech situation," in which the communicative possibilities available to elites appearing on the rostrum (where they could invent, articulate, exercise judgment, and win fame) were structurally different compared to those available to a plebeian audience confined to crowdlike, acclamatory reactions of "for" or "against."[28] Third, the tribunate also reflected the constraint of many-ness. While the tribunes of the plebs were empowered to prosecute high-ranking members of Rome's political and economic elite—and while the plebs could sit in judgment in courts constituted by the *comitia centuriata* and *comitia tributa*—such trials did not afford any space for ordinary citizens to deliberate or draw attention to themselves as individuals.[29] As in votes about laws, the plebs were constrained simply to vote up or down. Finally, the power of actual *crowds*—not just in the *contiones*, but within the military or in riots (especially frequent from the 50s BCE on)—was itself obviously constrained by manyness, as the crowd by its very nature operates only as a mass phenomenon.[30]

If the *comitia*, *contiones*, trials, and crowd-based behaviors evidence how popular power at Rome was mediated by manyness, for ordinary citizens within contemporary liberal democracies the condition of manyness is reflected in the primary manifestations of ordinary civic power today: elections, public opinion, and protest movements. In the case of elections, there is no question that the electorate, taken as a collective entity, has power, but this power is different from the power that individuals who comprise it have. For one thing, individuals have to face the problem that their individual vote makes but a negligible impact on the outcome of electoral contests—and that it is further subjected to the vagaries by which votes are aggregated and rendered authoritative. Even in the situation where I vote for the side that wins, I cannot experience this event as me caus-ing the victory of my favored side, but only me being fortuitously connected to a larger process of which I was some very small part. There is simply no space for my individuality to shine forth in the ballot booth. This in no way is to deny the very real effectivity the aggregation of such individual acts of engagement makes, but only to insist that this kind of empowerment relates first and foremost to the power of a collectively mobilized mass, not the power of an individual's speech, personal actions, or the consequent memorialization gained from these. With public opinion a similar situation obtains. Public opinion is a vital, if somewhat mysterious, force in a democracy. But leaving aside all the reasons to be skeptical about its operation—the degree to which it is controlled from above, the degree to which leaders respond to it not to obey it but merely to guide their rhetoric, and the difficulties surrounding precise calculations of its content or its impact—there is the fundamental fact that whatever power public opinion realizes is a power of an aggregated many. Likewise, manyness also informs protest move-ments: these have power, but they do not lead to any individual disclosure or commemoration, except in rare circumstances. For every Fannie Lou Hamer or Mohamed Bouazizi, there are thousands, if not millions, who will have contributed to the success of their movement without accreditation, acknowledgment, or other individualized form of empowerment. To be sure, such movements often exert great power: regimes are brought down from below, for example, when masses assemble, will not disperse, and pressure governmental bodies like the army to refuse commands from the existing leadership. Arendt, a great theorist of this phenomenon, accordingly differentiates the power of assembled publics—which can effect fundamental constitutional change and generate unpredictable events and new beginnings—from the mere force of those who control a government's capacity to inflict violence.[31] But what these assemblies usually do not do, *pace* Arendt, is empower ordinary individuals with the capacity to appear, distinguish themselves, and enjoy the sense of empowerment of speaking before an audience that will remember what they have done. Protest movements tend to be shaped by manyness, not togetherness.[32]

Citizens are of course free to enunciate more subtle, articulate, and original opinions in the public sphere (e.g., on the Internet), and they may strive to be the sparks of a new mass movement, but such attempts at a more far-reaching civic voice are not likely to involve nearly the kind of effectivity that is collectively achieved by elections, opinion polling, and protests. Indeed, it is just this separation of speaking (or expression in the full sense) from decision that defines the condition of manyness. When an ordinary citizen decides in a mass democracy, that citizen's expressive faculties are relatively muted. And when these faculties are exercised in an independent and genuinely authorial way, this almost certainly is coincident with the citizen being more separated from power than when voting, responding to polling, or protesting. The well-known communicative ideals of active public life—rhetoric, persuasion, deliberative discourse—do not occur for ordinary citizens, at least not in the clearest moments of their empowerment.

Manyness, then, means that the forms of empowerment available to ordinary citizens, while genuine, are nonetheless non-disclosive of the individual agents' distinct subjectivities. They neither require nor enable discretionary judgment from participants, they thus take the form of being "for" or "against" individuals and policies (rather than creating some initiative), and their primary purpose is to realize some worldly end rather than to gain for themselves a personal kind of power (e.g., prestige, wealth, or individual political influence).

2.5 Plutocracy

If remove and manyness were possibilities equally likely to be experienced by all and to an equal degree, or if they were universally capable of being escaped, their plebeian implications would be largely neutralized. However, experience of these structures is unevenly distributed due to the inequalities of social and economic life. Specifically, the impact of wealth on civic possibilities—on the likelihood of serving in office, influencing those in the highest positions of power, mobilizing fellow citizens under conditions of mass society, and, beyond government, realizing educational and economic opportunities—is itself part of the everyday phenomenon of ordinary political life. While the ideal of civic spaces uncontaminated by economic inequality is meaningful as something that can be more or less attained on a relative basis, it is unreal when considered as something that might be achieved in unadulterated form. The plebeian political philosophy I defend appeals to the reader's own phenomenological verification of the truth that we relate to our bank accounts not only economically as all-purpose means to realize merely private ends, but also *politically* as a rough (hardly fail-safe and hardly sole but nevertheless genuine) proxy of civic potency.[33] That is, phenomenologically speaking, we experience our wealth as something far from irrelevant to our political voice, but rather as having a bearing on the size, scope, and impact of that voice. And we do this, not simply because our polities have yet to implement certain reforms, but because no set of reforms could sufficiently disentangle economic and political power. What I am affirming, in other words, as a basic, plebeian structure of ordinary political life in contemporary liberal democracy is *plutocracy*—conceived not necessarily in terms of the conscious coordination of moneyed interests, but as the raw power of wealth to exert political force within civic spaces into which it is not supposed to tread. As the ordinary citizen of the late Roman Republic knew himself to be a plebeian in part (if not primarily) because he lacked great wealth—and for this reason was excluded from high politics[34]—so too, albeit in less extreme and less formal ways, is the ordinary experience of politics today mediated by an awareness that economic inequality has real, inescapable political consequences, which well-ordered liberal-democratic regimes (so long as they embrace private property and the family) can reduce but never entirely neutralize.

Put in more precise terms, by plutocracy I mean not necessarily oligarchy in any traditional sense but rather the power of inequalities in wealth to undermine equality of opportunity with regard to education and politics. With respect to education, a society is free from plutocracy to the extent that similarly talented and motivated children, regardless of their socioeconomic circumstances, can expect roughly equal prospects of "success" in life. With respect to politics, plutocracy is neutralized if similarly talented and motivated citizens, independent of their socioeconomic backgrounds, can expect to have roughly equal prospects of engaging in government. The ideal of a society where educational and political opportunities are insulated from the effects of economic inequality is a powerful and pervasive fixture of contemporary liberal-democratic thought, figuring prominently within recent influential philosophies of the liberal-democratic idea as well as the attitudes of ordinary citizens.[35] A plebeian philosophy of liberal democracy, of the kind I am defending in this book, argues that while such an ideal is noble and while there is always more that could be done to better approximate it within any given polity, it is a dereliction of both intellectual honesty and progressive purpose not to acknowledge at the same time that such ambitions are not fully realizable in a liberal-democratic regime. They are not so, not simply because every extant liberal democracy falls well short of the goal of a plutocracy-free society, but because, as I shall elucidate, the very institutions of private property and the family generate limits to a liberal-democratic society's capacity to neutralize its plutocratic elements. Private property is ultimately translatable into political influence and access—a truth virtually unanimously accepted by political thinkers prior to the nineteenth century, including those operating from a popular-republican standpoint, and virtually unanimously substantiated today by cross-national empirical studies on the impact of socioeconomic status on political influence and access. And the family constitutes a permanent engine whereby the arbitrary socioeconomic conditions of one's birth are made to have a formative significance for individual development. Liberalism, in other words, does not embody a unitary moral commitment, but a variety of rights—such as the protection of private property and the family, on the one hand, and equality of opportunity on the other—that are ultimately in tension with each other.[36] The problem of plutocracy is one main consequence of this tension.

Whereas liberal democrats today almost universally conceive of plutocracy as a problem that in principle will be satisfactorily corrected in a well-ordered liberal-democratic regime, plebeianism insists that in fact plutocracy is an inescapable problem that cannot be fully solved and thereby generates a second-order challenge: not just how to *reduce* plutocracy, but how to *retrospectively respond* to the plutocracy that always will have existed in liberal-democratic states.

In order to substantiate plutocracy as a permanent structure conditioning civic life in a liberal democracy, I begin by establishing how contemporary liberal-democratic thinkers evince a common failure to adequately recognize the intractability of plutocracy as a problem. Against this prevalent thinking, I then aim to demonstrate the truth of inescapable plutocracy by appealing both to the history of political thought (specifically, the broad consensus among political thinkers prior to the emergence of liberal democracy that economic and political power are necessarily intertwined) and to contemporary social-scientific research in political behavior (which provides a robust array of findings regarding the existence of plutocracy in all existing liberal-democratic regimes).

Varieties of Blindness to the Problem of Plutocracy: Denying, Ignoring, and Avoiding the Problem

The acknowledgment of permanent limits to the liberal-democratic project of a plutocracy-free society—and, with it, the recognition that a shadow of unfairness will be cast over even the most progressive and enlightened liberal-democratic regime—has almost entirely eluded political thinkers of the present generation. While few liberal democrats think that existing polities sufficiently realize the condition of non-plutocracy, by far the most common approach is to imagine that, with proper reforms, the problem of plutocracy might be satisfactorily addressed. Specifically, liberal democrats manifest an irrational and excessive sunniness regarding the problem of plutocracy in at least three different ways: the outright *denial* of plutocracy as an inescapable problem besetting liberal-democratic regimes, the *ignoring* of the problem through support of policies that, however substantial in their egalitarianism, clearly do not yield the promised neutralization of plutocracy, and the *avoidance* of the problem through the articulation of egalitarian ideals not directly bearing on fair equality of opportunity with regard to education and politics.

First of all, liberals who *deny* plutocracy usually do so by holding out the promise that reforms—ranging from campaign finance legislation, inheritance and estate taxation, and egalitarian social policies aimed at ensuring the wide dispersal of wealth within a polity—could create a society where socioeconomic factors would not interfere with opportunities for educational development and political influence. Consider, for example, John Rawls, one of the most influential political philosophers of the last century. To be sure, it must be admitted that Rawls in at least one key instance in his seminal *A Theory of Justice* (1971) veers in the direction of acknowledging something like the permanent problem of plutocracy, when he briefly admits that similarly talented and motivated children, even in the most well-ordered liberal-democratic regime, will have their life prospects affected by the socioeconomic conditions of the families into which they are born:

> The principle of fair opportunity [with regard to education] can be only imperfectly carried out, at least as long as the institution of the family exists. The extent to which natural capacities develop and reach fruition is affected by all kinds of social conditions and class attitudes. Even the willingness to make an effort, to try, and so to be deserving in the ordinary sense is itself dependent upon happy family and social circumstances. *It is impossible in practice to secure equal chances of achievement and culture for those similarly endowed.*[37]

But this honest acknowledgment of plutocracy—specifically, the power of wealth to intrude upon educational opportunity—is a highly anomalous moment within Rawls's philosophy which, in two different respects, must be said to have the opposite function of *denying* the problem of plutocracy. On the one hand, Rawls elsewhere and indeed for the most part describes fair equality of educational opportunity as something that is in fact fully realizable. In an article published four years prior to *A Theory of Justice*, Rawls could affirm, "Equality of opportunity is a certain set of institutions which assures equally good education and chances of culture for all."[38] And in a different passage from *A Theory of Justice*, Rawls writes, "Assuming there is a distribution of natural assets, those who are at the same level of talent and ability, and who have the same willingness to use them, should have the same prospects of success regardless of their initial place in the social system. . . . The expectations of those with the same abilities and aspirations should not be affected by their social class."[39] Rawls's later work is only more forceful in its confidence that an educational system can be free from the unfair influences of children's class backgrounds:

> Those who have the same level of talent and ability and the same willingness to use these gifts should have the same prospects of success regardless of their social class of origin, the class into which they are born and develop until the age of reason. In all parts of society there are to be roughly the same prospects of culture and achievement for those similarly endowed.[40]

On the other hand, when it comes to the capacity of a well-ordered liberal-democratic regime to entirely neutralize plutocracy with respect to the *political* opportunities afforded to its citizens, Rawls is altogether clear and unambiguous: he argues such a regime will guarantee what he calls the "fair value of political liberties," which "ensures that citizens similarly gifted and motivated have roughly an equal chance of influencing the government's policy and of attaining positions of authority irrespective of their economic and social class."[41] Rawls repeatedly emphasizes this element of his theory, insisting: "all citizens, whatever their economic or social position, must be sufficiently equal in the sense that all have a fair opportunity to hold public office and to affect the outcome of elections."[42] And again: "All citizens, whatever their social position, may be assured a fair opportunity to exert political influence."[43] While Rawls is all-too-brief in his account of the institutions whereby the fair value of political liberties might be instituted, he continually emphasizes at least two key reforms: campaign finance legislation (and other uses of electoral law to reduce the impact of private money in politics)[44] and various policies (like estate and inheritance taxes) that would serve to make the distribution of wealth much more dispersed than it is in conventional capitalist welfare states.[45]

Rawls is not alone in implying that the neutralization of plutocracy in politics and education is an essentially fully realizable goal. Not only do numerous subsequent liberal-democratic thinkers working within a Rawlsian paradigm repeat Rawls's idealism in this regard, especially with respect to equality of political opportunity,[46] but the denial of plutocracy as a permanent problem also finds voice among democratic thinkers working from different philosophical standpoints. Thus, the Marxist philosopher G. A. Cohen, whose luck-egalitarian account of justice departs from Rawls in numerous respects, affiliates himself with Rawls's confidence about generating a plutocracy-free society, arguing that "un-American experience shows that election regulation, of a sort Rawls would endorse, can produce political democracy under a wide inequality of income and wealth." Indeed, Cohen goes so far as to suggest some existing regimes outside of the United States have succeeded in "ensuring the people's opportunities to hold office and exercise political influence are substantially independent of their socioeconomic position"![47] Even libertarian thinkers, to the extent plutocracy is a concern, sometimes suggest the problem can be neutralized by reducing the scope of the state: if welfare and other state programs are dramatically curtailed, any disproportionate influence over and access to government on the part of the wealthy become less significant, since there is simply less to be won by effective political advocacy.[48] Of course, such an approach, if it is even plausible within the conditions of the vast and administratively complex nation-state, is far less plausible when it comes to the specific case of educational opportunity.

Liberal-democratic thinkers are not wrong to uphold fair equality of opportunity vis-à-vis education and politics as sacrosanct ideals. And it is clear that the policies they recommend would help to better realize such aspirations. But insofar as even the most radical schemes would still condone substantial inequalities,[49] insofar as the evidence is strong (as I shall relate) that even modest inequalities reproduce themselves in differential opportunities for education, politics, and even health, and insofar as liberal democrats have no answer to the permanent limits the family places on equality of educational opportunity, then even the most ambitious liberal-democratic projects for combatting inequality would only reduce, not eliminate, plutocracy from social life.

Second, blindness toward plutocracy is also reflected in the tendency of leading liberal-democratic philosophers to *ignore* it. This tendency can be found especially among thinkers who, more than Rawls, have thought through the specific details of the kinds of policies and programs required to combat plutocracy and who, consequently, are perhaps more aware that the reforms they support will lead to something less than the neutralization of socioeconomic status as a factor determining educational and political opportunity. But rather than confront this shortcoming head-on, contemporary political thinkers frequently subscribe to less-than-ideal proposals as if they were fully satisfactory.

Ronald Dworkin, for example, claims that if the underlying distribution of resources is itself justly organized within a liberal-democratic regime—which for Dworkin involves a society insuring all of its citizens against various forms of misfortune (e.g., poverty, disease, unemployment) as well as campaign finance legislation—both economic inequality and the political influence stemming from it will be very much reduced, so that "a great deal of the inequality in political influence of our own time" would be eliminated.[50] Like Rawls, Dworkin's ambition is that while inequality of political influence might continue to result from non-economic factors, such as the talent and commitment individuals bring to politics, the effects of wealth inequality on politics might come to be largely neutralized.[51] Yet, when Dworkin reflects on the ultimate impact of his proposed reforms, he states *not* that they will nullify the role of wealth in relation to political opportunity, but only that they will have the much more modest result of preventing the superrich from altogether monopolizing politics: "Moral agency is possible for all citizens in politics only if each has an opportunity to make *some* difference . . . enough to make political effort something other than pointless. . . . Citizen equality is destroyed when *only the rich* are players in the political contest."[52] If Dworkin's more sober assessment of the ultimate impact of his proposed reforms should be commended for its honesty, that the standard it embodies is something less than full-fledged equality of opportunity for political influence is barely admitted—and it certainly does not lead Dworkin to reflect on the enduring problem of plutocracy within his idealized account of the liberal-democratic regime.

The tendency toward ignoring, rather than simply denying, the problem of plutocracy can also be found in Tomasi's recent so-called bleeding-heart libertarian theory of social justice, in which a watered-down account of fair equality of opportunity regarding education—which promises only "*high quality* educational opportunities to all," not *equal* opportunities regardless of socioeconomic status, and which contains the caveat that this promise cannot necessarily be "guaranteed" by the market-based strategies Tomasi favors—is presented as a plausible interpretation of Rawls's idea of fair equality of opportunity, even though it is certain to lead to a circumstance in which similarly talented and motivated children will not expect to grow up with roughly equal prospects of "success" regardless of their class of origin.[53] From the other side of the political spectrum, one finds a similar ignoring of the problem of plutocracy when Freeman, after acknowledging that the family is a permanent barrier to the full realization of fair equality of opportunity, suggests that Rawls never sought the "practically impossible" rigorous goal that similarly talented and motivated children enjoy opportunities unaffected by their socioeconomic class of origin, but only intended that those with similarly *developed* abilities compete fairly for positions.[54] What is objectionable about this interpretation is not only that it conflicts with numerous passages where Rawls envisions an education system that will offer equal opportunities to the equally endowed, nor merely that Freeman's exposition becomes incoherent when he somehow thinks this reduced conceptualization of fair equality of opportunity is consistent with the ideal that "people, whatever . . . their social circumstances, be given the means to fully develop and effectively exercise the talents and abilities that they are endowed with, so that they may engage in public life as equal citizens."[55] What is also objectionable, at the most basic level, is that Freeman's approach leads him to look away from the problem that plutocracy will always be a feature of the liberal-democratic regime. In any case, in putting forward genuinely progressive reforms that nonetheless fall short of neutralizing plutocracy, philosophers in these instances emphasize their progressivism in such a way so as to ignore the lingering problems that would persist in even a significantly more egalitarian liberal-democratic polity.

Third, a final form of blindness toward the problem of plutocracy relates to the tendency of certain leading political philosophers to *avoid* it, by simply not addressing questions of fair equality of opportunity vis-à-vis politics and education when delineating the requirements of their otherwise progressive conceptions of liberal-democratic justice. For example, Sen's recent influential account of justice, which argues against ideal theorization in the name of comparative judgments of better versus worse arrangements that might be realized in the shorter term, articulates social justice in a way that need not face up to the truth that, even in the most progressive liberal-democratic regimes, similarly talented and motivated children will not enjoy roughly equal prospects of success regardless of socioeconomic background, nor will citizens possess roughly equal prospects of political influence independent of their class circumstances.[56]

Moreover, whenever some threshold level of welfare is upheld as providing the conditions for free and equal citizenship—with no additional attention to how citizens living above this minimum still experience differential political and educational opportunities—one finds liberal-democratic avoidance of the problem of plutocracy. For example, the capabilities approach to justice pursued by Nussbaum, among others, presents wealth and income in a just regime as susceptible to this kind of threshold analysis, whereby once sufficient economic resources are obtained, inequalities have no clear effect on civic relations of political equality.[57] Liberal republicans, like Pettit, draw on this capabilities idea when they argue that justice requires that citizens have sufficient resources so as to possess "the basic capabilities for functioning in society" and when they define the "socioeconomic independence" citizens in a just regime will enjoy in terms of escaping avoidable forms of domination (such as "being exploited or manipulated or intimidated by others"). Even as Pettit claims that such standards might require "the substantial reduction of certain material inequalities," and even as he presents his theory as something likely to appeal to "left-of-center liberals," his focus on the more rudimentary problem of non-domination means that his account does not face the plutocratic problem that inequalities in a condition of non-domination still, on average, generate disproportionate educational and political opportunities for the more wealthy.[58] To be sure, in his recent work especially Pettit affirms the ideal of equality of political opportunity, writing that "the citizens of a legitimate state have to enjoy equal access to a system of popular influence," which he defines in terms of "an opportunity for participation in that system that is available with equal ease to each citizen."[59] But because Pettit does not reflect on the way socioeconomic inequality above and beyond a threshold of non-domination shapes unequal opportunities for political influence, his appeal to equality of political opportunity seems empty, if not obfuscating, when he thinks it will be secured in the kind of liberal-republican order he defends.

In sum, then, whether by *denying, ignoring,* or *avoiding* the fact that even in a well-ordered liberal-democratic state fair equality of opportunity cannot be fully achieved for children with respect to education nor for citizens with respect to politics, leading political philosophers today manifest a blindness to the problem of plutocracy. The argument that follows, drawing both on the history of political thought and empirical studies in civic behavior, aims to overcome such blindness and to insist upon plutocracy as an intractable problem besetting even the most hypothetically advanced liberal-democratic regime.

Republican Honesty about Plutocracy

In claiming a necessary overlap between economic and political power, I am hardly stating a novel idea, but only repeating what centuries of political thinkers of various persuasions prior to the nineteenth century took for granted. Contemporary liberal-democratic theorists are the exception when they claim it is possible for relations of civic equality to be uncontaminated by the effects of economic inequality. The far more prevalent philosophy has been to recognize the impossibility of this ideal taken in its fullest sense. Not just Marxist critics (who argue that economic structures of private property and inequality must limit the meaning of juridical equality), and not just defenders of monarchy and aristocracy (who affirm the naturalness of hereditary political privileges for the wealthy and well-born), but the long premodern and early modern *republican tradition* of political thought expresses, in various ways, the basic assumption that wealth cannot be entirely separated from political power. Indeed, in affirming plutocracy I am only recalling (which is not to say returning to) an older, well-established understanding about the relationship between wealth and politics that was commonplace among republicans prior to the modern rebirth of democracy in the late eighteenth and early nineteenth centuries. For a vast range of republican thinkers, wealth was taken to be inseparable from political power. As Harrington put it, "Where there is inequality of estates there must be inequality of power."[60] Or, as Montesquieu could claim, "It is impossible that riches will not secure power."[61]

To be sure, republican thinkers confronted the necessary intersection of economic and political power in various different ways. For some, the inseparability of economic and political power was seen primarily as a problem, as numerous republican thinkers argued for curbing wealth inequality both to protect ordinary citizens from abuse from the very rich and to make political power more likely to be placed in the hands of merit rather than mere wealth.[62] Plato represents perhaps the most radical form of this way of thinking. Plato's scheme for a ruling elite of philosophically educated guardians required, he understood, that there be no property, and thus no economic inequality, among this class, because Plato accepted that economic divisions otherwise would interfere with the rule of reason and virtue. Plato's parallel requirement that the ruling elite forego the other main pillar of liberal-democratic society (and indeed of society pretty much everywhere)—the family—and that they raise their children collectively without knowing who are their biological relations followed a similar logic.

For other republicans, however, the problem rather was that the allegedly natural and proper political authority generated by property might be disrespected to the detriment of the stability of the state: hence, a long tradition of republicans, including Aristotle, Guicciardini, Montesquieu, Sieyès, and Guizot, proposed a variety of institutional measures for formally bestowing on the wealthy disproportionately greater political voice and opportunity, both as a necessary means of protecting property rights and on the assumption that the wealthy, due to their economic stake in society, would have a superior incentive to recognize and pursue the genuine public interest. Accordingly, prior to their gradual abolition over the last two centuries, wealth requirements shaped civic membership in virtually all premodern republics, whether as a minimal threshold level needed for active citizenship or also in the form of gradated civic classes based on degrees of property.

Interestingly, very often these two competing, almost opposite notions of the political potency of wealth—great wealth as a threat to political liberty and wealth as deserving class-based instantiation in formal political institutions—co-existed in the mind of single republican thinkers. Aristotle both expects a healthy republican regime will afford disproportionate influence to the wealthy and yet cautions against the excessively oligarchic exclusion of common citizens from deliberative institutions where they might participate and lend their

superior collective judgment.[63] Harrington at once affirms property requirements for citizens and gradations of two civic classes based on property (the
order of the foot and the order of the horse)[64] but at the same time calls for
land redistribution to prevent exorbitant accumulations that would undermine
the unity of the state.[65] Montesquieu's desire to replace the rule of wealth with
merit and virtue did not prevent him from excluding those without property
from civic membership, nor from advocating that the legislative power within a
modern republic ought to be divided between a lower chamber and a higher one
reserved for citizens "distinguished by birth, wealth, or honors."[66] Constitutional
framers in the United States aimed to create a regime that would "preserve the
spirit and the form of popular government" but at the same time would also
afford special respect to property both as a core political right and as something
that would lead its holders to play a disproportionate role of leadership in the
state.[67] A similar situation occurred in France, where the political rights affirmed
in the Declaration of the Rights of Man and of the Citizen (1789) were applied
unevenly, with property holders having them but not the propertyless.[68] Rather
than see this simultaneous effort to both *limit* and *enable* the disproportionate
influence of the propertied within republican regimes as schizophrenic or otherwise contradictory, it should be interpreted in light of an almost pretheoretical
republican acceptance that, within polities grounded on private property and
the family, wealth of course would carry with it political potency, thereby making the question for republican theorists one of *how*, rather than *whether*, the
disproportionate influence of the wealthy should be allowed to reveal itself.

The republican political thinker who provides what is likely the most important
theoretical bridge between the premodern republican outlook that so often took
for granted the propriety of affording *legalized* political privileges to the wealthy
and the modern liberal-democratic outlook that finds any such formal privileges
unacceptable given the moral premise of free and equal citizenship—*and who,
crucially, in spite of this transition, still expected property to exert disproportionate
influence within modern liberal-democratic politics*—is James Madison. Towards the
end of his life, Madison came to reject his earlier belief that the franchise should
be restricted to the propertied, since any denial of universal (male) suffrage, he
now argued, "violates the vital principle of free Govt. that those who are to be
bound by laws, ought to have a voice in making them."[69] But what deserves special emphasis is Madison's recognition that even within such an ethico-political
context—which clearly is the one occupied by today's liberal democracies where
any constitutionalization of political advantage for the wealthy would be seen as a
prima facie injustice—wealth would continue to exert disproportionate influence
in politics, albeit in indirect and informal ways. That is, Madison posits the natural
power of wealth to provide its holders with additional political clout even when
unaided by electoral institutions formally favoring the wealthy:

> Should . . . universal suffrage and very short periods of elections within
> contracted spheres be required for each branch of the Govt., the security
> for the holders of property when the minority, can only be derived from
> the *ordinary influence possessed by property*, & the superior information
> incident to its holders; from the popular sense of justice enlightened &
> enlarged by a diffusive education; and from the difficulty of combining
> & effectuating unjust purposes throughout an extensive country.[70]

Madison did not of course originate the idea that, in electoral republics especially, oligarchic tendencies would persist even when offices would be open
to all citizens regardless of social background—as the belief in the inherently oligarchic feature of elections (their tendency to favor the wealthy and
well-born) had informed much republican theorizing in the centuries prior
to Madison.[71] But Madison's reflections here are significant both because he
attends to the persistence of oligarchic effects within the much more egalitarian liberal-democratic regimes of the nineteenth century and because, in
delineating the different sources of such effects, he puts forward the central
idea of the "ordinary influence possessed by property" (an influence which
suggests something more general and widespread than the simple tendency
for the wealthy to be elected disproportionately to office). Madison, in other
words, has his finger on plutocracy—conceived not necessarily as the explicit
collusion of the rich to control the state, but rather as the raw power of wealth
to exert its force and influence within a formally (that is, juridically) equal
political system.

Plebeianism, of course, in no way shares Madison's approval that property
should exert disproportionate political influence within electoral systems.
Indeed, from a contemporary plebeian perspective, such influence poses a serious problem to the liberal-democratic ideal of a civic space of free and equal
citizenship untrammeled by the inequalities of wealth and social status. Given
this divergent normative emphasis, what is most of interest from the political-
philosophical perspective and deserving of further explication is not Madison's
familiar republican worry that property holders be afforded their proper (i.e.,
disproportionate yet not absolute) influence within a just liberal-democratic
state, but his understanding that property already by its very nature bestows
upon its owners an outsized political potency.

"The Ordinary Influence Possessed by Property"

What, after all, did Madison have in mind by "the ordinary influence possessed
by property"? And how might such ordinary influence be conceptualized today?
Three dynamics seem especially relevant.

First of all, one can point to the *fluidity of power* and in particular the fluidity of economic power, such that, at a certain level, wealth overlaps with various political potencies like the capacity to hold public office, influence the decisions of governments, and mobilize others to achieve policy aims.[72] Just as at a certain level of poverty other forms of empowerment become impossible or meaningless, so at a certain level of economic wealth there is an almost inescapable generation of extra-material, political forms of empowerment like fame, influence, and other informally derived opportunities for a more active political career. Such dynamics are reflected in the common practice of social scientists to rely on economic status as a proxy for status as such—a procedure that may be rough and reductive, but hardly incorrect.[73] The fluidity of power is perhaps best illustrated with respect to the relation between wealth and notoriety. It has long been understood that one of the liabilities of limited economic resources is that such a circumstance tends to render one invisible within a polity's social system. As John Adams put it, the poor man "feels himself out of the sight of others, groping in the dark. Mankind takes no notice of him. He rambles and wanders unheeded. In the midst of a crowd, at church, in the market . . . he is in as much obscurity as he would be in a garret or a cellar. He is not disapproved, censured, or reproached; *he is only not seen*."[74] From the other side, as Adam Smith among others recognized, one of the chief allures of wealth is the belief that it will gain for its holders the attention of others.[75] This combination of factors—wealth's capacity in itself to generate publicity as well as the resources to mobilize supporters and engage in political marketing—helps explain the long tradition of political thinkers who took it for granted that, within an electoral republic especially, the wealthy would have disproportionate advantages for pursuing active political life. The very wealthy are more proximate to political power, have more opportunities to get it, and can magnify their voices and influence in ways that ordinary citizens cannot. The United States Supreme Court's doctrine that money is speech for the purposes of jurisprudence regarding election law, and that therefore spending in politics deserves a high level of protection, may not be just as a matter of law (there might be more equitable campaign finance legislation which is currently being stymied by such jurisprudence) but it is accurate as a matter of political phenomenology.[76] Much like the Hegelian notion that quantity, after a certain level of magnitude, necessarily becomes quality, so does wealth become political power and political power wealth, at least at the highest levels of each.

Second, it is not just that great wealth inescapably becomes a political force, but that even more modest, incremental increases in economic resources raise the likelihood of political participation. Political scientists continually have shown that "the inequality of representation and influence are not randomly distributed but systematically biased in favor of more privileged citizens—those with higher incomes, greater wealth, and better education—and against less advantaged citizens."[77] Not only are the wealthy more likely to vote—a finding that has been corroborated for decades[78]—but wealth also contributes to the chances that one will engage in non-electoral forms of political participation, including campaigning, protesting, and other forms of community activism.[79] Such effects have been documented across various times and places.[80] In understanding the mechanisms whereby wealth contributes to greater likelihood of participation, the "civic voluntarism model" of Brady, Schlozman, and Verba is helpful. The model distinguishes between three sources supporting participation: resources (time, money, civic skills), engagement (including interest in politics, a sense of political efficacy, and the capacity to recognize the connection between one's preferences and ongoing public policy debates), and mobilization (that is, likelihood of being recruited to participate).[81] Wealth not only contributes to the first of these in a direct and obvious way, since wealth is a basic resource for political activity, but also connects to the latter two, insofar as material resources have been linked to political efficacy and greater chances of recruitment.[82] For these reasons, as I have mentioned, income and wealth often are considered not just an ingredient of socioeconomic status, but a proxy for it.[83]

Moreover, to the extent that wealth generates both an incentive to participate and a means of doing so, the wealthy will have a disproportionate advantage in politics. In conflicts between the haves and have-nots, the rich occupy a favored position not only because of their often superior resources and organization, but because such resources and organization can reveal themselves without explicit efforts at coordination. That is to say, to the extent that one of the political ambitions of the wealthy is to protect their wealth, the deployment of political resources toward this end need not require the same level of organized mobilization as those who, even if they potentially share a common commitment to redistribution, are more likely to suffer from the disaggregation generated by underprivilege and ideological difference.[84]

Third, another set of social-scientific findings supporting the phenomenological truth of plutocracy—specifically, ordinary citizens' experience of their economic status as not irrelevant to their political voice—concerns the extent to which inequality itself, beyond the material disadvantages of the less fortunate, has been shown to have a demotivating impact on political activity and a lessening of the quality of civic life.[85] The experience of being unequal in status, especially when the inequality is between segregated neighborhoods of better and less well-off, undermines efficacy in the less advantaged by eroding their capacity to trust and cooperate, preventing information flow (insofar as communication is hindered by homogeneity), and producing apathy.[86] Solt's cross-cultural study of five nations, for example, finds that "higher levels of income inequality powerfully depress political interest, the frequency of political discussion, and participation in elections among all but the most affluent citizens, providing compelling evidence that greater economic inequality yields greater political inequality."[87] Since those with fewer resources are less likely to be mobilized anyway, any added demobilization generated by inferior socioeconomic status would only exacerbate a prior tendency.[88]

The plutocratic effects of inequality itself (i.e., inequality independent of its material aspects) also can be seen in relation to health, where recent research has suggested that socioeconomic inequality reproduces itself in unequal health outcomes. The point is not simply the well-known correlation of low economic class with certain health risk factors (smoking, obesity, poor diet, exposure to pollution, and substandard housing)—as here such health inequalities could be addressed by raising the absolute material and educational standards of disadvantaged citizens so that they have the resources, information, and opportunity to engage in behaviors and choices no less healthy than those of their more well-off fellow citizens. Rather, what seems to reveal plutocracy in relation to health as an inescapable feature of civic life is the degree to which social inequality itself, divorced from its connection to material deprivation, has been shown to have negative health consequences. For example, the ongoing British Whitehall study, which has examined the health of more than 28,000 civil servants in England since 1967, has found that life expectancy increases at each grade of the civil service's socioeconomic ladder. The most junior employees like doorkeepers have death rates three times higher than the most senior administrators, even when controlling for numerous risk factors.[89] Similar findings about the effects of inequality on health outcomes have been documented in cross-national studies, which show that countries that enjoy lower levels of national wealth but higher levels of equality perform better on health measures than their counterparts.[90] If inequality itself has negative health consequences for those further down a socioeconomic hierarchy, by what mechanism does this process operate? Recent research suggests that lower socioeconomic status carries with it greater stress from not being in control of the conditions of one's life, whether in the form of being more likely to follow orders and obey a rigid schedule or in the form of lacking the predictability and stability afforded by higher status.[91] Accordingly, higher cortisol levels (associated with stress) and lower serotonin levels (associated with depression), both of which are detrimental to health, have been linked to low social status.[92] The plutocratic impact on health, if true, has profound political-philosophical implications. Whereas the intrusion of economic inequality into politics and education represents a failure to achieve a full-fledged meritocracy—since what plutocracy means in these contexts is that similarly talented and motivated citizens do not in fact have equal prospects of engaging in politics, and similarly talented and motivated children do not in fact have equal prospects of "success" in life—the epidemiological costs of socioeconomic inequality problematize the very aspiration of meritocracy.[93]

Overcoming the Enduring Refusal to See Plutocracy as an Inescapable Feature of Liberal Democracy

In analyzing the structure of plutocracy—the penetration of the effects of economic inequality into civic spheres (education, politics, health) that are supposed to be protected from any impact generated by differential socioeconomic status—I have emphasized numerous dynamics: the fluidity of power by which wealth at a certain level of magnitude must begin to contain political advantages; the various ways in which political and educational opportunities disproportionately accrue to the socioeconomically advantaged; and the possibility, underwritten by recent research, that inequality itself has a negative impact on the political activity as well as the bodily health of the less advantaged. Now it seems there are at least three main ways to resist such assertions of plutocracy as a basic structure of liberal democracies: to point out specific findings that do not cohere with it; to argue that its effects on politics are minimal, because participants have similar preferences as nonparticipants; and to argue that the situation is correctible (for example, that plutocracy is more of an American phenomenon that is largely neutralized in relatively egalitarian European societies). I take up these objections in turn.

With regard to the first challenge, there are admittedly exceptions to the general plutocratic relationship between socioeconomic status and political activism. For instance, in certain contexts and at certain levels of intensity, socioeconomic disadvantage can actually generate political activism.[94] And some well-known trends—like the correlation of education and political activity—are not absolute. For example, even though the level of education in many Western societies has risen over the last generation, it remains doubtful that such developments have contributed to greater political engagement. But, in response, it should be stressed that my purpose is to uncover only what is ordinary. *Ordinary citizens ordinarily* can expect, at least to some degree, wealth to intrude upon opportunities for political power, educational and career expectations, and health outcomes. As countless studies have demonstrated across various times and places, it is clearly the rule and not the exception that wealth promotes civic activity and influence.[95] Here it is worth repeating the conclusion of a landmark 1978 study, which I referenced in Chapter 1: "The political advantage of those citizens more advantaged in socioeconomic terms is found in all nations, certainly in all those for which we have data"[96]—a finding which is repeated in even stronger terms by a subsequent study two decades later (that I also quoted in the first chapter): "No democratic nation . . . lives up to the ideal of participatory equality."[97]

The second challenge to the idea of inescapable plutocracy argues that the consequences of unequal political participation are not that important, because the attitudes of participants are virtually the same as nonparticipants: thus, even if the median actual voter is more well-off than the median eligible voter, the ultimate policy consequences might be negligible. To be sure, some studies have found a close match between the policy preferences of voters and nonvoters— or that where there are differences they go in no particular ideological direction.[98] But we do a disservice to the phenomenology of everyday political life if we conclude from such findings that the effects of plutocracy are thereby neutralized. For one thing, while some studies find little difference, many others suggest both that there are differences and that these tend to relate specifically to redistributive policies.[99] Further, and more fundamentally, we need to look past mere policy preferences as an indication of similarity. What matters in politics is not just the content of preferences, but how preferences are prioritized. In the American context, for example, despite substantial overlap in the policy preferences of voters and nonvoters, those of lesser means (who disproportionately comprise non-voters) place a higher salience on certain issues—like education and "basic human needs"—and deprioritize other issues like non–tax-based economic issues, foreign policy, abortion, and the environment.[100] Also, to focus too heavily on any alleged correspondence between the policy preferences of voters and non-voters forgets that there are other forms of political activity beyond voting—many of which afford participants the opportunity to communicate and pursue objectives with at least somewhat more expressivity than the relatively mute, rare, often binary vote. Such extra-electoral kinds of engagement—activism, campaign work, fundraising and donations, contacting leadership—have been shown to be much more likely among socioeconomically advantaged people than the disadvantaged, pointing to a plutocratically determined differential in the amplitude, subtlety, and reach of the political voice available to citizens.[101]

Third, plutocracy might be resisted as only a contingent, but not necessary, feature of liberal-democratic civic life. One could object, for example, that while countries like the United States exhibit clear plutocratic tendencies (inequality is high, winner-take-all elections potentially underrepresent economic minorities, poverty and the depoliticization it threatens pose serious social problems, and onerous registration rules magnify the impact of socioeconomic factors on participation rates), other polities, like European and especially Nordic liberal democracies, counteract such plutocratic effects insofar as inequality in such countries tends to be lower, proportional representation incentivizes participation even from political minorities and the less powerful, poverty is contained, high voting rates minimize the effect of socioeconomic status on electoral participation, and educational systems better approximate the condition of providing similarly talented and motivated children roughly equal life prospects. To be sure, in the United States the effects of plutocracy seem especially strong.[102] And to the extent

American data has had an outsized impact in social-scientific studies on the effects of economic inequality in politics, there is a danger of distorting the degree of plutocracy in other parts of the world. But while it is important to recognize a wide diversity in the intensity of plutocracy in different nations, it is a mistake to allow such relative analyses to cover over the basic fact of plutocracy as a fundamental structure of political life in *all* liberal-democratic states. Europe and other relatively egalitarian societies differ in degree but not in kind from the United States. The most egalitarian European societies are still shaped by substantial inequalities in income and especially wealth and the basic plutocratic dynamic that socioeconomic status on average predicts various forms of political activity—whether voting or, even more, extra-electoral forms of engagement—is a widely recognized feature of European political behavior, even within the most egalitarian Nordic states.[103] Moreover, the fact that welfare programs in Europe are funded primarily through relatively regressive taxes on income rather than relatively progressive taxes on wealth—and that the very wealthy prevent more egalitarian transfers due to the threat of capital flight—indicate additional mechanisms by which plutocracy exerts itself in even the least unequal European societies.[104] The Nordic countries are not immune from such processes. Not only do they exhibit sizable inequalities in wealth,[105] but their political and educational systems—even if much more egalitarian than those of countries like the United States—are still overrepresented by the socioeconomically advantaged.[106] It is not surprising, therefore, that, as in the United States, the disproportionate political and civic capacity of the rich in the Nordic countries has generated social criticism.[107] The point, in other words, is that Europe is only *less* plutocratic, not without plutocracy.

In insisting upon the inescapability of plutocracy, the suggestion is not to reject the propriety of prevalent liberal-democratic norms of free and equal citizenship, nor in any way to depreciate efforts within specific societies to reduce their plutocratic elements. Clearly, even if plutocracy will remain a permanent problem, it can be contested and improved on a relative basis. But plutocracy in some form is a constitutive feature of liberal democracies grounded on the family and private property—and certainly persists in non-liberal and non-democratic states as well.[108] Those approaches have been most persuasive, therefore, which have framed reform not as what will cancel plutocracy but only as what can lead to the *diminishment* of plutocratic effects, whether Winters's call for "decreasing [their] intensity"[109] or Verba et al.'s appeal to government to "*modify* the socioeconomic" effect on civic life so that "the implicit class bias in politics can be *diminished.*"[110] While the power of such reforms to meaningfully uplift a particular civic culture ought not be underestimated, their partial nature—their inability to fully neutralize plutocracy—also needs to be appreciated as a core element of the *shadow of unfairness* that will inhabit even the most progressive liberal-democratic state and that will make it so ordinary citizenship in a liberal democracy is experienced in some key respects as second class.

2.6 Plebeian Indignation

These three structures conditioning the experience of everyday civic life in contemporary liberal democracy—remove, manyness, and plutocracy—not only challenge the more familiar understanding of democratic citizenship conceived strictly in terms of abstract principles, formal institutions, and empirical political behavior. Because they embody the condition of second-class citizenship, they also make clear why ordinary civic life in even the most progressive liberal-democratic regime cannot be altogether contented or satisfied. Specifically, whereas liberal democracy today presents itself as that system of government that uniquely affirms the so-called "dignity of man" (i.e., the metaphysical view that all humans have an inviolable, incomparable worth, which entitles them to free and equal treatment within their polities), it is also true that the phenomenological structures of remove, manyness, and plutocracy are among the most important reasons why the actual experience of democracy in its ordinary, everyday form is inescapably productive of *in-dignation*: a sense that however much liberal democracies do respect the dignity of their citizens, they do not do so completely, equally, or sufficiently.[111]

In attending to indignation, a plebeian theory of liberal democracy both draws upon yet goes beyond the historical legacy of the Roman plebs. On the one hand, indignation has long been recognized as a plebeian trait. In ancient Rome, numerous epithets customarily leveled at the plebs from aristocratic critics pointed precisely to the plebeians' vitriol as one of their objectionable qualities.[112] Machiavelli's more sympathetic account of the Roman plebeians nonetheless took it for granted that the mass of ordinary citizens within a republic would continually take on "ill humors" from having to confront the ambitions and usurpations of the nobles—such that a healthy republic, far from being free from tumult, would be one in which the plebs routinely needed to "vent [their] animus."[113] The plebeian theory of democracy I pursue in this book is clearly inspired by this historical legacy and, like Machiavelli, aims to demonstrate that indignation has a necessary role to play within a progressive approach to politics. But contemporary plebeianism differentiates itself from these earlier sources when it engages with the idea of indignation in a more precise and targeted way. The point is not simply that the nature of plebeian indignation is often left unelaborated within the prior tradition, whereas the account of plebeianism I defend clarifies how indignation is generated by remove, manyness,

and plutocracy. Nor is the point merely that when earlier authors reflect sympa-
thetically on plebeian indignation, they tend to assume, like Machiavelli, that it
relates to the threat of aristocratic violence and usurpation, whereas I mean to
emphasize the indignation that arises from being a second-class citizen. What
also is key is that plebeian indignation today draws its meaning from the specifically modern, indeed quite recent, idea that a just regime is one that respects
universal human dignity.

In order to understand the dynamics underlying plebeian indignation in its
contemporary liberal-democratic sense, one needs to take note of the particular
notion of dignity that has been invoked in conjunction with the rise of liberal-
democratic regimes over the last two centuries. Both the significance of dignity
within contemporary jurisprudence and its distinctive liberal-democratic form
are well expressed in the German Basic Law (*Grundgesetz*) whose first Article
asserts, "Human dignity is inviolable. To respect it and protect it is the duty
of all state power." Three crucial elements appear within this brief statement
about dignity. First, dignity is equal: all humans, or citizens within the state,
are equally dignified. Second, dignity is automatic and non-forfeitable: for
example, we do not lose our dignity when we act poorly.[114] And, third, because
it is automatic and non-forfeitable, the duties that dignity demands are placed
first and foremost on institutions rather than individuals: that is, it is above all
states and political organizations that have the responsibility to design legal and
social systems that properly respect individual dignity.[115] Something virtually
identical to the conception of dignity in the German Basic Law can be found
in numerous other liberal-democratic constitutions as well as in many of the
conventions and declarations that have guided and justified the spread of liberal democracy throughout the world.[116] A similar conception of dignity also is
invoked in prominent works of liberal-democratic philosophy.[117] Exponents of
the contemporary notion of dignity debate wherein dignity consists—whether
it is grounded in our capacity to exercise free choice and voluntary action (probably the dominant conception), our status as living human beings (frequently
invoked among Catholic thinkers and also recent bioethicists arguing for the
dignity of patients who have permanently lost all mental functioning), or (less
commonly but no less persuasively) our being born into conditions we did not
choose and hence do not deserve. But because dignity is seen in any of these
situations as being automatic and non-forfeitable, at least for conscious human
beings, it overrides any formal exclusion of citizens on the basis of inequalities
(e.g., aptitudes and characteristics like wealth, strength, intelligence, education,
birth, or talent) that anti-democratic thinkers throughout history have invoked
to justify hierarchy.[118]

It should be emphasized that this conception of dignity as equal, automatic,
and requisite of political (rather than individual) obligation is remarkably new.

It departs sharply from a much older, perhaps original Roman conception of dignity as *dignitas* or social standing—i.e., as something profoundly unequal, grounded on individual achievement (above all, achievement in politics), and thus requiring a *personal* responsibility to seek and earn renown.[119] It is also more recent than the rebirth of popular government at the end of the eighteenth century, as shown in the fact that it is absent within key documents like the French Declaration of the Rights of Man and of the Citizen (1789) or the American Declaration of Independence (1776) and Constitution (1787).[120]

The contemporary conception of dignity is as impressive and nascent an achievement as liberal democracy itself. It is remarkable in its call for a world where all human beings are respected as individuals of unique and incomparable worth. And it should be applauded to the extent it has inspired and shaped actual liberal-democratic constitutions and institutions over and against authoritarian, anti-democratic alternatives. But one consequence of such a grand, metaphysical, and inclusive notion of dignity that obligates states rather than individuals is that citizens are bound to be disappointed with how well their respective polities afford respect to the dignity of their persons. As Kateb, a recent student and celebrator of human dignity, has observed, "No society fully realizes the dignity of the individual, though some societies come closer than others."[121] Kateb does not elaborate the sources of this universal shortcoming, but my analysis has suggested that it arises not merely from generic imperfections preventing the full realization of any political goal, but, more severely, from the second-class civic structures impacting civic life in any conceivable liberal-democratic regime. That is, the very phenomenological structures conditioning the ordinary experience of politics—remove, manyness, and plutocracy—also undermine the capacity of liberal democracies to fully respect the dignity of their citizens. Especially when the grounds of dignity are conceived, as they most often are, as residing in human beings' capacity for free choice and autonomous action, ordinary civic experience seems to limit the full extent of the respect afforded the dignity of everyday citizens in even the most progressive liberal-democratic states. Remove, for example, means that the choices of ordinary citizens matter less than the choices of the select few who, closer to the centers of power, have their decisions more directly determine the fate of the polity. Manyness (in such forms as voting, public opinion, and protest) means that the power of ordinary citizens is not experienced as a fully autonomous phenomenon—as if the citizen's own will had made a tangible difference in politics—but as the fortuitous circumstance of having one's own perspective linked to a much larger body of like-minded individuals similarly constrained to a limited form of political expressivity and potency. And plutocracy means that one's state of remove and confinement to manyness are never merely a function of one's own choices and effort, but rather stem, at least on average and in part, from the way economic inequalities (which ought to play no role in the educational and life outcomes of children or the political influence of citizens) in fact excrete beyond the economic sphere and infect the realms of education and politics. For these reasons, the phenomenological correlate of the liberal-democratic commitment to universal dignity is not merely the experience of being respected in some key regards, but also, too, the experience of being not-fully-respected and so *indignant*.[122]

Plebeian indignation returns us to an idea that is often lost in the contemporary universalization of dignity as an equal, non-forfeitable, automatic achievement: namely that dignity is also a *burden*—and not just a gift, joy, or some other source of buoyancy.[123] For the Romans, for example, and for other cultures in which dignity was a relative, hierarchical possession that always was unevenly distributed within a populace, the burdensomeness of dignity inhered in the fact that its attainment required ongoing effort to win, maintain, and extend it.[124] Because it existed in degrees, one could always strive for more. Because it could be lost, one despaired about its actual or potential forfeiture.[125] In any case, it required persistent *political* achievement. While there is some debate as to whether this achievement fully constituted one's inner worth or only reflected it, success in the form of wealth, renown, and above all political office was a prerequisite for Roman *dignitas*. In a different yet parallel way, the idea of the burden of dignity was appreciated by earlier iterations of the "dignity of man"—such as those of Pico, Kames, Kant, or Schiller—which sometimes made dignity conditional on intellectual and moral achievement.[126]

Clearly, the plebeian burden of dignity is different from these two types. It is not the burden to achieve dignity in the world, but to withstand the tension of being *dignified yet ignoble*: that is, of being in principle but not fully in practice treated as free and equal citizens. After all, ignobility—the lack of wealth, political power, or renown (three things which overlap to a significant degree and, in their extremes, necessarily overflow into each other)—remains a feature of social life so long as political offices are limited, wealth unevenly distributed, and celebrity a scarce and valuable commodity. The removal of legalized nobility from a polity is therefore not the removal of ignobility from it. That there are neither legalized titles nor legalized exclusions from political life does not mean that all citizens are noble, nor that nobility itself in the sociological sense has been neutralized. What it does mean is that the experience of ignobility has only been transformed, and in most respects improved, but not cancelled. It means that ignobility becomes a function of demographics (the superabundance of the unknown, middling, and non-powerful relative to the famous, wealthy, and politically influential) and not of blood; that merit, rather than ascribed status, becomes the dominant principle for escaping ignobility; and that the possibility of escape is permanent, even if often negligible, rather than prohibited as a matter of law or deep-seated custom.

Thus, the contemporary universalization of human dignity has not meant universal nobility. However much ordinary citizens might have their dignity partially respected by such institutions as juridical equality, universal suffrage, and other rights, they nonetheless are forced to reconcile the idea of their absolute incomparable worth with their placement in social structures that leave them utterly unremarkable with respect to wealth, power, and notoriety and that, as I have shown, are constrained by the second-class civic structures of remove, manyness, and plutocracy. How to confront this tension between the idea of their dignity and the fact of their ignobility—*having* to confront it—is a central burden brought on by the contemporary celebration of universal human dignity. Dignity for the plebeian therefore is no simple joy or celebration of one's humanity, but also involves the *indignation* of living within political and economic systems that do not fully reflect that dignity.

Indignation is fundamental to a plebeian theory of liberal democracy on multiple levels. It is not just, as I have emphasized in this chapter, that indignation is a permanent *condition* within liberal democracy, which any honest philosophy of democracy ought to acknowledge and confront. Indignation is also important as one of the *motivations* for the proposals at the heart of plebeian progressivism, which I examine in the next chapter: namely, the identification and regulation of the most advantaged class. That is to say, one part of the justification for legally coercing a polity's best-off citizens to periodically engage in public acts of redress is that imposing regulatory burdens on the most advantaged might acknowledge, validate, channel, and partially ease plebeians' sense of indignation at being second-class citizens in a polity officially committed to undifferentiated free and equal citizenship. At the same time, however, plebeian indignation is still an *ethical problem* that must be faced by citizens committed to plebeian progressivism. As I further discuss in Chapter 4, even if indignation is an understandable reaction to second-class civic structures, and even if it is an appropriate motivation for certain plebeian political reforms, it nonetheless is a rancorous sentiment that transgresses prevailing norms of civility regarding citizens' public discourse in a liberal democracy. Thus plebeian indignation is unlikely to carry with it the proud, confident, exultant quality of "righteous indignation" which William Blake has in mind when he proclaims that "the voice of honest indignation is the voice of God." Instead plebeian indignation is one part of what I describe in Chapter 4 as the "principled vulgarity"—the ethically ambiguous but politically necessary commitments—plebeians must endure as part of their political maturity. Finally, indignation, with the displeasure it inherently involves, helps explain why the purpose of a plebeian theory of democracy is not only to improve politics but to help ordinary citizens find *solace* in the face of the inevitable unease their second-class status will generate for them. That egalitarian ideas and practices might themselves be a source of such solace is the possibility I pursue in the book's final chapter.

Reasonable Envy: The Heart
of Plebeian Progressivism

In the fate of being blindly subject to the unequal chances of our
unequal births we are all equals.

—Herbert Spiegelberg

3.1 The Idea of Reasonable Envy

One of the long-standing objections to the plebeian as a type—one of the
reasons the figure of the plebeian has a pejorative connotation—is its association with envy. Among historians of ancient Rome, Sallust, for example,
draws attention to the "violent envy" (*gravis invidia*) of the plebs.[1] And
Montesquieu likewise identifies a distinctly plebeian penchant for attacking
economic and political elites without cause.[2] More broadly, aristocratic critics of the alleged meanness of the lower orders have long affirmed that envy
is an especially plebeian trait. For Nietzsche, perhaps the most brutal critic
of plebeianism, for whom the plebeian designates less a Roman political class
than, more generally, an ignoble and ordinary kind of person, part of what is
so objectionable about the "plebeianism of the modern spirit" (*Plebejismus
des modernen Geistes*) is envious *ressentiment*: that is, an instinct, borne from
weakness, for revenge against the powerful, the joyful, and the healthy.[3] In
addition to "disgusting incontinence" and "a clumsy insistence that one is
always right," the "plebeian type" (*Pöbel-Typus*) is for Nietzsche defined by
"petty envy" (*Winkel-Neid*).[4]

It might seem that, to be persuasive, the development of a plebeian theory of
liberal democracy such as I pursue in this book would have to defend itself from
any association with envy. After all, envy is widely condemned, not just by aristocratic critics, but by broad segments of contemporary society who find it irrational, impious, or otherwise unsupportable. But this is not in fact the approach
I take. I accept the association of envy with plebeianism, but argue that this

linkage might be conceived in a progressive, non-pejorative light.[5] Specifically, I defend the idea of "reasonable envy"—a circumscribed kind of envy grounded on liberal-democratic ideals—as the core of plebeian progressivism.

The meaning of reasonable envy has two different applications, depending on how envy itself is defined. First, envy often is simply taken to mean any interest in imposing burdens on the well-off. On this rendering, one is envious, for example, to the extent one raises the question of whether the wealth and power of the most advantaged are fully just or whether society might be better off if this class were more rigorously regulated. This admittedly is a rather open-ended definition of envy, but it well describes the kind of envy that frequently is subjected to strong critique. Major contributions to modern liberal social philosophy, for example, have taken aim against envy in this general form, castigating it as a destructive, antisocial psychology.[6] The long-standing Christian objection to envy as one of the cardinal sins likewise often has in mind envy in this generalized sense of wishing to impose burdens on the more successful.[7] When a desire not to be guilty of envy has contributed to ordinary citizens' support for political positions especially beneficial to the very wealthy—such as reducing estate taxes or opposing any cap on the income or wealth of the most well-off—it is usually this conception of envy as any regulatory concern for the most advantaged that has been involved.[8]

Second, however, envy has a more precise, technical meaning: namely, the desire to make the powerful worse off even if doing so worsens one's own condition as well. Nietzsche speaks to this rendering of envy, and its connection to plebeianism, when he refers to "the plebeian [*Pöbelmann*] who cut ruthlessly into his own flesh, as he did into the flesh and heart of the 'noble.'"[9] If the first form of envy is not after all altogether without adherents in contemporary political culture, this second form of envy is almost universally opposed on the assumption that it is irrational, because it means supporting a situation that is a net loss, materially speaking, for all parties involved. Libertarians and other critics of redistributive schemes, for example, have long suggested that such schemes are rooted in envy in this secondary sense and are therefore invalid.[10] Many liberal egalitarians resist this charge, but not the assumption that, were liberal egalitarian principles indeed grounded in envy (i.e., in a desire to impose economic harm on the more advantaged in a manner that brought negative material benefit to the rest of society), this circumstance would be a check against those principles.[11]

The plebeian concept of "reasonable envy," which I defend in this chapter, stands for the idea that both forms of envy are wrongly denigrated in any absolute sense. Beneath the shadow of unfairness permanently cast in even the most advanced liberal-democratic states—where ordinary citizens are confined by remove and manyness, where representation is too uncertain to ever be fully definitive, and where plutocracy advantages the civic opportunities of the wealthy—there is a legitimate place for singling out the most advantaged class for unique regulatory attention and, further, there are some special circumstances when it is not irrational to impose costs on the most advantaged that have neutral or even negative material effects on the rest of society. In making these claims, I shall focus primarily on the most advantaged in the economic sense (i.e., the superrich), having already argued on behalf of imposing special burdens on the politically most advantaged (i.e., leaders in possession of great formal powers) in my earlier work.[12]

In defending both aspects of reasonable envy, I am inspired by the example of ancient plebeian republics which often differentiated the Few from the Many not just to aggrandize and celebrate the Few but to single them out for special public regulation, in a fashion that could hardly be said to have brought material benefit to the broader political community in all cases. The Athenian practice of ostracism, which exiled a citizen for ten years, is perhaps the starkest example in this regard. Not only was ostracism often imposed on individuals of great power and influence, but the procedure for deciding ostracism was wholly outside the judicial process and thus had no necessary connection to the remediation of concrete wrongdoing or illegality on the part of the ostracized. The Athenian Assembly voted annually whether it wished to impose an ostracism that year—and only following an affirmative response to this initial question would it later decide who the ostracized individual might be![13] What ostracism suggests, therefore, is the pure interest in burdening the Few as such, with the material benefit of such burdening a secondary, much more uncertain component of the process. Beyond ostracism, within the specific domain of the public burdening of *economic* elites that is the focus of this chapter, the Athenian Republic possessed numerous institutions that singled out the very wealthy and subjected them to special economic regulations.[14] The richest citizens were uniquely compelled to fund services or "liturgies" (*leitourgia*) to the state, like equipping triremes, sponsoring theatrical productions, financing gymnasia, subsidizing public dinners, and paying for delegations to other states.[15] The practice of *antidosis*, which in effect compelled the wealthy to police themselves as to which citizens were the very richest and thus obligated to pay the liturgies, only exacerbated the burden of the liturgies themselves.[16] In addition, the very wealthy also were singled out and forced to pay the *eisphora*, a special tax in times of war and other emergencies.[17] Further, should they hold formal positions of political power, the rich often provided public feasts upon attaining their magistracies and, in office, contributed personally to the administration of their official tasks.[18] In Rome, too, beyond the state supply of corn and land and the patronage of clients and electoral supporters, it was expected that the richest and most powerful citizens provide from their own pockets the funding of banquets, games, the construction of buildings, and sometimes the costs of the magistracies they held.[19] In both Athens and Rome, then, the economically most advantaged citizens had to incur special public economic burdens as a condition of their success—burdens which, even if they often served familiar fiscal interests in raising needed funds, also transcended narrow utilitarian considerations in compelling the very wealthy to acknowledge their ultimate deference to the state and their special obligation in a popular republic to recompense the public for their good fortune.[20]

It should be noted that, in a parallel fashion, *political* elites within both polities were made to endure their own similarly onerous set of regulations, as leading statesmen and officials had to face public audits following their terms of office,[21] withstand public fora where they might be subject to vitriolic critique and abuse,[22] and (in the case of Rome) wrestle with a tribunical power that among other capabilities could bring accusations against high officials in a trial (*iudicium*) before the amassed citizenry in the *comitia tributa*.[23] All in all, these ancient institutions—both economic and political—remind us that it is precisely the regulation of the most advantaged that distinguishes a plebeian republic from an oligarchic one: in both cases the Few are differentiated from the Many, but only in a plebeian regime does this differentiation serve to burden, and not just elevate, the most powerful members of the polity.

Such historical examples provide the basic template—sometimes crude but nonetheless instructive—of the kind of institutions a contemporary advocate of plebeianism, committed to the idea of reasonable envy, might support as part of the effort to progressively reform liberal democracy beneath the permanent shadow of unfairness. Of course, this template is, by itself, of limited use. Not only does it not detail how precisely reasonable envy might operate in the contemporary context, but it says nothing about the *grounds* on which reasonable envy might be justified within a liberal-democratic society. After all, how can the singling out of the very rich for special regulatory attention be considered legitimate, when it would seem that liberal democracies require *undifferentiated* civic relations making no appeal to social class? And how can the imposition of burdens on the superrich that have no material benefit for the rest of society be justified, even in the circumscribed and exceptional manner I shall clarify below, when a liberal-democratic order would appear to demand economic policies that contribute to the *reciprocal* advantages of all representative parties within a regime?

Answering these questions—and in so doing establishing the liberal-democratic credentials of reasonable envy—is the main focus of this chapter. I begin in Section 3.2 by drawing attention to an imbalance in the contemporary theory and practice of liberal democracy, whereby it is widely accepted that the least advantaged class ought to be singled out for special regulatory attention, but the most advantaged class remains unidentified and outside the scope of regulation. Section 3.3 aims to overcome this imbalance by demonstrating through a critical engagement with John Rawls—whose seminal theory of justice is perhaps the paradigmatic instance of this imbalance—that the same grounds on which a liberal-democratic society already finds it appropriate to regulate the least advantaged also justify it in identifying and regulating the most advantaged. The relevance of Rawls's philosophy stems, too, from the fact that it introduces, albeit quite briefly, the central idea I mean to defend and develop in this chapter: reasonable envy. My confrontation with Rawls in Section 3.3 is meant to demonstrate that this notion has a vital role to play in the implementation of social justice in a liberal-democratic society operating beneath the shadow of unfairness. I conclude, in Section 3.4, by explaining how the implications of these claims are not limited to an interpretation of Rawls's philosophy, but ought to encourage liberal democrats of diverse persuasions to endorse the identification and regulation of the most advantaged class as a legitimate and valuable liberal-democratic end. Taken together, these claims aim to justify reasonable envy on liberal-democratic grounds and, in so doing, more clearly specify the way it might function in contemporary liberal democracies.

3.2 The Imbalance in Contemporary Liberal Democracy Regarding the Identification and Regulation of Social Classes

Plebeianism does not aim to replace liberal democracy, but stands only for the further theoretical and institutional development of the liberal-democratic regime in light of the shadow of unfairness. Plebeianism, therefore, is rooted in the same moral ideal animating more familiar understandings of liberal democracy: the ideal of free and equal citizenship. Supporters of plebeianism, then, must demonstrate how the underlying standpoint informing plebeian progressivism—reasonable envy—is consistent with this ideal and, more generally, the values of a liberal-democratic society.

In establishing the liberal-democratic credentials of plebeian progressivism, my method is to engage in an *immanent critique* of prevailing liberal-democratic norms and, especially, the precise formulation these norms have received by the most influential recent theorist of liberal democracy, John Rawls. By immanent critique, I simply mean a method of argumentation that aims to improve an existing way of thinking, not by criticizing it from the outside on the basis of external normative standards, but by developing it in light of its own explicit and implicit moral commitments.

The point of departure for my immanent critique is the *imbalance* in contemporary liberal-democratic philosophy regarding the singling out of social classes for special regulatory treatment. Although the commitment to free and equal citizenship might seem to preclude any class-based differentiation among the citizenry, in fact liberal-democratic philosophies today frequently appeal to some notion of the least advantaged members of society as an essential socioeconomic category for reasoning about and implementing social justice. Yet this willingness to transact in class-based social differentiation has been largely one-sided, as an arresting lacuna within contemporary liberal-democratic philosophies is their general failure to treat the most advantaged citizens within a polity as a distinct class. The crux of my immanent critique is this: *The same grounds on which liberal democracies have felt justified in identifying and regulating the least advantaged class also suggest the basis on which the most advantaged class might be identified and regulated, sometimes even without material benefit for the rest of society.*

This tendency of recent liberal-democratic thought to operate with an explicit and lively concern for the least advantaged unparalleled by an equal concern for the most advantaged is most starkly evinced in John Rawls's highly influential theory of justice, which I consider in detail in Section 3.3. At the center of the Rawls's philosophy is the "difference principle," which holds that a system of inequalities is just only if it contributes to, and ideally maximizes, the prospects of the least favored class.[24] The difference principle, then, explicitly invokes the least advantaged class, but makes no direct mention of the most favored.

In devoting vastly disproportionate theoretical attention to the least favored vis-à-vis the most favored, Rawls is hardly idiosyncratic, but rather only the most well-known philosophical example of a broader trend underlying the dominant institutions and ideas informing the shape of present-day liberal democracies. Contemporary Rawlsians, who continue to work through the implications of the difference principle for both domestic and global politics, only perpetuate this privileging.[25] Beyond the Rawlsian paradigm, the philosophical theory that Rawls considered the strongest rival to his own account—a liberal utilitarian model that secures only a basic minimum for all citizens, in the manner of contemporary welfare-capitalist states, but does not call for the more egalitarian policies envisioned by the difference principle—parallels Rawls in defining social justice in a way that makes appeal to the least advantaged but not the most advantaged.[26] And more recent articulations of liberal justice, even if they depart from Rawls in other respects, repeat Rawls's relative blindness to the most favored members of society. Influential theories, like Dworkin's "equality of resources" model, for example, focus primarily on insulating democratic citizens from undeserved ill fortune rather than identifying and regulating the most advantaged as a class.[27] The same might be said of Ackerman and Alstott's "stakeholder society" proposal.[28] Capability theorists, like Sen and Nussbaum, who conceptualize justice as securing for all citizens the opportunity to realize certain basic human "functionings," likewise present the main thrust of liberal progressivism in terms of bettering the lot of the disadvantaged and also revising a merely economic conception of impoverishment.[29] Even many luck egalitarians, who roughly speaking are driven by the principle that only inequalities that stem from free choices as opposed to undeserved circumstances are just, often invoke this principle in order to combat, not all undeserved inequalities (including those of the most advantaged), but only the undeserved disadvantages besetting the least advantaged.[30]

Moreover, this philosophical trend of attending to the least advantaged class but not the most advantaged is paralleled by the prevalent institutions of the liberal-democratic welfare state, which are oriented around providing a social safety net rather than combating inequality as such. It is reflected, too, in the fact that in recent years numerous countries (e.g., Australia, Austria, New Zealand, Singapore, Sweden, and the United States) have reduced or repealed the estate tax, which primarily affects the wealthiest citizens.[31] Even the principle of progressive taxation has met growing resistance[32]—and taxation has been institutionalized in various nations through tax brackets that do not include a category for the superrich.[33]

From one perspective, liberal-democratic philosophy's relative blindness to the most advantaged is entirely understandable. It stems, for example, from a sensible concern with the poorest members of society, many of whom lack basic necessities like food, shelter, and safety. Yet notwithstanding this, there is reason to be suspicious of the imbalance in liberal-democratic theory. By focusing on the least advantaged much more than the most advantaged, prevailing theories of justice enforce a conception of the polity in which the basic distinction is between the many who are sufficiently well-off and the few who are disadvantaged, when it may be that the reverse diagnosis is more appropriate: a many who are relatively poor or powerless vis-à-vis an elite with great political power and wealth.[34] To the extent social scientific literature suggests that the economically most advantaged have disproportionate access to politics and influence over political decision-making, liberal-democratic philosophy's relative inattention to the most advantaged is not just groundless, but unwise as well.[35] As new social movements, like the Occupy Movement, have begun to challenge this prevalent silence about the most advantaged, there is perhaps only added urgency for a liberal-democratic society to clarify both to itself and its rivals what grounds if any there are for identifying and specially regulating the most favored class.

3.3 The Liberal-Democratic Credentials of Reasonable Envy: An Immanent Critique of John Rawls

In contesting contemporary liberal democracy's relative blindness to the most advantaged class—in establishing reasonable envy as a vital liberal-democratic end—I devote special attention to the highly influential political thought of John

Rawls. While symptomatic of liberal democracy's privileging of the least advantaged over the most advantaged when thinking about justice, Rawls's philosophy nonetheless suggests three reasons why the implementation of justice requires identifying and potentially regulating the economic expectations of the most advantaged, sometimes without any (or even negative) economic benefit to the rest of society. Specifically, I shall argue that the same three grounds on which Rawls explained the need for a just society to take a special interest in its least favored members—the *heuristic* grounds of using the expectations of the least favored to simplify complex judgments about just distributions, the *protective* grounds of insuring that the basic liberties of the poorest citizens not be undermined by insufficient material resources, and the *redressive* grounds of affording the least advantaged special attention as the class most likely disadvantaged by the arbitrary effects of the natural and social lotteries—also provide good reasons for expanding the regulatory attention of a just liberal-democratic order to include the economic expectations of the most advantaged. My claim, in other words, is that implementers of social justice in a liberal-democratic state have justification to single out and regulate the superrich as a way to help realize the difference principle in light of heuristic challenges regarding its application, as a means of counteracting excessive inequalities which undermine basic liberties (especially those pertaining to educational and political opportunity), and as redress for the fact that even the most well-ordered liberal-democratic societies cannot fully realize their commitment to free and equal citizenship.

My use of Rawls to defend the plebeian idea of reasonable envy is likely to meet two kinds of objections. On the one hand, certain Rawlsians will resist engagements with Rawls unrestricted to a faithful representation of the master's explicit intentions. On the other hand, certain critics of Rawls, especially those who object to the treatment his work receives as a "sacred" text in contemporary political philosophy, will wonder why it is necessary to develop liberal-democratic thought through appeal to Rawls at all.[36] Although very different, both objections unite around a resistance to critical appropriation: the one because the texts in question are considered final, the other because the texts in question are considered unnecessary or unworthy interlocutors. Against the first group, I say that political philosophy is historical—we philosophize in the present through conversation with past authors—and that Rawls himself both observed and exemplified this fact.[37] Rawls's later work admitted, moreover, that his philosophy was but one potential answer to how liberal democrats, taking citizens as free and equal members of a fair system of cooperation, might conceive of justice, thereby acknowledging the possibility of alternate arrangements that would be valid, if not superior, future alternatives to his own.[38] In any case, given plebeianism's ambition to further develop liberal democracy in light of the problem of the shadow of unfairness, it is hardly inappropriate to devote extensive theoretical attention to the leading philosopher of the liberal-democratic project in its current form. Against the second group of objectors, while I cannot defend Rawls's ideas as being categorically indispensable to any liberal-democratic philosophy of justice, it needs to be remembered that Rawls's stunning degree of influence within contemporary political thought is not without reason. That many of Rawls's greatest critics also have been among his greatest admirers, relying on Rawlsian concepts to develop their own competing theories of justice, is a sign that part of the importance of Rawls's work resides in the conceptual tools he developed to make his arguments about justice, rather than only the practical implications of the arguments themselves.[39] My own effort to rely on Rawlsian concepts to extend liberal-democratic theory to encompass an explicit, principled concern for the most advantaged class follows in this tradition of thinking simultaneously with and beyond Rawls.

Reasonable envy, it will be recalled, contains two ideas: first, that the most advantaged class ought to be singled out for special regulatory attention and, second, that in certain cases such regulation, though appropriate, will not materially benefit (and in fact might even harm) the economic prospects of the rest of society. The immanent critique of Rawls I undertake here is not limited to the first element of reasonable envy (establishing how regulation of the most advantaged class is consistent with the underlying values and commitments of Rawls's philosophy of justice), but includes the latter idea as well. That is, I aim to show that it is justifiable on Rawlsian grounds to sometimes impose costs on the most advantaged class with neutral or even negative economic impact on the broader society. Rawls is ripe for an immanent critique in this latter regard because he himself, albeit very briefly, introduces the idea that there are some circumstances when the normally irrational desire to see those with more have less, even if it results in our having less (or the same) too, is not irrational but in fact an appropriate response to a given political-economic situation. The few places where Rawls acknowledges conditions "where it would be unreasonable to expect someone to feel differently"—where envy is "excusable" or "not irrational"—represent a theoretical bridge between traditional liberal-democratic philosophy and the plebeian development of liberal democracy I defend in this book. Whereas the usual perspective is either to overlook Rawls's concept of reasonable envy altogether or to limit its meaning to an undesirable sentiment that will be curtailed in a well-ordered society such as the one Rawls proposed, in fact the idea has a more far-reaching and permanent relevance for those pursuing liberal-democratic justice beneath the shadow of unfairness. Properly understood, reasonable envy is not merely a sentiment ordinary citizens may feel under unideal conditions. It also stands for the idea that progressives committed to the implementation of social justice in a liberal democracy must sometimes support policies that in certain instances will impose economic costs on the most advantaged with negative or neutral economic impact on the rest of society. Therefore, in addition to implicitly suggesting the grounds on which a liberal-democratic society might rightly wish to identify and regulate the most advantaged class, Rawls's thought takes on special importance for plebeianism because Rawls is a key theorist, however incipiently, of the other key element of the plebeian idea of reasonable envy: envy in the sense of sometimes imposing costs on the most advantaged with negative or neutral impact on the rest of society.

In enlisting Rawls to defend the plebeian idea of reasonable envy, I develop mostly latent aspects of his thought. It is after all a striking feature of Rawls's philosophy that it makes virtually no direct appeal to the category of the most advantaged, let alone to situations when the most advantaged might rightly be burdened with no material benefit for the broader polity.[40] Even if one of the three justifications that I shall examine for implementers of liberal-democratic justice taking a special regulatory interest in the most advantaged—the protective grounds—finds some overt support in Rawls's writings, with respect to the other two justifications—the heuristic and redressive grounds—my argument clearly extends Rawlsian ideas beyond what Rawls explicitly argued.

But in thinking beyond Rawls, I mean less to disagree with him in any particular respect than to evolve his philosophy, showing that the same underlying grounds Rawls appealed to as justifying a liberal society's special concern for the least favored also support it taking a principled regulatory interest in the economic expectations of the most favored. It is significant to note in this regard that Rawls's own thinking vis-à-vis the singling out of particular classes for special regulatory concern underwent an evolution during his lifetime. Rawls initially in his early articles articulated his vision of social justice with much less concern for the category of the least favored: while he still made the *protective* argument that the realization of basic liberties requires a "social minimum,"[41] he presented the difference principle without appeal to any class, defining it only as the principle that "all" or "everyone" must be made to benefit from a social system generating economic inequalities.[42] From his 1967 article "Distributive Justice" onwards, however, Rawls relied additionally on the "final" or "full" conception of the difference principle (T, 60, 302/52, 266 rev), which he defined as the norm that inequalities are perfectly just "when the prospects of the least fortunate are as great as they can be."[43] Rawls, then, came to have a greater appreciation for the role of the least favored class in the implementation of social justice. Rawls's evolution in his thinking with regard to the least favored not only led him to reflect on two additional grounds (*heuristic* and *redressive*) on which a liberal society might legitimately single out a specific class for special concern, but ought to raise the possibility that this evolution is not complete: that, in particular, the same three grounds—*heuristic, protective, and redressive*—for devoting regulatory attention in a liberal-democratic society to the least favored also justify that society taking an active regulatory interest in the most advantaged.

The following three subsections take up each of these three grounds as bases for a liberal-democratic polity to identify and potentially limit the economic expectations of its most advantaged class. In the fourth subsection, I appeal to Rawls's often overlooked and incorrectly marginalized distinction between irrational and non-irrational forms of envy to support the idea that there are situations when it is in fact appropriate to impose economic costs on the most advantaged with neutral or even negative material consequences for the rest of society.

Extending the Heuristic Argument: The Importance of the Most Advantaged Class to the Implementation of the Difference Principle

One of Rawls's principal justifications for having liberal democrats identify and afford special concern to the least favored class is that the economic expectations of this class serve an important heuristic role in a society's effort to realize the difference principle. Rawls came to recognize that, without further specification, his initial criterion that everyone benefit from a system of inequality is indeterminate. In *A Theory of Justice*, Rawls admits that the notion of "everyone's advantage" is an "ambiguous phrase" (T, 61, 65/53, 57 rev)[44]—and that defining injustice as "simply inequalities that are not to the benefit of all . . . is extremely vague and requires interpretation" (T, 62/54 rev). Rawls's mature articulations of the difference principle correct this problem, specifying that just inequalities, in benefitting everyone, should specifically advantage—and ideally *maximally* advantage—the expectations of the *least favored*.[45] A related heuristic benefit of specifying the difference principle in terms of ideally maximizing the expectations of the least favored is greater ease in application. If the initial conception of the difference principle seemed to require measuring the benefits accruing to each representative person in a society, the expanded definition simply "selects one representative [the least advantaged] for a special role" (T, 97-8/83 rev) in this regard.

My claim is that even if this specification of the difference principle provides implementers of social justice with a clearer criterion by which to evaluate and enact just socioeconomic policies, it is not without its own heuristic challenges— challenges that are productively confronted and reduced by having ideal legislators explicitly integrate the economic expectations of the most favored class into their calculations. In order to understand both the endurance of heuristic challenges regarding implementation of the difference principle as well as the usefulness of the category of the most advantaged in helping to address them,

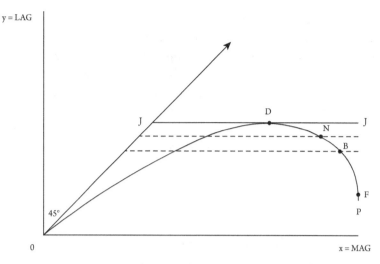

Figure 3.1 "In this figure the distances along the two axes are measured in terms of an index of primary goods, with the x-axis the more advantaged group (MAG), the y-axis the less advantaged (LAG). The line JJ parallel to the x-axis is the highest equal-justice line touched by the OP curve at its maximum at D. Note that D is the Pareto efficient point nearest to equality, represented by the 45-degree line. N is the Nash point, where the product of utilities is maximized (if we assume utilities to be linear in indexes of primary goods), and B is the Bentham point, where the sum of individual utilities is maximized (again with the same assumption). The set of Pareto efficient points goes from D to the feudal point F, at which the OP curve becomes vertical . . . *Society aims, other things equal, to reach the highest equal-justice line measured by the distance from O along the 45-degree line. To do this it moves as far northeast as possible along the OP curve and stops when this curve bends to the southeast*" (R, 62, emphasis added). Reprinted by permission of the publisher from JUSTICE AS FAIRNESS: A RESTATEMENT by John Rawls, pp. 62-63, Cambridge, Mass.: The Belknap Press of Harvard University Press, Copyright © 2001 by the President and Fellows of Harvard College.

consider Figure 3.1, one of Rawls's depictions of the meaning of the difference principle (simplified in this case because modeling only two representative positions). In attempting to legislate a just system of inequalities, ideal legislators are under two broad directives. First, they should seek a system of inequalities that approximates the point at which the least (or less[46]) favored maximally benefit (point D). How they do this depends on which part of the OP curve their society occupies. If it occupies a position of less-than-ideal levels of inequality (anywhere on the OP curve to the left of point D), legislators can favor a system of greater inequality so long as it raises the expectations of the least advantaged (and assumedly all other representative individuals). But if society occupies a position to the right of point D—where ongoing inequalities have been excessive insofar as they have not benefited, but in fact harmed, the expectations of the least advantaged (a space which Rawls calls the *"conflict segment"* [R, 124-127])—legislators must reform the basic structure in a way that reduces inequality and lowers the expectations of the more favored. Second, Rawls (T, 78-79/68 rev) is clear that equidistant misses of the ideal point D are not morally equal: a distribution to the left of D is "just throughout, but not the best just arrangement," whereas one within the conflict segment is "unjust."[47] This means that in attempting to approximate an ideal distribution, legislators have an obligation to avoid the conflict segment and thus should prefer any point to the left of D over one to the right.

What Rawls did not perceive is that the proper functioning of the difference principle, and in particular the proper policing of the conflict segment, would be aided if implementers of social justice made appeal to as finely calibrated a notion of the most advantaged (e.g., the superrich) as Rawls suggests they rely on for the least advantaged (e.g., "the unskilled worker" or "the lowest income class" [see T, 94, 307/84, 270]).[48] Specifically, they should supplement the ideal that the least favored maximally benefit from an ongoing system of inequalities with the ideal that the most favored appropriately contribute (i.e., the advantages accruing to the most favored class from an ongoing system of inequalities should not be excessive in the sense of harming the prospects of the least favored). From the perspective of the most abstracted conception of Rawlsian justice, where it is assumed point D will be achieved, this supplementary ideal appears superfluous: it is already contained in the former. But from the perspective of legislators, who must work to approximate point D in their specific societies, an explicit concern for the economic expectations of the most favored would serve at least three heuristic goals, all pertaining to the issue of how to hold on to a lively and rigorous conception of the conflict segment over and against various problems threatening to undermine its functionality.

First, insofar as determinations of whether and to what degree a society occupies the conflict segment depend on how finely the representative classes are calibrated, the formal integration of the most favored into the implementation of the difference principle promises to lend precision and greater effectivity to that principle. To the extent that Rawls presents the difference principle almost always without appeal to the most advantaged—and usually includes only the "more advantaged" which he opposes either to the "less advantaged" (in which case the "more advantaged" is 50% of the population) or to the "least advantaged" (in which case the "more advantaged" is a majority of the population, and a significant one at that)[49]—the difference principle would seem to lack the precision and sensitivity to combat any but the grossest instances of maldistribution. That is to say, without a notion of the "most advantaged," the conflict segment is limited to calculations that a great number of citizens (50%, if not a supermajority) prosper from a system of inequality to the detriment of the least or less advantaged, potentially failing to include situations, perhaps more numerous, when a system of inequality enables a small class of citizens (the most advantaged) to prosper with negative social impact.

Second, when the prospects of the most advantaged are explicitly integrated into efforts to implement the difference principle, the importance of the conflict segment—that is, the situation when a system of inequality is not benefitting the economic prospects of all representative members of society—is underlined, rather than marginalized. This might seem like a relatively small issue, but in fact the idea of the conflict segment is difficult to keep in view without a representative class—the most advantaged—whose expectations can serve as a point of reference in evaluating it. The temptation of uncritical market utopianism, which imagines any economic growth however distributed is to the benefit of all, is real. Rawls himself, after all, who operates effectively without a notion of the most advantaged, also evinces a tendency to relegate or ignore the conflict segment, even as he puts forward this crucial notion. Repeatedly, Rawls presents the difference principle in terms of the forward-looking rightward movement from O to D, rather than the retrospective, corrective, leftward movement from P to D. Even if technically speaking the difference principle calls for both movements, Rawls's rhetoric and argumentation often emphasize the former to the exclusion of the latter.[50] Given that the difference principle is itself to a certain extent marginalized within Rawls's theory,[51] the further marginalization of the conflict segment threatens to make that segment altogether neutralized. Insisting that the most favored class always has its expectations analyzed with respect to the evaluation of ongoing or proposed features of a society's underlying economic structure serves to maintain the vital, if overlooked and threatened, notion that decreasing inequalities can be just when it brings increased material benefit to the broader society.

Finally, the most advantaged class has a role to play—as the bearer of the "burden of proof" that a system of inequalities is not too excessive compared to the ideal distribution indicated by point D (i.e., that a society does not occupy the conflict segment)—within the context of uncertainty likely to surround any implementation of the difference principle. Rawls is clear that "there is often a wide variety of reasonable opinion as to whether the principle is satisfied."[52] Specifically, implementers face at least four sources of uncertainty: disagreement about the current diagnosis (who is relatively favored and unfavored at present), how a proposed policy will affect the relevant parties in the future, whether the policy will not only benefit the least favored but maximize their expectations compared to all other alternatives, and whether the selected policy has in fact achieved its aims. That the egalitarian element of the difference principle not be negated by the ability of opponents of justice to claim that their own preferred policies best serve the interests of the least favored (see R, 125), it is essential that the most advantaged class—as the best situated representative of the advantaged—bear the burden of proof within this context of uncertainty.[53] In saying that the most advantaged are "best situated," I mean that they have the most resources to withstand the costs of a less-than-perfect application of social justice, that their income and wealth most directly impact absolute levels of inequality, and that, under conditions of insufficient information, their expectations can serve as a proxy for the advantaged more generally.[54] Thus, when in doubt, legislators seeking to implement the difference principle should prefer to impose too many rather than too few economic costs on the most advantaged class, so as to veer toward too little rather than too much inequality.

It might seem that in attending to uncertainty in this way I am disagreeing with Rawls who argues (T, 201/176 rev) that citizens need to accept that on many questions of social and economic policy it is simply not clear what the difference principle requires—and that in such cases of indeterminacy, "we must fall back upon a notion of quasi-pure procedural justice" according to which the justice of a distributive scheme should be seen as inhering not in its substance (whether a system of inequalities is indeed mutually beneficial) but in its being enacted by a legitimate legislature. But even if such an approach requires that ordinary citizens relent from rigorism regarding the difference principle—since they must acknowledge that "the appeal to justice is not sufficiently clear and its resolution is best left to the political process"[55]—it still demands that legislators, within the political process, have some heuristic to guide their decision-making. Importantly, Rawls provides an account of what this heuristic should be. Recall that legislators committed to Rawlsian justice are under two moral directives: they should seek a system of inequalities that ideally maximizes the prospects of the least favored, but, additionally, in the event that their policies miss the ideal distribution (point D)—something virtually guaranteed under conditions of uncertainty—they are to prefer less-than-ideal rather than more-than-ideal levels of inequality (T, 78-79/68 rev). Taken together these two directives would appear to necessitate as a matter of effective legislative practice placing the burden of proof on the more—and in particular, as I am arguing here, the *most*—advantaged class. Legislators should identify the most advantaged as the class whose expectations are subject to special scrutiny in ensuring that a system of inequalities is not within the conflict segment.

When one considers the strong likelihood that the underappreciated conflict segment is precisely that part of the OP curve contemporary liberal-democratic societies occupy, any marginalization of that segment within a theory of justice is surely regrettable for liberal democrats committed to a notion of distributive justice more rigorous than the old, Lockean standard that the poor merely benefit at all from a system of inequality.[56] An advantage of a direct and explicit concern for the most favored is that it counteracts such marginalizing forces and more fully realizes a liberal-democratic society's commitment to a vision of social justice shaped by reciprocity and mutual benefit for all representative parties.

Extending the Protective Argument: The Threat to Liberty from the Most Advantaged

A second way in which those at the economic bottom of society enter into Rawls's theory of justice involves Rawls's argument that some minimum amount of income and wealth is required for the effective maintenance of basic liberties such as freedom of speech, religion, person, assembly, and so on. Prior to whatever additional gains the least favored receive through the difference principle, all citizens according to Rawls are to be guaranteed a "social minimum" as a condition of their basic liberties, on the assumption that there is a threshold level of resources without which other rights lose their meaning (PL, 228; R, 48, 162).

My claim—one which Rawls shares, even if its importance for singling out the most advantaged is something he does not strongly emphasize—is that the norm of protection justifies not just a floor on income and wealth, but potentially a ceiling. Like insufficient resources, too much inequality can also undermine the value of certain basic liberties. While Rawls's difference principle is explicitly opposed to making judgments about particular levels of inequality being intrinsically just or unjust (since it locates the justice of a system of inequalities in distributions that are mutually beneficial and ideally maximize the prospects of the least favored, regardless of how equal or unequal these distributions turn out to be), the difference principle is *not* the only distributive principle within Rawls's theory of justice. Beyond the difference principle there are two other crucial distributive principles within Rawls's system: the fair value of political liberties (which "ensures that citizens similarly gifted and motivated have roughly an equal chance of influencing the government's policy and of attaining positions of authority irrespective of their economic and social class" [R, 46; also see 149]) and fair equality of educational opportunity (i.e., "those who have the same level of talent and ability and the same willingness to use these gifts should have the same prospects of success regardless of their social class of origin, the class into which they are born and develop until the age of reason" [R, 44]).

There is nothing uniquely Rawlsian about Rawls's invocation of these two principles, since they reflect widely held norms that, ideally, a liberal democracy should afford educational and political opportunities to its citizens that are independent of the effects of socioeconomic status. That is, the two principles define the familiar liberal-democratic ambition—analyzed in Chapter 2—that a society's educational and political systems be free from plutocracy. But Rawls's specific account of these principles is important because, unlike many fellow travelers in the liberal-democratic tradition, he is explicit in understanding them as being endangered by too much inequality—or what he terms "excessive accumulations" or "excessive concentrations" of wealth and income.[57] Rawls does not extensively elaborate the nature of the "political domination" (R, 44) threatened by excessive inequalities.

But, as Freeman convincingly describes it, Rawls seems to mean that in the case of fair equality of educational opportunity, "there comes a point at which the degree of inequality is so great that, even if it satisfies the difference principle, . . . it nonetheless causes [the least favored] to feel diminished and less than civic equals of those who are more advantaged, leads them to see themselves as failures, and therefore neglect taking advantage of opportunities to educate and develop their capacities." In the case of the fair value of political liberties, as Freeman puts it, Rawls has in mind situations in which "because of the enormous inequalities of opportunities and unequal political influence that the capitalist welfare state allows, the less advantaged tend to withdraw from political and civic participation, seeing it as pointless, and suffer therewith a loss of their self-respect."[58]

Rawls, then, understands equality of opportunity as requiring not only familiar reforms pertaining to buttressing educational and political institutions against the intrusion of economic power, but the reduction of economic inequality itself when it reaches a level deemed to be so extreme that it undermines otherwise achievable relations of civic equality. Rawls does not define when accumulations of property become excessive and instead refers the question to political bodies, like legislatures.[59] But this is precisely why implementers of justice, who follow Rawls in understanding that excessive inequalities can undermine the capacity of free and equal citizens to enjoy civic equality with respect to education and politics, need to police the upper bounds of the distribution of income and wealth and, in so doing, operate with a lively sense of the most advantaged class.

Thus, even if Rawls does not explicitly say so, an inescapable implication of his concern with excessive inequalities is the need, on the grounds of protecting civil liberties, to identify and patrol the superrich.[60] This feature of Rawls's philosophy demonstrates the compatibility of a liberal-democratic polity with the ideology of historical plebeian republics which, in differentiating the Few from the Many for the purpose of regulating the Few, often did so for protective purposes. Because it was a frequent occurrence within premodern republican experience that wealthy families and individuals would undermine popular governments, rendering them more oligarchic and authoritarian or even placing them in foreign control,[61] republican theory and practice sometimes endorsed, in plebeian fashion, special bodies and offices, open only to citizens from the lower orders, with the purpose of vigilantly patrolling the rich and powerful.[62] Inspired in part by this legacy, John Adams put forward the idea of socioeconomically differentiated chambers of Congress for the nascent American republic, with the aim that this would in fact protect the country from the machinations of the wealthy elite.[63] Soon after Adams, William Manning, a radical farmer from Massachusetts, making direct appeal to ancient Roman plebeian structures like the tribunate, proposed creating a "Society of the Many or of Laborers," which would be comprised of laborers and other like-minded citizens (estimated to be approximately 92% of the citizenry), with the purpose of organizing and educating the Many so that their interests might prevail within electoral institutions that otherwise would be dominated by the very wealthy.[64] And much more recently, John McCormick's advocacy of "plebeian republicanism" likewise includes the proposal for a revived tribunate, to be composed of citizens chosen by lot from the bottom 90% of the economic distribution, with the power to initiate trials against political elites as well as veto certain laws.[65] Without justifying these plebeian proposals in their specifics, Rawls shows how their underlying logic of differentiating the Few from the Many so as to protect civic liberties is fully justifiable on liberal-democratic grounds.

There is, to be sure, a difference in the way protection is conceived in Rawls as opposed to these explicitly plebeian proposals. Plebeian thinkers and institutions traditionally have been concerned with actual usurpation: the danger that the socioeconomic elite within a society will deprive the less fortunate of basic freedoms.[66] Rawls, by contrast, gives voice to a different risk, namely that, independent of any insidious intentions of the wealthy and powerful, there are levels of inequality that at a certain degree of magnitude become so extreme that otherwise established liberties lose their *value* if not their formal instantiation: that is, that economic inequality can become so excessive that citizens come to feel that their ostensible political liberty to vote and engage in politics no longer enables them to make any impact in the electoral process and that, likewise, their formal right to apply for the same educational and professional opportunities no longer enables them to compete on fair terms with the wealthy and well-born.[67] The theory of plebeianism I defend here, however, embraces both protective concerns—the threat of usurpation and the threat of the demoralization generated by excessive inequalities—as grounding the need for a liberal-democratic society to at least actively police, if not necessarily limit, the upper bounds of an economic distribution.[68]

However much Rawls shares the same basic interest in protection that animates these plebeian efforts to identify and regulate the most advantaged class, the fact remains that, like other contemporary theorists of justice also worried about the threat to liberty posed by excessive inequalities, he does not directly propose singling out the superrich for special regulatory attention. Plebeianism, by contrast, calls for overcoming this reticence regarding the most advantaged class, insisting that the material preconditions of liberty require that a society take as lively an interest in its richest citizens as it must in its poorest.

Extending the Redressive Argument: The Need for Redress Beneath the Shadow of Unfairness

A third reason Rawls provides for singling out the least advantaged concerns redress: because the least favored on average have suffered the most from arbitrary disadvantages imposed by the natural and social lotteries, they have a claim to be privileged by the difference principle as the representative class whose income and wealth (along with other primary goods) ideally are to be maximized in the implementation of a just system of inequalities.[69] In justifying why the least favored in particular deserve to play a special heuristic role in the evaluation and implementation of justice, Rawls appeals to a redressive logic of compensation. To be clear, this form of compensation is distinct from the kind that is supposed to occur among reciprocally engaged free and equal citizens, whose inequalities are to be limited by the constraint that the less favored also benefit—or are compensated—by any system of inequalities (T, 102, 536/87, 470 rev). Rather, the compensation I mean to highlight, and the one that links Rawls's philosophy to a theory of redress, is the notion that when determining whether all citizens benefit from a system of inequalities, it is the expectations of the least advantaged that are to be singled out in the analysis because it is they who are most unfavored by the morally arbitrary distributions of the natural and social lotteries and by the imperfect capacity of a liberal-democratic society to partially correct for these in the sense of fully establishing fair equality of opportunity.[70] It is this latter kind of compensation that Rawls has in mind when he acknowledges, "It may appear that the difference principle is arbitrarily biased toward the least favored." Rawls's response is that "those favored by social and natural contingencies [should] regard themselves as already compensated, as it were, by advantages to which no one (including themselves) had a prior claim." Those who are not favored, the least advantaged, are entitled to their own kind of compensation in the form of a difference principle that privileges their interests when administering and evaluating justice.[71] Similarly, in one key passage from *A Theory of Justice* (73-4/63-4 rev; also see R, 124), Rawls argues that the least advantaged do not morally deserve their (on average) inferior placement in the natural lottery, nor is the principle of fair equality of opportunity fully realizable, and for these reasons they are entitled to play a unique role in the implementation of the difference principle.[72]

To be sure, in drawing attention to the redressive elements of Rawls's justification for singling out the least favored, I do not mean to attribute to Rawls the luck-egalitarian position that all undeserved inequalities are to be compensated. Clearly Rawls is not a luck egalitarian. He differentiates his theory from a wholesale philosophy of redress.[73] And he provides at least three reasons for allowing inequalities, even morally undeserved ones, to persist so long as they are part of a mutually beneficial social structure: the rationality of choosing absolute gains for all over the mere reduction of undeserved inequality (and, relatedly, the need for incentives for unequal rewards to motivate productive gains and the efficient allocation of resources) (T, 151/131 rev; R, 55, 203); the practical difficulty of enforcing a luck-egalitarian scheme (T, 87-88/76 rev; R, 68); and the entitlement (as opposed to moral desert) of individuals to be remunerated for their productivity (including individuals whose productivity is a function of morally arbitrary advantages).[74]

Still, if Rawls is opposed to efforts to neutralize all luck in an economic distribution, as I have indicated he is not altogether against redress, since his very particularization of the least favored as the class whose prospects are to be maximized in the implementation of the difference principle rests in part on redressive grounds. The question raised by Rawls's philosophy, then, is not *whether* misfortune should be mitigated at all, but *how much* mitigation should take place?

My claim is that there are Rawlsian grounds for extending redress to include the most advantaged, so that implementers of justice would aim not only to mitigate the arbitrary disadvantages of the least favored but the arbitrary advantages of the most favored. Underlying this argument is the problem that the two Rawlsian principles beyond the difference principle that I have already introduced—fair equality of opportunity with regard to both education and politics—are crucially important not simply because they are widely held by contemporary liberal-democratic philosophers and ordinary citizens alike, nor merely (following my discussion in the last subsection) because they are undermined by too much inequality, but because they will not be fully realizable in any conceivable liberal-democratic regime. As I argued in the discussion of plutocracy as a permanent civic structure in Chapter 2 (Section 2.5), private property and the family are so potent that it is impossible for a liberal democracy to maintain educational and political systems fully insulated from the intrusions of the effects of socioeconomic class. This circumstance is a crucial reason why even a so-called well-ordered society of the type Rawls hoped to see emerge will never be free from the shadow of unfairness. Such unfairness legitimates a claim of redress against the most favored class of society—the class prospering the most within an imperfectly fair system and thus, through costs placed upon it, best situated to *acknowledge* (and also remedy, however partially) the persistence of unfairness in an otherwise well-designed liberal-democratic regime.[75]

Rawls does not of course problematize the shadow of unfairness in any explicit way nor does he defend the propriety of seeking redress against the most advantaged in the face of this unfairness, but such positions ought to be considered justifiable extensions of his philosophy. At least with regard to one of the two principles calling for a plutocracy-free society—fair equality of opportunity with respect to education—Rawls occasionally admits that such an aspiration cannot be fully achieved in any imaginable liberal-democratic state. The principle that all similarly talented and motivated children should have the same prospect of "success" regardless of their social class of origin will never be fully realized, Rawls acknowledges, so long as there are institutions like the family. Here it is worth repeating, and indeed further contextualizing, a passage

I quoted in Chapter 2, since it is an important, if rare, instance of Rawls recognizing something like the shadow of unfairness with respect to liberal democracies' educational systems:

> The principle of fair opportunity can be only imperfectly carried out, at least as long as the institution of the family exists. The extent to which natural capacities develop and reach fruition is affected by all kinds of social conditions and class attitudes. Even the willingness to make an effort, to try, and so to be deserving in the ordinary sense is itself dependent upon happy family and social circumstances. *It is impossible in practice to secure equal chances of achievement and culture for those similarly endowed,* and therefore we may want to adopt a principle [i.e., the difference principle] which recognizes this fact and also mitigates the arbitrary effects of the natural lottery itself. (T, 74/64 rev, emphasis added)

While Rawls does not derive from this circumstance the need to seek redress against the most advantaged class, that he ought to have done so is lent force when one considers the unpersuasiveness of the two alternate solutions he pursues to the problem of plutocratic educational systems. One of these—if it can even be called a solution—is simply to deny the inevitability of plutocracy through repeatedly making claims, in contradiction to the above passage, that a properly reformed liberal democracy might after all fully achieve fair equality of opportunity with regard to education.[76] The other solution Rawls proposes, as the above passage suggests, is to invoke the fact of a liberal democracy being unable to satisfactorily implement fair equality of opportunity as a justification for the difference principle which, in privileging the least advantaged, "recognizes this fact" and mitigates it to some degree. But this solution is hardly convincing, since even if Rawls appeals to shortcomings in the implementation of fair equality of opportunity as an argument in favor of the difference principle, there is no escaping the problem that these shortcomings also disturb the difference principle itself. Although Rawls's argument in the above passage is to appeal to the imperfect realization of fair equality of opportunity to justify the difference principle, Rawls also repeatedly claims that the difference principle's refusal to understand particular distributions as being intrinsically just or unjust only works insofar as there is fair equality of opportunity:

> The role of the principle of fair opportunity is to insure that the system of cooperation is one of pure procedural justice [i.e., one in which there is no external standard of what constitutes a just distribution or excessive inequality, but only a procedure—in this case, the difference principle—that yields a limitless number of possible distributions, all

just]. Unless it is satisfied, distributive justice could not be left to take care of itself, even within a restricted range. (T, 87/76 rev; also see R, 46n)

Rawls may be correct in his claim that the difference principle mitigates some of the residual unfairness that accrues from a world without full fair equality of opportunity, but he does not pursue the further implication of this phenomenon: namely, that without more complete fair equality of opportunity, the difference principle's indifference toward wealth concentrations (so long as they are mutually beneficial) is no longer a fully fair mechanism of distribution. A liberal-democratic society's willingness to tolerate vast inequalities—to let "distributive justice . . . take care of itself"—erodes insofar as similarly talented and motivated individuals cannot expect similar prospects.[77] Due to the enduring impact of the social contingencies of one's birth on life expectations, the difference principle's insistence that citizens simply embrace any inequalities that are mutually beneficial loses some of its force.

Rawls, then, remains only dimly aware of the shadow of unfairness with regard to educational opportunity and his proposed solutions—denial or the difference principle—are too ineffectual to sufficiently address that shadow. Because some element of unfairness will always be with us—a point Rawls seems to acknowledge, however briefly—the plebeian approach is to develop the Rawlsian paradigm to include redress against the most advantaged class. That is to say, notwithstanding the substantial educational resources a liberal-democratic society will devote to all of its citizens—especially, perhaps, the least advantaged—it is nonetheless clear that given two equally talented and motivated children, the one born into a privileged background will have not only greater prospects of wealth, but greater prospects of culture, education, and "success" relative to a child born into an underprivileged background. This circumstance occurs not just in the United States, but even within the world's most egalitarian educational systems.[78] The impact of socioeconomic status on children's life prospects is unfair. It justifies a liberal-democratic society committed to free and equal citizenship in singling out the most advantaged, the group that has most prospered under an imperfectly fair system and that is therefore best able to provide redress in the form of the public acknowledgment and partial remediation of such unfairness.

The call for redress against the superrich will be seen as one of plebeianism's most controversial features, but this call is superior to other leading efforts to respond to the problem of plutocratically infected educational systems. For example, some have been led to take issue with the family itself on liberal grounds; but, here, the proposal seems patently undesirable and out of keeping with our mammalian roots. From the other side, libertarian critics like

Nozick have argued that the inability to fully realize fair equality of opportunity demonstrates its inappropriateness as a norm of justice, but such a critique conflates unenforceability with invalidity.[79] Finally, certain defenders of Rawls, like Freeman, have argued that the meaning of fair equality of opportunity is in fact more limited than guaranteeing similarly talented and motivated children roughly equal prospects of achievement: that it does not involve "requiring equal chances for the equally endowed" but only that citizens "have a fair opportunity to compete with others of similar abilities for positions within the range of their *developed* skills."[80] But, as I argued in the last chapter, this watered-down conception of fairness is unlikely to be fully satisfying to liberal democrats committed to the well-established ideal that children's career prospects not be affected by their socioeconomic status. Nor for that matter is it a compelling interpretation of Rawls, who explicitly and repeatedly calls for equal opportunities for the equally endowed—not the more minimal standard that those with similar *developed* skills have fair opportunity to compete with one another—as a condition of a just society.[81]

I have devoted special attention to the problem of plutocracy within educational systems because Rawls himself admits, albeit very briefly and not at all consistently, that no liberal-democratic society will be fully able to achieve fair equal equality of educational opportunity. Such a recognition is a point of connection between Rawls's political philosophy and plebeianism, suggesting that the plebeian idea of the shadow of unfairness, and with it the plebeian call for redress, might be justified on liberal-democratic grounds. But it is also important to attend to the other principle at play in the widely held liberal-democratic commitment to a plutocracy-free society: the principle that citizens have equal access to politics independent of their socioeconomic status—a principle Rawls designates as the fair value of the political liberties. Here too we ought to confront the inability of any conceivable liberal-democratic regime to fully realize this ambition, even if Rawls does not make an argument in this regard. As I argued in the previous chapter (Section 2.5), while a liberal-democratic society can always work to do better in approximating a situation in which all citizens, regardless of economic and social background, have an equal chance to hold office and influence election outcomes, a variety of factors make it impossible for this aim to be sufficiently realized: the fluidity of power by which wealth and political influence tend to translate into each other at their extreme magnitudes; the bevy of research in political behavior demonstrating the connection between socioeconomic status and the likelihood of various forms of political engagement; and the growing recognition of how simply being lower down within a socioeconomic hierarchy, independent of diminished material resources inherent in that placement, may undermine a sense of political efficacy as well as other components of a vibrant civic life. Rawls, it is true, does not confront plutocracy in the political system as a permanent problem. He does not hold the view that the scarcity of political offices in a mass liberal democracy itself prevents the fullest realization of equal political liberty.[82] And he thinks various liberal reforms, such as campaign finance legislation and the wider dispersal of capital within a society, can make it so the equally endowed and motivated "have roughly an equal chance of influencing the government's policy and of attaining positions of authority irrespective of their economic class" (R, 46). But while this ideal is noble and its approximation certainly worth striving for, the shadow of unfairness and the concomitant need for redress arise from the inescapable confluence of economic and political power that makes the economically well-off, on average, more likely than the less advantaged to exert political influence.[83]

That the shadow of unfairness is not limited to educational opportunity but also darkens the political realm is but another reason that a plebeian finds it appropriate to seek redress against the most advantaged class—the class that has prospered the most within a system that is not fully fair—and, in so doing, to extend Rawls's interest in mitigating the unfair disadvantages besetting the least favored class to also include an interest in mitigating the unfair advantages accruing to the most favored.[84]

Importantly, extending this logic of mitigation to also include the particularization of the most advantaged as a distinct class deserving special regulatory attention is fully compatible with the three limits on redress Rawls puts forward. First, because redress is constrained by the notion that all are supposed to benefit, there is no question of pursuing redress to a point that obviously leads to lower economic expectations for the rest of society. In this respect the redress argument is like the heuristic argument, but unlike the protective argument, in not wanting to impose burdens on the most advantaged that *clearly* lower the prospects of everyone else. But redress against the most favored would be grounds for reducing inequality when there is *neutral* material impact on the broader society, an issue about which Rawls is ambivalent.[85] Second, while it is true that the extension of redress to the most advantaged would require an additional set of applications (focusing on the most advantaged and not just the least advantaged), it would not result in the determination of desert and specific allocative shares for an entire population, something Rawls finds, rightly I believe, highly impractical. Finally, it is not correct to say that the extension of redress disrespects the entitlement of the most advantaged class to benefit from the productive use of their labor and capital, since any redress would only regulate the highest levels of income and wealth (above a threshold point), ensuring that those to whom it applied would retain their status as the wealthiest individuals (and retaining, too, their entitlement to remuneration for productive gains).

Clearly, the failure of a society to fully realize fair equality of opportunity with regard to education and politics is not as severe an injustice as despotism or other blatant violations of basic liberties. Nonetheless the principle of equal educational and political opportunity is fundamental not only to Rawls, but to multiple strands of liberal-democratic thought more generally and to the political attitudes of ordinary citizens.[86] Part of the rationale for my using the terminology *shadow* of unfairness is to designate precisely a residual unfairness that may not be enough to destabilize a regime through generating widespread disobedience and unrest, but nonetheless is sufficiently problematic so as to require some compensation from the class that most benefits from the inability of a liberal-democratic society to adequately escape the feudal confines of blood and lineage.

Defending Regulation of the Most Advantaged That Does Not Always Materially Benefit the Rest of Society

Recall that the concept of reasonable envy contains two distinct ideas. On the one hand, it stands for singling out and potentially regulating the economic expectations of the most advantaged class. On the other hand, it also includes the further claim that such regulation of the most advantaged sometimes should be carried out even if it generates neutral or negative economic outcomes for the rest of society. The immanent critique of Rawls I have conducted reflects this double meaning of reasonable envy. I have argued on three different grounds—heuristic, protective, and redressive—not simply that it is consistent with a Rawlsian conception of justice to identify and sometimes regulate the economic expectations of the most advantaged, but that as part of this process there are certain cases when it is legitimate to impose economic burdens on the most favored that have either a neutral or negative material impact for the broader populace. The protective argument, which aims to prevent inequalities that are so excessive that they threaten civic liberty, justifies regulation of the most advantaged even when the rest of society would be worse off in economic terms.[87] The redressive argument, as I have explained, legitimates the imposition of economic burdens on the most advantaged that would have a neutral material impact on other representative members of a political community. And while the heuristic argument does not sanction lowering the prospects of the most advantaged class when doing so *clearly* would have a negative or neutral impact on the rest of society, its support of having the most advantaged bear the burden of proof that a society's system of inequalities is outside the prohibited conflict segment means that it legitimates economic bias against the most advantaged under conditions of uncertainty.[88]

It is just this second element of reasonable envy—the imposition of economic burdens on the most advantaged class in certain situations where there is negative or neutral benefit to the rest of society—that I mean to further justify here, demonstrating that it is in fact consistent with the liberal-democratic ideal of free and equal citizenship and, specifically, with the canonical articulation this ideal has received in Rawls's philosophy. Before doing so, however, it should be stressed that when Rawls himself discusses envy he always has this second meaning in mind: that is, for Rawls, envy is not any regulatory concern for the more advantaged, but only the desire to impose costs on the more advantaged that have negative, or even neutral, economic impact on the broader economy.[89] Accordingly, my discussion in this subsection follows Rawls in discussing envy in this more restricted, secondary sense.

Critics will object that in defending potentially subjecting the most advantaged to costs without compensating economic benefit for the rest of society, my argument is not simply guilty of envy—the seemingly irrational desire for those with more to have less, even if it results in neutral or negative economic consequences for everyone else—but, in its enviousness, guilty of something widely opposed within the broader political culture and, in particular, by Rawls himself. Rawls, after all, explicitly defends the anti-envying mentality of "mutual disinterest," arguing that citizens must not be expected to have other-regarding sentiments—whether altruism or envy—when determining the content of social justice behind the so-called veil of ignorance (T, 128, 148, 253-4/111, 128, 223-4 rev). Rawls says citizens, so engaged, who are dismayed by another's economic success—if such success emerges from an underlying political and economic system that maximizes their own expectations—are "shortsighted" (T, 151)[90] because they are in effect preferring to have less simply so that others have less too. Rawls's apparent view about the irrationality of envy is by no means idiosyncratic, but, as I indicated in Section 3.1, reflective of a general opposition to envy among political philosophers and ordinary citizens alike.

Notwithstanding these considerations, however, such a one-sided account of Rawls's theory of envy is incomplete, unbalanced, and thus mistaken. Rawls's endorsement of mutual disinterest and his parallel critique of envy are not absolute: he makes an important distinction, often unobserved by Rawls scholars, between ordinary, irrational, inexcusable envy and another form which he describes as "not irrational"—an envy "where it would be unreasonable to expect someone to feel differently" (T, 534/468 rev; PL, 284; R, 88). The crucial claim I want to defend is both that this latter form of non-irrational envy has an important role to play in the *implementation* of Rawlsian justice and that the kinds of envy implicated in my defense of a liberal-democratic society regulating the most advantaged class fall within this category of non-irrational envy.

Rawls's delineation of the concept of non-irrational envy has not received sufficient attention, as numerous recent commentators have overlooked the notion altogether.[91] In part this is because Rawls himself only provides a brief sketch of the concept. But it is also a result of the fact that the usual treatment of the notion among scholars who have examined it is to marginalize non-irrational envy as having to do only with Rawls's arguments about the stability of his principles of justice (their capacity to generate the sources of their own support, in part by not producing rancorous sentiments, like envy, in the citizenry) and not also about the *implementation* of the principles themselves.[92] In other words, the usual reading of non-irrational envy is that Rawls appeals to it only as an *excusable rancorous sentiment* he thinks will be more curtailed in societies governed by his proposed principles of justice, not that it has any positive role to play in the effective instantiation of those principles *as the willingness of implementers of justice sometimes to impose costs on the advantaged without compensating economic benefit for the rest of society*.[93]

Although I find it incorrect, the reduction of non-irrational envy to excusable envy is understandable, if only because Rawls's most prolonged engagement with the concept of non-irrational envy confronts the notion in precisely this sense (T, 531-2, 534-41/466, 468-74 rev; R, 88, 180, 202). In these passages, Rawls argues that while normally it is irrational for individuals to want those with more to have less when doing so will have a negative impact on their own material welfare, there are circumstances when inequalities are so great that they harm the self-respect of ordinary citizens and thereby undo the irrationality normally attached to envious sentiments:

> A person's lesser position as measured by the index of objective primary goods may be so great as to wound his self-respect; and given his situation, we may sympathize with his sense of loss. . . . For those suffering this hurt, envious feelings are not irrational; the satisfaction of their rancor would make them better off. When envy is a reaction to the loss of self-respect in circumstances where it would be unreasonable to expect someone to feel differently, I shall say that it is excusable. (T, 534/468 rev, emphasis added)

Rawls thinks it an advantage of his proposed system of justice that it is less likely than alternative schemes, especially utilitarianism, to generate such excusable rancorous sentiments (T, 537/469-70 rev).

But this usual treatment of non-irrational envy is overly narrow on two grounds: it neglects the way in which envy has a role to play in the *implementation* of justice (and is therefore not just excusable but *reasonable*), and it forgets that beyond the problem of excessive inequalities there are at least two additional situations in which the normal irrationality of envy is abrogated. Both aspects of this richer, more expansive conception of envy are suggested in the following passage:

> A rational person . . . follows the plan which will satisfy more of his desires rather than less, and which has the greater chance of being

successfully executed . . . . A rational individual does not suffer from envy. He is not ready to accept a loss for himself if only others have less as well. He is not downcast by the knowledge or perception that others have a larger index of primary social goods. *Or at least this is true so long as the differences between himself and others do not exceed certain limits, and he does not believe that the existing inequalities are founded on injustice or are the result of letting chance work itself out for no compensating social purpose.* (T, 143/124 rev, emphasis added; also see T, 144, 530, 532, 533/124, 464, 466, 467 rev)

The first thing to note about this passage is that Rawls acknowledges there are *three* instances when envy is not irrational: excessive inequalities; inequalities that stem from an unjust basic structure, in which either basic liberties or fair equality of opportunity has not been fairly secured; and inequalities that do not satisfy the difference principle but involve an economic system in which income and wealth accrue to winners of the natural and social lotteries without less fortunate members of society also benefitting from the inequalities being generated (also see T, 530/464 rev).

The second crucial feature to note about this passage is that it comes, not from the final Part III of *A Theory of Justice* where Rawls engages with the issue of stability, but from Part I, "Theory" (specifically, Chapter 3, "The Original Position," Section 25: "The Rationality of the Parties"), where Rawls discusses the general conception of rationality presumed to govern the adoption and implementation of the principles of justice (T, 143/124 rev).[94] The suggestion, in other words, is that the three forms of non-irrational envy Rawls mentions arise in *two* separate contexts: not just in relation to the matter of stability (where theories of justice are evaluated with regard to how much excusable envy they generate[95]), but also in relation to the Original Position (where the three forms of non-irrational envy become contexts in which it becomes reasonable for implementers of justice to impose economic burdens on the advantaged with negative or neutral benefit for the rest of society).

To be sure, I do not mean to say that the initial *adoption* of the principles of justice is guided by envy for Rawls. In this regard, Rawls is clear that envy plays no role.[96] But, as Rawls explains, the Original Position can be disaggregated so as to refer to an initial adoption stage, where the principles are selected, and three successive stages—the constitutional convention (where equal basic liberties are constitutionalized), the legislative stage (where legislators select the social and economic policies required by justice), and the judicial stage (where particular cases are adjudicated)—all of which have to do, not with the selection of the principles, but their *implementation* (T, 195-201/171-6 rev). As the veil of ignorance is gradually lifted at each successive stage, each stage still models an ideal form of rationality pertaining to the implementation of justice.[97] If envy does have a potential role to play in the implementation of justice, as Rawls suggests, it would be at the legislative stage, where legislators ideally seek the passage of laws and policies that realize the social and economic conditions required by a just society—and do so with abundant information about the nature of the distributions within their society, with "the full range of general economic and social facts . . . brought to bear" (T, 199/175 rev).[98]

My claim is that any envy relating to the protective, heuristic, or redressive justifications for imposing regulatory burdens on the most favored can be seen as falling within the three categories of reasonable envy Rawls mentions: excessive inequalities, inequalities not bound by the difference principle, and inequalities founded on an unjust basic structure that does not properly respect fair equality of opportunity, respectively. The first of these assertions—that to the extent the protective grounds for capping the economic expectations of the most advantaged involves elements of envy (since such capping might very well lower everyone's material welfare), such envy is reasonable if it is part of the legislative effort to combat excessive inequalities—is straightforward and something Rawls clearly affirms. It is not simply that Rawls expects legislators to enact policies to counteract excessive accumulations of property.[99] What also is key is that Rawls explicitly argues that legislators so engaged are acting upon, or at least responding to, a non-irrational form of envy. In *Political Liberalism*, Rawls makes it clear that non-irrational envy is a *constraint* which legitimates laws and policies that limit the upper bounds of wealth: "[The principles of justice] also specify an ideal form for the basic structure in the light of which ongoing institutional and procedural processes are constrained and adjusted. Among these constraints are limits on the accumulation of property . . . that derive from the requirements of the fair value of political liberty and fair equality of opportunity, and the limits based on considerations of stability and excusable envy, both of which are connected to the essential primary good of self-respect. We need such an ideal to guide the adjustments necessary to preserve background justice" (PL, 284; also see T, 545/478 rev). By treating envy here as a constraint, Rawls specifies that it functions both in terms of stability and in terms of implementation—or that stability itself is more than a criterion for passively evaluating rival regimes, but a basis for implementers of justice to intervene in the economic structure of their society.

Second, the envious elements of the heuristic grounds for regulating the most advantaged should be seen as falling within the exception to the general irrationality of envy that arises when it is believed that "existing inequalities . . . are the result of letting chance work itself out for no compensating social purpose" (T, 143/124 rev). Given the uncertainty surrounding the successful implementation of the difference principle, the concern that a system of inequalities is too extreme, such that it passes into the conflict segment where it no longer

serves a compensating social purpose, will be an ongoing problem for legislators, even (and especially) ideally conceived ones. The context of uncertainty
means that legislators committed to justice cannot reliably achieve a precise
point on the OP curve (see Figure 3.1), but only a *range*. Their insistence that
the most advantaged bear the risks of this uncertainty, and with it their preference for less-than-ideal rather than more-than-ideal levels of inequality, means
that over time they will produce policies that tend to the left of the ideal distribution (point D) rather than to the right: it means that they will engineer a society
where all representative classes tend to have less-than-ideal as opposed to one
where only some do. Compare this to an alternate scenario where legislators,
under no compulsion to treat uncertainty in a biased way, simply could do their
best to reach the ideal distribution: over time they would produce a range of
systems of inequalities that straddled a space equidistant from both sides of the
ideal distribution. What justifies the former scenario over the latter one—and,
with it, a modicum of envy (since the former scenario is in effect the decision
for all to have less income and wealth over time than they would under the latter scenario)—is that the two sides of the curve are not morally equal. Because
the space to the right of D is one of injustice, but the space to the left is merely
less-than-perfect justice (T, 78-79/68 rev), a society has a moral reason to prefer
this otherwise irrational outcome. Since legislators cannot escape the possibility
that their polices will lead society into the conflict segment, it is reasonable for
them to operate on the basis of a heuristic device that, in privileging too much
over too little equality, over time will have the effect of making all members of
society materially worse off.

Finally, to the extent there is an element of envy in the redressive grounds for
regulating the most advantaged, which as I have discussed justifies placing economic burdens on the most advantaged even when doing so has a neutral material impact on the rest of society, such envy finds legitimation in Rawls's third
exception to the irrationality of envy: the belief that, within a society, "existing inequalities are founded on injustice" (T, 143/124 rev). Even if, as I have
indicated, the injustice in question is less one of gross and correctible injustice
than the residual unfairness stemming from an otherwise well-ordered society's
inability to fully realize fair equality of opportunity with regard to education and
politics, such unfairness is a basis for imposing redressive burdens on the most
advantaged which have no economic benefit for the rest of society.

I do not claim that the protective, heuristic, and redressive grounds for regulating the most advantaged exhaust the potential meaning of non-irrational envy
for Rawls, but only that, to the extent envy is involved in my three arguments for
extending social justice to include a concern for the most advantaged as lively
and explicit as normally evinced for the least favored, such envy falls within the
category of reasonable envy.[100]

Of course, it is important not to let the subtleties of my critical exegesis of Rawls obscure what should be the bigger point. That there is even a category of reasonable envy—that the imposition of economic costs on the advantaged without economic benefit for society has a role to play in the implementation of social justice—ought to be a corrective to the widespread denigration of envy within contemporary liberal-democratic philosophy and the broader political culture.[101]

It is worth recalling that the root meaning of *envy* comes from the Latin words "to see" (*videre*) and, specifically, "to regard maliciously" (*invidere*)—so that envy literally means a "hostile look"[102]—which reminds us that prior to any regulation and imposition of burdens, envy most basically involves a suspicion toward a particular person or class and, so, an identification of them. My arguments for regulating the most advantaged are at the most fundamental level arguments for *identifying* this class—a stipulation which might seem meager at first, but is actually quite substantial in light of the surprising absence of the most advantaged within major discourses of contemporary liberal-democratic thought, not to mention tax codes which define the upper bracket so low that the superrich remain hidden from view. Given the current context in which leading philosophies, civic attitudes, and political practices all align with a refusal to seek out the most favored members of society, such an identification would itself be a major, if initial, accomplishment of a liberal-democratic society's willingness to evolve its understanding of justice to more directly reflect, and indeed extend and further particularize, Rawls's (R, 125) insight: "In the well-ordered society of justice as fairness it seems that those most likely to be discontent are the more advantaged."

3.4 The Importance of Reasonable Envy to the Further Development of Liberal Democracy

My main purpose in this chapter has been to show that reasonable envy against the superrich is justifiable within the liberal-democratic paradigm of free and equal citizenship. Relying on an immanent critique of Rawls's philosophy of justice as the primary means of establishing the liberal-democratic credentials of reasonable envy, I have attended to situations in which envy is not a departure from liberal-democratic values, but instead a way to further realize them beneath the ever-present shadow of unfairness.

In conclusion, it is important to confront the objection that because my arguments in defense of plebeianism's call to identify and regulate the most advantaged class rely heavily on the language of Rawls's philosophy, they are of limited significance since Rawls is but one of many recent philosophers and has no monopoly on the meaning of liberal-democratic justice. Outside of the fact that Rawls is hardly an arbitrarily chosen philosopher, but the most influential liberal-democratic political thinker of recent times and someone whose thought often is heralded as summarizing the implicit moral logic of contemporary liberal-democratic states—and outside of the fact that Rawls after all introduces the very notion of reasonable envy that I have developed here—there are at least three reasons for understanding the immanent critique of Rawls pursued in this chapter as having a broader, more general significance for liberal democrats of all persuasions.

First, with regard to the heuristic grounds for identifying and regulating the most advantaged class, even if I have relied on the specifics of Rawls's difference principle to elucidate the heuristic logic for singling out the most advantaged class for special regulatory concern, the basic heuristic idea that the most advantaged class ought to play a role in the implementation of social policies under conditions of complexity and uncertainty has a relevance beyond the parameters of Rawls's philosophy. Virtually any account of liberal-democratic justice today will have to confront the problem that the precise nature of a polity's economic distribution as well as the impact of proposed socioeconomic policies on that distribution going forward are likely to be not-fully-known and thus contested.[103] The plebeian suggestion that the most advantaged are well-positioned to play an important heuristic role under such circumstances—since they occupy both an extreme point within the economic distribution and a position best able to absorb the risks of uncertainty—ought to find support, then, among a diversity of philosophical standpoints within the liberal-democratic tradition.

In insisting on the heuristic relevance of the most advantaged class, plebeianism is not engaged in the mere exegesis of Rawls, but rather stands for the refinement of the widespread liberal-democratic commitment to engage in class-based reasoning for heuristic purposes. After all, that the least advantaged members of society ought to play an essential heuristic role in a society's estimation of its commitment to social justice has long been understood. Gandhi is only the most famous of a robust tradition of thinkers who have asserted, "A nation's greatness is measured by how it treats its weakest members"—a statement which indicates the importance not only of benefiting the least advantaged members of society as a condition of social justice, but more basically of needing to identify the expectations of this group in order to even begin to evaluate a particular society's existing approach to social justice. Plebeianism extends this heuristic idea to the most advantaged, arguing that their economic expectations are essential to efforts to implement just socioeconomic policies.

Second, the immanent critique of Rawls I have carried out in this chapter has not primarily revolved around what is most particular to Rawls—the difference principle—but instead has concerned two other principles widely held by liberal-democratic thinkers and ordinary citizens alike: the principle that, regardless of socioeconomic status, similarly motivated and talented citizens should have roughly equal prospects of influencing politics (fair equality of political opportunity) and the principle that similarly talented and motivated children should have roughly equal prospects of occupational choice and other conventional criteria of success (fair equality of educational opportunity). Even if Rawls considers the liberties envisioned by these two principles with uncommon care and depth, they are in no way particular to his philosophy, as they form the basic idea of a meritocratically fair liberal-democratic order. Therefore, in claiming that the effective protection of these two sets of liberties requires greater regulatory attention to the most advantaged class, the argument I have pursued here has relevance for liberal-democratic thought in the most general sense, not merely for a particular Rawlsian version of it.

Of course, my claim in this chapter has not been merely that fair equality of opportunity with regard to education and politics is an important liberal-democratic norm, but that it is not fully realizable, thereby generating the logic for seeking redress against the superrich. As I demonstrated, Rawls begins to acknowledge this problem, admitting, however briefly, that the family imposes limits on how much equality of educational opportunity can be achieved (though failing to recognize parallel limits on the full realizability of equality of political opportunity). A crucial part of my critique of Rawls has been to argue for developing his very limited forthrightness in this regard into a much larger appreciation for the fundamental and inescapable shadow of unfairness darkening any conceivable liberal-democratic state.

A third reason my treatment of Rawls has an extra-Rawlsian relevance is that Rawls is hardly unique in being open to this kind of critique. Other leading liberal-democratic thinkers follow Rawls both in signaling a dim awareness that liberal-democratic norms are constitutively unrealizable and in nonetheless failing to present this circumstance as a full-fledged *problem* that ought to meaningfully alter how liberal democracy is conceived and pursued. Dworkin, for example, offhandedly references the fact that his proposals for distributive justice "cannot be realized perfectly."[104] He says something similar when he writes, "Self-government means more than equal suffrage and frequent elections. It means a partnership of equals, reasoning together about the common good. We can never fully achieve that ideal—no nation could."[105] But these acknowledgments do not lead Dworkin to what is, for the plebeian at least, the natural conclusion: that liberal democracy will always be conducted beneath a shadow of unfairness. Social scientists who have recognized that no existing nation fully lives up to liberal-democratic norms of participatory equality—but who fail to dwell on this at any length as an actual and urgent problem—embody a similar philosophical posture.[106] So, too, do many of the other figures I examined in Chapter 2 in my discussions of the varieties of contemporary blindness to the problem of plutocracy (Section 2.5). Insofar, then, as Rawls's all-too-incipient recognition of the shadow of unfairness is mirrored by numerous other contemporary approaches to the study of liberal democracy, the immanent critique of Rawls I have undertaken in this chapter, which insists on a far more direct and central confrontation with liberal democracy's inescapable inability to realize its fullest commitments, clearly has a broader application than a mere response to the particularities of Rawls's theory of justice.

Still, the ultimate defense of the singular attention I have devoted to Rawls is the significance of his philosophy to the contemporary understanding of liberal democracy. The point is not simply that Rawls is perhaps the most seminal liberal-democratic thinker of the last half-century and someone whose work often is seen as articulating the meaning of contemporary liberal-democratic institutions when viewed in their most idealized, aspirational light. Nor does Rawls's profound germaneness stem only from the fact that he is the paradigmatic philosophical example of the primary phenomenon I have subjected to immanent critique in this chapter: namely, the tendency of liberal democracy to operate on the basis of a profound imbalance whereby special regulatory concern is afforded to the least favored class but not also the most favored. What also justifies the special theoretical attention I have given to Rawls is that he does after all introduce the concept of "reasonable envy" and, with it, the suggestion that envy might have a legitimate function in a liberal-democratic regime. Rawls of course did not understand reasonable envy as a pioneering idea. But one cannot fully control the destinations to which one's thought is a bridge. And this is not only because one's thinking can be appropriated by perspectives antithetical to one's own, but because it is impossible to understand the full implications of one's own ideas when engaged in a philosophical project as progressive and evolutionary as the meaning of justice in a liberal-democratic regime.

Learning How Not to Be Good: A Plebeian Perspective

In the world there is no one but the vulgar.

—Machiavelli

4.1 The Problem of Principled Vulgarity

We miss out on the full meaning of plebeianism if we limit it to the *condition* of second-class citizenship or the *project* of identifying and regulating the most advantaged class. What plebeianism also involves is an account of why its theory will be difficult to accept among the very ordinary citizens it aims to serve, why it should still nevertheless be endorsed, and how its philosophy in this regard might embody a distinctly plebeian brand of political maturity.

What makes plebeianism challenging is that it requires from the ordinary citizen behaviors and commitments that, though necessary for a more honest and progressive pursuit of liberal democracy, are nonetheless morally ambiguous— a strange, almost paradoxical amalgam which I refer to as "principled vulgarity." I elaborate the particular elements of principled vulgarity in what follows, but in the most general sense it arises from the following dilemma: morally speaking, democracy would seem to stand for *undifferentiated free and equal citizenship* as the central norm informing its ethics and institutions, yet a plebeian philosophy of liberal democracy—*in the name of this very norm*—still finds itself insisting on the differentiation between the Few and the Many. This differentiation not only offends the morally powerful idea that democrats should commit themselves unqualifiedly to the generation of a classless society, but it also requires uncomfortable, always contestable decisions about where to draw the line in determining who belongs to each group. That the purpose of differentiating the Few from the Many is not at all an oligarchic one, but rather aims at burdening the most powerful members of a polity, only partially offsets plebeianism's moral fraughtness. For instance, because plebeianism partakes of envy—of aiming to burden the most powerful not for any concrete wrongdoing on their part and sometimes even when such regulation has negative material effect on the rest of society—its central proposals sit uneasily with pervasive moral sensibilities within contemporary culture. And even beyond its concern for regulating the Few, plebeianism's insistence that ordinary citizens understand themselves as second class—with political voices and civic opportunities systematically more attenuated than their more socioeconomically advantaged counterparts—will seem to some a demoralized ethical outlook, out of keeping with a virtuous faith in the enduring capacity of future reform to enable liberal democracy to fully realize its moral potential.

Thus far in this book I have emphasized the "principled" side of plebeian political ideas, arguing that the differentiation between the Few and the Many— and the imposition of burdens on the Few—is an appropriate way to acknowledge and respond to the shadow of unfairness that will be cast in any conceivable liberal-democratic regime. But it is also important to attend to the vulgar aspect. Because plebeianism involves elements offensive to widely held moral intuitions about democracy—because the shadow of unfairness darkens not merely the capacity of liberal democracy to fully implement its commitment to free and equal citizenship, but also the ethical horizon of ordinary citizens who strive to realize progressive ends under such conditions—part of the defense of plebeianism requires explaining to citizens why they should overcome their moral resistance to plebeian ideas and practices.

It might seem that such an explanation is impossible. After all, if plebeianism offends widely held moral norms, this would appear to represent a significant check against plebeianism. Or, from the other side, it might be thought that if plebeianism is correct as a political philosophy, the moral intuitions cautioning against plebeian ideas and practices, however pervasive, must themselves be incorrect. Such perspectives, which dissolve the problem of principled vulgarity at the outset by denying the very possibility of moral conflict, are unpersuasive not simply because they are blind to the tragic likelihood that in politics, if not elsewhere, not all good things ultimately coalesce in a single harmony, but because, in the specific case of plebeianism, there is a genuine dilemma: its advocacy of the Few-Many distinction aims to better achieve, yet at the same time also sullies, the liberal-democratic aspiration of free and equal citizenship. Thus, rather than disavow any element of ethical ambiguity, my defense of plebeianism proceeds in a different manner. I argue that the vulgar aspects of plebeian politics can be justified as a democratic appropriation of a long-standing (though admittedly still controversial) political idea: that political ethics are not reducible to morality and that political responsibility must therefore require, in the suggestive words of Machiavelli, "learning how not to be good."[1] As this chapter makes clear, within the history of political thought this kind of Machiavellian logic, according to which one must tarnish one's soul as a condition of serving the state, has almost always been restricted to a context of elite powerholding. What has not yet been sufficiently explored—and what plebeianism aims to accomplish—is the articulation of an account of politically responsible ethical ambiguity applicable on the level of ordinary citizenship.[2]

In making this case and defending the idea of principled vulgarity, I am here as elsewhere in this book inspired by the historical plebeians of late republican Rome. Indeed, the connection between plebeianism and vulgar or undignified modes of political expression is virtually as old as the notion of the plebs itself. However, if the traditional meaning of plebeian vulgarity has been pejorative and involved the castigation of the Roman plebs for degenerate behavior—as seen in such notions as the "depraved plebs" (*perdita plebs*),[3] the "dirty plebs" (*sordida plebs*),[4] the "low plebs" (*infima plebs*),[5] the "ignorant multitude" (*vulgus imperitum*),[6] or the "fickle plebs" (*ventosa plebs*)[7]—within the context of the contemporary and revitalized notion of plebeianism I defend, vulgarity becomes rather the specifically democratic form of ethical ambiguity that ordinary citizens will need to endure as they take up political responsibility beneath the shadow of unfairness. That the root meaning of vulgar is a popular one—designating the mass or crowd (*vulgus*)—only lends force to the idea that vulgarity might have an important and *principled*, albeit uneasy, role to play within the civic ethics of ordinary members of a liberal-democratic society.

My argument proceeds as follows. In Section 4.2 I detail how the basic idea of principled vulgarity has been surprisingly absent in the history of political thought. Following this, Section 4.3 discusses the main elements of the kind of principled vulgarity contemporary plebeians must endure, demonstrating how these depart from conventional and prevalent norms of civility. I conclude in Section 4.4 by reflecting more generally on the broader concept of political maturity implied by plebeianism, juxtaposing a plebeian conception of political maturity to two other leading understandings of the notion.

4.2 The Surprising Absence of the Idea of Principled Vulgarity in the History of Political Thought

In putting forward the notion that ordinary citizens must, as a condition of their political maturity, take on politically necessary but morally ambiguous behaviors and perspectives, the plebeian idea of principled vulgarity makes a claim remarkably absent in political thought, both historical and contemporary. Most obviously, principled vulgarity is a stark alternative to ethical paradigms that equate civic ethics with morality and thus recognize no such thing as morally ambiguous but politically necessary commitments. The idea of an ethically *unambiguous* civic ethics is perhaps best reflected in the influential Enlightenment tradition, which defines the good citizen as someone who is intellectually mature—whose general bearing is one of what Kant calls a "person of learning" (*Gelehrter*)—that is, someone whose most distinctive civic obligation is to engage fellow citizens with reasoned arguments in the public realm.[8] For Kant, and even more for the contemporary school of thought known as deliberative democracy (still one of the most dominant paradigms for citizenship today), the good citizen is modeled on the good scholar or the good parliamentarian: such persons think for themselves, give reasons for their views, seek persuasion rather than violence, and aim for laws that all might accept.[9] Because of its rationalism, this Enlightenment tradition does not face the tragic possibility that civic ethics are in fact irreducible to universal moral norms and thus require from their practitioners standpoints—like principled vulgarity—of a darker, more complicated hue.

But the idea of principled vulgarity—or a morally ambiguous but politically necessary ethics for *ordinary* citizens—is also surprisingly absent within the tradition one might expect to find it: the highly influential "dirty hands" or "Machiavellian" tradition, which emphasizes the need for a leader sometimes to act immorally in order to effectively execute the responsibilities of political office. I call this tradition Machiavellian, not necessarily because Machiavelli was the first to espouse it, but because he theorizes the idea of a morally ambiguous but political necessary kind of ethics with unmatched boldness and historical influence. Regardless of whether interpreters like Strauss are correct to call Machiavelli a "teacher of evil,"[10] it is clearly one of Machiavelli's central maxims that effective political actors, whether actual princes or leading politicians in republics (whom Machiavelli calls "princes of republics"[11]), must transact in practices that cannot be justified within familiar biblical, classical, or commonsensical moral paradigms. In Chapter 15 of *The Prince*, Machiavelli summarizes the transvaluation of moral values required by politics:

> A man who wants to make a profession of good in all regards must come to ruin among so many who are not good. Hence it is necessary to a prince, if he wants to maintain himself, to learn to be able not to be good, and to use this and not use it according to necessity.[12]

Machiavelli was not the first to suggest that a successful political leader would need to have a political ethics distinct from traditional accounts of virtue, as Quattrocento humanists, among others, also had taught that princes would be uniquely focused on providing security, managing military affairs, maintaining an active rather than contemplative existence, and practicing kingly virtues like *magnificentia* and *majestas*.[13] Where Machiavelli does break from the mirror-of-princes tradition—and from most prior political theory—is with his insistence that responsible political action would require the violation, and not the indirect realization, of traditional moral norms. Whereas medieval writers and earlier humanists had taught that the prince's political ethics were fully consistent with the four classical, "cardinal" virtues (fortitude, temperance, justice, and prudence) and the Christian virtues of faith, hope, and charity,[14] and assumed that any apparent transgression could be fully justified as what was necessary to realize the common good,[15] Machiavelli's singular importance as a moral philosopher resides in his stress that the prince's political ethics, far from supplementing or completing traditional morality, depend upon the acceptance that politics and morality cannot be fully reconciled. Even if this tragic outlook can be inferred in a few earlier authors,[16] Machiavelli's originality lies in his idea that the discontinuity between politics and morality needs to be actively *learned*: that there is a technology of politically expedient wrongdoing and that the ability to violate moral norms for the sake of politics (in the proper way) is not a capacity modern political leaders will find easy or natural but rather something about which they have to be persuaded and educated.[17]

Why does political responsibility sometimes require from leaders that they do immoral things? Later exponents of the Machiavellian tradition have pointed to numerous factors, including politics' necessary connection to violence, which is itself morally ambiguous;[18] the dilemma that effective political leadership requires the maintenance of a political machine whose values are to some extent at odds with democracy;[19] the alleged need for leaders to transgress the law in times of crisis;[20] and the problem that the calculus of moral judgment is different for political leaders, who must take responsibility for often millions of people, as compared to ordinary citizens who can make the choice "to do the right thing and suffer the consequences" without imposing burdens on an entire polity.[21]

The critique most commonly leveled against this Machiavellian tradition comes from philosophical frameworks that deny the possibility of moral dilemmas.[22] However, from a plebeian perspective, what is objectionable about the dirty hands tradition is not that it raises the issue of an ambiguous, uncomfortable political ethics discontinuous with traditional moral commitments, but that it does so only for *elite* citizens, especially the most powerful individual leaders within a state. The types of transgressions most often confronted within the dirty hands tradition—the alleged need in certain instances to deceive the masses, commit violence, or contravene laws in order to realize some end crucial to the defense and stability of the state—involve most obviously the ethical purview of leading statesmen and military commanders, not the perspective of ordinary citizens lacking special office within the polity. Given this emphasis on elite powerholders, the idea of principled vulgarity—with its focus on the ethical ambiguity required by politically responsible *everyday* citizens—has largely failed to appear within the dirty hands tradition.

In the case of Machiavelli, for example, his core teachings on how not to be good—involving the cultivation of capacities to instill fear, lie, break promises, simulate religious devotion, engage in cruelty, and attend to arms more than laws—all have as their explicit target the ethical horizon of elite political leaders, princes in both a literal and metaphorical sense, rather than the ethical situation of ordinary citizens. And when Machiavelli does address the ethics of ordinary citizens, he often appeals to the very traditional norms he otherwise aims to transcend—emphasizing, for example, the need for common citizens to be characterized by non-corruption,[23] goodness (*bontà*),[24] and decency (*onestà*).[25] At various points in the *Discourses on Livy*, for instance, Machiavelli clearly states the importance of citizens possessing religious piety and moral goodness if they are to perform the self-sacrifice and law-abidingness required for a healthy political community. He argues that in Rome, "religion served to command armies, to animate the plebs, to keep men good [*buoni*], to bring shame to the wicked."[26] He praises the plebs of the early Republic, whose trustworthiness made it possible for the Senate to propose that plebeian soldiers contribute one-tenth of their war booty on their honor without additional mechanisms for verifying their honesty, as an example which "shows how much goodness and how much religion were in the people, and how much good was to be hoped from it."[27] Machiavelli repeats the same phrase in his analysis of German tribes whose "goodness and religion" make it so that ordinary citizens contribute whatever taxes are required of them without additional oversight or threat of force.[28] While there are certain hints in Machiavelli's political philosophy suggesting something counter to his general moral traditionalism regarding non-elite citizens—for example, the People's alleged need to "vent its animus,"[29] its possession of "greater life, greater hatred, [and] more desire for revenge" than the Few when its liberty has been violated,[30] the suggestion that the plebeian desire not to be dominated stems not from any noble pacifism but from weakness,[31] and the precept that any authentic republican thinker must presuppose *all* individuals to be bad[32]—we are still left with the striking fact that Machiavelli, the great teacher of a political ethics discontinuous with ethics as such, confines this teaching, at least explicitly, to the Few.

Machiavelli is hardly alone in this regard, as other major figures within the dirty hands tradition similarly restrict their analyses to a situation involving significant powerholding. Certainly the few thinkers who prior to Machiavelli also put forward the idea of ethically ambiguous but politically necessary behavior have in mind a context of political leadership. Thucydides's account of the Mytilenean debate, for example, documents, even if it does not explicitly justify, the need for politically astute leaders to deceive those whom they serve.[33] Likewise, Kautilya's *Arthashastra*, written near the beginning of the third century BCE in India, instructs political leaders how to fight, kill, spy, break treaties, and protect against intrigue.[34] In the early modern era, when political thinkers besides Machiavelli conceptualized the idea of *raison d'état* as a political ethics not strictly continuous with traditional moral ideals, they too had in mind the ethical situation of monarchs and high officials, not ordinary citizens.[35] And more recent exponents of the dirty hands idea have continued to apply it primarily within a leadership context. For Max Weber, probably the most influential dirty hands thinker since Machiavelli, reflection on how political responsibility necessarily requires sometimes transgressing moral norms is explicitly directed toward the figure of leading politicians.[36] Debates about torture, which have been some of the most important recent contributions to the dirty hands tradition, tend to restrict their analyses to the ethical purview of government operatives who, even if they do not possess the highest authority within a state, clearly are distinguished from the situation of ordinary citizens.[37] Michael Walzer, it is true, concludes his essay on the dirty hands tradition with the proposal for institutions that might punish leaders for politically necessary but morally objectionable acts—and claims, in the essay's final sentence, that this would require everyday citizens, presumably involved in the punishing, "getting our own hands dirty."[38] But this proposal remains all-too-brief and its consequences entirely unelaborated with regard to just what dirty hands would mean for the non-elite citizen.

Rather than reject, as the Enlightenment critics do, the Machiavellian tradition for its central outlook—its insistence on the necessity of effective political action sometimes involving the transgression of conventional moral codes—the plebeian argues for its democratization. If there is a place for Machiavellian darkness in political theory, the applications of such a teaching ought to be extended to include not just the purview of princes and political elites but also the ethical horizon of ordinary citizens. The plebeian concept of principled vulgarity gives democratic content to the dirty hands idea, making it relevant to the lived experiences of everyday citizens in a liberal democracy.

Before discussing what learning how not to be good might mean on the plebeian level of ordinary citizenship, it is important to consider a third way in which the idea of principled vulgarity has barely penetrated political thought. Beyond Enlightenment thinkers who deny the very possibility of principled vulgarity by understanding political ethics as a subset of morality, and beyond Machiavellian thinkers who fail to recognize principled vulgarity by understanding ethical ambiguity as a problem limited to the powerful, probably the most surprising form of blindness to the notion of principled vulgarity comes from those few other contemporary thinkers operating, however incipiently, with an explicit notion of plebeianism. For example, in Breaugh's recent contribution, *The Plebeian Experience*—which after all is not a work in liberal democracy but

rather documents a series of historical events whereby the politically marginalized effectively contest governing power structures and achieve, at least for
a while, greater inclusivity and participation within the political system—the
so-called "plebeian principle" common to each of the historical episodes is the
utterly *unambiguous* "plebeian desire for freedom." As Breaugh puts it, " 'The
Plebs' is the name of an experience, that of achieving human dignity through
political agency."[39] Thus, the tragic aspect of Breaugh's plebeianism is only sociological (the plebeian pursuit of greater freedom can never finally overcome
the differentiation between the Few and the Many constitutive of all political
regimes) but not ethical (the plebeians who contest the Few in the name of
greater liberty do so without any threat or trace of a bad conscience).

The phenomenon of principled vulgarity is similarly absent within John
McCormick's book, *Machiavellian Democracy*, which occasionally presents
itself as an account of "plebeian republicanism" that can help the "plebeians of
modern republics" combat the ever-present threat of manipulation and domination from the most powerful members of society.[40] On the level of recom-
mendations for institutional reform, McCormick's contribution reflects the
core progressive ambition of plebeianism as I have defined it: the identification and regulation of the most advantaged. Specifically, McCormick's main
proposals for contemporary democracy—a tribunate composed of non-elite
citizens with the authority to veto laws and bring charges against the powerful, the use of sortition (in conjunction with election) for the nomination
and selection of leaders in order to break economic elites' hold on electoral
power, and an expanded capacity for ordinary citizens to deliberate and make
public judgments, especially judgments in political trials of leaders—follow the underlying plebeian logic of introducing differentiated citizenship
to *contest*, rather than to elevate, those with the most economic and political
power within a democracy. However, what appears to be mostly missing from
McCormick's account of plebeian democracy is Machiavellianism in its *moral*
sense: the idea that political maturity for the plebeian requires "learning how
not to be good." Ought not a so-called Machiavellian democracy demand that
its ordinary citizens be Machiavellian? Ought not plebeian proposals, which
explicitly aim to buttress the rights and liberties of the "ignobles,"[41] require
something ignoble, or *vulgar*, from those they are meant to serve? Much like
Machiavelli, these are questions about which McCormick remains reticent
and un-Machiavellian. Both in his interpretation of Machiavelli's account of
popular government and in his own statements about contemporary politics,
McCormick does not suggest that a committed plebeian will need to learn
to overcome—like a committed prince—his or her good conscience and
engage in politically necessary but morally dubious acts. McCormick continually applauds everyday citizens in a plebeian democracy in traditional moral

terms, speaking of "the trustworthy motives of the people,"[42] their tendency to use aggression and violence not at all or only in retribution for misdeeds from the nobles,[43] their superior capacity to embody norms of goodness and decency,[44] their fundamental disinclination toward domination,[45] and their proneness to good judgment.[46] McCormick sees Machiavelli as someone who, like himself, wants to "reeducate [conservative republicans] . . . on the honest or decent rather than insolent or licentious nature of the people."[47] To be sure, McCormick does acknowledge that the plebeians are not perfect, since they make mistakes in their decisions and are susceptible to being tricked,[48] but these imperfections are not seen as a *condition* of the functionality of plebeian democracy. Even if there are hints that McCormick might endorse my suggestion that plebeian democracy requires a Machiavellian moral outlook—i.e., *principled vulgarity*—such an outlook remains undeveloped in his contribution to plebeian political thought.[49]

Both Breaugh and McCormick, then, continually return to the moral goodness of ordinary citizens and the good conscience with which they can pursue the aims of a plebeian democracy. What this analysis leaves unexplored is the need for plebeians to undergo their own moral transvaluation, their own learning how not to be good—something parallel to, yet still different from, the moral transvaluation of the Machiavellian prince. What I mean to suggest, as I have indicated, is that the project of "ignobles" to avoid domination from political elites must of necessity contain something *ignoble* about it—and that this ignobility, far from disqualifying plebeian politics, would instead, in good Machiavellian fashion, simply be the populist-democratic correlate of the long-standing political wisdom that understands that political ethics are discontinuous with ethics as such and therefore require certain transgressions of conventional moral norms. In making this claim I do not mean to say the plebs are no different from the nobles and that both are animated by a common will to self-aggrandizement, for ordinary citizens occupy a substantially different political world from elite citizens and are not generally motivated by a desire for domination. Any extension of the Machiavellian teaching of learning how not to be good, therefore, should involve specific precepts for plebeians that are not the same as those for Machiavellian princes and political elites. What I do mean to suggest is that such an extension ought to be part of plebeian democracy, both because Machiavellian darkness should not belong to the Few alone and because, as a practical matter, the implementation and maintenance of the institutions of plebeian democracy—whether in the specific form advocated by McCormick (class-based representation, trials and other disruptions of elite power, the revival of the tribunate) or the more general form I have advocated in this book (the identification and regulation of the most advantaged as a class in need of special regulatory attention)—require overcoming the plebeian's good conscience and engaging in at least four commitments which, though necessary, are still ethically fraught and would demand from ordinary citizens the maturity to adulterate the purity of certain reigning moral, political, and social-scientific ideals. I consider these four commitments in the next section.

4.3 Principled Vulgarity as the Transgression of Civility: Four Examples

One way to understand the specific elements of plebeian vulgarity (and, with them, the bad conscience that the plebeian citizen must learn to endure) is plebeianism's transgression of well-established norms of civility. By civility, I understand most generally the habits and dispositions by which citizens manifest respect for each other, especially when they disagree. So conceived, civility is a core value of liberal democracy and often is treated as synonymous with good citizenship itself.[50] Now, to be clear, the "incivility" of plebeian vulgarity is circumscribed and chastened. It is more likely to frustrate and annoy opponents of plebeianism than permanently alienate them.[51] And it is limited to specific dynamics, the most important of which I shall presently discuss. Nonetheless, the ideas and commitments of plebeianism do contravene prevailing norms of civility in significant ways and, in so doing, demonstrate how plebeianism requires from its adherents a certain learning how not to be good.

Plebeianism's transgression of civility becomes especially vivid if civility is disaggregated to include four particular ethical directives: the duty to treat all citizens in public life identically as free and equal beings; the duty to make one's public appeals in terms all others might be able to accept (as opposed to putting forward arbitrary, idiosyncratic claims); the closely related duty to have one's public discourse guided by rational norms of deliberative speech (e.g., not just giving good reasons for one's view, but listening to the appeals of others with an open mind); and the duty to have one's public activity promote relations of civic friendship rather than rancor. These four components of civility are widely affirmed in contemporary political philosophy, especially by analysts and advocates of the concept of civility itself.[52] What I aim to show is that plebeianism violates—in partial yet still meaningful, *principled* ways—each of these four elements.

The Vulgarity of Class-Based Differentiated Citizenship

Plebeianism's insistence on class-based differentiated citizenship is, of course, limited. After all, when it comes to moral ideals, it is *undifferentiated* free and equal citizenship that plebeianism, along with all other paradigms of liberal democracy, affirms. But plebeianism stands for the idea that in two different ways this ideal cannot be the final word on the meaning and progressive pursuit of liberal democracy. On the one hand, despite the best efforts of even the most advanced and enlightened liberal-democratic regimes to realize conditions of free and equal citizenship, these regimes cannot cancel the second-class aspects of ordinary citizenship: above all, the *remove, manyness*, and *plutocracy* that constrain the civic lives of everyday people and thereby constitute crucial elements of the shadow of unfairness cast over civic relations in all liberal-democratic states. On the other hand, plebeianism moves beyond the simple and unambiguous commitment to free and equal citizenship when it argues that the key device for progressively responding to this shadow of unfairness is to identify the most advantaged class and to subject this class to special burdens (so as to serve a variety of heuristic, protective, and redressive purposes, which I examined in Chapter 3).[53] Even if these departures from the prevailing norm of undifferentiated citizenship are still animated by liberal-democratic principles, they nonetheless are likely to generate moral criticism against the plebeian who supports them, thereby raising the potential of a guilty conscience.

This guilty conscience arises, first of all, from the fact that the plebeian insisting on the second-class structures conditioning everyday civic life in liberal democracy understandably will be accused of putting forward a disenchanted account of the liberal-democratic regime. That is to say, with its fundamental and formal division between the Few and the Many, plebeianism sullies the idealism that would conceive of democratic life simply in terms of an undifferentiated notion of free and equal citizenship. While liberal-democratic regimes up until the 1960s effectively accepted differentiations based on race, ethnicity, class, and gender, it is distinctive of contemporary democratic experience that such differentiations are unjust. In America, for example, Rogers Smith describes the now conventional, idealistic objection to differentiation: "The dominant implication [of civil rights legislation and jurisprudence over the last half-century] is that differentiated citizenship is undesirable. . . . Uniform, formally identical treatment of citizens is generally regarded as the law's proper default position, with departures from such treatment requiring special justification."[54] A plebeian democrat does not of course reject the ideal of free and equal citizenship. But if the general trend in the political culture is either to assert that existing institutions already realize this commitment or to propose reforms that will enable polities to approximate it more closely, the plebeian—all the while supporting progressive efforts in this regard—*also* insists that the dream of free and equal citizenship will always remain to some very meaningful extent unfulfilled. Plebeian democracy thus carries with it the unwelcome insistence that a liberal-democratic state cannot become what its most idealistic exponents promised it would be: namely, a polity grounded in a uniform set of laws, applied to all citizens indiscriminately, reflecting a common human equality, which effectively overcomes, within a bounded political space, the social inequalities that hitherto have always infected political life. In denying the possibility of any future reform to generate a class-free society, plebeianism opens itself up to the charge of despondence and despair.

Differentiated citizenship threatens a guilty conscience not just by marking a fallen kind of liberal democracy, but in a second way as well: in raising the uncomfortable policy of singling out the most advantaged—and, in particular, the superrich—for special regulatory treatment. Even if plebeian differentiation in this regard is meant only to counteract the oligarchic and plutocratic elements that already persist within contemporary liberal democracies, there can be little doubt that opponents will charge plebeianism with irresponsible classism, that is, with unfair prejudice against the wealthy. After all, outside of the commitment to undifferentiated citizenship itself, numerous other factors undergird the widely held sensibility that any singling out of the superrich would be ethically and pragmatically misguided. These include, for example, the long-observed propensity of the less fortunate to celebrate and admire the very rich;[55] the widespread belief in the importance of incentives (and the inequalities they generate) to motivate productive gains and the efficient allocation of capital;[56] a tendency to worry more about political than economic elites;[57] the prevalence of so-called "conservative egalitarianism," according to which citizens favor equality of opportunity but reject any capping or other explicit regulation of the economic expectations of the very rich;[58] and an observed preference of citizens to address rising levels of inequality with minimal policy responses (incremental changes in trade and education policies) as opposed to more aggressive alternatives (higher taxes on the wealthy and transfers).[59] Even if plebeianism is not necessarily opposed to some of these standpoints (for example, it too recognizes the importance of incentives, and thus inequality, for maximizing productive gains), the fact that they contribute to a general unwillingness to countenance any regulatory concern with the superrich explains why the plebeian is likely to be accused of uncivil, *vulgar* classism.[60]

The Vulgarity of Arbitrariness

A second aspect of plebeian vulgarity is the *methodological vulgarity* that must attend any socioeconomic definition of who is a member of the most advantaged class. Outside of its high idealism, one of the appeals of the aspiration of undifferentiated free and equal citizenship is its felicitous methodology: it requires no untidy, contestable sociological divisions between nobles and ignobles, the Few and the Many, the rich and the middling. Plebeianism, by contrast, since it has as its central programmatic ambition the singling out of the most advantaged and the imposition of special economic and political burdens on this class, must operate with notions—"elite," "select few," "the specially empowered and favored"—that are infelicitous if only because their borders of inclusion are inescapably linked to the discretionary judgment of specific political bodies and cultures. While arguments can and should be made to explain why one cutoff point is better than another, plebeians must face up to the ineliminably arbitrary element in any differentiation of the Few from the Many. Such arbitrariness is vulgar because it offends what I have described as a crucial element of civility: that public appeals be made in terms that all other citizens might accept.

The problem of methodological vulgarity has not been confronted by other recent contributors to the nascent plebeian tradition. Consider, for example, McCormick's proposal for a revived tribunate in the United States that would exclude elite citizens from its membership. McCormick defines the elite in the following terms: "Political and economic elites are excluded from eligibility: that is, anyone who has held a major municipal, state, or federal office, elected or appointed, for two consecutive terms at any time in their life; and anyone whose net household worth exceeds $345,000 (i.e., members of the wealthiest 10% of family households as established by the most recent U.S. census data)."[61] My point is not to take issue with McCormick's proposal as such, but only to recognize, in a way that McCormick does not, that critics certainly will object that this definition is arbitrary and will ask why the cutoff should be the top 10% and not, for example, the wealthiest 1% or some other number. Even if the plebeian can make empirical arguments in defense of a particular delineation, such arguments will always be vulnerable to the challenge of a skeptic. This methodological vulgarity, this arbitrariness, thus represents another way in which the plebeian democrat, as a condition of his or her political maturity, must learn how not to be good.

But if the charge of arbitrariness cannot be refuted, it ought not in itself dissuade plebeians from their commitments. After all, theories of social justice have long made use of a notion of the "least advantaged"—a class which either possesses the minimal amount of resources or welfare a well-ordered society ought to guarantee its citizens (as in certain utilitarian schemes of social justice that rely on a notion of a basic minimum), or, following Rawls, the class which ought to have its prospects maximized for any ongoing system of inequalities to be just. But as Rawls among others has admitted, when it comes to any definition of the least favored, "it seems impossible to avoid a certain arbitrariness."[62] The plebeian can respond, therefore, that insofar as contemporary democracies already make use of a vivid and explicit (but arbitrary) category of the least favored as a class entitled to special regulatory attention, they should also be able to operate with a category of the most favored. Further, there are ways to soften the blows of methodological vulgarity: for example, if the most advantaged are subjected to burdens that only apply to income and wealth already above a certain cutoff, then they will not lose their status as the most advantaged in undergoing plebeian regulation.

Such responses do not, however, counteract the underlying charge: that plebeian proposals will always be to some degree arbitrary in how they differentiate citizens since judgments about who is part of the Few are inherently contestable. Being willing to persevere in the face of this difficulty—to make socioeconomic demarcations that are essential to plebeian progressivism but not fully explainable in terms all other citizens could be expected to accept—is thus a critical element of the plebeian bad conscience that will have to be endured as part of the commitment to plebeian progressivism.

The Vulgarity of Non-Deliberative Discourse

A third source of principled vulgarity relates to the problem that whereas civility involves the duty to have one's public discourse guided by so-called reasonable norms of deliberative speech (speech that engages in genuine conversations with one's political rivals and fellow citizens, in the sense of giving reasons, having an open mind, and speaking sincerely), plebeianism recognizes *non-deliberative discourse* as an intrinsic part of political advocacy, at least for ordinary citizens who simply do not normally find themselves in communicative contexts modeled on the form of a conversation. It is here we confront plebeian vulgarity in its most literal sense, as the recognition that the expressivity of the ordinary citizen is constrained by that citizen's confinement within a surrounding crowd (or *vulgus*), which thereby renders full-fledged deliberative speech impossible. In reflecting on the plebeian's non-deliberative discourse, I do not mean merely to repeat what I argued in Chapter 2 with regard to *manyness* (one of the principal second-class structures conditioning ordinary citizenship): namely, that the ordinary citizen usually can only achieve empowerment though having his or her voice affixed to a much larger mass of like-minded others (as in elections, protests, and public opinion polling), with the result that both the articulacy of that voice and its capacity for discretionary judgment are greatly diminished. The point I wish to introduce here is not simply that ordinary modes of civic empowerment do not attain the form of deliberative discourse, but that in those rare moments when everyday citizens do engage in a discursive exchange with powerful individuals in possession of substantial, discretionary decision-making authority, this engagement itself falls short of the communicativity at play in an authentic dialogue about norms and policies. For the ordinary citizen actually present at a deliberative exchange with the powerful, only three discursive options customarily are available: silent onlooking, circumscribed speech (e.g., being allowed to make a brief statement or ask a single question with little opportunity for follow-up), or disruption in the form of heckling, shouting down, or otherwise making a scene. None can be described as fully deliberative discourse and the third option—disruption—is especially vulgar in its willful disturbance of a conversation guided by norms of civility. But it is just this third option that needs to be appreciated as an authentically plebeian mode of political discourse—one which understandably will engender in the plebeian who engages in it some amount of guilt for interrupting a deliberative exchange, but which nonetheless has potential value both as an outlet for otherwise inhibited political expression and, more deeply, as a mechanism for attesting to the reality of the shadow of unfairness.

In affirming the importance of disruptive speech, plebeianism stands not for the wholesale rejection of deliberative discourse, but only for an appreciation of its limits. Plebeians do not question that, at the institutional level, laws can be rendered more rational and legitimate insofar as they emerge out of deliberative exchanges rather than mere negotiation, bargaining, voting, and political advertising. Nor do they question that, at the individual ethical level, parliamentarians and other citizens similarly situated at a decision-making table should pursue their aims through reasoned arguments, conducted in terms free and equal citizens of different backgrounds and worldviews might share, and informed by norms of sincerity, reciprocity, listening, mutual respect, and willingness to have one's perspective altered in light of what Habermas has called the "unforced force of the better argument."[63] But plebeianism objects to the implicit assumption of deliberative theories that the ordinary citizen first and foremost is—or could be made to be—a deliberator committed to legitimating laws and policies through deliberative discourse. The problem can be seen most vividly in the choice metaphor of deliberative democracy: the likening of the public to a *sphere*, where presumably all have some access, instead of, as a plebeian account would stress, to a *stage*, where access is of necessity restricted.[64] Specifically, whereas the notion of a public sphere reflects the idea that political communication might go on in a context where all citizens are included on free and equal terms, the plebeian metaphor of a public stage recognizes the fact that such inclusion cannot be fully realized: not only is political space divided disproportionately (with larger shares tending to go to those in possession of formal office, wealth, or fame), but political communication in contemporary mass democracies (and truly in all polities) contains an irreducible spectacular dimension (relating, in particular, to the theatrical nature of mass politics, its reliance on symbols and rhetoric rather than only rational discourse), which has the function of making ordinary addressees of political speech feel they are not simply would-be respondents in an ongoing conversation, but also recipients of messages which, whether manipulative or not, afford little opportunity for reply.

Likewise, whereas the deliberative metaphor of the public sphere imagines a single set of ethics applicable to all citizens, the plebeian idea of the public stage emphasizes the difference between ordinary and elite citizens and, thus, the possibility that civic ethics might require something different from powerholders (e.g., a parliamentarian, judge, high official, or leader—someone who *stands upon the public stage*) relative to ordinary citizens, without any formal outlet for making binding decisions beyond the vote, whose political lives are mediated by vicarious relations to more prominently situated *others*. Finally, whereas the metaphor of a public sphere suggests a political ethics devoted to the *full legitimation* of the laws, norms, and policies comprising public life, the stage, with its modeling of scarce and unequally divided political power, indicates an ethical landscape that is more fraught and ambiguous—a landscape in which office holders exert an impact upon public life that is not necessarily fully responsive or accountable to the great many without formal positions of political authority. The public stage, much better than the public sphere, models a politics that always will be at least somewhat darkened by the shadow of unfairness.

Confronted, then, with a public stage and not simply a public sphere, the plebeian understands that contemporary mass liberal democracy constitutively fails to attain full inclusivity, full political equality, and, thus, full moral legitimacy. Within such a context, non-deliberative discourse—and in particular *disruptive speech*—has a role to play, both as the kind of communication available to the ordinary citizen present at a public event and as a device for reminding those on the public stage that the legitimacy of their empowerment is not fully established or unmarred. Here it is important to remember that plebeianism does not stand only for the singling out and burdening of economic elites, but also for the burdening of *political* powerholders by subjecting them to contested forms of public appearances in which they do not control the means of their publicity: i.e., in which they must face the risk and uncertainty of genuinely spontaneous events. This latter element of plebeianism was the focus of my earlier book, *The Eyes of the People*, where I argued that there is democratic value in having leaders disrupted as they appear on the public stage, in part for the egalitarian reason that such disruption acknowledges the less-than-fully legitimate aspect of political authority.[65] But what that account mostly left out—and what I mean to emphasize here—is that ordinary citizens sometimes have a role to play in this disruption in the form of interruptive, heckling speech. Such interruptions will always seem vulgar when judged against prevailing standards of civility, but their expert use has an importance that has gone largely unnoticed within political science.

In particular, the figure of the shouter or heckler, who stands as the non-deliberative speaker par excellence, ought to be rehabilitated. At the very least, heckling should be evaluated from the perspective of the heckler: namely, as exhibiting a kind of political courage—the courage to speak out in a forum where one lacks standing—distinct to the ordinary, plebeian citizen. The history of heckling in democracy has yet to be written.[66] Such a history surely would include the classical prophets of the Bible who had to withstand heckling and abuse from the very crowds that validated their charismatic authority,[67] the shouting down (*thorubos*) of leaders as they addressed the popular Assembly in ancient Athens, the informal gathering of the Roman *contio* in which leading magistrates would address ordinary citizens and subject themselves to potential interruption from the crowd or effective cross-examination from rival leaders,[68] innovative nineteenth-century politicians like Andrew Johnson in the United States and William Gladstone in Britain who, much more than their predecessors, made extemporaneous public appeals where they were always in danger of being mocked and contested,[69] and more recent episodes of prominent politicians being heckled, like Harold Wilson in the 1960s and 1970s and John Kerry's infamous incident at the University of Florida in 2007. But as a matter of establishing its philosophical significance for democratic politics, one would do well to return to what is perhaps the earliest instance in the West's literary tradition of non-deliberative discourse deployed in an egalitarian direction: Thersites's heckling of Agamemnon in the Trojan War in the *Iliad*.

In a well-known scene, Thersites, the lowest of the Greek heroes, described in quasi-plebeian terms as "ill-favored beyond all the men that came to Troy" (II.216), brazenly upbraids Agamemnon, the head of the Greek army, in public for his mismanagement of the war, his unfair treatment of Achilles, and his enrichment from the struggle of others—abuses which justify, Thersites thinks, an abandonment of the entire war effort. But what distinguishes Thersites's political act is not so much the content of his arguments, but the non-deliberative form of their presentation. This can be seen most clearly in the fact that Thersites's political speech is deeply, and we learn habitually, disruptive. He is introduced in the following terms:

> As all the other rank-and-file sat down and stayed in their places, there
> was one alone who kept railing: Thersites, of measureless speech [*ame-troepys*], whose mind was full of a great store of disorderly words [*epea akosma*], wherewith to utter revilings against the kings, without result [*maps*], and not according to order [*ou kata kosmon*].[70]

Thersites disrupts the political order not simply because he is a lower-class Greek speaking out of turn, nor simply because given his low status it is only through some kind of transgressive disruption that he would be heard at all,[71] but because his speech itself lacks the dispassionate character of reasoned argument. It is disordered, then, not because it is unclear, but because it consists in the chiding and public shaming of leaders.[72] In addition to Thersites's specific upbraiding of Agamemnon, Thersites's penchant for non-deliberative discourse is repeatedly emphasized in his brief but memorable appearance in the Homeric epic.[73] Thersites is presented as one who "wrangles [*epizemenai*] with kings" (II.214); has the habit of "reviling [*neikeieske*]" (II.221) Odysseus and Achilles; deploys "shrill cries [*ozea keklygon*]" (II.222) and "loud shouting [*makra boon*]" (II.224); and of course "reviles [*neikee*]" (II.224; also see II.243) and "utters abuse at [*oneidea*]" (II.222; also see II.251) Agamemnon. For this reason, the major Greek leaders, despite their disagreements in other respects, are alike in their antipathy for Thersites.[74] It is significant, too, that Homer labels Thersites's speech "without result [*maps*]" (II.214): its purpose is not to realize some external end, but rather it represents an intrinsic interest in speaking out against the powerful.

When Odysseus rises to rebuke and then physically beat Thersites, his primary objection is not to the wrongness of Thersites's proposal to abandon the war, but to the unruly quality of Thersites's non-deliberative discourse:

> Thersites of reckless speech, clear-voiced talker though you are, restrain yourself, and do not be minded to quarrel with kings. For I think that there is no baser mortal than you among all the Greeks. You ought not take the name of kings in your mouth as you speak in assembly, nor cast reproaches on them.[75]

Thersites's greatest offense in the eyes of Odysseus is that he speaks publicly against elite leaders, that he calls them out by name in a public forum.

The *Iliad* is in fact as much about deliberative counsels as it is about war, with the epic staging at least six major political assemblies. The Greek heroes are experts not only at fighting, but at persuasive discourse among their fellow soldiers.[76] At the same time, deliberation is always under threat of dissipation. Usually three main obstacles prevent it, symbolized by each of the three main Greek heroes: the imposition of might and hierarchical authority over discourse (Agamemnon), trickery and manipulation rather than straightforward speech (Odysseus), and frustration at these two pathologies leading to withdrawal and even violence (Achilles). Thersites, however, models a fourth disruption to deliberation: the disruption of non-deliberative discourse, of speech aimed primarily at reviling leaders rather than solving problems. But Thersites's disruption of deliberative discourse can only be condemned, on par with the other three dysfunctions, if one adopts either an aristocratic ethic (which says, with Odysseus, that social inferiors should not participate in politics on equal terms) or an ethic of democratic idealism (which thinks it is possible to create a modern democratic polity entirely without traces of second-class citizenship, where all can in fact participate on free and equal terms). Insofar as the aristocratic ethic is morally untenable and democratic-idealistic ethic not fully practicable, Thersites's form of disruption stands as a kind of exemplar of plebeian ethics in a democratic age.

It is said of Thersites in one elusive passage that he speaks for the indignation of the people, or the collection of ordinary Greeks encamped at Troy: "With Thersites were the Greeks exceedingly angry and indignant in their hearts" (II.222-223). After Odysseus's physical beating of Thersites, however, the Greek rank and file turn against him, and numerous later commentators themselves have condemned Thersites and his envious spirit.[77] But because democratic ideals always will transcend any polity's ability to fully implement them, a certain level of indignation is constitutive of ordinary democratic experience and is therefore worthy of being channeled into the non-deliberative discourse uttered by the Thersiteses and other active plebeians of the world. Such discourse may be idle in the sense it does not produce legislative results, but it is not for that reason empty: at least not so long as there is performative value in having power-holders in a democratic society endure burdens on the public stage.

For ordinary citizens confronting their leaders, it is the possibility of out-of-order, *vulgar* interjections in the manner of heckling, rather than the chance to participate on free and equal terms in deliberation, that is the most usual opportunity afforded by a communicative setting. Accordingly, plebeianism recognizes in a way in which conventional accounts of civility do not that an ordinary citizen wishing to maximally participate in public discourse typically will have to do so in the manner of an *interjection* instead of conversation, that the structure of such interjections reflects second-class citizenship rather than overcomes it, and that there is an important if largely unrecognized form of political courage embodied in citizens, like hecklers, who are able to withstand the risks of making their voices heard within the crowds that almost always surround them whenever they might confront individuals of great power. Plebeianism, then, can sympathize with the admonition of Lentulus Marcellinus, Roman consul, to a crowd of largely plebeian citizens amassed in an informal assembly, or *contio*, in 56 BCE: "Shout! Shout, citizens, while you still can! Soon you will no longer be able to do so with impunity!"[78]

The Vulgarity of Rancorous Sentiments

A final form of vulgarity involves the vulgarity of rancorous sentiments, by which I mean not sentiments contributing to the destabilization of the very project of liberal democracy, but rather sentiments that make it difficult for this project to be conducted as a basis for civic friendship among its participants.[79] Three sentiments seem especially central in this regard.

First, underlying plebeian rancor is the sentiment of *indignation* I analyzed in Chapter 2 (Section 2.6), which arises from the problem that the second-class civic structures conditioning the ordinary experience of politics in any conceivable liberal-democratic regime—remove, manyness, and plutocracy—make it impossible for a liberal democracy to fully respect the dignity of its citizens. What needs to be stressed in this context is that indignation, even if understandable and appropriate, is likely to prevent a civic culture shaped by civic friendship and, for this reason, generate a bad conscience among indignant plebeians. The point is not simply that indignation keeps alive a vivid sense of the Few versus the Many—which obviously interferes with civic solidarity—but that the experience of indignation is itself unhappy and thus out of keeping with the good cheer required by a fully civil public life. The logic behind Auden's maxim—"Be happy and you will be good"—explains why the plebeian who cannot be fully happy in political life also will not be fully good, in the sense of being unable to always seek cooperation, compromise, and understanding with fellow citizens in a manner suggested by the ideal of civic friendship. After all, plebeianism involves a more disconsolate inner life for the ordinary citizen than that advertised by leading paradigms of democratic citizenship, whether the rancor-free rational psychology of deliberative ethics or the rancorous yet egalitarian psychology of so-called agonistic models.[80] The burden of understanding oneself as a second-class citizen, of feeling in danger of being oppressed by economic and political elites, and of acknowledging the inescapable seepage of the effects of economic inequality into a polity's educational and political systems—all of this suggests a less happy and more rancorous civic self-understanding than citizens in contemporary mass democracies normally are encouraged to experience. Other commentators on plebeian ethics generally have failed to appreciate the ethical ambiguity of plebeian indignation, precisely because they have not recognized the discontent that is inseparable from it.[81]

Such discontent, and the indignation that arouses it, are an important feature of political maturity from the plebeian point of view. They might be seen as the plebeian contribution to the long-standing tenet of political modernism that any authentic political theory must presuppose the human being to be fallen, if not evil—a dictum which finds famous articulations throughout the history of modern political thought. As Machiavelli puts it, "It is necessary to whoever disposes a republic and orders laws in it to presuppose that all men are bad, and that they always have to use the malignity of their spirit whenever they have a free opportunity for it."[82] David Hume similarly says, "It is . . . a just *political* maxim, that *every man must be considered a knave*: though, at the same time, it appears somewhat strange, that a maxim should be true in *politics* which is false in *fact*."[83] Carl Schmitt states the thesis even more boldly: "All genuine political theories presuppose man to be evil, i.e., by no means an unproblematic but a dangerous and dynamic being."[84] To this dark heuristic the plebeian democrat insists on the addendum: every authentic *democratic* theory must presuppose the ordinary citizen to be in some sense incensed, unsatisfied, frustrated, in a word, *unhappy*, at least within the circumscribed spaces of government and formal politics. Plebeianism's acceptance, and indeed productive generation, of this unhappiness is an important feature of what learning how not to be good would mean within a plebeian conception of liberal democracy.

A second rancorous sentiment of which the plebeian might be accused—and which is therefore likely to contribute to the plebeian bad conscience—is a certain *ingratitude*: what to critics will seem a hyperbolic dissatisfaction with today's most advanced liberal-democratic states, not for being inferior to other existing or historical regimes, but for failing to meet rigorous expectations of what democracy should be. After all, plebeianism does not necessarily deny that existing liberal democracies are better than all prior regimes.[85] But this means that a thinker or social scientist committed to restricting normative judgments in politics to comparative evaluations between regimes, thus dispensing with absolute evaluations of single regimes in light of an aspirational ideal, might accuse central features of plebeianism—its cultivation of indignation (rather than only responding to existing levels) and its call for penalizing elites for reasons other than only their own transgressions—of being emblematic of a faulty, dangerous philosophy of holding societies accountable to a criterion of perfection.[86]

While there may be counterarguments to make here, the plebeian would do better to accept some elements of the charge of ingratitude as a condition of political progressivism. What Susan B. Anthony said in the context of nineteenth-century feminism—"Our job is not to make young women grateful, it's to make them ungrateful"—is in fact applicable to any political theory that takes seriously the capacity of the future to surpass the past in what is politically possible. The plebeian, whose second-class status might be seen as a universalized and de-gendered version of the pre-liberation status of women in politics, must endure the bad conscience of offending the competing urge to embrace the status quo or to limit progressivism to the situation of the deeply underprivileged.[87]

Plebeianism's openness to the charge of ingratitude has tended to go unnoticed by other contemporary plebeian thinkers. It figures nowhere in Breaugh's account of historical plebeian regimes. McCormick's plebeian theory, likewise, focuses only on the relative difference between nobles and ignobles, emphasizing Machiavelli's claim that the Few are *more* ungrateful than the Many.[88] Not only does this forget that Machiavelli taught that *all* people—the Few and the Many alike—suffer from ingratitude, even if popular ingratitude is more mild than that of the powerful.[89] But it overlooks the problem that present-day plebeian reformers, insistent on addressing the various forms of unfairness hampering what is arguably the world's most progressive political regime (i.e., liberal democracy), will be said to suffer from their own ingratitude and all the vulgarity this entails.

Finally, a third rancorous sentiment likely conducive to the plebeian bad conscience relates to the plebeian's *quasi-vindictive desire to see the powerful especially burdened*—whether economically or politically—on the public stage. To be sure, in my discussion in Chapter 3 of the plebeian idea of reasonable envy I stressed the *reasonableness* of imposing burdens on the most advantaged members of society, explaining how such burdens are justifiable on liberal-democratic grounds and also limited in various ways. But the point I mean to raise here is that the motivations underlying plebeian proposals for regulating the most advantaged are not entirely reactive to the actual or threatened wrongdoing of concrete elite perpetrators, but stem too from the desire to see representatives of the Few (who may not be guilty of any specific offenses) compelled to engage in public acts of redress. Consider the Greek example of ostracism, which might be considered a prototype of plebeian institutions in general. As I discussed in the last chapter, what is so special, procedurally speaking, about ostracism is that the decision about whether anyone should be ostracized in a given year precedes (by many weeks) the question of who the ostracized individual, should there be one, will be.[90] In other words, the motivation to seek retribution against *any* elite precedes the motivation to seek remedial action against a particular transgressor. Such vengefulness is ethically ambiguous insofar as it takes satisfaction in the imposition of harms on individuals who are personally blameless—or whose only transgression is being powerful in a society darkened by the shadow of unfairness.

Other plebeian thinkers who have themselves called for specially burdening the most advantaged have not faced up to this ethical ambiguity, even as their theories clearly imply that part of what is at stake in plebeian institutions is a *symbolic and redressive*—rather than merely corrective and protective—interest in punishing the strong. Machiavelli, for example, who should be considered a plebeian thinker precisely insofar as he supported political institutions that single out the Few for special regulatory attention, implies something like this additional foundation for plebeianism when, in his discussion of political trials, he offers not one but two justifications for making it easy for citizens to bring forward charges of political crimes: not only will accusations and trials make it so citizens, especially elite ones, will be afraid to "attempt things against the state," but such institutions will enable the people to "vent . . . those humors that grow up in cities."[91] That the mass of ordinary citizens have a need to vent their "ill humors" is an important Machiavellian theme and something to which Machiavelli continually returns.[92] Although he does not fully elaborate the source of these ill humors, his clear implication is that they are part of what it means to be a plebeian: they stem from the frustration that arises from being a second-class citizen in a polity where first-class citizens not only threaten abuse, but win most of the honors, wealth, and power.[93] The ill humors, therefore, are not limited to responses to specific acts of transgression but have a more general and continual grounding.[94] Read in contemporary terms, the Machiavellian idea of "ill humors" would mean: insofar as liberal democracies are permanently unable to realize their own principles—because, for example, the effects of economic inequality inescapably infect political and education opportunity and key metrics of popular empowerment (e.g., representation) remain hard to verify—there are motivations for singling out and burdening the most advantaged in a way which, even if justified, is not justified in the sense of responding to a perpetrator of a concrete wrong. In other words, what a plebeian wants, in addition to protecting the polity from ongoing instances and future threats of elite domination, are political and economic acts of redress that acknowledge and also remedy the shadow of unfairness that remains in even the most progressive liberal-democratic society. But if this is true, the "nobles" forced to endure these burdens will not always be guilty of actual offenses, but will be made to suffer for a society's shortcomings vis-à-vis its own principles.[95]

Although he does not say so, a similar redressive (as opposed to merely corrective) logic informs McCormick's proposals for popular trials in which a revived tribunate would be able to accuse only three elite citizens per year (one each from the executive, legislative, and judicial branches of government). If the *raison d'être* of such investigations and trials is only the blameless desire to seek protection against threats from elites, as McCormick suggests, then one would expect there to be no limit on their number, allowing the factual determination of existing elite-imposed dangers to dictate whether to proceed with trials and how many there should be. In suggesting that something other than protection from actual or threatened wrongdoing motivates these trials, I do not mean to criticize the proposal for them, but only to suggest that their justification—and the justification for plebeianism in general—rests on additional foundations besides those of criminal justice (the bringing of offenders to justice): namely, the motivation to have the most advantaged members of society endure special economic and political burdens as *redress* for systematic social injustices for which no one individual is necessarily to blame.[96]

In drawing attention to the ethically ambiguous elements of plebeian rancorous sentiments—the unhappiness plebeianism condones and generates, the ingratitude of which it can be accused, and the partially vindictive nature of the redress it seeks—I do not mean to indict these sentiments, but only recognize that they are part of what learning how not to be good would mean on the level of plebeian psychopolitical life. They are what the plebeian must endure internally as part of the external effort to seek progressive liberal-democratic ends beneath the shadow of unfairness.

4.4 Political Maturity from the Plebeian Point of View

The elements of principled vulgarity I have described not only detail the particular aspects of the morally ambiguous but politically necessary commitments required by plebeian ethics. They also point to a more general doctrine of *political maturity* conceived from the plebeian point of view. While I am not inventing the concept of political maturity—since the term appears more or less explicitly in the work of many of the figures I have engaged in this chapter (especially Machiavelli, Kant, and Weber) and also has been confronted, however indirectly, by certain recent studies[97]—it is nonetheless true that it is not a widely employed notion, nor has its meaning been precisely defined. But maturity is a valuable concept that ought to exert greater influence in the study of citizenship. For one thing, because the concept of maturity suggests that the failure to be mature is something other than evil—arising from the inability to transcend some native childishness rather than from cruelty, a bad will, or barbarism—it promotes a kind of ethical analysis more chastened in its judgments as well as more respectful of those who do not follow its pronouncements. This mildness seems appropriate given that what is at stake in plebeian ethics is an account of how some citizens—ordinary ones—ought to consider political responsibility, not a universal theory of political morality for all citizens no matter how situated.

Most of all, the mature-childish contrast is useful because it builds off of an important feature of politics whose philosophical meaning too often goes unattended: namely, the fact that, while there may be occasional exceptions, it is one of the least controversial aspects of political life that *politics is not for children*.[98] It would seem that virtually all polities throughout history have had age rules for who can hold office and participate fully in government.[99] The exclusion of minors from formal political life is rarely seen as an injustice.[100] Likewise, the active inclusion of youth in politics—in the form of children soldiers or even perhaps the "Children's Crusade" in which American civil rights leaders recruited children to protest, confront potential violence, and suffer imprisonment as part of the 1963 Birmingham Campaign—usually is considered morally questionable if not outright wrong.[101] Such attitudes raise the question of what it is about politics that makes it unsuitable for the child and, from the other side, what kind of childishness is especially inappropriate within politics. In other words, what is the philosophy behind what appears to be this almost universal tenet that politics is not for children?

To respond to such questions merely by appealing to the developmental fact that in childhood one's rational faculties have not yet matured does not seem fully dispositive, especially when one considers that the age requirements for numerous offices (like the American Senate, 30 years old, and presidency, 35 years old) are higher than what would seem to be required for cognitive development. And the explanation suggested by the American Founders—that age makes it more likely that a potential leader's character will be known and established, thus lessening the uncertainty and risk attached to selecting electoral candidates—seems merely a prudential consideration based on the contingencies of a politics not yet inundated by modern technologies than a full-fledged account of why it is that politics, always it seems, has reflected a certain age bias.[102] The philosophical question remains, then: what is the meaning of the political maturity age is thought to bring?

To answer this question—or, more precisely, to show how plebeianism provides its own unique answer to it—it is necessary to take into account another important feature of the idea of maturity: not only does it invite philosophical reflection on the difference between political childishness and its opposite, but it suggests that part of what childishness means is the inability to face a particular, potentially unsettling *reality*. It is not by accident that one of the root meanings of maturity relates to the Latin word *mane*—that is, "early" or "of the morning"—suggesting that to be mature is to be awake in the sense of facing a reality that others may fail to acknowledge. With Thoreau, a great teacher of wakefulness and the obligation to confront what is real, the connection of such goals to the morning—or to maturity in this etymological sense—is made explicit. For Thoreau morning is less an actual time of day than the disposition of alert attentiveness to our surroundings:

> It matters not what the clocks say or the attitudes and labors of men. Morning is when I am awake and there is a dawn in me. Moral reform is the effort to throw off sleep. . . . The millions are awake enough for physical labor; but only one in a million is awake enough for effective intellectual exertion, only one in a hundred million to a poetic or divine life. To be awake is to be alive. I have never yet met a man who was quite awake. How could I have looked him in the face?[103]

As the last lines of this passage intimate, for Thoreau our wakefulness is never complete: "That man who does not believe that each day contains an earlier, more sacred, and auroral hour than he has yet profaned, has despaired of life, and is pursuing a descending and darkening way." As a result, even if Thoreau believes human beings have a natural desire for reality—"Be it life or death, we crave only reality"—he nonetheless understands our attunement to reality as perpetually unfinished and thus susceptible to ongoing improvement: "We must learn to reawaken and keep ourselves awake, not by mechanical aids, but by an infinite expectation of the dawn, which does not forsake us in our soundest sleep . . . Every man is tasked to make his life, even in its details, worthy of the contemplation of his most elevated and critical hour." Maturity, Thoreau suggests, consists in wakening to reality: "All memorable events, I should say, transpire in morning time and in a morning atmosphere." The last lines of *Walden* only emphasize this point, as Thoreau, in referring to "that morrow which mere lapse of time can never make to dawn," concludes: "The light which puts out our eyes is darkness to us. Only that day dawns to which we are awake. There is more day to dawn. The sun is but a morning star."[104]

Keeping in mind this root meaning of maturity as a capacity to operate in a "morning atmosphere" in which one is awakened to reality, it follows that the idea of *political* maturity would specify the ability to face a particular kind of *political reality*—one that many citizens will fail to acknowledge not necessarily because they are soporific or intellectually lazy as in Thoreau's critical diagnosis, but because the reality in question is disquieting, difficult, or unpleasant.

Now what is the nature of the reality that the politically mature citizen is able to successfully confront? What does it mean, politically speaking, not to be childish? There is no single answer to either of these questions. Rather, each of the three different traditions of civic ethics I have discussed in this chapter—the Enlightenment tradition evinced by Kant and more recent defenders of deliberative ethics, the dirty hands tradition defended by Machiavelli and other kindred thinkers, and the nascent plebeian tradition I have defended here with its idea of principled vulgarity—provides its own account of the kind of childishness that mature citizens, in facing reality, must be able to resist and overcome. Understanding the plebeian conception of political maturity, and its special suitability to ordinary citizens in today's liberal-democratic regimes, requires having some idea of the other two variants as well.

Within the Enlightenment tradition of political maturity, the reality to which many citizens fail to awaken is the fact that the world does not come to us already legitimated, but requires our own critical-rational engagement in order to inject an immanent rationality into an otherwise contingent set of political arrangements. That is to say, the Enlightenment tradition upholds the necessity of thinking, arguing, and deciding for oneself—both on the individual level and in the form of deliberative public institutions (like parliaments) where citizens' public reason might be brought to bear on the administrative and legislative output of the state—so as to overcome the fact that neither nature, nor tradition, nor revealed religion, nor mere technical efficiency can properly be the source of legitimacy in the modern world.[105] For the Enlightenment tradition, therefore, childishness is above all thoughtlessness and, with it, the abdication of employing one's critical rationality to authorize a society's norms, laws, and policies. This abdication can stem either from a literal *naïveté* (the belief, often grounded in an implicit traditionalism or deference to experts, that the world already is justified as it is)[106] or from *cynicism* (the belief that there can be no genuine legitimation, that might makes right, etc.). Political maturity on the Enlightenment account means overcoming both of these pathologies and instead exercising one's intellect, to repeat Kant's expression, in the manner of "a person of learning" (*Gelehrter*)—that is, someone whose primary civic purpose is to engage fellow citizens with deliberative arguments about the conduct of public affairs.[107]

With the dirty hands tradition, by contrast, the hard reality to be faced is the problem that in politics one always already finds oneself surrounded by enemies wishing to do one harm, that accordingly there can be no commitment to justice without the parallel commitment to *fight* for it, and that the logic of this fight (i.e., of effective struggle against opponents) introduces a second element of political ethics irreducible to—and at times in direct tension with—conventional understandings of moral goodness. That the ethics of a good political leader are distinct from ethics as such—this is the troubling truth that political maturity discloses according to the dirty hands tradition.[108] For exponents of this tradition childishness therefore appears as *innocence*: understood literally as the "absence of harm [from *in-* 'not' + *nocentem* 'harming']" both in the sense of not perceiving a world of harm (potential wrongdoers) and in the sense of being unable to commit the requisite harms (e.g., deception, violence, illegality) required at least occasionally by responsible political leadership. Political maturity requires overcoming one's innocence and accepting that political life cannot always be conducted by pure means.[109]

The plebeian idea of principled vulgarity borrows something from the Enlightenment and dirty hands traditions but, in synthesizing them, also moves beyond them in its conceptualization of the underlying reality that mature plebeian citizens must face. Like the Enlightenment account of political maturity, plebeianism understands advocacy in the public realm to be an essential part of politics, even as it insists that, for ordinary citizens, such advocacy sometimes will have to be characterized by uncivil forms of political communication (classism, arbitrariness, non-deliberative discourse, and rancor) opposed by the Enlightenment model. And like the dirty hands tradition of political maturity, plebeianism accepts the discontinuity between political ethics and ethics as such, but does so in a way focused on what this tragic circumstance means for ordinary citizens, not powerful leaders. As a result of this synthesis, however, the plebeian tradition understands the nature of the disconcerting reality confronted by the politically mature citizen in distinct terms. Rather than the default illegitimacy attached to unratified social norms or the inescapably warlike aspect of politics, for plebeians the reality which must be faced is their own relative *powerlessness*: the fact that they are not first-class citizens, that others besides themselves make the decisions most directly shaping the fate of their polity, and that their civic opportunities are darkened and circumscribed by the shadow of unfairness. That is to say, if both other models of maturity assume some kind of autonomy—the autonomy of authoring social norms collectively or the autonomy of a leader who can successfully navigate the challenges posed by opponents and the ethical ambiguities of political leadership—with plebeianism it is precisely *heteronomy* that constitutes what is difficult about the reality being faced. Learning to face and progressively cope with their heteronomy is the central inner-ethical challenge for plebeians.

Within the plebeian model, then, the childishness to be overcome by the politically mature citizen is neither naïveté/cynicism, nor innocence, but *infantile fantasies of omnipotence*. The association of childishness with such fantasies has long been a feature of various strains of psychoanalysis, first formulated in Freud's notion of "His Majesty the Baby."[110] But omnipotence has much less often been associated with notions of political immaturity.[111] Nonetheless, it is precisely a fantasy of omnipotence that defines the specifically plebeian brand of immaturity, whether in the form of plebeians presuming themselves to have much more power than they in fact do, or in the form of them presuming that the liberal democracies in which they live either are or could be made fully perfect with regard to fair equality of opportunity vis-à-vis education and politics. Such presumptions prevent the ordinary citizen from confronting his or her plebeian status, recognizing the propriety of plebeian reforms (such as the regulation of the most advantaged class), and acknowledging the need for a vulgar rather than merely civil ethics of political communication.

Of course, my point is not simply to introduce a plebeian conceptualization of political maturity as distinct from Enlightenment and dirty hands variants, but to defend the plebeian account as more appropriate for ordinary citizens than the other two. In making this claim it is helpful to consider yet another meaning of the idea of political maturity. Beyond the other valuable aspects of the concept of maturity I already have mentioned—the mildness of its judgments, its philosophization of the empirical exclusion of children from politics, and its disclosure of a troubling reality only the mature can face—maturity also refers to the situational awareness of doing that for which the time is ripe. This situational awareness—this second-order knowledge of *when* to engage in politically responsible, "adult" conduct—is implied in the fact that maturity after all is most basically an agricultural term, coming from the Latin *maturare*, which means "to ripen." On this reading, maturity is the time at which something bears fruit or comes to fruition—and being mature accordingly means doing that which is appropriate to the circumstances in which one finds oneself. Even if the Italian and German terminology on which Machiavelli, Kant, and Weber (among others) rely to develop the Enlightenment and dirty hands models of political maturity do not make use of this English word, the specifics of their accounts of political maturity clearly reflect the idea of timeliness. As much as Kant—and more recently many contemporary deliberative democrats—define political maturity in terms of the practices and values of deliberative discourse, they also recognize that not all times and places are suitable for deliberation.[112] Likewise, as much as exponents of the dirty hands tradition emphasize the political leader's need to commit morally dubious acts, there is a parallel, if secondary, teaching that the politically mature politician will economize such fraught practices, which in turn is only possible on the basis of a prior *situational* understanding that can separate out genuinely necessary moments of moral transgression from contexts in which such transgressions would be excessive and unwise.[113]

The importance of timeliness for a plebeian conception of political maturity is not simply that it reminds us that within the plebeian model too there must be some situational awareness regarding when and when not to engage in principled vulgarity, but that it is precisely the matter of timeliness that explains why the two prevailing paradigms of political maturity—the Enlightenment and dirty hands models—are not the most appropriate for ordinary, plebeian citizens in contemporary liberal democracies. Specifically, these two leading discourses, despite their differences, share the same presupposition that the citizen will possess substantial political power, either as a co-legislator in a formal parliament or informal public sphere, or as a leading politician entrusted with executive authority. This presupposition of power is out of keeping with the everyday structure of political experience in contemporary mass democracy, in which most citizens most of the time are neither legislators nor executives but rather members of a "Many" which rarely engages in political decision-making and, when it does, does so in ways that severely limit the expressivity of each individual member. If the dirty hands tradition speaks most appropriately to the condition of the One, and the Enlightenment tradition to that of the Few, what is needed—and what plebeianism supplies—is a notion of political maturity specifically designed for the context of the Many. It is immature not only to act like a child, but also to act according to a vision of maturity that does not speak to the situation in which one finds oneself.

5

Solace for the Plebeian: The Idea of Extrapoliticism

Teach us to care and not to care
Teach us to sit still.

—T. S. Eliot, "Ash Wednesday"

5.1 The Plebeian's Need for Solace

What remains to be considered within a plebeian theory of liberal democracy is the following problem: how to prevent the plebeian's second-class political status from altogether darkening the character of the plebeian's life. As I have argued in these pages, there can be no expectation of an ordinary citizen's political existence being a happy one. The emergence of liberal-democratic states may represent a remarkable achievement in political history, but the shadow of unfairness cast upon them means that individuals fated to live as ordinary citizens will likely endure various kinds of political discontent. The second-class civic structures conditioning everyday civic life in a liberal democracy (remove, manyness, and plutocracy) generate indignation at the knowledge that one's polity fails to fully realize free and equal citizenship. And the plebeian effort to seek progress under such circumstances through imposing special burdens on the most powerful members of society—with its elements of envy (however reasonable) and vulgarity (however principled)—likewise point to a political psychology of profound unease. Indeed, I have gone so far as to suggest that the plebeian has a responsibility to be unhappy in politics: to do otherwise would be to live in bad faith regarding the shadow of unfairness and the possibility of a more honest and progressive democracy that would arise from confronting it. But discontent in politics need not necessarily extend to an entirely discontented life. Here one might do well to reconsider the old, indeed foundational, liberal ideal of a separation between private and public. If the seventeenth-century origins of this idea related to keeping the individual's private religious conscience safe from a political realm no longer deemed an appropriate arbiter of theology, the idea I mean to raise here is rather how to protect the ordinary citizen's private happiness from the unhappiness that engagement in politics is so likely to generate beneath the shadow of unfairness.

A full account of plebeianism, then, should address how the plebeian citizen is supposed to manage the strains of political life. What behaviors and modes of thinking can plebeians rely on to maintain their spirit in the face of the various stresses and frustrations besetting plebeian politics?

One might object that such a question, though worth asking, does not belong within democratic theory, which—unlike, say, psychiatry—has no special competence in providing solace for psychological distress. What this objection forgets, however, is that egalitarianism—and, by extension, democracy—is a rich idea with a significance extending far beyond the narrow confines of politics conventionally construed. This broader, psychologically relevant understanding of egalitarianism is virtually unknown in contemporary democratic thought, but it figures prominently in the earliest, most ancient meditations on democracy and the idea of equality of which we have record. What is especially valuable about this ancient tradition—and what this chapter aims to recover—is the suggestion that democracy should be understood not only in its familiar, *political* or *governmental* sense (i.e., as a doctrine or state of affairs according to which citizens enjoy some kind of equality of access and influence regarding the political institutions of statecraft and lawmaking) but also in a less familiar, though still vital and historically accurate, *extrapolitical* sense as the *critical indifference* toward active and engaged political life. That is to say, I mean to excavate an ancient, though largely forgotten, democratic tradition which associates the egalitarian mindset with the tendency periodically *not to care* about politics— both in the sense of criticizing political life as disrespectful of human equality and, even more, in the sense of celebrating certain practices that draw on political ideals even as these are deployed in a non-political direction. For plebeians, whose relationship to liberal democracy is an ongoing source of consternation, such critical indifference has the potential to provide a distinctly *democratic* kind of solace: i.e., a partial shield, constructed from egalitarian materials, against the psychological tensions and strains of plebeian political life.

In referring to this ancient, too-often-neglected conceptualization of egalitarianism in terms of a critical indifference towards politics as *extrapolitical*, I introduce the neologism *extrapoliticism* so as to differentiate it from both *antipoliticism* and *mere apoliticism*. The critical indifference I mean to uncover is not antipolitical because it does not in fact represent a total, unconditional critique of active political life. Not only is such a wholesale critique perhaps impossible—since the active opposition to politics itself becomes political insofar as it aims to struggle for the realization of this ambition in the world—but it clearly misdescribes what is at stake within the ancient extrapolitical democratic tradition I shall discuss here, where the critical indifference toward politics is never entirely unrestrained or omnipresent, but only episodic. That is to say, an extrapolitical perspective does not reject politics once and for all, but looks to achieve only a temporary transcendence of political concerns, with the expectation of a future re-entry into political life. With regard to the second differentiation, the idea of extrapoliticism is meant to emphasize that what is at stake in the critical indifference toward politics is not any kind of apoliticism (which might have its basis in metaphysical sources, like an alleged equality before God, that diminish the perceived importance of temporal affairs), but a specific form of political indifference that relates to the redeployment and sublimation of the commitment to basic political values—such as equality, solidarity, free speech, and self-sufficiency—in an apolitical direction. Indeed, what is most significant about the egalitarian, extrapolitical tradition I mean to recover and defend in this chapter is its suggestion that certain seemingly political longings are in fact capable of being realized away from politics in the inspired relations of private life. One experiences extrapoliticism, then, not by losing all interest in political notions, but in pursuing them in apolitical form, outside the conventional political spaces of public advocacy, leadership, governance, administration, and legislation.

Because the extrapolitical meaning of democracy is something uniquely recognized by ancient political thinkers and almost entirely forgotten today, my elucidation of how extrapoliticism might function in the present context of contemporary liberal democracy leads me to the investigation of ancient sources. I begin in Section 5.2 with the Roman plebeians, my muse throughout this book, and consider how they may have found extrapolitical solace in the face of disappointment stemming from their second-class political lives. My analysis focuses on Epicureanism, the philosophy initially developed by the Greek philosopher Epicurus (341–270 BCE), which along with Stoicism was the dominant philosophical school in late republican Rome. What makes Epicureanism so interesting is not simply the extrapolitical significance of Epicurean notions that one should "live unnoticed"[1] and "avoid politics,"[2] but that it is a philosophy that appears to have been especially popular among Roman plebeians.[3] Cicero, for example, a leading statesman and philosopher of the late Republic with strong aristocratic leanings, goes so far as to lambast Epicureanism as a "plebeian philosophy."[4] But if Cicero intended this as an insult, I pursue the connection between Epicureanism and plebeianism in a more sympathetic light, exploring how Epicurean teachings, in their extrapoliticism, might have enabled plebeian citizens to cope in the face of their political mediocrity.

Epicureanism, however, is but one version of how an extrapolitical form of solace for the plebeian might take shape. I do not claim that Epicurean ideas are uniquely valuable to contemporary citizens. With this consideration in mind, in the second half of the chapter (Section 5.3), I situate Epicureanism within a broader tradition of ancient political thought that recognized that egalitarianism is not simply a political idea referring to government and lawmaking, but also implicates various extrapolitical ideas and practices. Section 5.4 defends the relevance of extrapoliticism to contemporary citizenship over and against concerns that it is irresponsibly quietistic.

Taken as a whole, my concern throughout this chapter is to return to some of the earliest sources of egalitarian thought in the West to suggest strategies and mindsets that might enable ordinary, plebeian citizens to resist the burdens of a political life that is constitutively disappointing and frustrating when seen from a liberal-democratic perspective. To be clear, I do not mean to redefine democracy in terms of a permanent withdrawal from politics, but only to include within the panoply of democratic ethics the idea that as a condition of their peace of mind ordinary citizens rightly will seek temporary self-distancing from their political lives. Plebeianism ought to be understood, therefore, not merely as the conditions and commitments that define active politics for ordinary citizens, but also as the *democratic rationale for* and *extrapolitical methods whereby* they periodically transcend the political as such.

5.2 Extrapoliticism and the Roman Plebeians: The Case of Epicureanism

Epicureanism's significance to a plebeian theory of democracy is not simply that it exemplifies what I am calling extrapoliticism—that is, the provision of solace to ordinary citizens through calling into question the desirability of high political office and offering practices whereby political longings temporarily might be sublimated in non-political form—but that, as a historical matter, Epicureanism was especially popular among plebeian citizens in late republican Rome, the political constituency that has most inspired this book's conceptualization of plebeianism as a theoretical construct for comprehending contemporary liberal democracy. This popularity was not just a function of the fact that Epicureanism was the most dominant philosophical school in late republican Rome and so, naturally, attractive to a large number of plebeians who were the most common type of citizen.[5] The connection between plebeianism and Epicureanism also follows from the degree to which Epicureanism has a strong egalitarian bent, thus potentially making it especially appealing to ordinary plebeian citizens. Epicurean communities in the ancient world were among the most inclusive philosophical schools, as lower-class citizens, along with women and slaves, were admitted as full members.[6] Moreover, to a greater extent than other Hellenistic schools, Epicureans actively sought to popularize their teachings and gain a wide array of new members.[7] This inclusivity stemmed directly from the fact that Epicurus's primary ethical teaching—that a good life consists in freedom from anxiety (*ataraxia*), the maximum overall increase of pleasure and reduction of pain (*aponia*), and bliss (*makaria*), all of which are usually best secured in friendship and philosophical discussion in *gardens*, real or metaphorical, far from the activities, concerns, and ambitions of engaged political and economic life— was formulated as a theory of happiness available to all regardless of their socioeconomic position. These considerations, along with certain proto-democratic aspects of Epicurus's thought (especially his implicit belief in human equality and his explicit contractarian notion of political justice as a mutual agreement among citizens not to harm each other[8]), make it credible to treat Epicureanism as an egalitarian philosophy, albeit one that continually challenges the integrity of political spaces rather than seeks to make them equally accessible to everyone. To be sure, ancient Epicurean communities drew adherents from all segments of society, but their egalitarian element, along with their popularity among the Roman plebs, suggest that one should take Cicero seriously when he describes Epicureanism as a "plebeian philosophy."

But if the special connection of Epicureanism to the plebeians of late republican Rome is well known, what has not been sufficiently recognized is the way this philosophical school may have functioned in providing extrapolitical solace to plebeian citizens—a solace with important resonances for ordinary citizens today. The extrapolitical potential of the Epicurean tradition has been overlooked due to the prevalence of interpretations emphasizing Epicureanism's antipolitical character. Even if I aim to resist such interpretations as the final word on Epicureanism, they are to be sure understandable. After all, in addition to their seemingly antipolitical admonition to "live unnoticed" and "avoid politics," Epicureans put forward the polemical and provocative idea that politics, usually at least, is a kind of *prison* (*desmoterion*).[9] While not denying political life altogether—since they recognize the importance of a minimal state in providing basic security, acknowledge that rare individuals might potentially find happiness in positions of governmental leadership, and also contemplate emergency situations in which more active participation might be necessary—the Epicureans' primary teaching is that in general a happy life is best secured outside of politics.[10]

Not surprisingly, the apparent antipoliticism of Epicureanism has made it a target of rebuke from generations of political thinkers, especially those espousing the importance of widespread participation in civic affairs to the health of a polity. For Cicero, the great critic of Epicureanism, part of what is so objectionable about the philosophy is that its ethic of political withdrawal, and its parallel limitation of civic activity to rare instances of emergency, denies a political community the services and civic training of otherwise talented and capable citizens.[11] Against the Epicureans, Cicero affirms his own abiding "care of the state" and his commitment to work day and night for the "freedom and safety of [his] fellow citizens."[12] Later political thinkers repeat the Ciceronian attack on Epicureanism as antipolitical and thus as something either irrelevant or detrimental to the requirements of a vibrant and just public sphere.[13] The assumption that Epicureanism is simply an antipolitical philosophy explains, perhaps, the surprisingly little attention Epicurus and his followers have received as political thinkers.[14]

But there is reason to move beyond a simplistic, merely antipolitical reading of the Epicurean tradition and to understand it as functioning in an additional, different, extrapolitical way: as standing less for the call to leave politics than as a teaching about how to endure the invisibility that already characterizes one's political position. After all, part of what makes the Epicurean concept of "living unnoticed" so poignant is that in any political society, including liberal-democratic ones, being unnoticed is as much a condition most will have to endure as it is something to which one might aspire. Given the scarcity of political office and the lack of meaningful forms of active engagement, most citizens find themselves politically unheralded—a condition which, especially in liberal democracies with their official doctrines of equal political influence for the similarly talented and motivated, is likely to be, for many at least, a source of anxiety. Because Epicureanism praises this very circumstance of being unnoticed, the meaning of Epicurean doctrines should be understood as inhering as much in their provision of solace to political beings confronted with the psychosocial tensions of political marginality as in their more common rendering as the call to abandon politics to the maximal extent possible. Such an alternative reading of Epicureanism finds support on numerous grounds. It is not just that, as I have described, Epicurus and his followers did not after all teach an absolute rejection of political life, nor that as a practical matter it would have been nearly impossible to entirely disentangle themselves from politics—an impossibility that seems even more pronounced today given the ever-widening reach of the state and the lack of spaces unclaimed by political sovereigns. Just as important as Epicurean doctrines is the *practice* of actual Epicureans who do not in all cases evince a total withdrawal from active political life. In Rome, for example, involvement in politics from professed Epicureans was not at all uncommon, suggesting that allegiance to Epicurean ideas did not necessarily translate into applying its call to avoid politics in a literal or complete fashion.[15] Indeed, the participation of Epicureans in Roman politics was sufficiently common that Cicero, who usually criticizes Epicurean teachings for encouraging disengagement from public affairs, occasionally also worries about the political *engagement* of Epicureans, whom he fears will have their public service corrupted by purely selfish considerations.[16] That Cicero voices concern about Epicureans' irresponsible involvement in politics—and not just their irresponsible withdrawal—is a clear reminder that we miss out on the full meaning of Epicureanism if it is reduced to an antipolitical standpoint and that, for some, the philosophy's apparent antipoliticism functioned more as an intellectual tonic for temporarily transcending the frustrations of political life than as a call to actually dispense with politics once and for all. When Epicureanism is interpreted in this broader fashion, Cicero's designation of Epicureanism as a "plebeian philosophy" ought to be read counter to the way he intended: not as an epithet disparaging Epicureanism's base antipolitical character, but as a recognition that Epicureanism has the potential to serve the psychological needs of plebeians in their very political status as second-class citizens struggling to come to terms with their ordinariness.

In attending to the extrapolitical function of the Epicurean tradition I do not mean to claim that extrapoliticism is the sole way to make sense of Epicurean ideas, as it is obvious that Epicureanism has also operated in the antipolitical fashion more familiar to generations of interpreters and critics. Nor do I mean to suggest that a theory of plebeianism such as I defend in this book could accept Epicureanism in its antipolitical form. Any transcendence of the political must function in conjunction with an active and engaged plebeian political agenda. The point, to paraphrase T. S. Eliot's line invoked as this chapter's epigraph, is to learn *to care and not to care about politics*, which is not at all the same thing as simply not caring. Epicureanism, and extrapoliticism more generally, are useful only in their capacity to provide an egalitarian kind of solace in the face of political reality, not as a seduction to turn away once and for all from this reality.

With these caveats in mind, I now detail the extrapolitical elements of Epicureanism. As I have indicated, in providing solace for political discontent, an extrapolitical standpoint operates in two related ways. It criticizes the dogged pursuit of political power as a loathsome path discordant with a life lived in full respect of human equality. And it celebrates certain practices that draw on egalitarian political ideals even as these are deployed in a nonpolitical direction. Accordingly, the discussion of Epicureanism that follows operates within these two dimensions. First, I argue for an understanding of the Epicurean call to "live unnoticed" and "avoid politics" in its *critical aspect* (i.e., its critique of active political life) rather than only in terms of its apparent celebration of a private existence. And second, I attend to how the specific teachings of Epicureanism (its call for equanimity, friendship, frank discussion, self-sufficiency, and the acceptance of one's mortality) are best understood as the *reconfiguration* and perhaps even *intensification* of political values (like equality, solidarity, free speech, and self-rule) rather than as the mere replacement of political objectives with apolitical ones. I conclude with a defense of Epicureanism, when conceived in extrapolitical terms, against the charge of civic irresponsibility.

The Epicurean Critique of Politics

Cicero and other critics are too quick when they dismiss Epicureanism as a selfish doctrine that privileges individual comfort and contentment over the sacrifices required for dedicated public service. Even if this critique is not entirely untrue, it is still incomplete because it neglects the fact that Epicureans are interested in politics if only as a singular object of disapproval. And this critique of the political is one important way in which Epicureanism has the ability to provide solace to ordinary, plebeian citizens who can expect no more than a highly marginal role within the state. In making the claim that the powerful and prominent do not on this basis enjoy a more pleasant life—and, even more, in suggesting that those vying for leading positions are especially prone to various forms of unhappiness—Epicurean teachings can reinforce in ordinary citizens the possibly true idea that their chance for happiness is not diminished by their socioeconomic middlingness. To be sure, any account of the sources of happiness will be viewed by the modern reader, cognizant of human diversity and the multiplicity of different ends an individual might seek to realize a good life, with a well-deserved skepticism. Still, the Epicurean criticism of the unhappiness likely generated by political ambition is nonetheless valuable, not only for suggesting how the historical Roman plebeians may have found extrapolitical solace, but for instilling in contemporary plebeian citizens an appreciation for the difference between socioeconomic success and happiness—and, with it, a tonic against the psychological strain arising from comparing one's mediocre civic station to that of the exceedingly powerful, wealthy, and acclaimed.

In elucidating the Epicurean critique of politics, it is helpful to keep in mind the central elements of Epicurean ethical theory. Continually the Epicurean tradition returns to the idea that a happy life—characterized, as I have said, by equanimity (*ataraxia*), a minimal amount of pain (*aponia*), and bliss (*makaria*),[17] spent in the company of friends—is best achieved through respecting the *limits* (*perata*) of life, a notion which should be understood in three different, closely related senses. One of these limits concerns the idea that "the limit of good things is easy to achieve,"[18] which means both that the good things in life are easily secured and that overindulgence in goods can render them sources of pain, sickness, and frustration. Epicureans differentiate natural, necessary desires like satisfying thirst through drinking from both unnecessary but natural desires (e.g., a thirst for drinking the finest beverages in the world) and unnatural desires (e.g., a thirst for glory).[19] In general, Epicureans teach limiting one's desires to the first category (what is natural and necessary) and, in any case, subjecting desires beyond these limits to careful scrutiny, ensuring that their fulfillment will indeed promote tranquility and lack of anguish.[20] What Epicureans find especially objectionable are those unnecessary desires (i.e., desires whose lack of fulfillment would produce no pain) that require much effort to realize and whose value depends merely on the "empty belief [*kenodoxian*] of mankind."[21] Against the proliferation of such unnecessary and unnatural desires, Epicureans insist on the idea of "enough"—that is, a limit to how much one needs in order to be satisfied—and they take aim at the unwisdom of those who cannot respect this limit: "Nothing is enough to someone for whom enough is little."[22] Thus, in addition to asserting "the limit of good things," the Epicureans also put forward a closely connected *second* idea: that *ataraxia* and freedom from anguish can only be achieved if one's desires are limited, that is, kept in check against the tendency to continually manufacture unnatural and unnecessary wants. Accordingly, it is a core Epicurean principle to teach "the limit of the desires"[23] and to assert that "even the greatest wealth is poverty when it comes to the unlimited desires."[24]

But what propels human beings to disrespect the limited nature of good things and to entertain unlimited desires? Underlying these two pathologies, Epicureans think, is the fear of death, which drives people, however impossibly, to deny their mortality through ambitions for prestige, status, and excessive wealth. Against this tendency, Epicureans assert the need for a third kind of limit: an acceptance of the limited human lifespan—that is, of death and the fundamental fact of human finitude. Accordingly, Epicureans teach:

> He who is assured of the limits [*perata*] of the lifespan knows how easy it is to take away the pain of want and to render the whole of life all-complete, so that there is no longer a need of things obtained in the manner of struggle [*agonas*: also "battle" or "assembly"].[25]

Overcoming the fear of death does not mean trying to remove the thought of it from one's mind. Even though Epicureans hold that death itself is "nothing" (something that cannot be experienced and thus nothing to dread),[26] the irrational fear of death which generates endless unnecessary desires is best counteracted by confronting, rather than turning away from, the limit of one's mortality.[27] Indeed, the repression of the fact of finitude seems to be the primary mechanism whereby the fear of death generates the production of limitless unhealthy needs and wants.[28]

With these three limits in mind—the limited nature of the good, the consequent need to limit one's own desires, and the fundamental limit of death attunement to which enables respect for the two other limits—it is possible to better understand what Epicureans find objectionable about most forms of political life and, more specifically, how their critique of politics may bring some solace and relief to ordinary, plebeian citizens with little power, wealth, or fame. What makes politics most suspect and worthy of critique, according to the Epicureans, is that it tends to violate each of these three limits.

First of all, against the civic-humanist teaching that active political life is the realization of a fully developed and happy human existence, Epicureans find that politics usually disrespects the limits of the good insofar as political figures typically are motivated by numerous unnecessary and unnatural desires, such the quest for glory, status, and power.[29] For Lucretius, the Roman Epicurean poet, war (and by extension a great deal of politics) is a result of the human failure to abide by a limited conception of the good: "Yes, all for nothing we wretched men toil on forever, and waste our lives on foolishness; clearly, because we never learned the limits of having, and where true pleasure's growth must end. And little by little this launched life toward the depths and up from the bottom stirred wars' wasteful waves."[30] To be sure, one can imagine political actors motivated by different factors—for example, a genuine interest in improving the public realm—but even here Epicureans would reply that the *struggle* that would seem always to characterize political action indicates that politics is not in itself easy or happy.[31] Such reasoning may be hard to accept for public-spirited progressives committed to achieving meaningful reform, whether through politics or the generation of prosperity, but even if such critics remain unpersuaded by the Epicurean injunction to withdraw from politics and socioeconomic competition, they can at least perhaps recognize some truth in the Epicurean idea that such pursuits are unlikely to be characterized by the tranquility Epicureans celebrate.[32] Insofar as tranquility might be understood as a kind of democratic value, something I elaborate below, its defense over and against active or excessive political involvement may be seen as having a justification beyond the purely selfish concern with one's own pleasure.

Second, it is not just that political life violates the limited nature of the good, but that in doing so it unleashes other desires that are themselves unlimited and thus almost certain to generate anxiety. As Lucretius describes it, a life bent on achieving rulership is likely to be "terrible" (*infestum*) because of its quest for goals that are endless, unreachable, and personally damaging. Political power is a desire unlikely to be sated since there is usually more of it to be had and since there are always threats from the ambitions of the less powerful against which one must be perpetually on guard.[33] What is also endless is the rulers' constant need to remain guided to some degree by the broader populace they lead. Lucretius says of political leaders, "All their wisdom is from others' lips" (*quandoquidem sapiunt alieno ex ore*)—meaning that they must constantly wage struggles based on the ideas of others which, as such, are subject to change, in some ways inconsistent with the politicians' own considered views, and likely never satisfactorily realized in the political actions politicians carry out.[34] On the basis of similar reasoning, the plebeian and sometime Epicurean poet Horace can claim that "free from the burden of unhappy ambition . . . I comfort myself with the thought I live more happily than if my grandfather had been a quaestor, and my father and uncle likewise."[35]

But, third, perhaps the most fundamental, if least elaborated, element of the Epicurean critique is the further consideration that a political mindset tends to cover over the basic fact of human mortality and thus prevent the kind of attunement to finitude Epicureans believe to be essential to achieving a happy, tranquil, and relatively pain-free existence. It is not simply that the lust for political power most often stems, in Epicureans' minds, from the fear of death—or, more precisely, from the repression of this fear, which produces, as Lucretius describes it, "care and vague desire" (*alia quavis scindunt cuppedine curae*), "an endless quest for change" (*quaerere semper commutare locum*), and the pursuit of "power that's vain and never granted [but which instead results in] hardship and endless pain" (*nam petere imperium, quod inanest nec datur umquam atque in eo semper durum sufferre laborem*).[36] Even more essentially, Epicureans suggest that politics promotes a temporal perspective that makes a healthy fixation on one's finitude impossible to cultivate or maintain. That is to say, one of the central Epicurean doctrines is that one must "remove the longing for immortality," but this ethic is perpetually undermined by active political life.[37] After all, in at least two respects, political life represents an attempted escape from the condition of human finitude. On the one hand, politics offers human beings, confined to a finite biological existence, the opportunity to in some sense overcome their mortality and achieve a partial kind of immortality through the memorialization of their persons or, in the form of legislation, their causes and conceptions of the public good. On the other hand, the state itself is immortal insofar as, unlike the human being, it is not obviously fated to die.[38] Appreciation of the death-defying aspect of politics is most closely associated with Hannah Arendt, for whom it is a basic postulate of her political philosophy. Arendt finds an essential purpose of the *polis* to be its capacity to provide a "guarantee against the futility of individual life," since the political realm is uniquely able to "transcend the life-span of mortal men . . . into a potential earthly immortality."[39] But such ideas are in fact hardly specific to Arendt. The relative immortality of the political realm is widely recognized within the tradition of political thought. Rousseau is a rare, if not sole, exception when he calls for states that will, like an Epicurean individual, remain attuned to their eventual passing from the world.[40] By contrast, Cicero's insistence upon the deathless state not only reflects the tacit assumption of most political philosophers, but unquestionably describes the political community's understanding of itself: "A city ought to be constituted that it would be everlasting. Therefore the annihilation of the republic is not natural, as is the annihilation of a human being, for whom death is not only necessary, but very often welcome. When a city, however, is destroyed, wiped out, and extinguished, it is as if—to compare small things to large ones—the entire world perished and dissolved."[41] Such a perspective is no less common among modern, postmetaphysical philosophers, with Hobbes, for example, enunciating the hope in his *Leviathan* that "there may Principles of Reason be found out, by industrious meditation, to make [the] constitution [of commonwealths] (excepting by externall violence) everlasting. And such are those which I have in this discourse set forth."[42]

Epicureans do not deny the difference between states and individuals regarding their mortality, but rather than derive from this difference the appeal of attempting to overcome human finitude through politics, they instead insist that it is precisely in the seduction of immortality that politics represents a danger to human happiness. Not only is the immortality of states merely relative, for they too ultimately will perish, but the posthumous memorialization promised by the public realm is something that cannot of course usually be enjoyed by the individuals who would seek it.[43] Crucial to Epicureanism is the discipline "not to try to achieve the impossible."[44] Even more fundamentally, the elongated temporal expanse of politics—its focus on both the past (e.g., adjudicating alleged wrongs) and the future (e.g., enacting legislation)—renders it suspect on Epicurean grounds, insofar as Epicureans' exhortation to live a life of tranquility and happiness among friends takes the shorter timeframe of the *day* as its basic horizon. The well-known Epicurean motto from Horace to "seize the day"—*carpe diem*—should be read not simply as a call to cease procrastination and make the most of the opportunities for fulfillment one finds before oneself, but to do so within the temporal unit of the day as opposed to the more long-term perspective of political life and socioeconomic competition.[45] Accordingly, an Epicurean motto holds, "We're born only once, and we cannot be born twice; and one must for all eternity exist no more. You are not in control of tomorrow yet you delay your [opportunity to] rejoice. Life is ruined by delay and each and every one of us dies without enjoying leisure."[46]

Epicureanism, then, operates as much as a critique of politics as it does as a simple call to avoid politics. This critical aspect is one important reason why one can speak of Epicureanism as providing a kind of solace for ordinary citizens confronting the frustrations and disappointments of a political life darkened by the shadow of unfairness. Epicureanism, of course, does not promise to cancel these frustrations and disappointments, but in suggesting that politics frustrates and disappoints everyone who engages in it, by insisting that a political mindset contradicts crucial elements of a distinctly human, mortal existence, and by therefore raising the possibility that those with limited political opportunities may find themselves with greater chances for contentment than those with active political careers, Epicureanism offers a kind of solace to those fated to endure an unremarkable, merely ordinary political existence.

Epicureanism as a Sublimation of Politics

The capacity of Epicureanism to provide solace for plebeian citizens inheres not simply in the fact that it criticizes the life of political prominence. Crucially, what also is key is that Epicurean practices, even if they involve withdrawal from active political life, still make appeal to political ideas and behaviors, employing these now for extrapolitical ends. Indeed, in the final analysis, the significance of Epicureanism for contemporary democratic theory is not that its specific ethical teachings are uniquely authoritative, but rather that it is a paradigmatic example of how a periodic withdrawal from politics might rest on some of the same basic egalitarian grounds that elsewhere and otherwise inspire political engagement.[47] What I mean to demonstrate, then, is that Epicureanism can be seen as *reconfiguring*, rather than rejecting outright, political, and especially democratic, ideas—and, furthermore, that this reconfiguration is not at all bizarre or idiosyncratic, but upon reflection compelling in its recognition that deeply held egalitarian values might be realized, perhaps even more intensely, in spaces beyond those of conventional political life. Specifically, in at least five different ways, Epicureanism represents an extrapolitical sublimation of egalitarian political commitments.

First, within the Epicurean paradigm the idea of equality takes on a psychological meaning—a mind (*animus*) that is equal, *equ-animity*, that is, a mind undominated by any particular passion—rather than only the standard institutional meaning (namely, the set of legal procedures by which citizens are treated equally vis-à-vis government and lawmaking). On the linguistic level, this extrapolitical appropriation of equality is perhaps best seen in Latin, where the word for equal, *aequus*, also means "calm." Thus, for Lucretius, as well as for Horace, the central Epicurean value of *ataraxia* (tranquility or equanimity) often is rendered in terms of an "equal mind" (*aequus animus*).[48] This idea of the democratic soul as an especially relaxed form of character is reflected in various sources even beyond the Epicurean tradition. Pericles's funeral oration, celebrating the democratic culture of fifth-century Athens, refers to the "relaxed way of life" (*rhathumia*) of Athenian citizens.[49] Likewise, Plato's depiction of the typical democratic character, which I consider in Section 5.3, includes the idea that such a person will "live from day to day, indulging the appetite of the moment," whether it be politics, philosophy, heavy drinking, flute playing, or just "idling and neglecting everything."[50] Epicurus's teachings can be read as a continuation of this tradition, but with the difference that for Epicureans political matters become the primary *obstacle* to equanimity rather than a potential site of its achievement.[51]

Second, the Epicurean framework also reimagines the very idea of human equality in a manner that undermines its functionality as a political notion. Ordinarily we think of political equality as something that, even if it is grounded on metaphysical ideas like universal human dignity, requires for its instantiation formal institutions affording equal respect and concern for the material interests of citizens. Yet, from the Epicurean perspective, human equality already exists outside of and independent from political life. On the one hand, such equality most basically inheres in the shared destination of death awaiting all human beings, which Epicureans believe ought to be a constant object of reflection. The Epicurean doctrine, "One can attain security against other things, but when it comes to death all men live in a city without walls,"[52] should be read not only as the assertion that death is inescapable and that we would do well to face rather than retreat from the fact of our finitude, but as the likening of this circumstance to a democratic city insofar as it imposes a kind of equality onto otherwise diverse and unequal citizens.[53]

On the other hand, such already-achieved equality arises from the degree to which Epicurean teachings about how to achieve happiness are accessible to virtually all people independent of their socioeconomic condition and political status. It is not simply that the poor, unknown, and unpowerful are no less able than the rich, famous, and dominant to achieve a life of *ataraxia*, bliss, and freedom from pain—but to a meaningful degree they are *better* able since, according to Epicurus, those who are seemingly privileged tend to be made unhappy by unending, extravagant desires and often fail to observe the simple, frugal existence that usually promotes more well-being than a life of luxury. Horace's cry, "Grant me, O Latona's son, to be content with what I have," finds echoes throughout the Epicurean tradition.[54] Those with less, who accept the idea of "enough" and learn to live with it, can free themselves from the pain of generating limitless needs that cannot be realized. At its extreme, such reasoning deconstructs the very idea of wealth—"Poverty, if measured by the goal of nature, is great wealth; and wealth, if limits are not set for it, is great poverty"[55]—and in so doing undermines the relevance of socioeconomic life and perhaps also of political life as well, since if material abundance is not correlated with human happiness, neither is a political realm working for the economic benefit of its citizens.

The point to emphasize, then, is that in its assertion that the socioeconomically disadvantaged are as likely if not more likely to achieve happiness than the advantaged, Epicureanism rests on a kind of egalitarianism that marginalizes the significance of politics. This teaching might be accused of quietism if Epicureans practiced it in complete, unadulterated fashion. But if we interpret Epicureanism *extrapolitically*, as a kind of solace for those who are, inescapably, caught up in political and socioeconomic hierarchies, the Epicurean deconstruction of wealth and advantage ought to be understood as a periodic measure by which ordinary citizens can be eased by the thought that the equality they seek unsuccessfully in political life might be temporarily rediscovered in their relation to death and in their equal opportunity for equanimity, bliss, and freedom from pain.[56]

A third way in which Epicureanism represents a kind of appropriation and sublimation of egalitarian political values concerns the concept of *solidarity*: rather than seek solidarity in political relations of citizenship, Epicureans affirm that it is more meaningfully sought in private relations of friendship beyond the confines of public life, such as occurred in the Garden Epicurus himself set up just outside of Athens's city walls. As Epicurus taught, "Of those things which wisdom provides for the blessedness of one's whole life, by far the greatest is the possession of friendship."[57] The ancient Epicureans were not alone in praising friendship, as it was a recurring idea in Greek philosophy that citizens in a well-ordered polis would be friends, but they departed from conventional approaches when they sharply differentiated civic friendship (the kind of solidarity occurring between fellow co-participants in governmental and lawmaking processes) from what they considered the more genuine friendship between private individuals.[58] Philodemus, a popular Epicurean poet and philosopher who lived in late republican Rome and then in nearby Herculaneum, expressed the basic idea when he wrote, "If a man undertook a systematic enquiry to find what is most hostile to friendship and most productive of enmity, he would find it in the City."[59]

Now why do Epicureans privilege private over civic friendship, taking it to be a deeper and more genuine form of solidarity? One answer is that they think relations with private friends are better than those with fellow citizens in providing the tranquility, bliss, and freedom from pain they prize—that, specifically, friendship helps one to recognize the three limits I have discussed above (the limited nature of the good, the need to limit the desires, and the need to confront the ultimate limit of death), the appreciation of which usually produces happiness. Such a claim is implied in the Epicurean doctrine that friendship is a superior source of security (*asphaleian*) than civic relations when confronting bad things.[60] For this argument to make full sense, it would seem that the safety provided by private friendships lies not only in their capacity to prevent certain harms (like the loss of physical safety), which might after all be best achieved through political relations, but in their special ability to make us see that much of what worries us (our middling levels of wealth, our lack of fame or great prominence, etc.) ought not do so, something for which political life, with its distribution of glory and commitment to generating prosperity, is ill-suited. In any case, the point to stress is that while Epicureans in the ancient world repeat numerous aspects of more conventional understandings of friendship, they uniquely raise the issue of the *setting* in which solidarity might be forged, claiming that a richer variant can be pursued and realized outside of politics. Thus, the Epicureans in effect take a political idea—solidarity with fellow citizens and the *protection* such solidarity affords—and argue that its fullest expression would need to take place beyond the confines of political life. Such a conviction has obvious relevance to ordinary plebeian citizens whose opportunities for civically mediated solidarity are hampered by diminished chances for public speech, office-holding, and individuated judgment. After all, it is simply not possible for plebeians, qua citizens, to construct more than haphazard and superficial relationships in the political spaces within which they are marginalized. But Epicureanism stands for the idea that political marginality in no way means the denial of opportunities for friendship, as these are best conducted *off* the public stage, not upon it.[61]

A fourth element of the Epicurean extrapolitical appropriation of political ideas—and one that further explains the Epicurean preference for private friendship over civic friendship—concerns the idea of *free speech*, specifically the notion of *parrhesia*. Initially, *parrhesia* had a specifically political and indeed governmental meaning, designating primarily the practice of free speech among citizens as they address each other in public. But as the classical polis gave way to Hellenistic polities less shaped by norms of political equality, *parrhesia* became increasingly redefined in relation to a private virtue of frank and candid discourse.[62] The ancient Epicureans, who conceived of *parrhesia* in this latter fashion, were thus part of a larger movement of thinkers engaged in the reconsideration of the meaning of free speech. Importantly, however, whereas other writers and thinkers still tended to emphasize the power-laden significance of frank and candid speech—above all, its use within increasingly hierarchical societies of differentiating a true friend from a flatterer, since *parrhesia* (with its strong tendency toward critique) was considered something friends but not flatterers would do[63]—for Epicureans the idea of free speech is even more stripped of political function, as *parrhesia* for them indicates above all the value of speaking truly and deeply with one's friends, often for the sake of philosophical inquiry or the moral reform of participants in the discussion.[64] Consider the Epicurean teacher Philodemus's insistence: "Although many fine things result from friendship, there is nothing so grand as having one to whom one will say what is in one's heart and who will listen when one speaks. For our nature strongly desires to reveal to some people what it thinks."[65] Such a celebration of free speech, and the friendship that enables it, presupposes that most of the time—especially in politics—we do not fully reveal our thoughts, concerns, and feelings, indicating yet again how private relations among friends might more deeply realize a value originating in the public sphere. It is within this context of privileging intimate, honest, and revelatory speech that the Epicurean endorsement of wine-drinking ought to be understood—as light inebriation not only facilitates such speech but resembles it in being something that cannot usually occur within the practice of governance.[66] In any case, the ancient Epicureans appealed to the political ideal of *parrhesia* even as they reinterpreted this ideal in extrapolitical terms. That is, they suggest that meaningful, unconstrained speech before one's equals—hitherto conceived as an egalitarian political value—might be realized, potentially in purer form, beyond the institutions of political life.[67] Such a teaching is a solace to plebeian citizens who, as such, lack opportunities for full-fledged political speech.

Finally, a fifth way in which the Epicurean tradition represents an extrapolitical reconfiguration of formerly political notions concerns the idea of self-sufficiency, or *autarkeia*. Arguably, the primary meaning of *autarkeia*, initially at least, was as a political concept. With Aristotle, for example, *autarkeia* usually is presented as a feature of a city-state capable of living on its own;[68] or, if it does designate an individual's own independence, it is an independence that is secured through a robust political regime, an adequate amount of wealth and power, or a well-ordered marketplace facilitating trade.[69] That is to say, although there are exceptions, within Aristotle's account *autarkeia* is first and foremost a quality that either refers to or is ensured by political and socioeconomic structures.[70] With the Epicureans, by contrast, *autarkeia* is continually theorized as a quality of persons rather than economies and states, and furthermore as a quality that is usually best realized through the internal regulation of wants rather than through public achievement. To be sure, Epicureans do not deny that some basic amount of political security is useful for self-sufficiency or that wealth in certain cases is something to enjoy. But their major focus is to explain, on the one hand, how *autarkeia* can be attained without great wealth or power, and, on the other hand, how the active pursuit of wealth and power would likely erode *autarkeia*.

With regard to the former of these, Epicureanism emphasizes how a frugal life usually maximizes pleasure and makes periods of abundance more enjoyable, whereas habituation to luxury poses obstacles to such things. To be self-sufficient, then, does not require much.[71] In part because self-sufficiency can be achieved with few resources, ancient Epicureans taught the importance of taking inventory of one's desires, constantly thinking through whether equanimity might be better served by curtailing rather than fulfilling one's wants.[72] What this inventory most often reveals, they believe, is that whatever amount of goods one already possesses is enough to achieve a happy life, full of personal fulfillment and generosity toward friends. In affirming a conception of self-sufficiency that requires little in the way of material resources or worldly achievements, Epicureanism also takes aim, more generally, at external validations of one's worth. Hence the doctrine: "Natural philosophy does not create boastful men nor chatterboxes nor men who show off the 'culture' which many quarrel over, but rather strong and self-sufficient men, who pride themselves on their own personal goods, not those of external circumstances."[73] Thus the Epicurean view that "the greatest fruit of self-sufficiency is freedom [*eleutheria*, especially the negative freedom of not being a slave]" relates in particular to the freedom from servitude, however severe or mild, to the opinions and preferences of others.[74] Epicureans do not seek total avoidance of social interactions, but rather only oppose the active seeking after fame, wealth, and success: "Praise from other men must come of its own accord, as we must be concerned with healing ourselves."[75]

With respect to the latter concern—a critique of how the pursuit of wealth and power undermine self-sufficiency—Epicurean thought continually emphasizes the idea that, more often than not, the fulfillment of numerous desires—above all the desire for economic and political power—is not in fact conducive to the minimizing of pain and anxiety. Consider Epicurus's doctrine: "The disturbance of the soul will not be dissolved nor will considerable joy be produced by the presence of the greatest wealth, nor by honor and admiration among the many, nor by anything which is a result of indefinite causes."[76] In labeling the improper and ineffective sources of happiness "indefinite" (*adioristous*), Epicurus objects not just to their uncertain relationship to human fulfillment, but also to their endless quality, since part of the reason the pursuit of wealth and fame so often leads to unhappiness is that they always seem to leave their seekers wanting more. Horace, likewise, can state, "As money grows, care and greed for greater riches follow after."[77] Horace inveighs against the curse of wealth, declaring, "To those who seek for much, much is ever lacking; blest is he to whom the god with chary hand has given just enough."[78] In its account of self-sufficiency, then, Epicureanism continually aims to expose apparent needs as merely unnatural or unnecessary desires and thus expose, too, the way human life often frustrates itself in what Lucretius calls "empty cares" (*curis inanibus*), among which political ambition is a paradigmatic example.[79]

The ancient Epicureans were not unique in presenting *autarkeia* in a largely internal rather than political and economic fashion, as Stoics, for example, defined the good life as stemming from virtue alone (disconnected from any attainment of wealth and power),[80] and Cynics like Diogenes, with their rejection of property and most norms of civilization, practiced an austerity more radical than the Epicureans.[81] Nor is it true that this internal conception of *autarkeia* was entirely unknown prior to the emergence of Epicureanism and other Hellenistic schools in the fourth-century BCE.[82] But what is distinctive about Epicureanism, especially in contrast to the Stoics, is that the idea of self-sufficiency is theorized and practiced in an explicit, targeted opposition to active political life and the kind of freedom politics promises.[83] This feature makes it especially relevant to plebeians because it suggests that even if they cannot enjoy the fullest kind of independence offered by politics, even if their role with their states lacks anything resembling autonomy in the literal sense of self-legislation, they can still engage in the management of their desires and in so doing find another kind of self-sufficiency.

In these five respects, then—as a psychological account of equality in the form of equanimity, as an insistence on a human equality transcending all political relations, as a call for a deeper form of solidarity than that offered by politics, as a defense of a purer and more intimate free speech than the kind practiced on the public stage, and as a defense of an internalized form of self-sufficiency—the Epicurean tradition translates political values into commitments that find their fullest realization outside of politics. This sublimation not only reminds us, *pace*

Cicero and many later critics, of the enduring connection of Epicureanism to politics, but also demonstrates how Epicurean practices may operate as effective antidotes to the psychic strains of plebeian political life. The Epicurean can live outside of conventional political spaces without entirely sacrificing—and indeed in a certain sense gaining—some of the core elements of what egalitarian politics has to offer.

Why Epicureanism Is Not Necessarily Civically Irresponsible

What makes the extrapolitical elements of the Epicurean tradition instructive for contemporary liberal-democratic citizens living beneath the shadow of unfairness and wrestling with the discontent of their second-class civic status is not necessarily the specific doctrines of the Epicureans—which can hardly claim to have definitively unlocked the path toward happiness—but the more general reminder of something which is all but forgotten today: namely, that democratic ideas and practices are wrongly limited to their conventional political context, but have applications that involve the transcendence of a political mentality and, with it, a transcendence of the uneasiness emanating from a frustrated, second-class, plebeian mode of civic life. Of course, for such transcendence to be meaningful to a plebeian theory of liberal democracy such as I defend in this book, it can only be periodic and must be complemented by an enduring willingness to pursue plebeian political objectives (like the regulation of the most advantaged class) within the second-class civic conditions (such as remove, manyness, and plutocracy) constraining the full effectivity of political advocacy. It might seem that the combination of a temporary transcendence of politics with an abiding engagement in the political realm—even if both emanate from a common set of egalitarian ideals—is contradictory. But this would be to confuse the plebeian's need to find a balance between conflicting impulses with the despair that such a balance is impossible. Those Roman citizens whose Epicureanism did not prevent political engagement are a historical reminder that balancing of this kind is certainly conceivable. Indeed, with Horace, the virtue of achieving a mix of political activism and periodic transcendence of politics is thematized and celebrated: "Accept the gift of pleasure when it's given. Be willing *for now* to be a private person, unworried about the city and how it's doing. Put serious things aside."[84]

That such a balance is worth striving for—that we should learn *to care and not to care* about politics and that egalitarianism has a vital role to play in both ventures—will be difficult to accept by citizens who worry that any interest in even a temporary transcendence of the political is civically irresponsible. Some plebeians will be tempted to agree with Cicero when he fears that citizens under the sway of Epicureanism—and by extension of extrapoliticism in any form—either will not perform acts of public service or will have their service corrupted by a philosophy that renders their civic engagement conditional on purely private considerations. But plebeians would do well to resist this temptation and not let worries about civic irresponsibility undermine a legitimate interest in seeking extrapolitical solace for their political discontent. Critiques like Cicero's only make sense to the extent citizens actually enjoy opportunities for meaningful political engagement. Were all citizens in fact to have the same chance for an equally impactful political life, Cicero's concern about the alleged deleterious impact of Epicureanism would have more merit. But insofar as political opportunity is not equally shared and some systematically enjoy more of it than others, worries about the dangers of Epicureanism to the vitality of the state must be exposed as hyperbolic. After all, as I have claimed, in even the most progressive liberal-democratic regime, "living unnoticed" is something likely to characterize most citizens' political lives, regardless of whether they choose to embrace this condition as Epicureans urge. The effort to draw on egalitarian ideas to find solace in the face of political marginality—and not merely to contest this marginality—is therefore a legitimate democratic goal. I have suggested that Epicurean doctrines do this insofar as they imply that the private lives of unknown plebeian citizens still afford meaningful opportunities for fulfilling basic political longings and that, conversely, the lives of active public servants are not as admirable, or as consistent with norms of free speech, self-sufficiency, and civic equality, as republicans like Cicero believe. When conceived more as solace for citizens without fully satisfying opportunities for a meaningful political existence than as a call for citizens to squander whatever political potential they possess, Epicureanism is not detrimental to the health of a polity, but instead stands only as a way of coping with the psychosocial dilemmas of a plebeian political existence.

To be sure, concern about the irresponsibility of Epicureanism, and of extrapoliticism more generally, might take a somewhat different form—one that finds special emphasis among contemporary critics. This is the idea that transcendence of the political is irresponsible because it is defeatist: it unnecessarily accepts as inevitable various forms of correctible political pathologies. Something like this critique appears, for example, when it is suggested that Epicureanism is symptomatic of political decline, such as occurred following the demise of democratic city-states in Greece in the Hellenistic period or the decline and fall of the Roman republic.[85] The implicit idea, in other words, is that reformist energies should be deployed toward improving underlying institutions (e.g., restoring popular government over and against tyranny and absolutism) rather than devising therapeutic strategies for enduring disappointment. While one might resist this critique on the historical level and point to circumstances in which Epicurean revivals have not in fact been precisely contemporaneous with political decline,[86] on the philosophical level a different kind of counterargument seems no less germane: namely that "political decline," if it signifies a regime that is less than fully fair or inclusive, is never entirely escapable. This tragic truth is the most basic meaning of the shadow of unfairness. While one certainly can strive to achieve better rather than worse outcomes, our liberal democracies always will fall short of their ideals for reasons this book repeatedly has emphasized, including the inevitable incursion of socioeconomic status into political and educational opportunities. In the face of this shadow of unfairness haunting even the most progressive liberal-democratic states, it is not misguided—it is not irresponsible—to seek strategies for enduring the strains of political life, especially when it is possible for citizens to combine, in the course of a day, active commitment to plebeian political reforms and extrapolitical efforts to transcend the inevitable difficulties and disappointments of a political consciousness.

When Epicureanism is interpreted as a distinctly plebeian mode of thought—something suggested after all by the popularity of Epicureanism among the Roman plebs as well as Cicero's denigration of Epicureanism as a "plebeian philosophy"—the solace offered by Epicurean ideas and practices can be seen as periodic, not omnipresent, and thus as something that complements, rather than replaces, whatever kind of political impact plebeians might be able to realize within the unexceptional circumstances they inhabit. Given this double focus of plebeianism on caring and not caring about politics, the ultimate significance of Epicureanism for contemporary democratic theory is that is a quintessential instance of how a periodic, principled, and solace-driven withdrawal from politics might rest on some of the same basic egalitarian grounds that elsewhere and otherwise inspire political engagement.

5.3 The Broader Tradition of Extrapoliticism

I have placed special emphasis on the Epicurean tradition both because it bears an important historical affiliation with the plebeians of the late Roman Republic and because it appears as a paradigmatic example of a kind of political theory that combines egalitarianism with a critique of politics—a critique that, as I have shown, redeploys political values in a non-political direction, suggesting that our deepest political longings may find some satisfaction outside of active political life. But Epicureanism is not the sole instance of this extrapolitical dynamic whereby individuals experience and justify a call to transcend political sensibilities on egalitarian grounds. Indeed, it is perhaps not an exaggeration to say that the idea and practice of extrapoliticism are as old as the concept of egalitarianism itself. To substantiate this claim, my aim in the conclusion of this chapter is to situate Epicureanism in a wider context of ancient political thought and to demonstrate that its teachings are not an aberration but rather part of a broader classical conception of democracy that conceives of egalitarianism also *in opposition to politics*, and not just as the widespread dissemination of possibilities for rule.

In consulting some of the earliest records of egalitarian thinking in the West, my purpose is neither arcane nor antiquarian, but rather shaped by the present-oriented desire to bring to the attention of contemporary liberal-democratic citizens—strained by the psychological challenges of living beneath the shadow of unfairness—the possibility that the egalitarianism at the heart of their commitment to democratic politics might also function in generating non-political mentalities that can mitigate the impact of their political discontent. Of course, if the extrapolitical solace of egalitarianism were already well-known, an excavation of ancient texts would be less necessary. At most it would only further establish that egalitarian-inspired extrapoliticism is not a bizarre or otherwise marginal element of democratic ethics, but a fundamental and originary aspect of democracy. But democracy's extrapolitical meaning is not at all well-known. True, the notion of a non-political form of egalitarianism can be found in religion (when it postulates human equality before an otherworldly divine power) and in art (in whose perspective the poor and powerless are as worthy objects of depiction as the wealthy and powerful)—both of which are well-reflected in the lines of Ginsberg's "Footnote" to *Howl*: "Everyman's an angel! The bum's as holy as the seraphim!"[87] But the notion that the radicalization of the very ideas and practices at play in democratic politics might also induce the transcendence of the political—this extrapolitical potential of democracy and the solace it offers—is simply unrecognized in postclassical democratic thought. One must consult the ancient Greek conceptualization of democracy, therefore, not to revisit something that has long been recognized and studied, but to disclose, almost for the first time, a forgotten conception of democracy of clear relevance to ordinary, second-class citizens in *contemporary* liberal-democratic states.

Over and against the seemingly obvious and commonsensical modern understanding of democratic ethics as being necessarily connected to political participation and engagement, Greek thought continually presents indifference to politics as a *democratic* phenomenon that emerges out of the very egalitarian principles elsewhere and otherwise undergirding the institutions of popular government. To be clear, in drawing attention to the importance of extrapoliticism within ancient egalitarian thinking, I do not mean simply to take aim at what sometimes appears as a false universalization of political activism in overly stylized accounts of "ancient" or "classical" political thought.[88] That not all Greek or Roman ethics are reducible to political activism—that there are alternate classical traditions with a more ambiguous if not opposed relation to active political life—is well-known.[89] Even in the heyday of Athenian democracy, for example, important constituencies such as peasant farmers, contemplative philosophers, and rich elitists suspicious of popular government gave voice to the idea of *apragmosune,* or non-engagement in the city's public affairs.[90] And there are various figures in Greek poetry and drama who enunciate the notion that political life is a source of strain usually not worth the effort.[91] But rather than attend to these generic forms of apoliticism in the ancient world, what I mean to emphasize is the specific apolitical tradition that I am describing as *extrapolitical*: that is, that particular form of apoliticism that is periodic (not total) and that is motivated and shaped by some of the same egalitarian political values informing active civic engagement in a democratic society.

Evidence for the ancient recognition of political indifference as a democratic mode of being-in-the-world comes, above all, from three of the earliest sources of egalitarian thinking in the West. In literature, the Homeric epic, with its story of Achilles, presents loss of care for politics and commitment to human equality as synonymous forces. In philosophy, one of the main reasons Plato opposes the democratic regime is precisely that it engenders indifference among the citizenry. And in history, Herodotus's account of the first debate on constitutions reveals an ancient egalitarian interest in using democracy to quell, rather than encourage, political behavior. These three sources, which stand at the origins of Western literature, political philosophy, and history, show how egalitarianism might be experienced as a set of commitments that can just as easily direct one to withdraw from politics as engage in political pursuits. By virtue of their originary status and inner logic, they offer support to plebeian efforts to periodically transcend political life and find solace in the face of its frustrations.[92]

Achilles's Extrapoliticism

To recognize the capacity of the idea of equality to be radicalized in an extrapolitical form, which calls into question the very meaning and importance of political life, one need only confront the following thought experiment. Imagine that you consider all human lives to be of equal value and worth, so that it is no longer possible to say that the destitute beggar on the street has a life any less desirable than a billionaire or some head of state. If you were to actually think this, not only would you be espousing an extreme kind of egalitarianism—one grounded on a spiritual belief in the equality of all fates, independent of all materialist considerations—but it would be impossible to hold on to a lively conception of politics, since your perspective would erode your capacity to understand basic political considerations like the difference between profit and loss, benefit and harm, justice and injustice.

This radical kind of egalitarianism, which dissolves political sensibilities rather than seeks the instantiation of equal political rights in familiar democratic institutions, is hardly uncommon within ancient Greek egalitarian thinking. It can be located as early as the Homeric epic which dates from approximately the eighth-century BCE. The *Iliad* depicts extrapoliticism and egalitarianism as almost synonymous forces that appear, not antagonistically, but with the highest consonance and cooperation. The key figure is Achilles, whose withdrawal from war and politics is perhaps the earliest portrayal of political indifference within the world's literary tradition and whose egalitarian insight into the equality of all fates also makes him one of the very first exponents of an egalitarian ethos. To be sure, Achilles's apoliticism is complex and varied. His apoliticism at the end of Book 1 is an altogether different phenomenon from his apoliticism in the *Iliad's* central Book 9. At the end of the first book, Achilles withdraws out of protest. He will no longer fight Trojans nor deliberate with once-fellow Greeks because he believes himself to have been spurned in the distribution of war booty, above all in being asked to give up the slave girl Briseis. Dishonored and belittled, Achilles decides to make his presence felt by his absence. He resolves to sit on the shores of Troy and to watch the struggle, in quasi-plebeian fashion, as a spectator. Disappointed in his efforts to win distinction helping the Greek cause, Achilles exiles himself, wishing destruction upon his former allies, so that through Greek defeat he might finally gain an overdue, if perverse, renown. Achilles's outrage at the system of distributive justice practiced at Troy makes it difficult to characterize this initial period political withdrawal in terms of extrapoliticism or any other kind of critical indifference toward politics as such. So long as Achilles feels himself to have been wronged by a corrupt regime, his political silence does not reflect an aversion to war and politics themselves, but only to their particular conduct by the general Agamemnon in the ninth year of the campaign at Troy. Achilles, initially at least, continues to wage a silent war through his very refusal to participate. Book 1 concludes, "Never did he go to the place of assembly, where men win glory, nor ever to war, but allowed his heart to waste away, as he remained there; *and he longed for the war cry and battle.*"[93]

Achilles is not heard from again until the epic's ninth book. But when he is, the situation is altogether different. Now it is a loss of feeling for political life itself, rather than protest, that defines his civic disengagement. If previously Achilles had sought to win acclaim through his absence, by Book 9 he has come to disdain the struggle for distinction as such. Three eminent Greek leaders, Odysseus, Ajax, and Phoenix, visit Achilles in his hut where they find him transformed, now as a *bard* "delighting his heart" with a lyre, singing songs of "the glorious deeds of warriors."[94] To this poet Achilles, this Achilles turned Homer, they offer to return the controversial slave girl Briseis and to bestow upon him treasure, vast property, and titles to rule. Yet Achilles, curiously immune to the desire for worldly distinction that had led him to rage in Book 1, now announces that he will neither accept the gifts nor return to the struggles of war and politics, but will begin to prepare for his homecoming to Phthia. The strangeness of Achilles's position must be appreciated. Having been raised by his father to lead an eminently political life, "to strive for glory in assembly among men" and to "always be best," and having acted on the public stage for nine years at Troy, Achilles, in his indifference to politics in Book 9, appears suddenly as a squanderer of political potential.[95] What reason does he have not to participate now that the wrongs have been righted and he is duly honored? Neither oppression, nor material deprivation, nor lack of an education in politics appears to underlie Achilles's apoliticism. Rather, his abstention from political life seems to have no other cause than his own purely held preference not to engage in its struggles. The specifically *extrapolitical* character of this preference—that is, its critical aspect and its grounding in egalitarian values and ideas—is made most manifest when Achilles, in explaining to the three emissaries his refusal to return to war and politics, associates his newfound unwillingness to participate in public affairs with an egalitarian ethos:

> An equal fate [*isē moira*] to the one who stays behind as to the one who struggles well. In a single honor are held both the low [*kakos*] and the high [*esthlos*].[96]

Achilles's insight into the equality of all fates is thus *coincident* with his political indifference. It is only when Achilles withdraws from political assembly with fellow Greeks and from war against Trojans that he recognizes an irrepressible human equality surpassing the divisions of class, caste, and *ethnos*. So long as Achilles had participated in war and politics, he sought to fulfill his father's wish that he be the "best of the Achaeans" and, so, cultivated value distinctions between himself and others and, by extension, between the high (*esthloi*) and the low (*kakoi*). It is Achilles's abstention from the agonism at the core of war and politics alike that provides the context for his democratic awakening and his resulting incapacity to distinguish between high and low. Linguistically, Achilles's egalitarianism and political apathy are more than coincident; they are identical. Achilles uses the very same words to express both his sudden indifference to politics and war and also his recognition of human equality. "We are all held in a single honor"—thus Achilles will no longer bother himself with winning an ephemeral and false distinction on the public stage. "We are all held in a single honor"—this is also how Achilles affirms the equality of all fates.[97]

Achilles's political indifference is, of course, short-lived, as he soon rejoins the Greek war effort to avenge the death of his friend Patroclus. But the period of Achilles's withdrawal has great poignancy, not only because, from a literary perspective, the decision of the mightiest warrior in the Trojan War not to fight constitutes one of the *Iliad's* central actions, but because, from a political-philosophical standpoint, it indicates how old, if not primordial, is the extrapolitical meaning of egalitarianism. Achilles, the leading character of the Greek world's leading epic, is at his most egalitarian not when pursuing political life in a public arena, but when seeking to transcend the confines of the political through the intensification and sublimation of political values. This intensification and sublimation stem not merely from the fact that Achilles relates to the idea of human equality in a fashion that, as I have just described, undermines rather than enables active political life. Also important is the way in which solidarity is practiced by Achilles in Book 9, so that it stands no longer for a broad and abstract allegiance to the Greek war host, but rather for an immediate, face-to-face fellowship with friends. In Book 9, Achilles will not return to the Greek cause, nor for that matter will he side with the Trojans, but he does dwell in his tent with his friend Patroclus and, it should be emphasized, invite the Greek emissaries whom he otherwise rebuffs to enter his domain and eat and drink strong wine together.[98] Furthermore, if Achilles's withdrawal obviates political speech such as occurs before an assembly of one's peers, it makes possible other forms of arguably freer speech, above all the poetic speech of *song about politics*, which Achilles is found joyously singing upon the three emissaries' arrival. It is worth pointing out, too, in this regard that Achilles's response to the emissaries includes the memorable lines spoken not just specifically against Odysseus but also more generally against strategic (i.e., political) speech as such: "Hateful in my eyes, even as the gates of Hades, is that man that hides one thing in his mind and says another."[99] Thus, in his relationship to equality, in his solidarity with Patroclus and to a lesser extent the emissaries, and in the free speech of his poetic and non-strategic discourse, Achilles sublimates political values in an extrapolitical direction and, in so doing, finds a joy and ease that eludes him so long as he lives in pursuit of political concerns.

I do not mean to suggest that Achillean apoliticism is the only or even primary way egalitarianism is presented in the *Iliad* or the broader political culture of ancient Greece. In both the fictional world of the *Iliad* and the actual world of Greek politics, for instance, the idea of *isomoira* (the equality of fates) is not limited to an extrapolitical mantra, but just as often formulated as an ideology upon which a radically redistributive politics might be grounded and organized.[100] If Achilles, in the intoxication of his joyful extrapoliticism, interprets *isomoira* to mean that all humans are equal in the here-and-now regardless of material differences, political activists frequently appealed to *isomoira* to emphasize ongoing *inequalities* in the material world that are in need of immediate, corrective political action. But one should refrain from making a judgment as to which of these conceptions of *isomoira* represents a more radical brand of egalitarianism: whether that of the activists for bringing the idea of equality to bear upon the material world or Achilles's for refusing to look upon the material world in terms of the high–low distinction. The fact that the Greek word for fate, *moira,* has the secondary meaning of portion or share suggests the co-originality of ideal-istic and materialistic conceptions of *isomoira*. The idealistic variant, which con-ceives of an ineradicable human equality superseding all worldly distinctions and thereby dissolving the proclivity and passion for politics, may not be the only form that egalitarian thinking can take, but it is nonetheless true that the idea of human equality does contain this extrapolitical potential. Accordingly, any conception of the full meaning of egalitarianism ought to include some notion of the extrapolitical. The point is not to replace the familiar egalitarian ethics of political activism with an unfamiliar egalitarian ethics of withdrawal, but to see the latter as playing a vital role *in conjunction with the former*—both together comprising a more comprehensive, therapeutically attuned conception of egalitarianism well-suited to the lived experiences of actual, ordinary, plebe-ian citizens.

Plato's Critique of Extrapolitical Democrats

The possibility that a radical egalitarianism might inform not just political insti-tutions but, in addition, a temporary and carefree transcendence of political concerns might strike the reader as highly unconventional. Yet it actually figures prominently in what is arguably the earliest and most influential philosophical treatment of democracy from the ancient world: Plato's critique of the demo-cratic regime in *The Republic* authored in the beginning of the fourth-century BCE. Within this critique, there are indications of an awareness of the Achillean phenomenon in which an individual is contentedly drained of political energies as a consequence of an all-encompassing egalitarianism.[101] Indeed, Plato was especially well positioned to connect periodic political indifference to democ-racy because his philosophy insists that the meaning of each political regime exceeds the governmental structure it specifies and also refers to a type of per-sonality likely to flourish within a particular political community. For Plato, democracy does not simply designate the social arrangement in which political power originates from the majority, but also marks a way of life likely to be pur-sued by typical democratic citizens. And what is distinctive about the democratic person, Plato thinks, is the ever-present risk that this person's political energies will evaporate, due to an extreme egalitarianism that renders all pursuits equally attractive and valuable. The democratic individual:

> . . . lives on, yielding day by day to the desire at hand. Sometimes he drinks heavily while listening to the flute; at other times, he drinks only water and is on a diet; sometimes he goes in for physical training; at other times, he's idle and neglects everything; and sometimes he even occupies himself with what he takes to be philosophy. He often engages

in politics, leaping up from his seat and saying and doing whatever comes into his mind. If he happens to admire soldiers, he's carried in that direction, if money-makers, in that one. There's neither order nor necessity in his life, but he calls it pleasant, free, blessedly happy, and he follows it for as long as he lives.[102]

Plato intends this depiction of the democratic character to be damning. The democratic person, in Plato's view, is someone incapable of taking up genuine political responsibility, since one lives democratically, Plato claims, when one is unable or unwilling to possess stable ethical values, when the question of "time not misspent" remains unanswered in any sort of durable or consistent manner. The chaotic cycle of inebriation, military exercise, and philosophy symbolizes the equal claims of the three parts of the Platonic soul—appetite (*epithumia*), spirit (*thumos*), and reason (*logos*)—which compete against each other, unsuccessfully, for rule of the democratic person, making the democratic life full of transience, dilettantism, and the attention-deficit disorder. For Plato, then, the equality of all impulses and inclinations within the democratic personality precludes the cultivation and maintenance of *values as such,* since values are always hierarchically organized and specify the relative importance of some concern vis-à-vis others. And it is the valuelessness of the democratic individual—the incapacity to take a meaningful stand on behalf of a cause and the absolute failure to maintain any durability, consistency, or commitment—that underlies the political irresponsibility of the democratic form of life. Thus, in Plato's view what is problematic about democracy is that there is a tension between its institutional and individual manifestations. From the perspective of a polity's institutions, democracy characterizes that regime in which the entire citizen body finds itself with the power to determine the norms that will govern the political community. On the individual level, however, the democratic personality refers precisely to the failure to behave with the modicum of selfsameness and durability required by serious political action. To be sure, Plato's commitment to an ahistorical conception of rationality and to standards of propriety independent of their popularity should not be forgotten as important sources of his antagonism toward the democratic regime; indeed, Plato's insistence that the authentic political leader be understood as a trained expert, equivalent to a doctor or a captain of a ship, obviously makes it impossible for him to embrace the democratic notion that social norms have no other foundation than the *demos* which defines them. Nonetheless, what also figures prominently within Plato's critique of democracy is the concern that a radical, psychological egalitarianism would dissolve the capacity for genuine political commitment.

But one does not have to accept Plato's anti-democratic message to recognize the truth of his insight that someone might be led, on egalitarian grounds, to withdraw from active political life from time to time. It is possible, after all, to conceive of a periodic political withdrawal that does not destabilize a primary and foundational commitment to public affairs. Plato himself admits that the democratic character uniquely prone to political indifference is still someone who "often engages in politics," reminding us of the key point that extrapoliticism stands not for the total or even frequent abdication of political responsibility, but only the episodic transcendence of political concerns. True, Plato suggests that even the political engagement of democratic citizens is politically irresponsible since their political pursuits are destabilized by the same incessant fluctuation that elsewhere leads them not to care about politics at all. If Plato were correct in this regard, then both democracy and the idea of extrapoliticism would have to be viewed with profound suspicion. But if Plato is wrong—if it is possible both to care and not to care about public affairs in a democratic society—then his account of the democratic individual should be read in an altogether different, non-critical light: as the reminder that the desire to experience forms of life that are "pleasant, free, [and] blessedly happy" is a legitimate, authentically egalitarian ambition justifying the occasional suspension of political mentalities unlikely to serve that goal. Plebeianism in any case embraces this double promise of egalitarianism, finding it as a basis both to care and sometimes not to care about a political life permanently darkened by the shadow of unfairness.

Herodotus's Account of the Extrapolitical Democratic Wish

Beyond the Homeric epic and Platonic philosophy, the extrapolitical potential of egalitarianism finds documentation in no less a noteworthy source than the first coherent presentation of the democratic dream within political theory: the debate on constitutions reported by Herodotus in his *Histories* (written around 450 BCE). Here an egalitarian mindset is associated with both the commitment to egalitarian government and the desire to overcome—or at least quell—certain political sensibilities.

The crucial passage comes from Book 3 of the *Histories* in which Herodotus relates the rise of Persian power in the East. Following the overthrow of the pseudo-Smerdis by seven co-conspirators, Persia is left without a form of government as no clear successor has emerged from the political shuffling. This leads to a debate among the conspirators about which form of government they should institute, thereby bringing the central question of the "best regime" into the tradition of recorded political thought.[103] Three speeches follow, each supporting a different form of government: egalitarian, oligarchic, and monarchic. When monarchy is selected, Otanes, the defender of egalitarianism, makes a final request from his fellow conspirators that they ultimately grant: namely, that he not be subject to the jurisdiction of the new regime and that he be permitted to live outside its boundaries. In making this request, Otanes explains that his primary desire is "neither to rule nor to be ruled"[104]—an arresting reversal of the much more familiar conceptualization of democracy, canonical since Aristotle, of ruling and being ruled in turn. Otanes, then, who might be considered the first (albeit likely fictional) democratic theorist of whom we have record, provides another example of extrapoliticism. He is both a supporter of a regime that affords political equality to all of its citizens and, at the same time, someone who, on the individual level, aims to escape politics, however impossibly or imperfectly, in order to transcend the confines of the insufficiently egalitarian circumstances in which he finds himself.

If Otanes's extrapoliticism is revealed most clearly in his articulation of the desire to leave behind politics, it also can be located, in more indirect, partial, and tacit form, in the proposals that he makes for the egalitarian government he supports. Otanes defends egalitarian political institutions, not because they will make subjects into rulers through extending monarchical autonomy to the entire citizenry, but rather because they will abate the competitive passions that have hitherto been so fundamental to political experience. He declares that government in the hands of the majority "does none of those things that single rulers do."[105] And what characterizes the politics of single rulers is an unquenchable agonal energy, an irrepressible urge for distinction and self-aggrandizement that leads to arrogance (*hubris*) and ill-will (*phthonos*).[106] If democracy is idealized today, it is usually because it is seen as that form of government in which there is an identity between the rulers and the ruled so that the law's addressees might also understand themselves to be the law's authors. The important suggestion from Herodotus's debate on constitutions, however, is that the very notion of rule—even when it is evenly distributed in the form of *collective* authorship and autonomy—is a value of kings.

It is not by chance that the word Otanes uses to describe the egalitarian form of government he promotes is not *demokratia* (the rule of the people), but *isonomia* (equality before the law). The difference is important because it reflects perfectly Otanes's desire for egalitarian government to be something other than a community of rulers. *Demokratia* shares with the two other forms of government (oligarchy and monarchy) the fact that it is a form of rule (*arche* or *kratos*). *Isonomia,* on the other hand, does not derive its meaning from the idea of rule. In this respect, then, Otanes's wish to "neither to rule nor to be ruled" should be understood as referring not simply to Otanes's attempt to escape politics after his egalitarian proposal is rejected, but in a sense to the nature of the proposal itself.

Otanes's interest in diluting politics of its central element of rule is evidenced in the three main institutional features of *isonomia* that he proposes and that were implemented by some of the earliest egalitarian regimes on record: the empowerment of a popular assembly to deliberate upon all questions of public policy (which prevents the consolidation of power in the hands of single rulers); the selection of magistrates by lot (which diminishes the agonism of politics); and the examination of public officials following their terms of service (which burdens powerholders). [107] It is the second of these—sortition—that is perhaps the most antipolitical of political structures because it circumvents the competition for offices, disconnecting positions of leadership from human effort and the machinations of party, faction, or demagogue. The struggle for power that figures so prominently within conventional politics has little function when leadership is determined by the free play of chance.[108] Of course, it must be remembered that the actual implementation of *isonomia* never attained the idealization that surrounded it. If the philosophical and moral appeal of *isonomia* resided in its attempt to depoliticize the *polis* through quelling the passions for ruling and being ruled, the fact remains that in reality *isonomia* was often no more than a euphemism used by popular leaders to describe demagoguery.[109] Moreover, in Athens, the full proliferation of election by lot was always held in check by the popular election of military leaders and economic administrators as well as by screening processes that limited who was eligible for offices selected through sortition.[110] But these limitations restricting the realization of Otanes's isonomic vision need not conceal the philosophical insight contained within it: namely, that the political meaning of egalitarianism ought to be conceived not merely as the sharing of political rights and powers, but also as the attempt to limit, quell, or otherwise challenge the integrity of the political as such.

In these two roles—as an enunciator of the wish to leave behind politics and as a supporter of a form of government that would restrict the competition for and practice of rule—Otanes stands as an important exemplar of the too-often-forgotten extrapolitical aspect of egalitarianism. If we see both of these roles as recurring rather than sequential—that is, if we understand Otanes as someone who fluctuates on an ongoing basis between efforts at egalitarian reform and attempts to transcend politics altogether—we find in him perhaps a classical incarnation of the modern plebeian, who, as I am arguing, will be shaped by the double desire to both reform and sometimes escape a politics that always falls short of liberal-democratic ideals.

The fact that Achilles becomes an egalitarian only once he is outside of the political community, that Plato worries about the political indifference of the democratic individual, and that the earliest defender of egalitarian government, Otanes, seeks to reduce the sphere of political competition and then tries to escape politics—all of this suggests that an egalitarian ethos is wrongly reduced to that which motivates a popular form of government, but in fact is also consistent with the urge to get beyond the limits of a political mentality. The modern optimism that equality might be secured through active participation in political life would have struck ancient theorists of egalitarianism as a rather strange and counterintuitive ideal. Surely, there was an appreciation for the capacity of legal communities to carve out a space of equality in a world otherwise characterized by gross disparities in power, wealth, and privilege. Aristotle, for example, credits the *polis* for bringing together unequal individuals into a limited and circumscribed sphere of legal equality.[111] But to expect that the political activities that went on within this space might themselves cohere with egalitarian principles—this notion would have been inconceivable to the ancients. Because a life lived in respect of human equality was recognized as being in some tension with the political life, part of the meaning of egalitarianism was understood to involve efforts to transcend, temporarily, the political as such.

5.4   The Unquiet Quietism of Plebeianism

Guided by the historical examples of some of the earliest recorded instances of egalitarian thinking in the West, I have argued that democracy might stand for something beyond a political arrangement approximating an equal distribution of rights, powers, and opportunities: namely, a basis for both criticizing and temporarily transcending the political itself. Because no regime can fully live up to the ideal of free and equal citizenship, a democratic sensibility grounds criticism of the life of political prominence, calling into question the ultimate compatibility of this life with egalitarian values and raising the possibility that it is in fact the experiences of the politically marginalized that are most consonant with democratic ethics. Further, insofar as unfulfilled egalitarian political longings—such as longings for equality itself, free speech, solidarity, and self-sufficiency—might be realized in reconfigured, sublimated form outside of politics, a democrat possesses an egalitarian rationale as well as an egalitarian means for transcending the political as such. Both elements—the criticism and the transcendence—point to how the democratic commitment to human equality might provide a kind of solace to ordinary citizens fated to endure the disappointment and frustration of ordinary, plebeian political existence.

The most likely criticism to be leveled against my elaboration and defense of this democratically inflected extrapolitical tradition is that it amounts to nothing more than quietism: a passive retreat from public life and, with it, a sad forsaking of the rights of active citizenship that, even if imperfect, are precious and hard-won through centuries of political struggle. At one level, the honest response to this criticism is to acknowledge its veracity. My point is precisely that ordinary citizens have good reason to sometimes seek an extrapolitical transcendence of the political, so that any simple, universalized embrace of active citizenship would be not only naïve (insofar as conditions do not allow its full realization) but inaccurate in its reduction of what a democratic sensibility has meant in the past and should mean going forward. At the same time, however, it is important to stress at least three ways in which the kind of quietism I am defending is something different from, and much less sad or quiet than, the quietism objected to in this hypothetical critique.

First of all, it should be emphasized that there is no obvious connection between a withdrawal from politics and a psychology of unhappiness. Political apathy needs to be distinguished from apathy as such. In fact, if anything, political indifference, far from promoting a further disengagement from non-political pursuits, may be a precondition for various forms of enthusiasm—whether artistic, intimate, or otherwise—that active political existence must repress or disallow. With Nietzsche, for example, it is a general principle that ecstasy—the orgiastic standing beside oneself—depends upon the suspension of the political instincts:

> One feels in every case in which Dionysian excitement gains any significant extent, how the Dionysian liberation from the fetters of the individual finds expression first of all in a diminution of, in indifference to, indeed, in hostility to, the political instincts. Just as certainly, Apollo who forms states is also a genius of the *principium individuationis* [the principle of individuation], and state and patriotism cannot live without an affirmation of the individual personality.[112]

Nietzsche may overstate the incompatibility between politics and ecstasy, but his underlying insight that political indifference is hardly inconsistent with joyful enthusiasm finds support in most of the figures analyzed in this chapter's discussion of extrapoliticism, including the Epicureans' pursuit of bliss in gardens outside of politics, Achilles's exultant, song-filled period of political disengagement in the *Iliad*, and Plato's account of the carefree democratic personality who sometimes loses interest in civic behavior. Because it may be the case that political withdrawal provides the opportunity for numerous forms of passion otherwise occluded by politics, any worry about the melancholy element of extrapoliticism ought to be strongly tempered.

Second, as my elaboration and defense of extrapoliticism has emphasized, periods of plebeian indifference to politics are supposed to be only *temporary*. The plebeian withdrawal from politics is meant to be practiced in tandem with whatever active political energies might be mustered, not in replacement of them. A more thorough or complete doctrine of apoliticism therefore must be strenuously resisted. Importantly, the specific exponents of extrapoliticism discussed in this chapter reflect a periodic, rather than omnipresent, form of political withdrawal. Achilles's retreat from war and politics is brief and temporary.

Otanes only seeks to escape the confines of the political after trying, unsuccessfully, to reform it. Plato's prototypical democrat, while often dropping out from active political life, also continually returns to it. And the Epicurean tradition, even if it teaches political indifference, not only recognizes special circumstances when committed political engagement is called for, but as a historical matter has been practiced by individuals who often involved themselves in politics. Given these considerations, a more appropriate motto for extrapoliticism than the oft-cited Epicurean dictum to "live unnoticed," which seems to denote (however inaccurately) a complete and final withdrawal from political life, would be something like Horace's exhortation, put in the mouth of the mythological Greek hero Teucer but intended to have a general significance: "My brave fellows! You have often suffered worse things at my side. Banish your worries now with wine. Tomorrow we shall set out once more over the boundless sea."[113] In other words, we who have suffered in politics and will suffer again are right to withdraw from time to time and seek pleasure and contentment beyond the ordinary confines of political life—especially, it should be added, when such pleasure and contentment are themselves informed by extrapolitically modulated egalitarian values.

Horace's urging to seek temporary transcendence through wine points to a third sense in which the quietism of extrapoliticism is something less than fully quiet. To the extent that plebeian transcendence is achieved not just through purely inner psychological transformation but from without via the assistance of wine and other similar substances—and it is not by chance, I think, that Achilles, Plato's idealized democrat, Horace, and the Epicurean tradition more generally all achieve or defend a tranquility aided by wine—there may after all be a kind of politics implicit in the very effort to periodically escape politics: namely, the struggle against unjust restriction of those means conducive to extrapolitical sublimation of the political instincts. To be sure, such matters are vast and complex. They extend beyond the purview of a plebeian theory of democracy for which they are only one small element. And their precise determination at any point in time must rest on a panoply of considerations, of which political philosophy is but one. Nonetheless, plebeianism offers a specifically "democratic" reason—beyond the more-often invoked libertarian, prudential, or medical rationales—for enabling citizens more rather than less access to the means of achieving bliss. By "democratic," I do not simply mean the majority's right to access those substances it deems worthy of consumption—an idea eloquently expressed a century ago in the context of alcohol prohibition by New York City mayor Fiorello LaGuardia when he said, "Prohibition cannot be enforced for the simple reason that the majority of American people do not want it enforced and are resisting its enforcement. That being so, the orderly thing to do under our form of government is to abolish a law which cannot be enforced, a law which the people of the country do not want enforced." Beyond this logic, insofar as relaxation is itself a democratic value—something strongly suggested in the ancient Greek understanding of egalitarianism—and, furthermore, insofar as politics seen from the democratic point of view always will generate frustrations and strains that need to be transcended in some way, a plebeian sensibility recognizes something like a right to intoxication. Pater Liber, the patron deity of the Roman plebeians, is after all the god of wine. Here, once again, plebeians can follow Horace when he embraces wine as something "to bestow fresh hopes, and powerful to wash away the bitterness of care"—and when, inspired by drink, he can declare, "Put aside delay and thirst for gain, and, mindful of Death's dark fires, mingle, while you can, brief folly with your projects. 'Tis sweet at the fitting time to be foolish."[114]

ACKNOWLEDGMENTS

In the seven years I devoted to this book I benefitted from the help of many. I owe special thanks to friends who propelled me to stay on track and generously gave of their time and attention. Countless discussions with Adam Mohr were a well of inspiration. Corey Brettschneider's encouragement was instrumental to the initial draft. Aziz Rana's perceptive suggestions revealed so many fruitful avenues for improvement. And once the manuscript had been accepted for publication, Brendhain Diamond's brassy worry that I possibly "don't know how to write at all" helped me see that much more work still needed to be done.

I am fortunate to have undertaken this project at the University of Pennsylvania, where numerous colleagues and students—including Michaël Aklin, Osman Balkan, Nancy Hirschmann, Ellen Kennedy, Matt Levendusky, Julia Lynch, Ed Mansfield, Marc Meredith, Anne Norton, Brendan O'Leary, Eric Orts, Rogers Smith, Vesa Soini, Peter Struck, Kok-Chor Tan, Alec Webley, and Jeff Weintraub—offered valuable information, insight, and support.

For their continued guidance and example, I am grateful to Bruce Ackerman, Sharon Krause, Nancy Rosenblum, and Dennis Thompson.

The project gained immensely from the work of six research assistants— Xavier Flory, Nicole Hammons, Ben Horn, Ting Lau, Nate Shils, and Stephan Stohler—to whom I am indebted. In addition, I am thankful to Josh Stanfield whose careful readings of the completed manuscript led to numerous late-stage corrections and improvements.

I presented material from the book at colloquia and conferences at Brown, Carleton, Columbia, Cornell, Duke, Fudan, Harvard, and Yale Universities; the Annenberg School for Communication at Penn; The New School for Social Research; the Philomathean Society at Penn; the Tri-Co Political Theory Workshop sponsored by Bryn Mawr, Haverford, and Swarthmore Colleges; and the Universities of California-Davis, Copenhagen, Edinburgh, Florida, Havana,

Maryland, Warwick, and Wisconsin–Madison. Portions of the project were also presented at annual meetings of the American Political Science Association, Association for Political Theory, and Western Political Science Association. I owe a big debt of gratitude for all the critical feedback I received at these events, including comments from Rick Avramenko, Sam Bagg, Eric Beerbohm, Anders Berg-Sørensen, Kevin Elliott, David Estlund, Jill Frank, Michael Frazer, Bryan Garsten, Aaron Gavin, Michael Gillespie, James Glass, Bjorn Wee Gomes, Turku Isiksel, Anna Jurkevics, Andreas Kalyvas, Hélène Landemore, Haimo Li, Jason Maloy, Luke Mayville, Don Moon, Jim Morone, Shmulik Nili, Guido Parietti, Ed Quish, Hari Ramesh, Amit Ron, Joel Schlosser, Melissa Schwartzberg, George Shulman, Annie Stilz, Shannon Stimson, Robert Taylor, Brandon Terry, Mathias Thaler, Les Thiele, Andrea Tivig, John Tomasi, Richard Tuck, Nadia Urbinati, and Daniel Viehoff.

Outside of these venues, conversations and exchanges with Martin Breaugh, Filipe Campante, Erlend MacGillivray, Murad Idris, Joe Mazor, Kirstie McClure, John McCormick, Russ Muirhead, and Tomer Seifan were invaluable.

A Ryskamp Fellowship from the American Council of Learned Societies allowed me to devote the entirety of 2013–14 to completing the initial manuscript. I thank the ACLS for its generosity. I am also appreciative of research funding provided by Penn's Provost Office.

The book draws on six of my previously published essays: "Liberalism and the Problem of Plutocracy," *Constellations: An International Journal of Critical and Democratic Theory* 23.1 (2016): 84–95; "Solace for the Frustrations of Silent Citizenship: The Case of Epicureanism," *Citizenship Studies* 19.5 (2015): 492–506; "Rawls and the Forgotten Figure of the Most Advantaged: In Defense of Reasonable Envy Toward the Superrich," *American Political Science Review* 107.1 (2013): 123–138; "Learning How Not to Be Good: A Plebeian Perspective," *The Good Society*, 20.2 (2011): 184–202; "Analyzing Legislative Performance: A Plebeian Perspective," *Democratization* 20.3 (2013): 417–437; and "Apathy: The Democratic Disease," *Philosophy & Social Criticism*, 30.5–6 (2004): 745–768. I thank the editors and publishers of these journals for permission to reprint parts of those pieces here.

For his patient encouragement of my work, I am deeply appreciative of David McBride at Oxford University Press and the rest of his team. The two anonymous reviewers supplied by the Press offered critical feedback that led me to strengthen the manuscript in significant ways.

Above all, I am thankful to my wife Amy for going through the last seven years with me, helping in so many aspects of the book's production, and illuminating my life with her kindness and wisdom. I am no less grateful to and for our children, Kitty, Stella, and Morris, who have enlivened these years beyond measure and made me better understand Novalis when he says, "Where there are children, there is a golden age." I am fortunate to have had the support of many other members of my family, especially Helen and Oscar, Ebba and Johan, August and Ija, and Andy and my sister, Julie.

I dedicate this book to my parents, Joan and Franklin Green, in love, admiration, and gratitude.

JEG
Philadelphia, PA
March 2016

NOTES

Preface

1. Thomas Hobbes, *Leviathan*, ed. Richard Tuck (Cambridge: Cambridge University Press, 1996), Introduction, 10.
2. Ralph Waldo Emerson, "Self-Reliance," in *Self-Reliance and Other Essays* (Mineola, NY: Dover Publications, 1993), 31.
3. Niccolò Machiavelli, *Il Principe* (Milan: Mondadori, 1986), 4.
4. Niccolò Machiavelli, *Discourses on Livy*, trans. Harvey C. Mansfield and Nathan Tarcov (Chicago: University of Chicago Press, 1996), Preface to Book I.
5. Friedrich Nietzsche, *On the Advantage and Disadvantage of History for Life*, trans. Peter Preuss (Indianapolis: Hackett, 1980), 7.

Chapter 1

1. John Rawls, *Justice as Fairness: A Restatement* (Cambridge, MA: Belknap Press of Harvard University Press, 2001), 57.
2. Jürgen Habermas, *Between Facts and Norms: Contributions to a Discourse Theory of Law and Democracy*, trans. William Rehg (Cambridge, MA: MIT Press, 1996), 7.
3. Martha C. Nussbaum, *Sex and Social Justice* (New York: Oxford University Press, 1999), 46.
4. Ronald Dworkin, "A New Map of Censorship," *Index on Censorship* 35:1 (2006): 130–33, 131.
5. The United Nations Universal Declaration of Human Rights (1948), for example, does not rest with the delineation of specific rights just liberal-democratic regimes ought to implement, but upholds the promise of civic relations in which "all human beings . . . are endowed with reason and conscience and should act toward one another in a spirit of brotherhood" (Article 1).
6. For a recent overview of the representation of public opinion in governmental policy which, though generally positive about the functionality of representation, still recognizes these sources preventing full confidence—especially, the problem of the absence of an agreed-upon standard for measuring opinion, policy, and their interrelation—see Paul Burstein, "Public Opinion, Public Policy, and Democracy," in Kevin T. Leicht and J. Craig Jenkins, eds., *Handbook of Politics: State and Society in Global Perspective* (New York: Springer, 2010), 63–79.
7. James A. Stimson, Michael B. MacKuen, and Robert S. Erikson, "Dynamic Representation," *American Political Science Review* 89.3 (1995): 543–65, 557; James Stimson, "Perspectives on Representation: Asking the Right Questions and Getting the Right Answers," in Russell J. Dalton and Hans-Dieter Klingemann, eds., *The Oxford Handbook of Political Behavior* (New York: Oxford University Press, 2007), 850–862, 861.
8. One finds this kind of sunniness when influential reports on the governments of the world, in comparing liberal-democratic regimes to non-democratic and illiberal ones, attribute to the

former something akin to political perfection. For instance, *The Economist's* popular "democracy index" refers to the countries receiving more than 8 out of 10 as "full democracies," which in 2014 included 24 polities. "Democracy Index 2014: Democracy and Its Discontents," *The Economist* Intelligence Unit, 2015. Freedom House's annual rankings likewise deem the group of countries best realizing liberal-democratic norms as "free" as opposed to the next group which are labeled "partially free." Within the Polity IV Project, conducted by the Center for Systemic Peace, levels of autocracy and democracy are scored on a ten-point scale, with a "fully institutionalized autocracy" receiving -10 and a "fully institutionalized democracy" receiving +10. In recent years it has been thought that some liberal democracies have attained the +10 level: "A perfect +10 *democracy*, like Australia, Greece, or Sweden, has institutionalized procedures for open, competitive, and deliberative political participation; chooses and replaces chief executives in open, competitive elections; and imposes substantial checks and balances on the discretionary powers of the chief executive." Monty G. Marshall and Benjamin R. Cole, *Global Report 2011: Conflict, Governance, and State Fragility* (Vienna, VA: Center for Systemic Peace, 2011), 8–9. The 2014 edition of the report substitutes "A fully institutionalized (+10) democracy" for "A perfect (+10) democracy." See Monty G. Marshall and Benjamin R. Cole, *Global Report 2014: Conflict, Governance, and State Fragility* (Vienna, VA: Center for Systemic Peace, 2014), 20.

9. See, e.g., John Dewey, "Creative Democracy—The Task Before Us," in Jo Ann Boydston, ed., *The Later Works, 1925-1953* (Carbondale: South Illinois Press, 1988), Vol. 14, 224–30.

10. Sidney Verba, Norman H. Nie, and Jae-on Kim, *Participation and Political Equality: A Seven-Nation Comparison* (Chicago: University of Chicago Press, 1978), 1; Sidney Verba, Kay Lehman Schlozman, and Henry E. Brady, *Voice and Equality: Civic Voluntarism in America* (Cambridge, MA: Harvard University Press, 1995), 1.

11. John Rawls, *Justice as Fairness: A Restatement*, 149, 44.

12. To be sure, as Breaugh has recently shown, numerous thinkers occasionally have made use of the category "plebeian," often with the Roman plebeians in mind, in an approving and emancipatory spirit, including Machiavelli, Montesquieu, Vico, Pierre-Simon Ballanche, Daniel De Leon, Foucault, and Rancière. Martin Breaugh, *The Plebeian Experience: A Discontinuous History of Political Freedom*, trans. Lazer Lederhendler (New York: Columbia University Press, 2013), 44–102. And one might add to this list other figures, such as William Manning and John McCormick. Of course, favorable reference to the plebeian is not the same as theorizing a notion of plebeianism, and very often this tradition has limited itself to the former. In any case, my purpose is to lend greater theoretical comprehensiveness to a notion of a plebeianism that at present is at best marginal, incipient, and not sufficiently well-defined. Such a project means that my approach is at least somewhat close to Breaugh's own effort, on the basis of his historical analysis, to derive a unifying "plebeian principle." And it is also close to McCormick, when he very briefly suggests that the so-called "Machiavellian Democracy" he defends be understood as a kind of "plebeian republicanism." John P. McCormick, *Machiavellian Democracy* (Princeton: Princeton University Press, 2011), 147. But Breaugh and McCormick—to the extent they conceptualize plebeianism—understand by it only one of the four aspects I shall emphasize in this book (a differentiation between the Few and the Many that serves to contest the Few for progressive ends), having little or nothing to say about the other three elements that I elaborate: the problem that ordinary citizenship always will be experienced as second class (i.e., an explanation for why it is, even in advanced liberal-democratic states, that the Few-Many distinction will continue to endure); the ethical challenges that must inform plebeian political advocacy; and the consequent need for solace in the face of a political life that is constitutively disconcerting. Moreover, whereas Breaugh's study of "plebeian experience" focuses primarily on historical moments of popular resistance in ancient Rome, early modern Europe, eighteenth century England, the French Revolution, and the Paris Commune, my own account of plebeianism is intended as a framework for understanding the nature of the *contemporary liberal-democratic* regime in its *everyday aspect*.

13. To be clear, plebeian progressivism centers on demanding from the most advantaged members of society, defined in terms of *both economic and political power*, that they bear special, legally imposed economic and political burdens as a condition of their preeminence within imperfectly free and equal liberal-democratic societies. However, in my earlier book, *The Eyes*

of the People: Democracy in an Age of Spectatorship (Oxford: Oxford University Press, 2010), I already analyzed and defended the singling out of *political* elites (i.e., leading politicians and high officials) for special regulatory attention; I also proposed a hitherto neglected norm for such regulation: the norm that political leaders be forced to appear in public under conditions they do not control. In further developing the plebeian idea that the most advantaged class ought to be subject to special regulatory burdens, this book concerns itself primarily with *economic* elites, a group I neglected to consider in my earlier work.

14. Consider the observation of Erik Olin Wright, a defender of radical alternatives to conventional capitalist societies (including an unconditional basic income for all, worker-owned cooperatives, and, more generally, the capacity of voluntary and reciprocal social relations to better control economic and political power): "Pure communism is . . . a utopian fantasy, since a complex society could not function without some sort of authoritative means of making and enforcing binding rules (a 'state')." Erik Olin Wright, *Envisioning Real Utopias* (London: Verso, 2010), 124.

15. Even as he continues to affiliate himself with communism, Alain Badiou recently acknowledged on the British TV show *HARDtalk*, "The failure of all socialist and communist experiences in the last century has the consequence that we have no, today, great and clear idea of another world" (24 March 2009). Available online at: https://www.youtube.com/watch?v=NPCCNmE7b9g. Relatedly, Chris Hedges, though an advocate of socialism (albeit in a "democratic socialist" form that may after all be fully consistent with a liberal-democratic regime grounded on private property and the family), admits, "The inability [of the left] to articulate a viable socialism has been our gravest mistake." Hedges, "Why I Am a Socialist," *Truthdig.com* (29 December 2008). Available online: http://www.truthdig.com/report/item/20081229_why_i_am_a_socialist. In a similar vein, Slavoj Žižek, who identifies as a communist, nonetheless has said on a different episode of *HARDtalk*, "I think that the communism of the twentieth century—more specifically, all the network of phenomena we refer to as Stalinism—are maybe the worst ideological, political, ethical, social catastrophe in the history of humanity." And, of the present moment, he adds: "Except for some old Keynesian formulas, I'm not aware of any convincing radical left alternatives." (24 November 2009). Available online: https://www.youtube.com/watch?v=w8cIagiKwkw.

16. On the idea of false necessity and the call for possibilities as such, see Roberto Mangabeira Unger, *False Necessity: Anti-Necessitarian Social Theory in the Service of Radical Democracy* (Cambridge: Cambridge University Press, 1987).

17. To be sure, it should be stressed that whereas aristocratic critics of democracy have long employed terms like *plebeian* to criticize, *from the outside*, the integrity of popular government, this book's appropriation of such terminology is different since it aims to say that those sympathetic to popular government would do well to recognize how the liberal-democratic project of realizing free and equal citizenship is not quite as pristine or ethically uncomplicated as its central purveyors have suggested.

18. This end was initiated with Caesar's appointment as dictator for life in 44 BCE, then wrought with fifteen years of civil wars that followed Caesar's assassination in the same year, and finally consolidated with Octavian's assertion of imperial control when the Senate in 27 BCE declared him both "Augustus" and "*Princeps*" and, along with other electoral and popular bodies, lost effective control of the state.

19. See e.g., Andrew Lintott, *The Constitution of the Roman Republic* (Oxford: Oxford University Press, 1999); Fergus Millar, *The Crowd in Rome in the Late Republic* (Ann Arbor: University of Michigan Press, 2002); and Claude Nicolet, *The World of the Citizen in Republican Rome*, trans. P. S. Falla (Berkeley, CA: University of California Press, 1980). I elaborate the specifics of the conditions of the Roman plebs, and their similarity to the structure of ordinary citizenship in today's liberal-democratic regimes, in Chapter 2.

20. Euergetism is distinct from charity or fiscal responsibility, and is better conceived as gifts—often in the form of immediately consumable feasts and games or non-consumable monuments, processions, and the like—than as distributional exchanges in the manner of public welfare. See Paul Veyne, *Bread and Circuses: Historical Sociology and Political Pluralism,* ed. Oswyn Murray and trans. Brian Pearce (London: Penguin, 1990).

21. Among Roman sources, see Sallust, *The War with Catiline* and *The War with Jugurtha*, trans. J. C. Rolfe and revised by John T. Ramsey (Cambridge, MA: Harvard University Press, 2013). Sallust attributes to the plebs a penchant for revolution (*The War with Catiline*, §37) as well as ill-will, indignation, and envy [*gravis invidia*] (*The War with Jugurtha*, §30). Montesquieu likewise describes the plebs as evincing both a disrespect for wealth and a tendency, "due to a malady eternal in man," to use their tribunes not just for defense against concrete abuse from elites but as a device for proactive attacks. Montesquieu, *Considerations on the Causes of the Greatness of the Romans and Their Decline*, trans. David Lowenthal (Indianapolis: Hackett, 1999), 83–85. For these and other reasons, the plebeians were subject to numerous epithets: see, e.g., Zvi Yavetz, *Plebs and Princeps* (Oxford: Oxford University Press, 1969), 141–42.

22. I detail the popularity of Epicureanism in late republican Rome, especially among the plebeians, in Chapter 5.

23. Otherwise diverse philosophical traditions affirm this goal: see, e.g., Leo Strauss, *What Is Political Philosophy? And Other Studies* (Chicago: University of Chicago Press, 1959), 11; Sheldon S. Wolin, "Political Theory as a Vocation," *American Political Science Review* 63.4 (1969): 1062–82, 1078; Rawls, *Justice as Fairness: A Restatement*, 2–3.

24. Rawls, for example, admits that his conceptualization of the state as a voluntary system of cooperation does not fully describe reality (and, by implication, thus has a metaphorical aspect): "No society can, of course, be a scheme of cooperation which men enter voluntarily in a literal sense; each person finds himself placed at birth in some particular position in some particular society, and that nature of this position materially affects his life prospects. Yet a society satisfying the principles of justice as fairness comes as close as a society can to being a voluntary scheme, for it meets the principles which free and equal persons would assent to under circumstances that are fair." John Rawls, *A Theory of Justice* (Cambridge, MA: Belknap Press of Harvard University Press, 1971), 13; also see Rawls, *A Theory of Justice: Revised Edition* [hereafter in this chapter "rev"] (Cambridge, MA: Belknap Press of Harvard University Press, 1999), 12. Even Schmitt, who really does want to understand political relations as those between friends and enemies, still has to acknowledge that political enmity is in principle fully separable from psychological feelings of hate and animosity. See Carl Schmitt, *The Concept of the Political*, trans. George Schwab (Chicago: University of Chicago Press, 1996), 28–29.

25. See, e.g., Nicolet, *World of the Citizen in Republican Rome*, 22. That, technically speaking, the *civitas* may have designated a space somewhat larger than the town, or *urbs*, and included the land surrounding the town (or *ager*), need not disturb the basic point: that the word for citizenship evokes a local form of politics centered upon a city.

26. See, e.g., Philip Manow, *In the King's Shadow: The Political Anatomy of Democratic Representation* (Cambridge: Polity, 2010), 1: "Although not completely undisputed, this idea of parliamentary representation of the sovereign people still dominates our democratic imaginary."

27. On this tendency, see Jeffrey Edward Green, *The Eyes of the People: Democracy in an Age of Spectatorship* (New York: Oxford University Press, 2010), 68–70, 74–118.

28. J. G. A. Pocock, "The Ideal of Citizenship Since Classical Times," in Ronald Beiner, ed., *Theorizing Citizenship* (Albany: State University of New York Press, 1995), 29.

29. Aristotle, *Politics*, trans. H. Rackham (Cambridge, MA: Harvard University Press, 1932), 1275a23–4.

30. See ibid., 1277b22–4.

31. It is true that Locke argues for the fundamental difference between paternal and political power. But it is still the case that in invoking children's implicit consent as the grounds of legitimate parental power, Locke understands children and the People (which itself must consent, tacitly or explicitly, to legitimate government) in parallel terms. See, e.g., Locke, *Second Treatise on Government*, §75: it is "almost natural for Children by a tacit, and scarce avoidable consent to make way for the *Father's Authority and Government*" (Peter Laslett, ed., *Locke: Two Treatises on Government* (Cambridge: Cambridge University Press, 2000), 317). This linkage between the consent of the governed within politics and the consent of children within the family, given special force by the dominance of Locke's educational (and not just political) writings in eighteenth-century Anglo-American culture, is pursued by Gillian Brown,

The Consent of the Governed: The Lockean Legacy in Early American Culture (Cambridge, MA: Belknap Press of Harvard University Press, 2001).

32. If Kant is correct and every authentic moral theory already implies its practicability—if *ought* really does imply *can*—then this benefit of analogical normative theory will be seen as superfluous: all that matters is affirming the right ideals and practicality will take care of itself. But insofar as the precise formulation of ideals is in dispute, it would seem that a theory that already could prove its ability to be implemented would carry with it extra philosophical support. At the very least it would be immune from the charge of impracticality so often leveled against aspirational political thought.

33. I defend an approach to political theory that melds historical and philosophical approaches in Jeffrey Edward Green, "Political Theory as Both Philosophy and History: A Defense Against Methodological Militancy," *Annual Review of Political Science* 18 (2015): 425–41; Green, "On the Difference Between a Pupil and a Historian of Ideas," *Journal of the Philosophy of History* 6.1 (2012): 86–112.

34. Antoine de Baecque, *The Body Politic: Corporeal Metaphor in Revolutionary France, 1770–1800* (Palo Alto: Stanford University Press, 1997), 7.

35. Jacques Rancière, *Disagreement: Politics and Philosophy* (Minneapolis: University of Minnesota Press, 1999), 60.

36. Held, for example, in interpreting democratic realism as a feature of certain pluralist models of democracy (and also as an implication of the democratic theories of Weber and Schumpeter), writes, "Their 'realism' entailed conceiving of democracy in terms of the actual features of Western polities. . . . Questions about the nature and appropriate extent of citizen participation, the proper scope of political rule and the most suitable spheres of democratic regulation—questions that have been part of democratic theory from Athens to nineteenth-century England—are put aside, or, rather, answered merely by reference to current practice. The ideals and methods of democracy become, by default, the ideals and methods of the existing democratic systems. Since the critical criterion for adjudicating between theories of democracy is their degree of 'realism,' models which depart from, or are in tension with, current democratic practice can be dismissed as empirically inaccurate, 'unreal' and undesirable." David Held, *Models of Democracy*, 3rd edition (Cambridge: Polity, 2006), 166.

37. Most often minimalism has involved conceiving of democracy in terms of elections for leadership selection, without direct or meaningful control by ordinary citizens over the selection of actual policies. Hindness, for example, refers to "realist theories of democracies" as "one of the most influential doctrines in twentieth century political science," standing for the idea that democracies are "governed by a combination of elected officials and professional state bureaucracies, and the people decide who is elected to rule them, not the substantive policies which their government is to pursue" (Barry Hindness, "Citizenship and Empire," in Thomas Blom Hansen and Finn Stepputat, eds., *Sovereign Bodies: Citizens, Migrants, and States in the Postcolonial World* (Princeton: Princeton University Press, 2005), 252). Sometimes minimalism arises because it is thought that more robust moral ideas are undesirable, as when Ferree refers to "the tradition of 'democratic realism'—the belief that ordinary citizens are poorly informed about public affairs, have no serious interest in, and are generally ill-equipped for political participation. . . . Those who want to be represented have the political obligation to use the representative process" (Myra Marx Ferree, *Shaping Abortion Discourse: Democracy and the Public Sphere in Germany and the United States* (Cambridge: Cambridge University Press, 2002), 297). In a similar vein, Blaug interprets democratic realists as those who "highlight the threat posed to democracy by excessive participation" (Ricardo Blaug, *Democracy: A Reader* (New York: Columbia University Press, 2001), 440). However, minimalism also arises when more robust ideals are considered unattainable. For Przeworski, for example, democracy becomes reduced to processes that enable the peaceful transfer of power, divorced from allegedly impossible ideals of rationality, equality, and representation (Adam Przeworski, "A Minimalist Conception of Democracy: A Defense," in Ian Shapiro and Casiano Hacker-Cordón, eds., *Democracy's Value* (Cambridge: Cambridge University Press, 1999), 23–55). Similarly, others appeal to the notion of minimalism to conceptualize what they take to be the inescapability of elitism within contemporary democracies. As Faulks, for example, writes, "Weber and Schumpeter accept the 'realist' approach of Mosca and see elite leadership

as inevitable" (Keith Faulks, *Political Sociology: A Critical Introduction* (New York: New York University Press, 2000), 43). Also see Raymond D. Boisvert, *John Dewey: Rethinking Our Time* (Albany: State University of New York Press, 1998), 74; Frank Hendricks, *Vital Democracy: A Theory of Democracy in Action* (Oxford: Oxford University Press, 2010), 61. Spragens likewise associates democratic realism with minimalism in the sense of avoiding higher goals unlikely to be achieved: "Preoccupied as they are with what they see as the persistently demanding tasks of maintaining a moderate, peaceful, and nontyrannical social order, democratic realists tend to look with suspicion upon 'higher' democratic goals. They recognize that the goals of moderation, stability, and social peace seem rather pedestrian to many of more hopeful or idealistic disposition. But they are dubious about the capacity of any political regime—and certainly about the capacity of liberal regimes that by definition allow space for very imperfect human beings to pursue their own purposes—to do much in the way of improving character, creating community, or answering to some other high moral ideal. . . . As for the central political goals that animate democratic realism—civil peace, stability, and personal security—no one can reasonably gainsay their importance" (Thomas A. Spragens, *Civic Liberalism* (Lanham, MD: Rowman & Littlefield, 1999), 7–8, 15).

38. For the claim that the integrity, protection, and endurance of democratic institutions require that they be dissociated from moral norms of social progress and social justice, see Giuseppe Di Palma, *To Craft Democracies: An Essay on Democratic Transitions* (Berkeley: University of California Press, 1990), 23; Samuel P. Huntington, *The Third Wave: Democratization in the Late Twentieth Century* (Norman: University of Oklahoma Press, 1991), 165–69; also see Ian Shapiro, *The Real World of Democratic Theory* (Princeton: Princeton University Press, 2011), 10. For concerns about the ineffectuality of excessive idealism, see, e.g., Posner's linkage of his pragmatic democratic theory to "classical realism"—one feature of which in his view is an objection to overidealistic forms of normative theorizing as being pointless. Richard A. Posner, *Law, Pragmatism, and Democracy* (Cambridge, MA: Harvard University Press, 2003), 44; also see Brian Leiter, "Classical Realism," 11 *Philosophical Issues* 24 (2001): 245. Also relevant in this regard is Mantena's analysis of the tradition of "moderating realism," which is concerned with how "absolutist ethics, ideological certitude, and utopian schemes can threaten political order and lead to unrestrained uses of power." Karuna Mantena, "Another Realism: The Politics of Gandhian Nonviolence," *American Political Science Review* 106.2 (2012): 455–70, 455.

39. William E. Connolly, *The Ethos of Pluralization* (Minneapolis: University of Minnesota Press, 1995), 140; Posner, *Law, Pragmatism, and Democracy*, 44. Other accounts of political realism as a standpoint opposed to idealism—whether something that aims to minimize the meaning of ideals, reject the universality of certain reigning ideals, or insist on the fraught political dimensions of certain ideals—include Mark Philp, *Political Conduct* (Cambridge, MA: Harvard University Press, 2007), 74; William Galston, "Realism in Political Theory," *European Journal of Political Theory* 9.4 (2010): 385–411.

40. See Spragens, *Civic Liberalism*, 15–17. As Allan Bloom put it, though not with democracy per se in mind, "We need to criticize false understandings of Utopia, but the easy way out provided by realism is deadly." Allan Bloom, *The Closing of the American Mind: How Higher Education Has Failed Democracy and Impoverished the Souls of Today's Students* (Chicago: University of Chicago Press, 1987), 67.

41. Here I follow Geuss when he says, "The opposite of reality or the correct perception of reality is in any case not the imagination [i.e., any idealistic conception of what a more just politics might look like] but illusion." Raymond Geuss, *Philosophy and Real Politics* (Princeton: Princeton University Press, 2008), 11.

42. T. S. Eliot, *Four Quartets* (Orlando, FL: Harcourt, 1971), 14. Slavoj Žižek, *Welcome to the Desert of the Real: Five Essays on September 11 and Related Dates* (New York: Verso, 2002).

43. See, e.g., E. E. Schattschneider, *The Semisovereign People: A Realist's View of Democracy in America* (New York: Holt, Rinehart and Winston, 1960), 139: "The beginning of wisdom in democratic theory is to distinguish between the things the people can do and the things the people cannot do. The worst possible disservice that can be done to the democratic cause is to attribute to the people a mystical, magical omnipotence which takes no cognizance of what

very large numbers of people cannot do by the sheer weight of numbers. At this point the common definition of democracy has invited us to make fools of ourselves."

44. See, e.g., E. E. Schattschneider, *Two Hundred Million People in Search of a Government* (New York: Holt, Rinehart and Winston, 1969), 46: "Democracy begins as an act of imagination about people. For this reason, democracy is a doctrine of social criticism."

45. Although political realism for Williams still makes appeal to the normative dimension of "legitimation" (which defines when power is warranted), it does not "make the moral prior to the political." Williams, *In the Beginning Was the Deed: Realism and Moralism in Political Argument* (Princeton: Princeton University Press, 2005), especially 1–3, 77. Likewise, Geuss invokes realism less to diminish normative theory—since he acknowledges that politics "is not and cannot be a strictly value-free enterprise"—than to insist that ethical analysis emerges out of a prior, historical engagement with actual institutions and motivations: "A 'realist' in the sense in which I am using the term will . . . start from an account of our existing motivations and our political and social institutions (not from a set of abstract 'rights' or from our intuition)" (Geuss, *Philosophy and Real Politics*, 1, 59; also see, 6–7, 13). As Geuss further explains, "Political philosophy must be realist. That means, roughly speaking, that it must start from and be concerned in the first instance not with how people ought ideally (or ought 'rationally') to act, what they ought to desire, or value, the kind of people they ought to be, etc., but, rather, with the way the social, economic, political, etc., institutions actually operate in some society at some given time, and what really does move human beings to act in given circumstances" (ibid., 9).

46. Reinhold Niebuhr, *Moral Man and Immoral Society* (Louisville, KY: Westminster John Knox Press, 2013), 275. Also see xxxiv: "What is lacking among all these moralists, whether religious or rational, is an understanding of the brutal character of the behavior of all human collectivities, and the power of self-interest and collective egoism in all intergroup relations. Failure to recognize the stubborn resistance of group egoism to all moral and inclusive social objectives inevitably involves them in unrealistic and confused political thought. They regard social conflict either as an impossible method of achieving morally approved ends or as a momentary expedient which a more perfect education or a purer religion will make unnecessary. They do not see that the limitations of the human imagination, the easy subservience of reason to prejudice and passion, and the consequent persistence of irrational egoism, particularly in group behavior, make social conflict an inevitability in human history, probably to its very end." Also see Tillich's notion of "belief-ful realism." Paul Tillich, *The Religious Situation* (New York: Meridian Books, 1967), 116.

47. Geuss, for example, observes, "Every theory is 'partisan' . . . and [involves] taking a position in the world" (Geuss, *Philosophy and Real Politics*, 29). Spragens also alludes to this dynamic when, in his account of democratic realism, he writes, following Alexander Hamilton, "The central task of democratic government . . . becomes to deal successfully with . . . forces and tendencies that constantly threaten to undermine it. No democratic regime can expect to survive, realists would argue, unless its leaders avoid what Alexander Hamilton called 'those reveries which would seduce us into an expectation of peace and cordiality' or 'deceitful dreams of a golden age' and instead focus constructively on the kinds of problems that 'continually agitated' the 'petty republics of Greece and Italy' and kept them 'in a state of perpetual vibration between the extremes of tyranny and anarchy' " (Spragens, *Civic Liberalism*, 4). Also see William E. Scheuerman, *The Realist Case for Global Reform* (Cambridge: Polity, 2011), 4–5.

48. See, e.g., A. John Simmons, "Ideal and Nonideal Theory," *Philosophy & Public Affairs* 38.1 (2010): 5–36.

49. According to Rawls, "The circumstances of justice may be described as the normal conditions under which human cooperation is both possible and necessary." Rawls, *A Theory of Justice*, 126/109 rev. For similar statements, see: H. L. A. Hart, *The Concept of Law* (Oxford: Clarendon Press, 1961), 189–95; J. R. Lucas, *The Principles of Politics* (Oxford: Clarendon Press, 1966), 1–10. On the particular issue of moderate scarcity, Rawls explains, "There is the condition of moderate scarcity understood to cover a wide range of situations. Natural and other resources are not so abundant that schemes of cooperation become superfluous, nor are conditions so harsh that fruitful ventures must inevitably break down. While mutually

advantageous arrangements are feasible, the benefits they yield fall short of the demands men put forward." Rawls, *A Theory of Justice*, 127/110 rev. On the issue of the inescapable pluralism of worldviews, see Rawls, *Justice as Fairness: A Restatement*, 4, 35–37; *A Theory of Justice*, 127/110 rev. On the issue of primary goods all rational individuals are presupposed to want, see *A Theory of Justice*, 90–95/78–81 rev.

50. For the critique of ideal theory as a kind of "applied ethics," see Geuss, *Philosophy and Real Politics*, 23.

51. Legislators, Rawls acknowledges, not only operate with more information about the distribution of wealth and income in a given society, but also have to confront the problem of uncertainty (as it is rarely altogether clear how proposed policies will affect distributions going forward). The challenge of uncertainty leads Rawls to posit that, when making decisions about which tax structure and economic system to implement, ideal legislators must veer toward too little rather than too much inequality—a bias which has no place in the initial conceptualization and justification of the principles of justice. Rawls, *A Theory of Justice*, 78–9/68–9 rev; also see 195–201/171–76 rev; *Justice as Fairness: A Restatement*, 48, 112, 114, 172–74.

52. Ronald Dworkin, *Is Democracy Possible Here? Principles for a New Political Debate* (Princeton: Princeton University Press, 2006), 108. The acknowledged inability to fully realize his distributive principle contributes to Dworkin's decision to favor implementation only along the lines of *ex ante equality* (where citizens are insured against various negative outcomes), thus excluding a commitment to *ex post equality* (which would have aimed to neutralize the positive, undeserved benefits of being born with talent or being lucky in other respects). Ibid., 104–6; also see Dworkin, *Sovereign Virtue: The Theory and Practice of Equality* (Cambridge: Harvard University Press, 2000), Chapter 2.

53. Tan, for example, defines luck egalitarianism in terms of the principles that justify institutional arrangements, not as the institutional arrangements themselves. Further, he sketches a scenario where, due to the difficulties of separating choice from luck, it would be appropriate to support Rawls's difference principle as an institution for implementing luck egalitarianism, even though the difference principle aims only to have the least favored maximally benefit from an ongoing system of inequalities, not to neutralize all the arbitrary effects of luck within an economic distribution. Kok-Chor Tan, *Justice, Institutions, and Luck: The Site, Ground, and Scope of Equality* (Oxford: Oxford University Press, 2012), 109–14.

54. For the former, consider Ackerman, an otherwise great defender of civility in the form of dialogic discourse, who says of those who in Nietzschean fashion conceive of themselves as supermen and deny free and equal citizenship: "And if they do declare themselves supermen, they surely will understand me when I say that I'm willing to fight for my rival understanding of the world." Bruce Ackerman, *Social Justice in the Liberal State* (New Haven, CT: Yale University Press, 1981), 17. In appealing to this kind of struggle, Ackerman is not affirming value pluralism in the manner of a skeptic, but acknowledging that there are perspectives that will resist his own account of moral objectivity, such that the commitment to his view is not just reasoned defense (though it is primarily that), but an identification of whom he will need to struggle against *politically* and not just intellectually. For the latter, consider how prevailing paradigms of liberal justice often include some attention to "nonideal theory"—especially the way political responsibility shifts in contexts of gross injustice by sanctioning, for example, civil disobedience. See, e.g., Rawls, *A Theory of Justice*, 363–91/319–43 rev; Amy Gutmann and Dennis Thompson, *Why Deliberative Democracy* (Princeton: Princeton University Press, 2004), 51.

55. Geuss, for example, acknowledges with regard to his own essay on realism, "One might worry that the form of 'realism' described in the foregoing is so broadly construed as to be vacuous, excluding nothing" (Geuss, *Philosophy and Real Politics*, 59). Spragens's account of democratic realism arguably is overbroad as it includes an extremely wide spectrum of thinkers who only "have in common a clear tendency to view the possibilities of liberal politics with a sober and skeptical eye." As Spragens elaborates, "The realists' political heroes thus are the brokers, the peacemakers, the compromisers, the deal-makers, and the head-knockers, who make the governing process work while maintaining some semblance of social comity" (Spragens, *Civic Liberalism*, 3, 13).

56. Thus, I disagree with Geuss when he divorces his defense of realism from specific political proposals: "If politics should be concrete, oriented toward action, and 'partisan,' what particular politics do I, Raymond Geuss, advocate? This is in principle a perfectly legitimate question, but one that is misplaced here" (Geuss, *Philosophy and Real Politics*, 95). Geuss does point the reader, however, to work that does provide some substantive direction. See, e.g., Geuss, "The Politics of Managing Decline," *Theoria* 52.108 (2005): 1–12. I think Zolo has it better when he links realism to taking aim at the theodicies of the present day. See Danilo Zolo, *Democracy and Complexity: A Realist Approach* (Cambridge: Polity, 1992), vii.

57. I have discussed elements of this unreality, in particular "democratic theory's tendency toward self-deception—specifically, its strange capacity to remain blind in theory to pathologies and disappointments that are obvious features of the actual experience of democratic life ... What seems especially true is the insight that democratic theory is dispositionally challenged in its ability to confront the obvious—nonparticipation, nondecision, hierarchy, nonpreference, spectatorial passivity—as foundational features of everyday political life in today's democracies" (Jeffrey Edward Green, "Three Theses on Schumpeter: Response to Mackie," *Political Theory* 38.2 (2010): 268–75, 272, 273).

58. Juvenal, *Satires*. In *Juvenal and Persius*, translated by Susanna Morton. Cambridge, MA: Harvard University Press, 2004.

59. Green, *The Eyes of the People*, 122–26.

Chapter 2

1. Aristotle, *Nicomachean Ethics*, trans. H. Rackham (Cambridge, MA: Harvard University Press, 1934), 1134b29-30. For a similar account of the meaning of nature in Aristotle—and its use for contemporary social science—see Jill Frank, "Citizens, Slaves, and Foreigners: Aristotle on Human Nature," *American Political Science Review* 98.1 (2004): 91–104; Stephen G. Salkever, *Finding the Mean: Theory and Practice in Aristotelian Political Philosophy* (Princeton: Princeton University Press, 1990), 13–104. Also see David R. Mayhew, "Political Science and Political Philosophy: Ontological Not Normative," *PS: Political Science & Politics* (2000): 192–93. Mayhew argues for understanding the purpose of political theory as being first and foremost "a source of ontological illumination—that is, as a window to the nature of political reality" (192).

2. On the restriction of magistracies to the aristocratic classes, see Bernard Manin, *Principles of Representative Government* (Cambridge: Cambridge University Press, 1997), 46; Fergus Millar, "The Political Character of the Classical Roman Republic, 200–151 B.C.," *The Journal of Roman Studies* 74: 1–19, 11, 18; Matthias Gelzer, *The Roman Nobility*, trans. Robin Seager (Oxford: Blackwell, 1969), 12–13; Claude Nicolet, "Le cens sénatorial sous le République et sous Auguste," *Journal of Roman Studies* 66 (1976): 20–38, 20.

3. On the non-deliberative quality of the legislative assemblies in which plebeians were restricted to yes-no votes, with effectively no capacity to set the agenda or engage in discussion, see Lily Ross Taylor, *Roman Voting Assemblies from the Hannibalic War to Dictatorship of Caesar* (Ann Arbor: University of Michigan Press, 1966); Claude Nicolet, *The World of the Citizen in Republican Rome*, trans. P. S. Falla (Berkeley, CA: University of California Press, 1980), 254–55.

4. To be sure, the older notion of a hereditary, not-strictly-socioeconomic plebeianism lived on (as certain offices, like the Tribunate, were restricted to members of traditional plebeian families, so that Clodius in 59 BCE had to renounce his patrician heritage and seek adoption from a plebeian family in order to attain the office), but plebeianism as I shall employ the term, and as the term came increasingly to be employed, refers to the *multitude*, the mass of ordinary citizens unelevated in status, wealth, or renown. On this rendering of plebeianism, both in the late Republic and early Empire, see Sallust, *The War with Jugurtha*, in *The War with Catiline* and *The War with Jugurtha*, trans. J. C. Rolfe and revised by John T. Ramsey (Cambridge, MA: Harvard University Press, 2013), §63; Horace, *Epistles*, in *Satires, Epistles, and Ars Poetica*, trans. H. R. Fairclough (Cambridge, MA: Harvard University Press, 1929), II.1.182–86; Tacitus, *Histories: Books I–III*, trans. Clifford H. Moore (Cambridge, MA: Harvard University Press, 1925), 1.4; Niccolò Machiavelli, *Discourses on Livy*, trans. Harvey C. Mansfield and

Nathan Tarcov (Chicago: University of Chicago Press, 1996), I.29–31; Henrik Mouritsen, *Plebs and Politics in the Late Roman Republic* (Cambridge: Cambridge University Press, 2001), 76; Matthias Gelzer, *The Roman Nobility*, 21; John P. McCormick, *Machiavellian Democracy* (Cambridge: Cambridge University Press, 2011), 31. Also see Marcus Tullius Cicero, *Letters to Atticus: Volume I*, trans. D. R. Shackleton Bailey (Cambridge, MA: Harvard University Press, 1999), #16, 86–89; Montesquieu, *Considerations on the Causes of the Greatness of the Romans and their Decline*, trans. David Lowenthal (Indianapolis: Hackett, 1999), 85. Yavetz provides helpful discussion of the complexity of the issue, but his basic conclusion nonetheless is straightforward: "One has to understand the terms *plebs, vulgus*, etc. as designations of persons who belonged neither to the *ordo senatorius* nor to the *ordo equester* [i.e., persons defined by their lack of elite status]." Zvi Yavetz, *Plebs and Princeps* (London: Oxford University Press, 1969), 154.

5. Horace, *Epistles*, 1.1.57–59 (my translation). Tacitus, too, even though writing about life in the early Empire, captures this socioeconomic conception of the plebs when he differentiates the Senators, the Equestrians, *and* the "respectable portion of the people, which was connected with the great families" from the "*plebs sordida*" (i.e., "the dirty plebs" or those with neither noble nor high economic status). Tacitus, *Histories*, 1.4; also see 3.74 for another usage of *plebs sordida*.

6. The existence of politically negligible but socially influential aristocratic orders and titles within certain liberal democracies, as in the noble and monarchical families in numerous European countries, is a partial exception to this larger tradition. See Ellis Wasson, *Aristocracy and the Modern World* (New York: Palgrave Macmillan, 2006).

7. To be sure, certain differentiations remain, as age, immigration status, criminal record, and mental disability can generate something less than full political rights of citizenship. Still, even if some of these restrictions may be violations of the requirements of free and equal citizenship, they are not unambiguously so—and in any case, the formal institutions of contemporary mass democracy can be said to reflect, on a level never previously achieved, the norm of free and equal citizenship.

8. Edmund Husserl, *Ideas: General Introduction to Pure Phenomenology*, trans. W. R. Boyce Gibson (New York: Collier, 1931), 91.

9. For Husserl, phenomenology means "experiences [*Erlebnisse*] intuitively seizable and analyzable in the generality of their essence, not experiences empirically perceived and treated as real facts." Edmund Husserl, *Logical Investigations*, trans. J. N. Findlay and revised by Dermot Moran, 2 vols. (London: Routledge, 2001), 2:166.

10. Martin Heidegger, *Being and Time*, trans. John Macquarrie and Edward Robinson (New York: Harper Perennial, 2008), Section 4, 32–35.

11. Richard Schmitt, "Phenomenology," in Paul Edwards, ed., *The Encyclopedia of Philosophy* (New York: Macmillan, 1967), 138. Jung describes phenomenology as "radical empiricism" (Hwa Hol Jung, *Rethinking Political Theory: Essays in Phenomenology and the Study of Politics* (Athens, Ohio: Ohio University Press, 1993), 7, 30)—an idea that repeats Husserl's claim, "We phenomenologists are the true empiricists." The idea of political theory as radically empiricist—as treating facts in a way that that exceeds what is usually taken as empirical by behavioralist social science—is also expressed by Wolin when he writes, "Facts . . . are more multi-faceted than a rigid conception of empirical theory would allow" (Sheldon S. Wolin, "Political Theory as a Vocation," *American Political Science Review* 63.4 (1969): 1062–82, 1073).

12. Heidegger, *Being and Time*, Section 7, 59. As Heidegger elaborates, "The idea of grasping and explicating phenomena in a way which is 'original' and 'intuitive' is directly opposed to the *naïveté* of a haphazard, 'immediate,' and unreflective 'beholding' [*Schauen*]" (ibid., 61).

13. Even in Switzerland, which has perhaps the most frequent elections of any liberal democracy, voting—on the national level at least—occurs only about four times per year.

14. See, e.g., Steven Galt Crowell, "Who Is the Political Actor? An Existential Phenomenological Approach," in Kevin Thompson and Lester Embree, eds., *Phenomenology of the Political* (Dordrecht: Kluwer, 2000). Crowell's analysis of political phenomenology treats the citizen as a political *actor*, as someone "who deliberates and decides" (18). Because Crowell treats the ordinary citizen and officeholder as exhibiting "a common intentional feature" (18), his analysis

of voting is biased toward choice rather than the non-chosen limitations reducing that choice. Likewise, Jung's phenomenology privileges an active, deliberating, co-equal form of citizenship, with Jung asserting, "Since the human being is an active and social being, freedom and responsibility are two main modalities of action in the social world." Jung treats responsibility as "both the capacity and demand to respond to the call of others" without differentiating alternate forms of responsibility based on one's placement in a hierarchical political space affording radically different communicative opportunities to citizens. Jung, *Rethinking Political Theory*, 20–21. There are, to be sure, certain exceptions to a political phenomenology that favors analysis of elite or exceptional modes of political experience. See, e.g., Aristotle's brief but important discussion of "being ruled," in *Politics*, trans. H. Rackham (Cambridge, MA: Harvard University Press, 1932), 1277a26–1277b30. More recently, see accounts of democratic listening: Susan Bickford, *The Dissonance of Democracy: Listening, Conflict, and Citizenship* (Ithaca, NY: Cornell University Press, 1996); Andrew Dobson, *Listening for Democracy: Recognition, Representation, Reconciliation* (Oxford: Oxford University Press, 2014).

15. Sweden, for example, has a low Gini coefficient for income (.31), but not for wealth (.79). David Domeij and Paul Klein, "Public Pensions: To What Extent Do They Account for Swedish Wealth Inequality?" *Review of Economic Dynamics* 5.3 (2002): 503–34. As of 2011, the wealthiest 20% in Sweden owned approximately 73% of the wealth (compared to 84% in the United States). See, e.g., http://blogs.reuters.com/felix-salmon/2011/03/25/swedish-inequality-datapoint-of-the-day/.

16. Guicciardini argued that even when all citizens were eligible to run for office, electoral systems would tend to empower the same types of leaders as under regimes that restricted eligibility for magistracies to an economic and aristocratic elite. Francesco Guicciardini, *Discorso di Logrogno*, in Athanasios Moulakis, ed. and trans., *Republican Realism in Renaissance Florence: Francesco Guicciardini's Discorso di Logrogno* (Lanham, MD: Rowman & Littlefield, 1998), 122–23; "Considerations of the *Discourses* of Niccolò Machiavelli," in James B. Atkinson and David Sices, eds. and trans., *The Sweetness of Power: Machiavelli's Discourses & Guicciardini's Considerations* (DeKalb, IL: Northern Illinois University Press, 2002), 381–483. Also see *The Federalist*, ed. Terrence Ball (Cambridge: Cambridge University Press, 2003), Nos. 10, 37, 39, 57, 60, 63; Manin, *Principles of Representative Government*, 43–44, 57; McCormick, *Machiavellian Democracy*, 107–108. Would sortition cancel remove? It would certainly lessen it, since if implemented to the fullest extent all citizens would feel a genuine possibility of being selected for leadership. But because sortition would not solve the problem of plutocracy (at least with regard to education), nor the problem of manyness, nor the difficulties surrounding the measurement of representation (see Section 1.1), I do not understand it as a fully satisfactory solution to the shadow of unfairness.

17. To be sure, there are exceptions—for example, certain neo-populists recognize the constitutive marginality of ordinary citizenship. See, e.g., Jacques Rancière, *Disagreement: Politics and Philosophy*, trans. Julie Rose (Minneapolis: University of Minnesota Press, 1999). But it seems the prevalence of other leading discourses which deny remove makes attention to it neither redundant nor without critical purchase.

18. John Rawls, "Justice as Reciprocity" [1971], in Samuel Freeman, ed., *John Rawls: Collected Papers* (Cambridge, MA: Harvard University Press, 2001), 195. Rawls further explains that one can rightly object to the particular pattern of honors, offices, etc., but not the existence of such a distribution itself. See Rawls, "Justice as Fairness" [1958], in *Collected Papers*, 50; "The Sense of Justice" [1963], in *Collected Papers*, 75.

19. Without invoking the game metaphor, Dworkin repeats Rawls's claim that the distribution of citizens into office holders with vast decision-making authority and non–office holders without such authority is not itself a mark against the ideal requirements of free and equal citizenship. "It makes no sense," he writes, "even as an unattainable ideal, to call for vertical equality of impact in a structure of representative government, because a representative structure is necessarily one in which impact is sharply different, from a vertical perspective" (Ronald Dworkin, *Sovereign Virtue: The Theory and Practice of Equality* (Cambridge, MA: Harvard University Press, 2000), 192).

20. Of course there was even some possibility of social mobility within ancient Rome, especially in the late Republic when wealth had relatively more sociopolitical importance: plebeians, for

example, could potentially enter the Equestrian order during their lifetime. And Equestrians with no tradition of consular rank in their families, while usually confined to lesser offices, could potentially gain the consulship, as Cicero did, thereby becoming a *novus homo*. Meanwhile, the social mobility of contemporary societies is consistently overestimated. See, e.g., John P. McCormick, "Contain the Wealthy and Patrol the Magistrates: Restoring Elite Accountability," *American Political Science Review* 100.2 (2006): 147–63, 153: "Social mobility . . . is too frequently underestimated in the context of pre-eighteenth-century republics and notoriously overestimated in the context of contemporary ones—and in neither case does it obviate the objective reality or political ramifications of class divisions." Also see Bill Keller, ed., *Class Matters* (New York: Times Books, 2005).

21. Fair equality of opportunity, for instance, often is defined by liberals less as the principle that all similarly talented and motivated *people* can have the same prospects of success than as the norm that all similarly talented and motivated *children* not be disadvantaged by the economic and social circumstances of their birth. See, e.g., John Rawls, *Justice as Fairness: A Restatement* (Cambridge, MA: Belknap Press of Harvard University Press, 2001), 44.

22. On togetherness, see Hannah Arendt, *The Human Condition* (Chicago: University of Chicago Press, 1958), 180: "This revelatory quality of speech and action comes to the fore where people are with others and neither for nor against them—that is, in sheer human togetherness." For sameness, see ibid., 214–15, 309. Sameness, Arendt explains, "occurs not only in isolation but in utter loneliness, where no true communication, let alone association and community, is possible" (215).

23. Arendt distinguishes the political labor movement (committed to effecting radical change) from trade-unionism (which seeks only to have its interests heeded to some greater degree within existing institutions). See Arendt, *The Human Condition*, 215–16.

24. Ibid., 180.

25. As Katz explains, "Even when a choice was allowed in elections, the choice was tightly controlled by the presiding magistrate. Legislative votes were simply 'yes' and 'no' decisions on a question with no amendments possible. In addition to the limits on the people's freedom of choice, the presiding magistrate in particular, and the ruling class in general, had a variety of institutional and procedural devices by means of which they could control the outcome of a vote" (Richard S. Katz, *Democracy and Elections* (Oxford: Oxford University Press, 1997), 14). Also see Mouritsen, *Plebs and Politics in the Late Roman Republic*, 63; Nicolet, *The World of the Citizen in Republican Rome*, 254–55; Andrew Lintott, *The Constitution of the Roman Republic* (Oxford: Oxford University Press, 1999), 42–49; Fergus Millar, "The Political Character of the Classical Roman Republic." Such restrictions were equally present in the plebeian assembly—the *concilium plebis*—where tribunes controlled all aspects of the assembly besides the ultimate vote.

26. Lintott, *The Constitution of the Roman Republic*, 42: "A *contio* might elicit an impression of popular feeling through applause and shouts, but did not create any decision."

27. Nicolet notes that those "who were allowed to speak at *contiones* . . . apparently . . . were seldom below the rank of praetor" (Nicolet, *World of the Citizen in Republican Rome*, 286). Mouritsen likewise finds "the most striking aspect of the Roman *contio* is the fact that, unlike the Athenian assemblies, it was not open for everyone to put forward their views. The *contio* remained under the control of the presiding magistrate, and only with his permission could others be allowed to address the meeting" (Mouritsen, *Plebs and Politics in Late Republican Rome*, 46). Given its limited accessibility, Taylor likens the *contio* to a modern press conference (Taylor, *Roman Voting Assemblies*, 20). And even Millar, who appeals to the *contiones* as a key institution constituting popular sovereignty at Rome, admits, "The right to speak at public meetings (*contiones*) does seem to have been controlled by whoever called the meeting, and normally was restricted to officeholders or ex-officeholders" (Fergus Millar, *The Roman Republic in Political Thought* (Hanover, NH: University Press of New England, 2002), 144). If ordinary citizens were called to the rostrum to testify or make a statement, this was both rather rare and at the discretion of magistrates and tribunes who, as with the legislative and judicial assemblies, controlled when and whether the *contiones* were to take place. Machiavelli, however, takes a more participatory view of the *contio*, arguing that "it [was] permitted to every citizen" to speak in one (*Discourses*, III.34, 289). Also see Lintott, *The Constitution of the*

Roman Republic, 47, where he remarks that, within the *contio*, "private citizens had to be given an opportunity to speak about a bill before it was either put to the vote or vetoed"—but this need not mean that all, or even any, plebeians had the right to speak.

28. On the *contio* as a "hierarchical communication situation" but one where elites were exposed to potential critique, see Robert Morstein-Marx, *Mass Oratory and Political Power* (Cambridge: Cambridge University Press, 2004), 4, 9, 119, 127–28, 132, 165, 170–71; also see, Peter O'Neill, "Going Round in Circles: Popular Speech in Ancient Rome," *Classical Antiquity* 22.1 (2003): 135–76, 147. Even if the *contio* was a place where plebeians might be heard, this still took the form of shouting, hissing, heckling, and perhaps question-asking—modes which even if vital for destabilizing powerholders as they appeared on the public stage brought nothing in the way of self-disclosure or authorial expressivity to the plebs who uttered them. That is to say, while one should not underestimate the real popular potential of the *contiones*—as a source of information often presented in a critical, quasi-deliberative fashion by competing politicians, as a vehicle for communicating mass preferences, and as an injection of *agonism* into elite life (insofar as the *contio* was a place where leading politicians had to face both their rivals and the unpredictable, sometimes hostile interjections of the amassed crowd)—it would be a mistake to forget that such processes in no way identified or empowered distinct plebeian subjectivities, but only a collective mass preference deeply constrained in its communicativity. This means that when Millar (*Roman Republic in Political Thought*, 146) says of the *contiones* that "the crowds present could and did make their reactions very clear" and that such processes therefore ought to be seen as "participationist" or "communitarian," it needs to be remembered that the genuine populism at play here is still constrained by a collective, inarticulate, and blunt form of expressivity, definitive of the phenomenon of manyness.

29. Millar, "The Political Character of the Classical Roman Republic," 2: "The people enjoyed the three basic constitutional rights of direct voting on legislation, including declarations of war and the making of peace-treaties; of electing all the annual holders of political and military office; and of judging in popular courts constituted by the *comitia centuriata* and *comitia tributa*." None of these enabled the individual self-disclosure of plebeian citizens. On the tribunes' right to accuse socioeconomic elites, see William Smith, "Tribunus," in *Dictionary of Greek and Roman Antiquities* (Boston: Longwood Press, 1977), 1151.

30. On the potency of crowds in the late Republic and early empire, see Millar, *Roman Republic in Political Thought*, 154–55; Yavetz, *Plebs and Princeps*, 9–37; J. S. McClelland, *The Crowd and the Mob: From Plato to Canetti* (London: Routledge, 2011), 34–59.

31. Hannah Arendt, *On Violence* (New York: Harcourt, Brace & World, 1970).

32. In other words, Arendt's account of the salutary benefits of political assembly links together two different effects—their potency vis-à-vis mere force and their enabling of individual self-disclosure—which need not appear in tandem with each other. Indeed, my claim is that the forms of mass protest accessible to ordinary citizens are much more likely to produce the former than the latter effect.

33. To be clear, in focusing on "civic potency," I mean not only how economic inequalities reproduce themselves in political processes (e.g., participation in, access to, and influence over government), but also how one's socioeconomic background affects educational and career attainment.

34. While all male citizens could vote, the votes of poorer citizens were formally diluted in various ways. One of the main legislative and electoral assemblies, the *comitia centuriata*, divided citizens into five or six property-based classes, with the richer classes having disproportionate votes relative to the poorer. Even the most popular of the assemblies, the *comitia tributa*, disadvantaged the poorest citizens—the urban plebs—by limiting them, despite their great numbers, to only four of the thirty-five tribes comprising the assembly. As Katz summarizes, "All Roman voting assemblies were weighted in favor of the rich" (Katz, *Democracy and Elections*, 15). Even if the tribunes of the plebs were plebeians and unlikely to have wealth on the level of the aristocratic classes, they too were much more likely to be wealthy than not. See McCormick, *Machiavellian Democracy*, 93: "The wealthiest or most notable citizens among the plebs were certainly most likely to become tribunes on a fairly consistent basis, but these notable plebeians were generally not the very richest and most prominent citizens in the republic as a whole." Also see Lintott, *The Constitution of the Roman Republic*, 120.

35. For the pervasiveness of the ideal of a plutocracy-free society within the attitudes of ordinary citizens, see, e.g., Benjamin I. Page and Lawrence R. Jacobs, *Class War? What Americans Really Think about Economic Inequality* (Chicago: University of Chicago Press, 2009), 2–3; also see Larry M. Bartels, *Unequal Democracy: The Political Economy of the New Gilded Age* (Princeton: Princeton University Press, 2010), 127–61. I demonstrate its pervasiveness within contemporary liberal-democratic philosophy in the argument that follows in the main text.

36. While not confronting the problem of plutocracy per se, John Gray does depart from the perspective of most contemporary liberals when he insists upon liberalism's internal pluralism: its diverse and competing set of moral commitments. My argument here is in the spirit of Gray's "agonistic liberalism." See Gray, *Two Faces of Liberalism* (New York: The New Press, 2000), 14, 32, 34, 69–104; Gray, *Berlin* (London: Fontana Press, 1995), 141–68.

37. John Rawls, *A Theory of Justice* (Cambridge, MA: Belknap Press of Harvard University Press, 1971), 74; *A Theory of Justice: Revised Edition* [hereafter in this chapter "rev"] (Cambridge, MA: Belknap Press of Harvard University Press, 1999), 64.

38. Rawls, "Distributive Justice" [1967], in *Collected Papers*, 143.

39. Rawls, *A Theory of Justice*, 73/63 rev; also see 93/80 rev.

40. Rawls, *Justice as Fairness: A Restatement*, 44.

41. Ibid., 46.

42. Ibid., 149.

43. Ibid., 177.

44. Rawls, *Political Liberalism* (New York: Columbia University Press, 2005), 358; Rawls, *Justice as Fairness: A Restatement*, 149.

45. Rawls, *A Theory of Justice*, 73/63 rev; *Justice as Fairness: A Restatement*, 44, 46n, 161; "Justice as Fairness," 52–3; "Distributive Justice," 140–41. Rawls's defense of social policies that would make the distribution of wealth much more broadly dispersed is important not simply because it suggests the potential radicalism of Rawls's model, but also because it indicates that one of the principal liberal-democratic strategies for reducing plutocracy involves the reduction of inequality itself. The rigor of Rawls's egalitarianism, often overlooked, is given special emphasis by a recent set of commentators who emphasize how the later Rawls's notion of "property-owning democracy" carried with it the call for the wide dispersal of capital through such policies that would block "the intergenerational transmission of advantage" (e.g., significant inheritance, estate, and gift taxes) and policies that would aggressively protect political discourse from the intrusion of money (e.g., "campaign finance reform, public funding of political parties, public provision of forums for political debate, and other measures to block the influence of wealth on politics . . . perhaps including publicly funded elections"). See Martin O'Neill and Thad Williamson, eds., *Property-Owning Democracy: Rawls and Beyond* (Hoboken, NJ: Wiley-Blackwell, 2014), 81, passim.

46. For example, the full realizability of the fair value of political liberties is claimed by Martin O'Neill, "Free (and Fair) Markets without Capitalism: Political Values, Principles of Justice, and Property-Owning Democracy," in Martin O'Neill and Thad Williamson, eds., *Property-Owning Democracy: Rawls and Beyond* (Hoboken, NY: Wiley-Blackwell, 2014), 75–100; Samuel Freeman, *Justice and the Social Contract* (New York: Oxford University Press, 2007), 107.

47. G. A. Cohen, *Rescuing Justice and Equality* (Cambridge, MA: Harvard University Press, 2009), 385. Even if Cohen incorrectly reduces Rawls's proposals for combating plutocracy in politics to those pertaining to campaign finance legislation, thus forgetting that Rawls also thought the reduction of inequality was essential to neutralizing the unfair influence of wealth in politics, the basic point to emphasize is that Cohen too denies plutocracy as a permanent problem within a liberal-democratic society.

48. John Tomasi, *Free Market Fairness* (Princeton: Princeton University Press, 2012), 252; H.A. Scott Trask, "William Graham Sumner: Against Democracy, Plutocracy, and Imperialism," *Journal of Libertarian Studies* 18.4 (2004): 1–27.

49. For example, even a well-ordered Rawlsian regime would still be characterized by what one radical Rawlsian describes as "moderate, ethically justifiable inequalities." Further, given that the most radical liberal proposals usually target the intergenerational transfer of wealth, there is reason to suspect that *intra*-generational inequalities would still be significant under most

liberal schemes. See Thad Williamson, "Is Property-Owning Democracy a Politically Viable Aspiration?" in Martin O'Neill and Thad Williamson, eds., *Property-Owning Democracy: Rawls and Beyond* (Hoboken, NY: Wiley-Blackwell, 2014), 288.

50. Dworkin, *Sovereign Virtue*, 199.
51. Dworkin, *Is Democracy Possible Here? Principles for a New Political Debate* (Princeton: Princeton University Press, 2006), 150–54; *Sovereign Virtue*, 195, 197, 199, 351–85.
52. Dworkin, *Sovereign Virtue*, 230, 385 (emphasis added).
53. Tomasi, *Free Market Fairness*, 243–44 (emphasis added).
54. Freeman, *Rawls* (London: Routledge, 2007), 98.
55. Freeman, *Justice and the Social Contract*, 98.
56. Amartya Sen, *The Idea of Justice* (Cambridge, MA: Belknap Press of Harvard University Press, 2009), 97.
57. Martha C. Nussbaum, *Frontiers of Justice: Disability, Nationality, Species Membership* (Cambridge: Harvard University Press, 2006), 291–93. On the tendency of purveyors of the capabilities model to interpret capabilities in terms of "sufficiency" levels, see Jonathan Wolff, "Social Justice and Public Policy: A View from Political Philosophy," in Gary Craig, Tania Burchardt, and David Gordon, eds., *Social Justice and Public Policy: Seeking Fairness in Diverse Societies* (Bristol, UK: Policy Press, 2008), 23.
58. Philip Pettit, *Republicanism: A Theory of Freedom and Government* (Oxford: Oxford University Press, 1997), 10, 159, 161–63; also see Pettit, *On the People's Terms: A Republican Theory and Model of Democracy* (Cambridge: Cambridge University Press, 2013), 84–88, 90–91, 298.
59. Pettit, *On the People's Terms*, 169–70.
60. James Harrington *The Commonwealth of Oceana*, in J. G. A. Pocock, ed., *The Commonwealth of Oceana and A System of Politics* (Cambridge: Cambridge University Press, 1992), 57. Even if Harrington thought much of this inequality could be corrected—since, in the very next clause, he writes, "and where there is inequality of power there can be no commonwealth"— he also expected wealthier citizens to have disproportionate political opportunities (as seen in his call for two orders, the foot and the horse, and his exclusion of the propertyless from citizenship), acknowledging in his own ideal proposals the place for seemingly inescapable economically generated political inequality.
61. Montesquieu, *Ouevres Complètes* (Paris: Chez Lefevre, 1835), 145: "Il est impossible que les richesses ne donnent du pouvoir." This passage comes from Montesquieu, *Considerations on the Causes of the Greatness of the Romans and Their Decline* [1734] (Indianapolis: Hackett, 1999), 85 (my translation is slightly altered). Even if Montesquieu writes this in critique of excessive economic inequality—and holds that less inequality within a polity will enable talent and virtue, rather than mere wealth, to attain power—the statement still can be read as Montesquieu's reflection about a general feature of all politics. In spite of his call for meritocracy, for example, Montesquieu still expected the propertyless to be excluded from full citizenship, arguing that "in choosing a representative, all citizens in the various districts should have the right to vote except those whose estate is so humble that they are deemed to have no will of their own." And he still argued for two separate legislative chambers, with one reserved for a noble class defined in part by great wealth. Montesquieu, *The Spirit of the Laws*, trans. Anne M. Cohler, Basia Carolyn Miller, and Harold Samuel Stone (Cambridge: Cambridge University Press, 1989), 160.
62. On republican calls to curb economic inequality so as to protect ordinary citizens from potential abuse, see Aristotle, *Politics*, 1295b4–15; Thomas More, *The Complete Works of St. Thomas More* (New Haven, CT: Yale University Press, 1963), 67; Thomas Jefferson, *Writings* (New York: Library of America, 1984), 841. On republican interest in reducing inequality for meritocratic reasons, see Plato, *The Collected Dialogues of Plato*, eds. Edith Hamilton and Huntington Cairns (Princeton: Princeton University Press, 1996), 584d, 737e; Harrington, *The Commonwealth of Oceana*, 202, 231; Harrington, *A System of Politics*, in J. G. A. Pocock, ed., *The Commonwealth of Oceana and A System of Politics* (Cambridge: Cambridge University Press), 460; Montesquieu, *The Spirit of the Laws*, 44–45, 94–96. For an informative account, see Eric Nelson, *The Greek Tradition in Republican Thought* (Cambridge: Cambridge University Press, 2004), which details a long-standing "Greek" tradition of republican

thought, grounded precisely on combating economic inequality so that virtue and merit, rather than mere wealth, better determine who holds political power.

63. Aristotle, *Politics*, 1281a40-b10, 1283a40-b1, 1283b23-35, 1286125-32, 1287b12-30, 1332130-35.

64. Harrington proposes a division of the citizenry which "distributes the citizens into horse and foot by the cense or valuation of their estates; they who have above £100 a year in lands, goods, or monies, being obliged to be of the horse, and they who have under to be of the foot. But if a man has prodigally wasted and spent his patrimony, he is neither capable of magistracy, office nor suffrage in the commonwealth." Harrington, *The Commonwealth of Oceana*, 76.

65. Ibid., 76, 234. As Harrington explains, "The centre or fundamental laws are, first, the agrarian, proportioned at £2,000 a year in land, lying and being within the proper territory of Oceana, and stating property in land at such a balance, that the power can never swerve out of the hands of the many" (ibid., 234).

66. Montesquieu, *The Spirit of the Laws*, 160.

67. James Madison, "No. 10," in *The Federalist*, 40–46. See also Alexander Hamilton, who expects "land-holders, merchants, and men of the learned professions" will dominate the political life of the nascent American republic ("No. 35," in *The Federalist*, 161).

68. William Doyle, *The Oxford History of the French Revolution* (Oxford: Clarendon Press, 1989), 124, 420. Jack R. Censer and Lynn Hunt, *Liberty, Equality, Fraternity: Exploring the French Revolution* (University Park: Pennsylvania State University Press, 2001), 55; Jeremy D. Popkin, *A History of Modern France* (Upper Saddle River, NJ: Pearson, 2006), 46, 124, 420.

69. James Madison, "Note to His Speech on the Right of Suffrage (1821)," in Philip B. Kurland and Ralph Lerner, eds., *The Founders' Constitution* (Chicago: University of Chicago Press, 1987), Vol. 1, 602.

70. Ibid., 603.

71. See note 16.

72. On this last, see Jeffrey A. Winters, *Oligarchy* (Cambridge: Cambridge University Press, 2011), 11–20.

73. Wilkinson's cross-national analysis leads him to conclude that it is almost impossible to distinguish between wealth and income, on the one hand, and status, power, and prestige on the other (Richard Wilkinson, *The Impact of Inequality: How to Make Sick Societies Healthier* (New York: New Press, 2006), 71–72).

74. John Adams, *Discourses on Davila*, in Charles Francis Adams, ed., *The Works of John Adams, Second President of the United States* (Boston: Little, Brown, 1851 [1790]), Vol. 6, 239.

75. Adam Smith, *The Theory of Moral Sentiments* (London: Penguin, 2010), 46–47: "It is because mankind are disposed to sympathize more entirely with our joy than with our sorrow, that we make parade of our riches, and conceal our poverty. . . . Nay, it is chiefly from this regard to the sentiments of mankind, that we pursue riches and avoid poverty. . . . To be observed, to be attended to, to be taken notice of with sympathy, complacency, and approbation, are all the advantages which we can propose to derive from [wealth]. It is the vanity, not the ease, or the pleasure, which interests us . . . The rich man glories in his riches, because he feels that they naturally draw upon him the attention of the world, and that mankind are disposed to go along with him in all those agreeable emotions with which the advantages of his situation so readily inspire him. At the thought of this, his heart seems to swell and dilate itself within him, and he is fonder of his wealth, upon this account, than for all the other advantages it procures him. The poor man, on the contrary, is ashamed of his poverty. He feels that it either places him out of the sight of mankind, or, that if they take any notice of him, they have, however, scarce any fellow-feeling with the misery and distress which he suffers. He is mortified upon both accounts. For though to be overlooked, and to be disapproved of, are things entirely different, yet as obscurity covers us from the daylight of honour and approbation, to feel that we are taken no notice of, necessarily damps the most agreeable hope, and disappoints the most ardent desire, of human nature."

76. As the Supreme Court reasoned in *Buckley v. Valeo*, 424 U.S. 1, 19 (1976): "A restriction on the amount of money a person or group can spend on political communication during a campaign necessarily reduces the quantity of expression by restricting the number of issues

discussed, the depth of their exploration, and the size of the audience reached. This is because virtually every means of communicating ideas in today's mass society requires the expenditure of money."

77. Arend Lijphart, "Unequal Participation: Democracy's Unresolved Dilemma," *American Political Science Review* 91.1 (1997): 1–14. Also see Pippa Norris, *Democratic Phoenix: Reinventing Political Activism* (Cambridge: Cambridge University Press, 2002); Katherine Cramer Walsh, M. Kent Jennings, and Laura Stoker, "The Effects of Social Class Identification on Participatory Orientations Towards Government," *British Journal of Political Science* 34.3 (2004): 469–95; Lester W. Milbrath and Madan Lal Goel, *Political Participation: How and Why Do People Get Involved in Politics?*, 2nd edition (Chicago: Rand McNally, 1977); Christopher J. Anderson and Pablo Beramendi, "Income, Inequality, and Electoral Participation," in Pablo Beramendi and Christopher J. Anderson, eds., *Democracy, Inequality, and Representation: A Comparative Perspective* (New York: Russell Sage Foundation, 2008), 299 ("The effect of income on electoral participation at the individual level is basically linear and positive. That is, those with relatively higher incomes participate more and those with lower incomes relative to the median income participate less in elections"); Jan Teorell, Mariano Torcal, and José Ramón Montero, "Political Participation: Mapping the Terrain," in Jan W. van Deth, José Ramón Montero, and Anders Westholm, eds., *Citizenship and Involvement in European Democracies: A Comparative Analysis* (London: Routledge, 2007); and Sidney Verba, "Would the Dream of Political Equality Turn Out to Be a Nightmare?" *Perspectives on Politics* 1.4 (2003): 663–77, 666 ("In general, citizens who are advantaged when it comes to education, income, social standing, race, ethnicity, or gender are more politically active than those who are not").

78. Robert J. Franzese and Jude C. Hays, "Inequality and Unemployment, Redistribution and Social Insurance, and Participation: A Theoretical Model and an Empirical System of Endogenous Equations," in Pablo Baramendi and Christopher J. Anderson, eds., *Democracy, Inequality, and Representation: A Comparative Perspective* (New York: Russell Sage Foundation, 2008), 239–40 ("As is well-established empirically . . . the relatively wealthy have a higher propensity to vote than the relatively poor"). Franzese also has shown that under general conditions the median voter will be poorer as participation increases. Franzese, *Macroeconomic Policies of Developed Democracies* (Cambridge: Cambridge University Press, 2002). Also see Margaret Conway, *Political Participation in the United States* (Washington: Congressional Quarterly Press, 1986); Martin Harrop and William L. Miller, *Elections and Voters: A Comparative Introduction* (New York: New Amsterdam Books, 1987); Raymond E. Wolfinger and Steven J. Rosenstone, *Who Votes?* (New Haven, CT: Yale University Press, 1980); Steven J. Rosenstone and John Mark Hansen, *Mobilization, Participation, and Democracy in America* (New York: Longman, 1993); Sidney Verba, Norman H. Nie, and Jae-on Kim, *Participation and Political Equality: A Seven-Nation Comparison* (Cambridge: Cambridge University Press, 1978).

79. Lijphart, for example, states, "This systematic class bias applies with special force to the more intensive and time-consuming forms of participation" ("Unequal Participation," 1). Likewise, Rosenstone and Hansen (*Mobilization, Participation, and Democracy*) find that the fewer participants in a political activity, the greater the socioeconomic inequality likely to characterize it.

80. Anderson and Beramendi, "Income, Inequality, and Electoral Participation," 287–88: "A substantial literature has documented that higher levels of education and social status (measured by income or social class) are the most consistently significant predictors of political action across a variety of countries." Also see Verba, Nie, and Kim, *Participation and Political Equality*, 1.

81. Sidney Verba, Kay Lehman Schlozman, and Henry Brady, *Voice and Equality: Civic Voluntarism in American Politics* (Cambridge, MA: Harvard University Press, 1995).

82. On the correlation between wealth and political efficacy, see Frederick Solt, "Economic Inequality and Democratic Political Engagement," *American Journal of Political Science* 52.1 (2008): 48–60. On the correlation of wealth to likelihood of recruitment, see Robert Huckfeldt and John Sprague, "Political Parties and Electoral Mobilization: Political Structure, Social Structure, and the Party Canvass," *American Political Science Review* 86.1 (1992): 70–86; Steven J. Rosenstone and John Mark Hansen, *Mobilization, Participation, and Democracy*.

Further, another relevant dynamic is the correlation between wealth and education, which is important due to the impact of education on the likelihood of participating in politics. See, e.g., Wolfinger and Rosenstone, *Who Votes?*, Chapter 3; Verba, Schlozman, and Brady, *Voice and Equality*, 5, 18, passim; Milbrath and Goel, *Political Participation*.

83. Anderson and Beramendi, "Income, Inequality, and Electoral Participation," 280–81.

84. See, e.g., Jeffrey A. Winters and Benjamin I. Page, "Oligarchy in the United States?" *Perspectives on Politics* 7 (2009): 731–51; Robert Goodin and John Dryzek, "Rational Participation: The Politics of Relative Power," *British Journal of Political Science* 10.3 (1980): 273–92; Peter Bachrach and Morton S. Baratz, *Power and Poverty: Theory and Practice* (Oxford: Oxford University Press, 1970), 6–11; E. E. Schattschneider, *The Semisovereign People: A Realist's View of Democracy in America* (New York: Holt, Rinehart and Winston, 1960), 106. Solt describes how the wealthy can successfully promote their interests: "No coordination—or even intent—is required for this to occur: by using their money to amplify their own speech in arguments on some issues, more affluent people can drown the voices of poorer citizens and so keep the issues they would raise from being discussed" (Solt, "Economic Inequality and Democratic Political Engagement," 49). Also see Winters, *Oligarchy*, 18, 20.

85. Anderson and Beramendi, "Income, Inequality, and Electoral Participation," 299: "Inequality affects participation negatively—and it does so regardless of whether income is more concentrated at the upper or lower end of the income distribution." Solt similarly finds that, across five industrialized democracies, inequality at the national level depresses interest in politics, the frequency of political discussion, and the likelihood of having ever voted, particularly for lower-income citizens (Solt, "Economic Inequality and Democratic Political Engagement"). Also see David Campbell, *Why We Vote: How Schools and Communities Shape Our Civic Life* (Princeton: Princeton University Press, 2006).

86. On the relationship of increased inequality to declining levels of trust and cooperation, see Alberto Alesina and Eliana La Ferrara, "Who Trusts Others?," *Journal of Public Economics* 85.2 (2002): 207–234; Robert J. Boeckmann and Tom R. Tyler, "Trust, Respect, and the Psychology of Political Engagement," *Journal of Applied Social Psychology* 32.10 (2002): 2067–88; Eric M. Uslaner and Mitchell Brown, "Inequality, Trust, and Civic Engagement," *American Politics Research* 33.6 (2005): 868–94. On inequality as a potential blockage to information flow, see Robert Huckfeldt, Jeanette Morehouse Mendez, and Tracy Osborn, "Disagreement, Ambivalence, and Engagement: The Political Consequences of Heterogeneous Networks," *Political Psychology* 25.1 (2004): 65–95. On the relationship of inequality to the production of apathy, see John Gaventa, *Power and Powerlessness: Quiescence and Rebellion in an Appalachian Valley* (Urbana: University of Illinois Press, 1980).

87. Solt, "Economic Inequality and Democratic Political Engagement," 48. Also see Goodin and Dryzek, who find that the relationship between income inequality and electoral participation was strongly negative across 38 democracies in the late 1950s and 42 American metropolitan areas in the early 1960s. Robert Goodin and John Dryzek, "Rational Participation." For the effect of inequality on participation at the sub-national level, see Carles Boix, *Democracy and Redistribution* (Cambridge: Cambridge University Press, 2003); Frederick Solt, "Civics or Structure? Revisiting the Origins of Democratic Quality in the Italian Regions," *British Journal of Political Science* 34.1 (2004): 123–35.

88. On the lesser likelihood of poorer citizens being mobilized relative to the more advantaged, see Solt, "Civics or Structure?"; Goodin and Dryzek, "Rational Participation"; Boix, *Democracy and Redistribution*; Verba, "Would the Dream of Political Equality Turn Out to Be a Nightmare?"

89. Richard Wilkinson and Kate Pickett, *The Spirit Level: Why Greater Equality Makes Societies Stronger* (New York: Bloomsbury Press, 2011), 75. Also see, M. G. Marmot, G. Rose, M. Shipley, and P. J. Hamilton, "Employment Grade and Coronary Heart Disease in British Civil Servants," *Journal of Epidemiology and Community Health* 32.4 (1978): 244–249. As Wilkinson and Pickett explain, "There are now numerous studies that show the same thing, in different societies and for most kinds of ill-health—low social status has a clear impact on physical health, and not just for the people at the very bottom of the social hierarchy. . . . There is a social gradient in health running right across society, and where we are placed in relation to other people matters; those above us have better health, and those below us

have worse health, from the very bottom to the very top" (*The Spirit Level*, 75–76). Also see Wilkinson, *The Impact of Inequality*, 16, 18, 20, 23.

90. Wilkinson and Pickett, *The Spirit Level*, 20, 30.

91. For the former, see H. Kuper and M. Marmot, "Job Strain, Job Demands, Decision Latitude, and the Risk of Coronary Heart Disease within the Whitehall II Study," *Journal of Epidemiology and Community Health* 57.2 (2003): 147–153; Wilkinson, *The Impact of Inequality*, 60. For the latter, see Ari Väänänen et al., "Lack of Predictability at Work and Risk of Acute Myocardial Infarction: An 18-Year Prospective Study of Industrial Employees," *American Journal of Public Health* 98.12 (2008): 2264–71.

92. For cortisol, see T. Chandola, A. Britton, E. Brunner, H. Hemingway, M. Malik, M. Kumari, E. Badrick, and M. Kivimaki, "Work Stress and Coronary Heart Disease: What Are the Mechanisms?" *European Heart Journal* 29.5 (2008): 640–48; Wilkinson, *The Impact of Inequality*, 275. For serotonin, see Robbert J. Verkes et al., "Mood Correlates with Blood Serotonin, but not with Glucose Measures in Patients with Recurrent Suicidal Behavior," *Psychiatry Research* 80 (1998): 239–48; Peter D. Kramer, *Listening to Prozac* (New York: Penguin, 1993); Wilkinson, *The Impact of Inequality*, 87–88, 280.

93. As Wilkinson observes, "Even if it were possible to give people an equal opportunity to end up in an inferior position, that would not make it any more tolerable . . . To know that you are fairly allocated to poverty is little comfort and may actually increase the stigma attached to it; it certainly does nothing to reduce the pain of exclusion. The substitution of equality of opportunity for equality of outcome as a political aim reflects a monumental failure even to begin thinking seriously about the nature of society's problems." Wilkinson, *The Impact of Inequality*, 284.

94. Oliver, for example, finds that socioeconomically diverse communities tend to vote and engage in informal civic activity to a larger extent than do citizens in more homogenous areas. Eric J. Oliver, *Democracy in Suburbia* (Princeton: Princeton University Press, 2001), Chapter 3. Moreover, Campbell finds that greater inequalities in municipalities appear to raise the rates of donating money or time to campaigns and that, within certain counties, inequality may raise the likelihood of voting. Campbell, *Why We Vote*, 13–75. One theory for such effects is that as average incomes grow farther apart, preferences for taxes and other economic policies become more polarized and generate greater political energy: see Henry E. Brady, "An Analytic Perspective on Participatory Inequality and Income Inequality," in Kathryn M. Neckerman, ed., *Social Inequality* (New York: Russell Sage Foundation, 2004), 667–702.

95. For example, Roller and Rudi conclude that the civic voluntarism model (which predicts that greater socioeconomic status generates greater likelihood of political participation) "seems to be a universal model of political participation that is not only valid for the United States but also for Western as well as Central and Eastern European democracies." Edeltraud Roller and Tatjana Rudi, "Explaining Level and Equality of Political Participation: The Role of Social Capital, Socioeconomic Modernity, and Political Institutions," in Heiner Meulemann, ed., *Social Capital in Europe: Similarity of Countries and Diversity of People? Multi-Level Analyses of the European Social Survey 2002* (Leiden: Brill, 2008), 269, 278. Likewise, while Verba recognizes that underprivileged citizens can be mobilized around a particular issue—and counteract the effect of economic inequality on politics—he still acknowledges the general norm that "recruitment to activity more often reinforces the socioeconomic stratification of political participation, as recruiters seek those who have the resource capacity to be effective activists" ("Dream of Political Equality," 667). Verba, Schlozman, and Brady capture the default quality of plutocratic processes, that is, their status as an ordinary feature of political life in contemporary mass democracies, when they conclude that while "it is impossible to specify [exactly] what one person, one vote would look like," nonetheless "we must recognize a systematic bias in representation through participation. Over and over, our data showed that participatory input is tilted in the direction of the more advantaged groups in society—especially in terms of economic and educational position." (*Voice and Equality*, 512; also see 532). Also see Henry E. Brady, Sidney Verba, and Kay Lehman Schlozman, "Prospecting for Participants: Rational Expectations and the Recruitment of Political Activists," *American Political Science Review* 93:1 (1999): 153–68.

96. Verba, Nie, and Kim, *Participation and Political Equality*, 1.
97. Verba, Schlozman, and Brady, *Voice and Equality*, 1.
98. Peter Enns and Christopher Wlezien, eds., *Who Gets Represented?* (New York: Russell Sage Foundation, 2011); Stephen Shaffer, "Policy Differences between Voters and Non-Voters in American Elections," *The Western Political Quarterly* 35.4 (1982): 496–510; Verba, Schlozman, and Brady, *Voice and Equality*, 204; Wolfinger and Rosenstone, *Who Votes?*, 105–14.
99. Stephen Earl Bennett and David Resnick, for example, while acknowledging numerous instances of close similarity in the preferences of American voters and non-voters, still find that non-voting "does have an impact on some domestic policies, especially spending on welfare programs" (Bennett and Resnick, "The Implications of Nonvoting for Democracy in the United States," *American Journal of Political Science* 34.3 (1990): 771–802). Verba et al. (*Voice and Equality*, 167, 206) find "some tilt in a liberal direction among non-voters" and, "a small but consistent tendency for those who are more conservative in attitude or Republican in party identification to be more active." And Verba ("The Dream of Political Equality," 670) argues that with regard to similarities in the preferences of participants and nonparticipants, the "magnitude can be overstated." A similar point is made by Michael M. Gant and William Lyons, "Democratic Theory, Nonvoting, and Public Policy: The 1972–1988 Presidential Elections," *American Politics Quarterly* 21 (1993): 185–204.
100. Verba, Schlozman, and Brady, *Voice and Equality*, 221; Verba, "Would the Dream of Political Equality Turn Out to Be a Nightmare?"
101. Verba, Schlozman, and Brady, *Voice and Equality*, 197, 202, 205, 213, 512. As Verba explains, "We find that active and inactive citizens are not the same. Differential voice means that different things are being said—especially by activities that can easily carry a message. . . . The divide between the active and inactive citizens increases with the difficulty of the act" ("Dream of Political Equality," 670).
102. On the United States as a country with perhaps the largest economic inequality of any industrialized democracy—and a country whose inequality in wealth and income has dramatically increased over the last generation (so that, as of 2009, the top 1% of income holders earned approximately 17% of all income, the wealthiest 1% owned approximately 34% of the wealth, the bottom 90% possessed only 57.5% of the nation's income and 29% of the nation's wealth, and the top 101 wealth holders were worth an average of $8 billion or 59,619 times more than the average member of the bottom 90%)—see Page and Jacobs, *Class War?*, 4–9. Inequality in America has only further intensified in the last few years. As of 2012, the wealthiest 1% owned more than 40% of the nation's wealth, with the wealthiest 10% owning more than 75% of it. Emmanuel Saez and Gabriel Zucman, "Wealth Inequality in the United States since 1913: Evidence from Capitalized Income Tax Data," National Bureau of Economic Research, Working Paper 20625 (2014), 54–55 (Figures 6 and 7). Available online: http://gabriel-zucman.eu/files/SaezZucman2014.pdf. It is widely accepted that economic inequality in America has translated into significantly unequal political opportunities. See, e.g., Kay Lehman Schlozman et al., "Inequalities of Political Voice," in Lawrence R. Jacobs and Theda Skocpol, eds., *Inequality and American Democracy: What We Know and What We Need to Learn* (New York: Russell Sage Foundation, 2005), 19. Also see Kevin Phillips, *Wealth and Democracy: A Political History of the American Rich* (New York: Broadway Books, 2002), 4; Kay Lehman Schlozman, Sidney Verba, and Henry E. Brady, *The Unheavenly Chorus: Unequal Political Voice and the Broken Promise of American Democracy* (Princeton: Princeton University Press, 2012); Bartels, *Unequal Democracy*; Winters and Page, "Oligarchy in the United States?"; Martin Gilens, *Affluence and Influence: Economic Inequality and Political Power in America* (Princeton: Princeton University Press, 2012); Martin Gilens and Benjamin I. Page, "Testing Theories of American Politics: Elites, Interest Groups, and Average Citizens," *Perspectives on Politics* 12.3 (2014): 564–81. Hacker and Pierson suggest that growth in inequality over the last three decades in the United States has been caused by government policies serving the interests of the wealthy. Jacob S. Hacker and Paul Pierson, *Winner-Take-All Politics: How Washington Made the Rich Richer—And Turned Its Back on the Middle Class* (New York: Simon and Schuster, 2010).

103. On the general effects of European socioeconomic inequality on politics, see Verba, Nie, and Kim, *Participation and Political Equality*, 1–22, 286–309; Erik Oppenhuis, *Voting Behavior in Europe: A Comparative Analysis of Electoral Participation and Party Choice* (Amsterdam: Het Spinhuis, 1995), 21–22; and Jan Teorell, Paul Sum, and Mette Tobiasen, "Participation and Political Equality: An Assessment of Large-Scale Democracy," in Jan W. van Deth, José Ramón Montero, and Anders Westholm, eds., *Citizenship and Involvement in European Democracies*, 388, 403. On the effects of European socioeconomic inequality on non-electoral forms of political participation in particular, see Roller and Rudi, "Explaining Level and Equality of Political Participation," 253, 267. Also see Gabriel Badescu and Katja Neller, "Explaining Associational Involvement," in Deth, Montero, and Westholm, eds., *Citizenship and Involvement in European Democracies*, 160, 184. ("Citizens with higher levels of education and income are more likely to participate in voluntary organizations. . . . Socio-economic resources and indicators of social integration as well as factors indexing social orientations, norms, and motivations prove to be important predictors of organizational involvement. The effects of resources and levels of social integration are consistent across the majority of countries.")

104. Pablo Beramendi and Christopher J. Anderson, "Inequality and Democratic Representation: The Road Traveled and the Path Ahead," in Pablo Beramendi and Christopher J. Anderson, eds., *Democracy, Inequality, and Representation: A Comparative Perspective* (New York: Russell Sage Foundation, 2008), 402. Also see Beramendi and Rueda, "Social Democracy Constrained: Indirect Taxation in Industrialized Democracies," *British Journal of Political Science* 37.4 (2007): 619–41: "Thus, to ensure that redistribution is promoted through generous expenditure policies, social democratic parties in highly co-ordinated environments find themselves in a paradoxical situation. They need to support the welfare state by taxing labour more than capital and . . . by relying on regressive indirect taxation" (627). Thomas R. Cusack and Pablo Beramendi, "Taxing Work," *European Journal of Political Research* 45.1 (2006): 43–73. Also see Verba et al., *Elites and the Idea of Equality: A Comparison of Japan, Sweden, and the United States* (Cambridge, MA: Harvard University Press, 1987), 37; Winters, *Oligarchy*, xiii.

105. In the Nordic countries, as of 2008 the wealthiest 10% owned the following percentages of national wealth: Denmark (65%), Finland (42%), Norway (51%), Sweden (59%)—lower than the US (70%) but still sizable. James B. Davies et al., "The World Distribution of Household Wealth," in James B. Davies, ed., *Personal Wealth from a Global Perspective* (Oxford: Oxford University Press, 2008). The inequality is even greater for the super-rich. In Finland, for example, a recent study found that the richest 0.5% of the population owns 71.6% of capital market wealth (as opposed to 41% in the United States). Jussi Karhunen and Matti Keloharju, "Shareowning Wealth in Finland 2000," *Liiketaloudellinen Aikakauskirja / The Finnish Journal of Business Economics* 2.1 (2001): 188–226. As Winters puts it, "Although society is far more equal in Finland than in the United States when making broad Gini comparisons of large swaths of the population at the top and bottom, wealth is at least as concentrated in the hands of a fraction of the top 1% in Finland as in the United States, and perhaps more so" (Winters, *Oligarchy*, 279). In Sweden, not only is there a similar concentration of shareholding wealth, but in that country the top quintile owns 73% of wealth (as opposed to 84% in the US): see http://www.thefiscaltimes.com/Articles/2011/03/25/Wealth-Debate-How-Two-Economists-Stacked-the-Deck.aspx#page1 and http://blogs.reuters.com/felix-salmon/2011/03/25/swedish-inequality-datapoint-of-the-day/.

106. The overrepresentation of the wealthy in Nordic societies—i.e., plutocracy—can be seen in at least three different respects. First, ordinary citizens clearly *perceive* it to be the case that children's socioeconomic conditions have consequences for their opportunities in life. A recent survey found that only 15% of Swedes believe that coming from a wealthy family is "not important at all" for "getting ahead in life," with 46% believing that it is either essential, very important, or fairly important. Nearly identical results were found with regard to having well-educated parents, as 91% thought this would have at least some significance for career advancement. In Finland, a parallel survey produced similar results: 78% of Finns believe

that having wealthy parents has at least some relevance for getting ahead in life and 79% think that having well-educated parents does: Jonas Edlund and Stefan Svallfors, "ISSP 2009—Social Inequality IV: Sweden," Umeå University, Department of Sociology, 2009. Gothenburg, Sweden: Swedish National Data Service (SND), available online: http:// snd.gu.se/en/catalogue/study/577; Raimo Blom, Harri Melin, and Eero Tanskanen, "Social Inequality IV: Finnish Data," FSD2514 International Social Survey Programme, 2009, 14–15. Second, Nordic plutocracy is reflected in individual political behavior. In Sweden, for example, activism in civil society is correlated with socioeconomic status. Amnå finds that "socioeconomic background and particular social circumstances" impact the younger generation's associational life—and, specifically, that "the expected relative importance of SES is verified for all three modes of political participation: capacity to appeal (0.39), collective protesting (0.30), and voting in the last election (0.16)." More generally, Amnå reports, "From the standpoint of occupational status, disposable income, and education, the data reveal a general pattern in which upper-level, white-collar employees, the highly educated, and those with high incomes are overrepresented in associational life as a whole, while manual laborers, the poorly educated, and those with low incomes are underrepresented. This applies to associations concerned with politics, the environment, special interests, women's rights, housing, international solidarity, and lifestyles" (Erik Amnå, "Associations, Youth, and Political Capital Formation in Sweden: Historical Legacies and Contemporary Trends," in Lars Trägårdh, ed., *State and Civil Society in Northern Europe: The Swedish Model Reconsidered* (Oxford: Berghahn, 2007), 184–85, 171–72). Also see Douglas Baer, "Voluntary Association Involvement in Comparative Perspective," in Trägårdh, ed., *State and Civil Society in Northern Europe*, 98. Third, the plutocratic aspects of Nordic politics are arguably seen in tax policy, as it appears the power of wealth, grounded in the threat of capital flight, has made it so welfare programs are funded primarily through regressive, indirect taxation rather than more progressive wealth taxes. As Kenworthy's study concludes, "High-tax countries such as Sweden, Denmark, and Finland rely heavily on consumption taxes, the burden of which is shared broadly across the citizenry rather than concentrated on firms and affluent individuals" (Lane Kenworthy, "Tax Myths," *Contexts* 8.3 (2009): 28–32, 29). Somewhat similarly, Baramendi and Anderson, noting the much higher levels of wealth inequality as opposed to income inequality in Northern European countries, argue, "The gap between the distributions of income and wealth in Scandinavia is particularly interesting, as it seems to confirm recent accounts that redistribution in the most egalitarian societies is mostly a matter of conflict within labor rather than between capital and labor" (Beramendi and Anderson, "Inequality and Democratic Representation: The Road Traveled and the Path Ahead," 402).

107. Nora Mueller, Sandra Buchholz, and Hans-Peter Blossfeld, "Wealth Inequality in Europe and the Delusive Egalitarianism of Scandinavian Countries," MPRA Paper 35307 (University Library of Munich, Germany, 2011); Bengt Ericson, *Den Nya Överklassen: En Bok Om Sveriges Ekonomiska Elit* (Stockholm: Fischer & Co., 2010).

108. I agree, then, with Winters and Page when they write, "We believe that minority power is a fact of life in any complex society, with representative government changing the character and extent, but not the fact, of majority exclusion" ("Oligarchy in the United States?," 731).

109. Winters, *Oligarchy*, 285.

110. Verba, Nie, and Kim, *Participation and Political Equality*, 2, 307 (emphasis added).

111. By "inescapable," I mean not necessarily that all citizens in a liberal democracy will experience indignation, but the more minimal empirical prediction that some significant number always will as well as the normative point that those who do have a rational basis for doing so.

112. Consider, for example, such epithets as "fanatical multitude" (*fanatica multitudo*) (Tacitus, *Histories*, 2.61); "the crowd, prone to suspicion" (*vulgus, pronum ad suspiciones*) (Tacitus, *Histories*, 2.21); and "shameless or ignorant crowd" (*volgus impudens vel imprudens*) (Lucius Annaeus Seneca, "On the Shortness of Life," in *Moral Essays: Volume II*, trans. John W. Basore (Cambridge, MA: Harvard University Press, 1932), §1, 286).

113. Machiavelli, *Discourses*, I.7, 24. Also see Anthony J. Parel, *The Machiavellian Cosmos* (New Haven, CT: Yale University Press, 1992): 82–89.

114. As Kateb puts it, "I believe that though a human being can never forfeit his or her dignity . . . one assaults one's dignity when one is a party to serious injustice." George Kateb, *Human Dignity* (Cambridge, MA: Belknap Press of Harvard University Press, 2011), 13. Kateb also speaks to the automatic aspect of dignity: "Every human being is unique and individual [i.e., dignified] without having to try to be" (ibid., 12). The idea of equal, non-forfeitable, automatic human dignity has found perhaps its starkest expression in defenders of the dignity of patients without functioning mental faculties or consciousness.

115. Rosen recognizes how the contemporary conception of dignity obligates institutions more than individuals when he writes that, for some at least, dignity "gives a foundational reason for their having basic entitlements in relation to the actions of the state and fellow members of the human race (or, to put that mouthful in more simple terms: *human rights*)." Michael Rosen, *Dignity: Its History and Meaning* (Cambridge, MA: Harvard University Press, 2012), 6. And Rosen adds, "Dignity is central to modern human rights discourse, the closest that we have to an internationally accepted framework for the normative regulation of political life, and it is embedded in numerous constitutions, international conventions, and declarations" (ibid., 1–2).

116. For examples of the role of dignity within modern constitutions, consider, e.g., The Political Constitution of the United States of Mexico (1917), Article I: "All types of discrimination . . . which attack human dignity and have as an objective to destroy the rights and liberties of the people are forbidden"; Constitution of the Republic of Chile (1980), Article 1: "All men are born free and equal, in dignity and rights"; and Constitution of Peru (1993), Article 1: "The defense of the human person and respect for his dignity are the supreme purpose of society and the State." For the importance of dignity within conventions and declarations, see, e.g., United Nations Universal Declaration of Human Rights (1948), Article 1: "All human beings are born free and equal in dignity and rights. They are endowed with reason and conscience and should act toward one another in a spirit of brotherhood"; American Convention on Human Rights (1969): "Everyone has the right to have his honor respected and his dignity recognized"; African Charter on Human and Peoples' Rights (1981), Article 5: "Every individual shall have the right to the respect of the dignity inherent in a human being." Also see United Nations International Covenant on Civil and Political Rights (1966); UNESCO and Council of Europe, *Convention for the Protection of Human Rights and Dignity of the Human Being with Regard to the Application of Biology and Medicine* (1997).

117. See, e.g., Ronald Dworkin, *Justice for Hedgehogs* (Cambridge: Belknap Press of Harvard University Press, 2011); Dworkin, *Is Democracy Possible Here?*; Nussbaum, *Frontiers of Justice*, 17, 53, 174, 411, 179–95; Sen, *The Idea of Justice*, vii, 116; John Rawls, *A Theory of Justice*, 329, 586/289, 513 rev;. Cohen, *Rescuing Justice and Equality*, 80; Alan Gewirth, *Self-Fulfillment* (Princeton: Princeton University Press, 2009), 159–74.

118. See Jennifer Tolbert Roberts, *Athens on Trial: The Antidemocratic Tradition in Western Thought* (Princeton: Princeton University Press, 1994).

119. For the Romans, *dignitas* was a hierarchical notion, which some had and others lacked, based on the achievement of wealth, fame, and political success within a polity. Cicero, for example, refers to Marcus Attilus Regulus's "rank and *dignitas* as an ex-consul" (Cicero, *On Duties*, trans. Walter Miller (Cambridge, MA: Harvard University Press, 1913), III.99). And it was common to refer to one type of citizen as having more dignity than another, as in the view that the Senatorial order's *dignitas* was greater than that of the Equestrian order. See, e.g., Cicero, "Oration for His House," in *The Orations of Marcus Tullius Cicero*, trans. C. D. Yonge (London: George Bell and Sons, 1875), §74; Suetonius, *Life of Vespasian*, in *The Lives of the Caesars*, trans. J. C. Rolfe (Cambridge, MA: Harvard University Press, 1914), Vol. 2, §9.2. Likewise, Tacitus can refer to his own *dignitas* as something that "started, grew, and advanced." Tacitus, *Histories*, 1.1. Caesar's famous lines from his *Commentaries on the Civil War*—that he crossed the Rubicon in order to protect his *dignitas*, something he valued more than his life—was not at all the equal dignity to which all citizens were entitled, but a differentiated and hierarchical notion (Julius Caesar, *Civil Wars*, trans. A. G. Peskett (Cambridge, MA: Harvard University Press, 1914), I.9). Hobbes draws on the Roman notion of *dignitas* when he writes that the "public worth of a man, which is the value set on him by the commonwealth, is that which men commonly call 'dignity.' And this value of him by the commonwealth, is understood, by offices of command, judicature, public

employment; or by names and titles, introduced for distinction of such value" (Thomas Hobbes, *Leviathan*, ed. Richard Tuck (Cambridge: Cambridge University Press, 1991), Chapter 10, 63–64). Accordingly, Hobbes understands the fact that "men are continually in competition for honour and dignity" as a main source of human conflict (ibid., Chapter 17, 119), arguing that one of the principal functions of sovereign authority is to bestow dignity (ibid., Chapter 18, 126). Kateb, in my view, understates the hierarchical aspect of *dignitas* when he writes, "It would seem that, conceptually, human dignity was for a long time just a matter of stature, of humanity's superiority to all other beings on earth, although it was a superiority that only the few high and great ones proved or at least made vivid" (Kateb, *Human Dignity*, 8). It is not simply that in Rome only a few citizens had a full opportunity to have their "humanity" shine forth, but that what was being manifested in the expression of *dignitas* was less humanity than the differentiated *excellence* of the dignified individual.

120. The Declaration of the Rights of Man and of the Citizen does invoke the idea of dignity in Article VI, but in the pre-liberal-democratic sense of a limited number of "dignities" and offices for which all citizens are to have the right to compete: "Tous les Citoyens étant égaux à ses yeux sont également admissibles à toutes dignités, places et emplois publics, selon leur capacité, et sans autre distinction que celle de leurs vertus et de leurs talents." The absence of the contemporary conception of dignity in eighteenth-century documents such as this suggest what likely gave rise to the contemporary conception: the negative experience of the horrors of the twentieth century and the positive commitment to an egalitarianism exceeding the outlook of eighteenth-century founders who confined membership of their new republics on the basis of property, race, and gender.

121. Kateb, *Human Dignity*, ix.

122. Other models of dignity—which ground it not in the capacity for autonomy, but in life itself or the undeservedness of unequal status by birth—ought to be no less offended by the second-class civic experience instantiated by remove, manyness, and plutocracy.

123. But see Kateb, who refers to the "burdens of human dignity" (*Human Dignity*, 12).

124. Thus Cicero complains of democracy in *On the Commonwealth* that it allows "no degrees of status [*dignitas*]." Cicero, *On the Commonwealth*, in James E. G. Zetzel, ed., *On the Commonwealth* and *On the Laws* (Cambridge: Cambridge University Press, 1999), I.43. Also see Cicero, *On Duties*, I.38, I.42, I.45, I. 138–9, II.22, III.87. To be sure, there is some evidence in Cicero of one's capacity for justice and virtue generating *dignitas*—which would suggest that it is equally shared, at least in potential. See, e.g., Cicero, *Rhetorici Libri Duo Qui Vocantur De Inventione*, ed. Eduard Ströbel (Leipzig: Teubner, 1915), 2.160, 2.166.

125. Cicero, e.g., speaks about how his *dignitas* has been restored upon his return from exile in 57 BCE. Cicero, "In the Senate After His Return," in *The Orations of Marcus Tullius Cicero*, trans. C. D. Yonge (London: George Bell and Sons, 1875), §1.

126. Indeed, even if much of Kant's seminal account of dignity mirrors, if not inspires, the contemporary liberal-democratic conception as an automatic, inalienable human quality (in particular, Kant's notion of a universal dignity inhering in all individuals insofar as they rational beings, which requires respect in the form of a liberal legal order, or *Rechtstaat*), it is nonetheless the case that Kant, in a few passages at least, treats dignity as contingent on moral action, and so as something human beings forfeit when they fail to act morally. In the *Grundlegung*, for example, Kant argues that dignity is not simply the grounds of moral action, but contingent upon it: "The dignity of humanity consists just in its capacity to legislate universal law, though with the condition of humanity's being at the same time itself subject to this very same legislation." Immanuel Kant, *Grounding for the Metaphysics of Morals*, trans. James W. Ellington (Indianapolis: Hackett, 1993), 44 [440]. In the *Metaphysics of Morals*, Kant likewise claims that the "humanity in [a man's] person is the object of the respect which he can demand from every other human being, *but which he must also not forfeit.* . . ."—and, in a similar way, he writes, "By a lie a human being throws away and, as it were, annihilates his dignity as a human being." Kant, *Metaphysics of Morals*, trans. Mary Gregor (Cambridge: Cambridge University Press, 1996), 186–87 [435], 182 [429] (emphasis added). The implication from these passages is a model where dignity is

equal *in potentia*, but is conditional on our being moral and, to this degree, forfeitable and not automatic. Within the contemporary liberal-democratic paradigm of dignity, by contrast, individuals do not owe duties to themselves as a consequence of their dignity, but rather it is the state, legal order, and overall social system that are obliged to respect the inherent dignity of human beings.

Chapter 3

1. Sallust, *The War with Jugurtha*, in *The War with Catiline* and *The War with Jugurtha*, trans. J. C. Rolfe and revised by John T. Ramsey (Cambridge, MA: Harvard University Press, 2013), §30, 230–31.
2. Montesquieu, *Considerations on the Causes of the Greatness of the Romans and Their Decline*, trans. David Lowenthal (Indianapolis: Hackett, 1999), 83–85.
3. Friedrich Nietzsche, *On the Genealogy of Morals*, in *On the Genealogy of Morals* and *Ecce Homo*, trans. Walter Kaufmann (New York: Vintage, 1969), §1.4, 28. Also see Nietzsche, *Twilight of the Idols*, where, in his critique of Sainte-Beuve, Nietzsche writes, "In his fundamental instincts he is plebeian [*Plebejisch*] and next of kin to Rousseau's resentful spirit: consequently he is a Romanticist—for beneath all romanticism Rousseau's instinct for revenge grunts and frets" (*Twilight of the Idols*, in *Twilight of the Idols/The Anti-Christ*, trans. R. J. Hollingdale (London: Penguin, 1990), 79).
4. Friedrich Nietzsche, *Beyond Good and Evil: Prelude to a Philosophy of the Future*, trans. Walter Kaufmann (New York: Vintage, 1966), section §264, 214. I translate *Winkel-Neid* as "petty envy" rather than Kaufmann's more literal, but enigmatic, translation as "nook envy."
5. In rehabilitating a progressive conception of envy, I am inspired by earlier understandings of envy that differentiated between morally better and worse forms. Hesiod, for example, distinguishes two kinds of struggle—one leading to war and conflict, the other to work and industry. In elaborating this latter variant, Hesiod associates it with a benign form of envy (*phthonos*): "potter strives with potter and craftsman with craftsman, and beggar is envious [*phthoneei*] of beggar and singer of singer" (Hesiod, *Works and Days*, in *Theogony, Works and Days, Testimonia*, trans. Glenn W. Most (Cambridge, MA: Harvard University Press), lines 25–26, 88–89 (translation altered)). Hippias (*Anthologium* 3, 38, 32 = Hippias DK B 16) likewise claims there are two forms of envy (*phthonos*), with the morally superior variant involving the envy one feels at the unjust when they are wrongly honored. For these and other Greek distinctions among variations of envy, see Peter Walcot, *Envy and the Greeks: A Study of Human Behaviour* (Warminster, UK: Aris & Phillips, 1978), 12, passim. In the early modern period, Francis Bacon's essay "Of Envy" differentiates a normal, debased envy from a special kind of "public envy" about which "there is yet some good." Bacon writes, "For public envy is as an ostracism, that eclipseth men, when they grow too great. And therefore it is a bridle also to great ones, to keep them within bounds" (Bacon, "Of Envy," in *The Essays* (London: Penguin, 1985), 86).
6. J. S. Mill, *On Liberty and Other Essays*, ed. John Gray (Oxford: Oxford University Press, 1998), 87, 250; Alexis de Tocqueville, *Democracy in America*, trans. Harvey C. Mansfield and Delba Winthrop (Chicago: University of Chicago Press, 2000), 189, 479–82.
7. See Gonzalo Fernández de la Mora and Antonio De Nicolas, *Egalitarian Envy: The Political Foundations of Social Justice* (New York: Paragon House, 1987), 19–32; Joseph Epstein, *Envy* (Oxford: Oxford University Press, 2003), xi, 87.
8. Page and Jacobs, for example, have found that while Americans support policies that would institute equality of opportunity, "they oppose putting limits on how much people can earn and they do not envy or resent the rich" (Benjamin I. Page and Lawrence R. Jacobs, *Class War? What Americans Really Think About Politics* (Chicago: University of Chicago Press, 2009), 31; also see 14, 101). Also see Leslie McCall and Lane Kenworthy, "Americans' Social Policy Preferences in the Era of Rising Inequality," *Perspectives on Politics* 7.3 (2009): 459–84, 462; Jennifer L. Hochschild, *What's Fair: American Beliefs about Distributive Justice* (Cambridge, MA: Harvard University Press, 1981), 132, 218, 56, 14, 89, 211. On the role of envy-avoidance in contributing to support for rolling back estates taxes, see Michael J. Graetz and Ian Shapiro, *Death by a Thousand Cuts: The Fight over Taxing Inherited Wealth* (Princeton: Princeton University Press, 2006), 213.

9. Nietzsche, *Beyond Good and Evil*, §212, 138.

10. F. A. Hayek, *The Constitution of Liberty* (Chicago: University of Chicago Press, 1960), 93; David E. Cooper, "Equality and Envy," *Journal of Philosophy of Education* 16 (1982): 35–47; Robert Nozick, *Anarchy, State, and Utopia* (New York: Basic Books, 1974); Sigmund Freud, *Group Psychology and the Analysis of the Ego*, trans. James Strachey (New York: Liverwright, 1949); Nietzsche, *On the Genealogy of Morals*.

11. Richard Norman, "Equality, Envy, and the Sense of Justice," *Journal of Applied Philosophy* 19.1 (2002): 43–53; Robert Young, "Egalitarianism and Envy," *Philosophical Studies* 52 (1989): 261–76. Even theories affirming the ideal of comparative fairness do not ground themselves in, and often explicitly differentiate themselves from, an affirmation of envy. See, e.g., Larry S. Temkin, "Egalitarianism Defended," *Ethics* 113 (July 2003): 764–82, 768–69; John Broome, *Weighing Goods: Equality, Uncertainty, and Time* (Oxford: Basil Blackwell, 1995), 168–69.

12. See Jeffrey Edward Green, *The Eyes of the People: Democracy in an Age of Spectatorship* (Oxford: Oxford University Press, 2010), 7–29, 140–200.

13. See Sara Forsdyke, *Exile, Ostracism, and Democracy: The Politics of Expulsion in Ancient Greece* (Princeton: Princeton University Press, 2005); David J. Bederman, *The Classical Foundations of the American Constitution: Prevailing Wisdom* (Cambridge: Cambridge University Press, 2008), 195.

14. Athens is rightly conceived along with Rome as a plebeian republic because, even though more egalitarian than Rome, Athens still had its politics shaped by a basic division between the rich and the poor as well as at least a formal differentiation of citizens based on property classes. See Paul MacKendrick, *The Athenian Aristocracy: 399 to 31 B.C.* (Cambridge, MA: Harvard University Press, 1969); Mogens Herman Hansen, *The Athenian Democracy in the Age of Demosthenes: Structure, Principles, and Ideology* (Oxford: Oxford University Press, 1991), 109–10; Josiah Ober, *Mass and Elite in Democratic Athens: Rhetoric, Ideology, and the Power of the People* (Princeton: Princeton University Press, 1989), 117–18.

15. Hansen, *The Athenian Democracy*, 110–12; Ober, *Mass and Elite in Democratic Athens*, 199.

16. Because they were obligations restricted to the rich, part of the enforcement of the liturgies required identifying just who the wealthiest citizens were. Through the institution of antidosis, or "exchange," if a citizen did not want to pay for the liturgy to which he was called because he thought some other citizen was richer than he, he could bring a legal action against that citizen who would then have three choices: to pay the liturgy instead; if he claimed to be poorer, to exchange all of his property with the accusing citizen and then pay the liturgy; or to have the matter of who was richer settled by a court. As MacDowell explains, "If the man challenged chose the second alternative, to exchange property, each of them swore an oath . . . and within three days had to produce an inventory of his own possessions, showing debts and liabilities as well as assets. Each could also, if he wished, go with witnesses to the other's house or estate to observe what was there and seal the doors of the barns or store-rooms, to check that his opponent not remove anything surreptitiously" (Douglass A. MacDowell, *The Law in Classical Athens* (Ithaca, NY: Cornell University Press, 1978), 162). Also see Matthew Christ, "Liturgy Avoidance and Antidosis in Classical Athens," *Transactions of the American Philological Association* 120 (1990): 147–69. This procedure exemplifies the general plebeian principle that popular empowerment should involve the imposition of burdens on the most advantaged, as the obvious effect of the antidosis was to compel the wealthy to themselves determine (with all the concomitant costs in time, effort, and risk) who among them was the richest.

17. Hansen, *The Athenian Democracy*, 112–15; Ober, *Mass and Elite in Democratic Athens*, 28, 199–200.

18. See, e.g., Paul Veyne, *Bread and Circuses: Historical Sociology and Political Pluralism*, ed. Oswyn Murray and trans. Brian Pearce (London: Penguin, 1990), 118–20; also see Ober, *Mass and Elite in Democratic Athens*, 232.

19. Fergus Millar, *The Crowd in Rome in the Late Republic* (Ann Arbor: University of Michigan, 1998), 73–94, passim; Veyne, *Bread and Circuses*, 201–345; Andrew Lintott, *The Constitution of the Roman Republic* (Oxford: Oxford University, 1999), 94–121.

20. On the idea of this form of compensation in the Hellenistic and Roman contexts, see Veyne, *Bread and Circuses*, 93, 118.

21. On the Athenian *euthunoi* (public audits of magistrates upon leaving office), see Ober, *Mass and Elite in Democratic Athens,* 230, 267, 329; Hansen, *The Athenian Democracy,* 222–24. For the Spartan use of the audit, see Bederman, *Classical Foundations of the American Constitution,* 63. In the Roman context, for the *lex repetundarum,* which mandated audits of higher magistrates by judges from the relatively lower-class Equestrian order, see M. H. Crawford, ed., *Roman Statutes,* (London: Institute of Classical Studies, University of London, 1996), Vol. 1, 65; Bederman, *Classical Foundations of the American Constitution,* 195. On the audit of dictators, see ibid., 146–47.

22. On the Greek practice of *thorubos* (shouting down elite speakers), see Judith Tacon, "Ecclesiastic *Thorubos*: Interventions, Interruptions, and Popular Involvement in the Athenian Assembly," *Greece & Rome* 48.2 (2001): 173–92; Josiah Ober, *The Athenian Revolution: Essays on Ancient Greek Democracy and Political Theory* (Princeton: Princeton University Press, 1996), 18–31. On the Roman *contio* (an informal public meeting) as a "hierarchical communication situation" limited to elite speakers but one where such elites were exposed to critique from rivals as well as the interruptions of the crowd, see Robert Morstein-Marx, *Mass Oratory and Political Power* (Cambridge: Cambridge University Press, 2004), 4, 9, 119, 127–28, 132, 165, 170–71; also see Lily Ross Taylor, *Roman Voting Assemblies from the Hannibalic War to the Dictatorship of Caesar* (Ann Arbor: University of Michigan Press, 1996), Chapter 2; Karl-J. Hölkeskamp, "Conquest, Competition and Consensus: Roman Expansion in Italy and the Rise of the Nobilitas," *Historia* 42 (1993): 12–39, 26–30; Henrik Mouritsen, *Plebs and Politics in the Late Roman Republic* (Cambridge: Cambridge University Press, 2001), 38–62; Peter O'Neill, "Going Round in Circles: Popular Speech in Ancient Rome," *Classical Antiquity* 22.1 (2003): 135–76, 147.

23. Millar, *The Crowd in Rome,* 14. As Millar explains, there is scholarly disagreement about the precise functioning of these trials. See A. H. M. Jones, *The Criminal Courts of the Roman Republic and Principate* (Oxford: Blackwell, 1992), Chapter 1, "*Iudicia Populi.*" In a sense, an analogous situation existed in Athens whenever prominent citizens would contest each other in trials before the assembled people. See Richard A. Bauman, *Political Trials in Ancient Greece* (London: Routledge, 1990).

24. John Rawls, "Distributive Justice" [1967], in Samuel Freeman, ed., *John Rawls: Collected Papers* [hereafter in this chapter "CP"] (Cambridge: Harvard University Press, 1999), 134–40; Rawls, "Distributive Justice: Some Addenda" [1968] in CP, 163; Rawls, *A Theory of Justice* [hereafter in this chapter "T"] (Cambridge: Belknap Press of Harvard University Press, 1971); Rawls, *A Theory of Justice: Revised Edition* [hereafter in this chapter "rev"] (Cambridge, MA: Belknap Press of Harvard University Press, 1999).

25. Chris Wyatt, *The Difference Principle Beyond Rawls* (New York: Continuum, 2012); Joshua Cohen, *The Arc of the Moral Universe and Other Essays* (Cambridge, MA: Harvard University Press, 2010), 99–128; Thomas Pogge, *John Rawls: His Life and Theory of Justice* (Oxford: Oxford University Press, 2007), 272–73.

26. Rawls, *Justice as Fairness: A Restatement* [hereafter in this chapter "R"] (Cambridge: Belknap Press of Harvard University Press, 2001), 120.

27. Even if Dworkin defends a theory of justice in which individuals' resources are to stem from morally deserved sources like their free choices rather than morally arbitrary sources such as luck, his proposed hypothetical insurance market that is to realize this vision is more concerned with the undeserved disadvantages of the unfortunate than with the undeserved advantages of the fortunate. Dworkin's scheme is designed primarily to compensate those who are low skilled, unemployed, disabled, or otherwise unable to secure a reasonable standard of living. It does not aim to neutralize the luck of investment income and other forms of "option luck." And it insists on an *ex ante* approach to equality (which aims to distribute the costs of insuring against possible risks) over an *ex post* approach (which aims to neutralize undeserved distributions after they have occurred). Furthermore, Dworkin calls into question the very notion of the most advantaged, by suggesting that those who doggedly pursue and obtain wealth suffer from an absurd conception of the good. Finally, despite its ideal of making all inequalities the result of ambition and choice rather than endowment and luck, Dworkin's plan recognizes, *and accepts without problem,* that the relatively talented and lucky will continue to have more than the untalented and unlucky. Ronald Dworkin, *Is Democracy Possible Here? Principles for a*

New Political Debate (Princeton: Princeton University Press, 2006), 108; *Sovereign Virtue: The Theory and Practice of Equality* (Cambridge, MA: Harvard University Press, 2002), 104–107.

28. Ackerman and Alstott propose giving each citizen $80,000, funded by a tax on the wealthiest 41% of the country, in order to supply all members of society with the resources to be effective democratic citizens, not to identify or regulate the most advantaged as such. Bruce Ackerman and Anne Alstott, *The Stakeholder Society* (New Haven, CT: Yale University Press, 2000).

29. Nussbaum, for example, lists ten essential human capabilities—including "bodily health"; "bodily integrity"; the ability "to imagine, to think, and to reason"; the capacity to form a conception of the good; and "play"—meant to describe the minimum conditions for "a life worthy of human dignity." Martha C. Nussbaum, *Frontiers of Justice: Disability, Nationality, Species Membership* (Cambridge, MA: Harvard University Press, 2006), 76–78.

30. Arneson, for example, defends a prioritarian version of luck egalitarianism which holds that "justice requires us to maximize a function of human well-being that gives priority to improving the well-being of those who are badly off and those who, if badly off, are not substantially responsible for their condition in virtue of their prior conduct" (Richard Arneson, "Luck Egalitarianism and Prioritarianism," *Ethics* 110 (2000): 339–49, 340). Cohen, however, does present a version of luck egalitarianism more directed against unjust advantages and my argument here is in the spirit of his liberal egalitarianism. See, e.g., G. A. Cohen, *Rescuing Justice and Equality* (Cambridge, MA: Harvard University Press, 2008).

31. Kenneth Scheve and David Stasavage, "Democracy, War and Wealth: Lessons from Two Centuries of Inheritance Taxation," *American Political Science Review* 106.1 (2012): 81–102; David Duff, "Abolition of Wealth Transfer Taxes: Lessons from Canada, Australia, and New Zealand," *Pittsburgh Tax Review* 3 (2005): 71–120.

32. See Graetz and Shapiro, *Death by a Thousand Cuts: The Fight Over Taxing Inherited Wealth,* especially 4–5, 266–67.

33. Consider, for example, the top income tax brackets for the following countries in 2015: Canada ($138,586), UK (£150,000), Australia ($180,000), and the United States ($413,200).

34. See Jacob S. Hacker and Paul Pierson, *Winner-Take-All Politics: How Washington Made the Rich Richer—and Turned Its Back on the Middle Class* (New York: Simon and Schuster, 2010); Steve Fraser and Gary Gerstle, eds., *Ruling America: A History of Wealth and Power in a Democracy* (Cambridge, MA: Harvard University Press, 2005); Paul Krugman, *The Great Unraveling: Losing Our Way in the New Century* (New York: Norton, 2003). Kevin Phillips, *Wealth and Democracy: A Political History of the American Rich* (New York: Broadway Books, 2002). Of course much depends on specific cases. See, e.g., Lupu and Pontusson's finding (2011) that the allegiance of middle-income voters is affected by the *structure of inequality*: they are more likely to ally with the poor and support redistribution when the distance between the middle and the poor is smaller relative to the distance between the middle and the rich. Noam Lupu and Jonas Pontusson, "The Structure of Inequality and the Politics of Distribution," *American Political Science Review* 105.2 (2011): 316–36.

35. In the United States, for example, much evidence points to the disproportionate political advantage of the very wealthy. See Jeffrey A. Winters and Benjamin I. Page, "Oligarchy in the United States?" *Perspectives on Politics* 7 (2009): 731–51; Larry M. Bartels, *Unequal Democracy: The Political Economy of the New Gilded Age* (Princeton: Princeton University Press, 2008); Lawrence Jacobs and Theda Skocpol, eds., *Inequality and American Democracy: What We Know and What We Need to Learn* (New York: Russell Sage Foundation, 2005); Martin Gilens, *Affluence and Influence: Economic Inequality and Political Power in America* (Princeton: Princeton University Press, 2012); Martin Gilens and Benjamin I. Page, "Testing Theories of American Politics: Elites, Interest Groups, and Average Citizens," *Perspectives on Politics* 12.3 (2014): 564–81.

36. See, e.g., Matthew Scherer, "Saint John: The Miracle of Secular Reason," in Hent de Vries and Lawrence E. Sullivan, eds., *Political Theologies: Public Religions in a Post-Secular World* (New York: Fordham University Press, 2006).

37. In a reflection on his pedagogy, Rawls says he followed Kant's view, as articulated in *The Critique of Pure Reason* B866: "We cannot learn philosophy; for where is it, who is in possession of it, and how shall we recognize it? We can only learn to philosophize, that is, to exercise the talent of reason, in accordance with its universal principles, on certain actually

existing attempts at philosophy, always, however, reserving the right of reason to investigate, to confirm, or to reject these principles in their very sources." Rawls, *Lectures on the History of Moral Philosophy*, Barbara Herman, ed. (Cambridge, MA: Harvard University Press, 2000), xvii. Rawls's *Theory of Justice* can be seen as a critical appropriation of the social contract tradition, particularly Kantian deontology and Rousseau's notion of the general will, to model the modern requirements of justice. Cohen reports, "Rawls . . . once said . . . that his two principles of justice could be understood as an effort to spell out the content of [Rousseau's idea of] the general will." Joshua Cohen, *Rousseau: A Free Community of Equals* (Oxford: Oxford University Press, 2010), 2.

38. John Rawls, *Political Liberalism* [hereafter in this chapter "PL"] (New York: Columbia University Press, 1996), xlviii–xlix.

39. For example, Dworkin pursues an alternative liberal vision in part "through an analysis of John Rawls's powerful and influential theory of justice" (Dworkin, *Taking Rights Seriously* (Cambridge: Harvard University Press, 1977), xii). Nozick's seminal statement of libertarian political philosophy devotes more than fifty pages to Rawls's *Theory of Justice*, claiming, "Political philosophers now must either work within Rawls' theory or explain why not." Nozick, *Anarchy, State, and Utopia*, 183. G. A. Cohen, one of Rawls's most strident critics in recent years, working from a luck-egalitarian perspective, begins his critique of Rawls with remarkable praise: "At most two books in the history of Western political philosophy have a claim to be regarded as greater than *A Theory of Justice*: Plato's *Republic* and Hobbes's *Leviathan*." Cohen, *Rescuing Justice and Equality*, 11.

40. If Rawls does briefly refer to the contrast between the "most favored" and "least advantaged" (T, 76/66 rev) and also, in explicating notions like "chain connection" and "close-knitness," to a three-way contrast between the "most favored," "least favored," and someone in-between (T, 81-3/70-3 rev), much more common are contrasts not invoking the most favored: "more advantaged" versus "least advantaged" (T, 157/136 rev; R, 124; "Distributive Justice," 138; "Distributive Justice: Some Addenda," 169, 170; "A Kantian Conception of Equality" [1975], in CP, 263) or "more advantaged" versus "less advantaged" (R, 62, 123–30). Now it is true that Rawls does discuss something like the superrich in confronting a hypothetical situation in which close-knitness does not apply (i.e., when it might happen that altering the prospects of the more advantaged has no effect on the least advantaged). Rawls clarifies that the difference principle, here, should be seen as "the lexical difference principle," which holds, "In a basic structure with n relevant representatives, first maximize the welfare of the worst-off representative man; second, for equal welfare of the worst-off representative, maximize the welfare of the second worst-off representative man, and so on until the last case which is, for equal welfare of all the preceding n–1 representatives, maximize the welfare of the *best-off representative man*" (emphasis added). Yet, if this is a circumstance in which Rawls does appeal to the "best off," it is also one where he marginalizes the very category, as Rawls immediately adds that he "shall always use the difference principle in the simpler form" (T, 83/72 rev), i.e., not in a form that might require explicit and direct attention to the most favored, in part because he believes "in actual cases [the lexical difference principle] is unlikely to be relevant" (T, 72 rev).

41. Rawls, "Constitutional Liberty and the Concept of Justice" [1963], in CP, 88–89.

42. Rawls, "Justice as Fairness" [1958], in CP, 48, 50; "Constitutional Liberty and the Concept of Justice," 75, 76; "The Sense of Justice" [1963], in CP, 98.

43. Rawls, "Distributive Justice," 138.

44. Also see Rawls, "Distributive Justice," 134–40; "Distributive Justice: Some Addenda," 154.

45. Rawls, "Distributive Justice: Some Addenda," 163. Also see "Distributive Justice," 134–40; "A Kantian Conception of Equality," 263; T, passim; PL, 6, 261, 271; R, 42–43, 59, 65, 99–100. Rawls also sometimes describes the difference principle in terms of the *less* favored, especially in simplified hypothetical cases involving only two representative positions (R, 62, 123–13), but this ought not be seen as challenging the primacy, for Rawls, of the least favored as the class whose prospects ideally are to be maximized. For passages where Rawls uses the *less* and *least* advantaged interchangeably, see T, 75, 104–5, 536/65, 89, 470 rev. Also, see T, 98 (not in the rev), where Rawls defines the less advantaged as synonymous with the least

advantaged: "Surely this gap . . . the social distance between those who have least and the average citizen . . . is an essential feature of the less favored members of society."

46. See note 45.

47. Rawls explains, "There is a significant distinction between the cases that fall short of the best arrangement. A society should try to avoid the region where the marginal contributions of those better off are negative since, other things equal, this seems a greater fault than falling short of the best scheme when these contributions are positive" (T, 79/68-9 rev).

48. For examples of this differential in calibration (e.g., Rawls's tendency to compare the prospects of the *more* advantaged with those of the *least* advantaged), see: T, 157/136 rev; R, 124; "Distributive Justice," 138; "Distributive Justice: Some Addenda," 169, 170; "A Kantian Conception of Equality," 263. Rawls appears to acknowledge this differential when he explains that in applying the difference principle, "It is unnecessary to define weights for the more favored positions in any detail" (T, 94/80 rev).

49. Figure 3.1, which is from R, 62, demonstrates the first of these formulations (also see R, 123-130; "A Kantian Conception of Equality," 263–64), while the latter formulation occurs in "Distributive Justice," 138; "Distributive Justice: Some Addenda," 169, 170; T, 157/136 rev; "A Kantian Conception of Equality," 263; R, 124.

50. Typical is the following statement: "The crucial point is that the difference principle can be regarded as an agreement to consider the distribution of natural assets as common property and *to share in the benefits* of this distribution whatever it turns out to be. Those who have been favored by nature . . . *may gain from their good fortune only on terms that improve the situation* of those who have done less well. . . . One is led to the difference principle if one wishes to frame the social system so that no person gains or loses from his arbitrary place in the distribution of natural endowments or from his *initial position* in society without going on to receive *compensating benefits* in return" (Rawls, "Distributive Justice: Some Addenda," 165, emphasis added). Also see Rawls, "Justice as Fairness," 50; "Constitutional Liberty and the Concept of Justice," 82; "Justice as Reciprocity" [1971], in CP, 203; "A Kantian Conception of Equality," 262; T, 131 rev.

51. The difference principle is marginalized in the sense that it is lexically posterior to the provision of equal basic liberties and fair equality of opportunity. Further, due to the inevitable uncertainty and controversy Rawls thinks will surround its precise requirements, the difference principle is not to be written into a polity's constitution; rather, particular legislatures, guided by the difference principle, will give it provisional shape (R, 47–8). For the same reason, Rawls also thinks the difference principle is not properly considered an object of civil disobedience, which instead should be limited to severe, and so *clear*, violations of the provision of equal basic liberties as well as fair equality of opportunity. Rawls, "The Justification of Civil Disobedience" [1969], in CP, 184.

52. Rawls, "The Justification of Civil Disobedience," 184; also see 185; R, 48.

53. Rawls himself anticipates this threat of elite manipulation. See R, 125.

54. The third of these extends Rawls's own reasoning: just as Rawls informally assumes "chain-connection" whereby the maximization of the prospects of the least favored is presumed to raise the prospects of everyone else (T, 80–81/69–71 rev), so can we make a parallel assumption that a society in which the most advantaged are not benefitting unfairly is likely, or more likely, to be one where other advantaged classes are not either.

55. Rawls, "The Justification of Civil Disobedience," 184.

56. The critique most frequently leveled against contemporary liberal-democratic societies is not that they do not permit sufficient inequalities to enable productive gains, nor that the least advantaged have not gained at all in absolute terms from the economic and political system generating inequalities, but that these productive gains have not been fairly distributed: that the less advantaged would be better off if the underlying system of inequalities were less unequal. See Hacker and Pierson, *Winner-Take-All Politics*; Bartels, *Unequal Democracy*; Krugman, *The Great Unraveling*.

57. Rawls, "Justice as Fairness," 52–53; "The Sense of Justice," 77, 89; "Distributive Justice," 140, 141; "Distributive Justice: Some Addenda," 161; T, 73/63 rev; R, 44, 161. In an important footnote to *Justice as Fairness: A Restatement*, Rawls emphasizes that the two principles of political and educational opportunity, even if they do not look to allocate specific shares in a

predetermined manner, are very much concerned with relative distributions and the problem of *excessive inequalities*: "It is sometimes objected to the difference principle as a principle of distributive justice that it contains no restrictions on the overall nature of permissible distributions. It is concerned, the objection runs, solely with the least advantaged. But this objection is incorrect: it overlooks the fact that the parts of the two principles of justice are designed to work in tandem and apply as a unit. *The requirements of the prior principles have important distributive effects.* Consider the effects of fair value equality of opportunity as applied to education, say, or the distributive effects of the fair value of political liberties. We cannot possibly take the difference principle seriously so long as we think of it by itself, apart from its setting within prior principles" (R, 46n, emphasis added). Since, as I argue in the following subsection (as well as in Section 2.5 of the previous chapter), these liberties are not fully realizable, what is undermined by excessive accumulations is the amount of these liberties that can be realized.

58. Samuel Freeman, *Rawls* (London: Routledge, 2007), 131, 132–33; see T, 277–8/245–6 rev; R, 51, 159.

59. Rawls, "Distributive Justice," 143. While Rawls makes it clear that a well-ordered property-owning democracy will not permit "very large inequalities . . . so that the control of the economy and much of political life rests in a few hands" (R, 138)—and while he argues that campaign finance legislation is one key component of this effort (PL, 356-363)—Freeman (*Rawls*, 90) is correct, I think, when he argues that Rawls's account of what constitutes excessive accumulations "is left quite vague."

60. Although Rawls does advocate intervention in the economy to combat excessive inequalities undermining fair equality of opportunity with regard to education and politics (e.g., the regulation of inheritances), the figure of the most advantaged remains almost entirely absent in his philosophy. Dworkin, though potentially supportive of steeply progressive taxation, also provides scant attention to the most favored, arguing that various campaign finance reforms and a robust social insurance system will counteract a great deal of the negative effects of excessive inequalities (*Sovereign Virtue*, 199, 351–85; *Is Democracy Possible Here?*, 150–54).

61. On this threat see John P. McCormick, "Contain the Wealthy and Patrol the Magistrates: Restoring Elite Accountability to Popular Government," *American Political Science Review* 100.2 (2006), 147; Peter R. Baehr, *Caesar and the Fading of the Roman World: A Study in Republicanism and Caesarism* (New Brunswick, NJ: Transaction Press, 1997); Lauro Martines, *Power and Imagination: City-States in Renaissance Italy* (New York: Alfred Knopf, 1979); Anthony Molho, Kurt Raaflaub, and Julia Emlen, eds., *City-States in Classical Antiquity and Medieval Italy* (Ann Arbor: University of Michigan Press, 1991), 251–354.

62. Martines, *Power and Imagination*, 34–62; McCormick, "Contain the Wealthy and Patrol the Magistrates"; Niccolò Machiavelli, *Discourses on Livy*, trans. Harvey C. Mansfield and Nathan Tarcov (Chicago: University of Chicago Press, 1996), I.3.

63. John Adams, *Discourses on Davila*, in Charles Francis Adams, ed., *The Works of John Adams, Second President of the United Statest* (Boston: Little, Brown, 1851 [1790]), Vol. 6, 280.

64. William Manning, *The Key of Liberty: The Life and Democratic Writings of William Manning "A Laborer," 1747–1814*, eds. Michael Merrill and Sean Wilenz (Cambridge, MA: Harvard University Press, 1993), 143, 153; on Manning's appeal to Roman plebeian structures, see 127, 163.

65. McCormick, *Machiavellian Democracy*, 170–78.

66. Manning, for instance, attributes to the Few nothing less than the desire to realize "schemes to destroy free government" (*The Key of Liberty*, 138). McCormick argues that in a democracy or popular republic the threat posed by the wealthy is hardly neutralized but in some sense only aggravated: "The widespread freedom that republics afford *all* social actors, not just average people, invariably enables some citizens to amass greater material resources than others; moreover, political necessity *always* permits public officials within every regime type, even democracies, considerable prerogative in the exercise of their duties. As a result of these two facts, republics, democracies, and popular governments have eternally suffered attempts by wealthy citizens to manipulate politics to their own benefit. . . . Thus, the common citizens of regimes characterized by the very highest levels of political freedom and socioeconomic equality must always confront the political influence of those who possess greater resources

and the political power of those who actually hold office" (McCormick, *Machiavellian Democracy*, 15).

67. See, e.g., Rawls, "Justice as Fairness," 52–53; "Constitutional Liberty and the Concept of Justice," 77, 89; "Distributive Justice," 140, 141; "Distributive Justice: Some Addenda," 161; T, 73, 277–8/63, 245–6 rev; R, 44, 51, 159, 161. Also see Dworkin, *Sovereign Virtue*, 195, 203, 385; *Is Democracy Possible Here?*, 128; and Samuel Freeman, *Justice and the Social Contract* (Oxford: Oxford University Press, 2007), 131, 132–33.

68. As some of the historical examples indicate, such policing and regulating need not mean curtailing wealth but perhaps other measures: e.g., excluding the very wealthy from certain offices, making them subject to special audits, or perhaps restricting what money can buy. On this last form of regulation, see Michael J. Sandel, *What Money Can't Buy: The Moral Limits of Markets* (New York: Farrar, Straus and Giroux, 2012).

69. On the disadvantage of the least favored with regard to the natural and social lotteries, see Rawls, "A Kantian Conception of Equality," 258–59.

70. On two different senses of compensation in Rawls, see Freeman, *Justice and the Social Contract*, 118.

71. Rawls, "A Kantian Conception of Equality," 263–64.

72. I cannot accept that Rawls's claim that his account of justice would mitigate some of the effects of the social and natural lotteries is a mere "informal argument" intended only to refute libertarianism (Samuel Scheffler, "What Is Egalitarianism?," *Philosophy & Public Affairs* 31.1 (2003): 5–39, 9). While it is true that when Rawls invokes luck mitigation in section 12 of *A Theory of Justice* he observes that his discussion here is not "strictly speaking" a grounds for the difference principle (T, 75/65 rev), his appeal to luck mitigation occurs in numerous other contexts without this caveat: see, e.g., Rawls, "Distributive Justice," 140; "Distributive Justice: Some Addenda," 161–62; "A Kantian Conception of Equality," 263–64; T, 96, 101, 123/82, 87, 106–107 rev. Moreover, critics who argue that Rawls was no luck egalitarian, that he did not aim to altogether *neutralize* morally arbitrary factors, still recognize that he sought to *mitigate* these factors, at least in the context of combating gross inequality (see, e.g., Freeman, *Justice and the Social Contract*, 117).

73. Rawls speaks to the subtlety of his approach—his support of a partial, but not full, commitment to luck mitigation—when he acknowledges, "Although the difference principle is not the same as that of redress, it does achieve some of the intent of the latter principle" (T, 101/87 rev; also see T, 100/86 rev; "Distributive Justice: Some Addenda,"155).

74. On this last, see Rawls, "Justice as Fairness," 48; "Distributive Justice," 152; "Distributive Justice: Some Addenda," 170.

75. To avoid misunderstanding, two points of clarification should be made. First, as I elaborate in the final part of Section 3.3, redress ought not be imposed when doing so *clearly* makes the rest of society worse off—though where there is uncertainty about this, there is room for redress. Second, while my argument does not specify precisely what kinds of policies ought to define redress, it is helpful to envision redress as involving, not mere tax payments, but direct financing of public goods like schools, infrastructure, and public monuments—similar to the burdens placed on economic elites in ancient popular republics like Athens and Rome. See Hansen, *The Athenian Democracy*, 110–15; Ober, *Mass and Elite in Democratic Athens*, 199–234; Millar, *The Crowd in Rome*, 73–94; Lintott, *The Constitution of the Roman Republic*, 94–121. As a public acknowledgment of a liberal-democratic society's failure to realize fully its own principles, redress needs to be more than merely a cost placed on the most advantaged, but a *public* burden which the rest of society might witness—and so also perhaps a kind of quasi-honor in the manner of a legalized and compulsory *noblesse oblige*.

76. See, e.g., T, 73/63 rev: "Those who are at the same level of talent and ability, and who have the same willingness to use them, should have the same prospects of success regardless of their initial place in the social system. . . . In all sectors of society there should be roughly equal prospects of culture and achievement for everyone similarly motivated and endowed. The expectations of those with the same abilities and aspirations should not be affected by their social class." Also see T, 93/80 rev; R, 44; "Distributive Justice," 143. Thus, even if Rawls very occasionally acknowledges (e.g., "Distributive Justice: Some Addenda," 162; T, 74/64 rev) that fair equality of opportunity cannot be fully realized within his system, he elsewhere— and, indeed, much more often—suggests the full realization of fair equality of opportunity

as a condition of a just society. I detail Rawls's inconsistency in this regard in Chapter 2 (Section 2.5).

77. The family is clearly one key cause of this unfair distortion of expectations; relatedly, much social scientific research demonstrates how the class structure into which a child is born is a strong predictive factor of the economic and social opportunities experienced as an adult. See Peter Sacks, *Tearing Down the Gates: Confronting the Class Divide in American Education* (Berkeley: University of California Press, 2007); Samuel Bowles, Herbert Gintis, and Melissa Osborne Groves, *Unequal Chances: Family Background and Economic Success* (Princeton: Princeton University Press, 2005).

78. On the importance of parents' educational attainment to children's life prospects in relatively egalitarian Australia, see Bill Martin and Judy Wajcman, "Understanding Class Inequality in Australia," in Fiona Devine and Mary Waters, eds., *Social Inequalities in Comparative Perspective* (Malden, MA: Blackwell, 2004): 163–90, 177–79. In Sweden, a recent study found that 84% of Swedes think having wealthy parents is at least somewhat relevant to "getting ahead in life," and 90% believe that having well-educated parents is. Using the same survey questions, a Finnish study found that 78% of Finns believe coming from a wealthy family has at least some significance for career advancement, and 79% think that having well-educated parents does (Jonas Edlund and Stefan Svallfors, "ISSP 2009—Social Inequality IV: Sweden," Umeå University, Department of Sociology, 2009. Gothenburg, Sweden: Swedish National Data Service (SND), available online: http://snd.gu.se/en/catalogue/study/577; Raimo Blom, Harri Melin, and Eero Tanskanen. "Social Inequality IV: Finnish Data," FSD2514 International Social Survey Programme, 2009, 14–15).

79. Nozick, *Anarchy, State, and Utopia,* 167.

80. Freeman, *Rawls,* 98 (emphasis added).

81. See note 76.

82. Rawls, "Justice as Fairness," 50; "Constitutional Liberty and the Concept of Justice," 75; "Justice as Reciprocity," 195.

83. See Chapter 2 (Section 2.5) for a detailed explanation of this phenomenon.

84. It is important to remember that the plebeian idea of redress has two different applications: not just redress against the most advantaged *economic* class (i.e., the superrich) which I am examining here, but also redress against the most advantaged *political* class (i.e., political leaders) which I defended in my earlier work in conjunction with its call for subjecting politicians and other high officials to contested forms of publicity. See Green, *The Eyes of the People,* 17, 23, 137–39, 198, 203.

85. On Rawls's ambivalence regarding the permissibility of reducing inequalities when doing so would only have a neutral material impact on the least favored, see Philippe Van Parijs, "Difference Principles," in Samuel Freeman, ed., *The Cambridge Companion to Rawls* (Cambridge: Cambridge University Press, 2003). Against Van Parijs's opposite recommendation (ibid., 232), the plebeian idea of redress I am defending here would be a reason for resolving this ambivalence in an egalitarian direction, at least as it pertains to the most favored class.

86. On fair equality of opportunity as a widely endorsed principle, see McCall and Kenworthy, "Americans' Social Policy Preferences in the Era of Rising Inequality"; Page and Jacobs, *Class War?*; Martin Gilens, *Why Americans Hate Welfare* (Chicago: University of Chicago Press, 2000); Hochschild, *What's Fair?*; Eliot R. Smith and James Kluegel, *Beliefs About Inequality: Americans' Views of What Is and What Ought to Be* (New York: A. de Gruyter, 1986). For Rawls's own seeming endorsement of the full realization of fair equality of opportunity as a condition of a just society, see note 76.

87. To be sure, Rawls's system of justice—which makes the provision of basic liberties and fair equality of opportunity lexically prior to the difference principle—already contemplates situations where the pursuit of social justice sometimes will mean the sacrifice of economic gains for all. But if the prior principles of justice require policies that sometimes leave society materially worse off (e.g., freedom of speech is still to be maintained even if it were shown that limiting it would lead to economic gains for all), I understand the costs at stake in envy (both in its irrational and reasonable forms) as directly economic (not the indirect consequences of securing prior rights) and directly targeted against the better off (not something distributed indiscriminately among wide segments of the society, rich and poor alike) (see T, 532, 535-6/

466, 469 rev). Thus, even if the protective limiting of excessive inequalities has as its purpose the securing of political and educational liberties, because it imposes direct economic costs uniquely on the most advantaged it should be seen as an instance of (reasonable) envy.

88. I explain in the discussion that follows why this bias might be considered collectively disadvantageous, economically speaking, over the long term.

89. Rawls's explicit definitions of envy (T, 144, 532, 533, 535–6/124, 466, 467, 469 rev) limit it to situations in which the imposition of costs on the advantaged has a *negative* impact on the rest of society, rather than also a *neutral* one. But insofar as Rawls is ambivalent about the latter circumstance—sometimes appearing to treat it too as irrational (see T, 82–3/72 rev; also see Van Parijs, "Difference Principles")—and insofar as others have treated the latter explicitly as envy (e.g., Nozick, *Anarchy, State, and Utopia*, 239), I consider both phenomena under the heading of envy.

90. The revised edition does not include this phrase, but Rawls elsewhere invokes the same idea of the irrationality of envy as something "collectively disadvantageous" (T, 144, 532/124, 466 rev), writing, "Envy tends to make everyone worse off" (T, 144/124 rev) and, as such, "tends to harm both its object and its subject" (T, 533/467 rev).

91. See, e.g., Robert S. Taylor, *Reconstructing Rawls: The Kantian Foundations of Justice as Fairness* (University Park: Penn State Press, 2011); Paul Voice, *Rawls Explained: From Fairness to Utopia* (Chicago: Open Court, 2011); Percy B. Lehning, *John Rawls: An Introduction* (Cambridge: Cambridge University Press, 2009); Pogge, *John Rawls*.

92. See, e.g., Freeman, *Rawls*, 269; Jon Mandle, *Rawls's A Theory of Justice: An Introduction* (Cambridge: Cambridge University Press, 2009), 130–32; also see Sebastian Maffettone, *Rawls: An Introduction* (Cambridge: Polity, 2011), 111. Tomlin, however, argues that the relegation of envy to issues of stability is untenable: that because envy is a fact of human psychology it ought to enter deliberations in the Original Position and be allowed to alter the selection and justification of principles of justice (Patrick Tomlin, "Envy, Facts and Justice: A Critique of the Treatment of Envy in Justice as Fairness," *Res Publica* 14 (2008):101–16). But my focus is to explore the role of envy, neither in the selection of principles nor primarily as pertains to stability, but as regards the *implementation* of justice—and to show that Rawls's theory already suggests that envy (the imposition of costs on the advantaged even when it leads to non-beneficial economic consequences for all) has a role to play in this context.

93. Reasonable envy, therefore, would relate primarily to the *policy* of imposing costs on the advantaged that tend to make everyone worse off economically (T, 144, 532, 533/124, 466, 467 rev), not the various "destructive feelings" (T, 144/125 rev)—"lack of confidence," "impotence," "anguish," "inferiority," and "hostility" (T, 532, 535–6/466, 469 rev)—Rawls treats as causes and consequences of envy conceived as an excusable rancorous sentiment. Nonetheless, as I discuss in Chapter 4 (especially Section 4.3), a trace of rancor remains in reasonable envy, in the form of the quasi-vindictive desire to see the powerful (economic and political elites) specially burdened on the public stage, even if they are in no way personally guilty of any concrete wrongdoing.

94. Likewise, when Rawls does launch his discussion of excusable envy in conjunction with stability in Part III, he suggests that the idea of a non-irrational form of envy is not new, but has been implicated "throughout [the book]" (T, 530/rev 464).

95. To be sure, though, Rawls explicitly links "excusable envy" only to one of these three forms: excessive inequalities (T, 530–41/464–74 rev).

96. See T, 538/471 rev: "To insist upon equality as the two principles of justice define it is not to give voice to envy" as "the claims to equality supported by the two principles do not spring from these feelings." Also see T, 144, 151, 530/124, 131, 465 rev; R, 87–8.

97. As Rawls explains, "It is essential to keep in mind that the four-stage sequence is a device for applying the principles of justice. This scheme is part of the theory of justice as fairness and not an account of how constitutional conventions and legislatures actually proceed. It sets out points of view from which the different problems of justice are to be settled" (T, 200/176 rev). Or, as he later puts it, "The four-stage sequence describes neither an actual political process, nor a purely theoretical one. Rather, it is part of justice as fairness and constitutes part of a framework of thought that citizens in civil society who accept justice as fairness are to use in applying its concepts and principles" (PL, 397).

98. I decline to use the term "nonideal theory" to describe matters of implementation, both because Rawls is clear that the implementation of domestic principles of justice, especially by the ideal legislators I have in mind, is still part of ideal analysis (T, 195–201/171–76 rev; PL, 397–8; R, 48, 172–4) and because Rawls tends to reserve the concept of nonideal theory for gross injustice, in particular the "substantial and clear injustice" arising from "serious infringements" of basic liberties or "blatant violations" of fair equality of opportunity, both of which might demand civil disobedience (T, 8, 372/8, 326 rev; see A. John Simmons, "Ideal and Nonideal Theory," *Philosophy & Public Affairs* 38.1 (2010): 5–36).

99. Rawls, "Distributive Justice," 143.

100. If one of the three situations grounding non-irrational envy—*excessive inequalities*—might appear necessarily to concern the most advantaged, it is conceivable that the other two situations (failure to realize the difference principle and failure to secure the basic liberties or fair equality of opportunity) potentially involve placing compensatory costs on a wider segment of society. My argument for devoting regulatory attention to the most advantaged does not rely, then, on logical features of reasonable envy itself, but rather on the heuristic, protective, and redressive grounds discussed in the three previous sections.

101. Given my treatment of reasonable envy in this chapter more as a *policy* (the willingness, as part of the implementation of justice, to impose costs on the more advantaged with neutral or negative economic effect on the rest of society) than as a *rancorous psychology* of ill-will (see note 93), it might be asked whether the envious elements of the heuristic, protective, and redressive grounds for regulating the most advantaged are better described in terms of resentment, not envy—where resentment is defined, as Rawls defines it, as a *moral* critique of others having more than us, when we have reason to think that their having more is a consequence of "unjust institutions . . . or wrongful conduct on their part" (T, 533/467 rev). But there are at least three reasons for preferring "reasonable envy" to "resentment." First of all, Rawls does not treat as an explicit or necessary element of resentment what is essential to his (and my own) notion of envy: an imposition of costs on the advantaged that tends to make everyone worse off in material terms. Second, none of the three cases fits perfectly within the rubric of resentment. The inequalities lessened by the protective grounds for regulating the most advantaged stem neither from gross injustice (the failure to realize principles of justice, independent of issues pertaining to their fair value) nor from the wrongful conduct of any individual. Indeed, Rawls explicitly links such counteracting of excessive inequalities to the reduction of excusable envy in the citizenry (PL, 284, also see T, 545/478 rev), not the satisfaction of resentment. The heuristic grounds for imposing costs on the most advantaged with potential negative impact on the rest of society relate to preventing the *possibility* of injustice under circumstances of uncertainty (not rectifying concrete injustice) and likewise involve no accusation of wrongdoing on the part of the most advantaged. And if the redressive grounds for reasonable envy do find support in the residual unfairness stemming from a society's inability fully to realize fair equality of opportunity with regard to education and politics, the injustice in question is not an avoidable offense, nor are the most advantaged guilty of any wrongdoing in this case either. Third, because Rawls himself presents non-irrational envy—specifically the excusable envy generated by excessive inequalities—as a situation that demonstrates "we can resent being made envious" (T, 534/468 rev), it would seem that, when it comes to non-irrational envy, its distinction vis-à-vis resentment is frayed and that one of the defining features of non-irrational envy is precisely its *moral element*. Of course, this interpenetration of envy and morality cuts both ways. It also means that those adopting the standpoint I am defending in this chapter—reasonable envy against the superrich—are prone to experience some degree of ethical ambiguity in making their call for imposing economic burdens on the most advantaged. Not only will they likely feel guilty when criticized by those espousing a purely anti-classist, anti-envy mentality, but as I discuss in the next chapter (Section 4.3), reasonable envy contains an element of rancor insofar as the redress it seeks satisfies the quasi-vindictive desire to see the powerful burdened as such, even when they have done nothing personally unjust. For these and other reasons, the question of how the plebeian might endure this bad conscience—what I term "principled vulgarity"—is an important concern for a plebeian theory of liberal democracy and, accordingly, the topic of Chapter 4.

102. Helmut Schoeck, *Envy: A Theory of Social Behavior* (New York: Harcourt, Brace & World, 1969), 197.

103. For an instance of a luck egalitarian recognizing the practical difficulty of knowing when inequalities stem from morally deserved sources like choices instead of morally undeserved ones like luck, see Kok-Chor Tan, *Justice, Institutions, and Luck: The Site, Ground, and Scope of Equality* (Oxford: Oxford University Press, 2012), 109–14.
104. Ronald Dworkin, *Is Democracy Possible Here?*, 108.
105. Dworkin, *Sovereign Virtue*, 385; also see 195, 203.
106. Consider Sidney Verba, Kay Lehman Schlozman, and Henry E. Brady, *Voice and Equality: Civic Voluntarism in America* (Cambridge: Harvard University Press, 1995), 1; Sidney Verba, Norman H. Nie, and Jae-on Kim, *Participation and Political Equality: A Seven-Nation Comparison* (Chicago: University of Chicago Press, 1978), 1.

Chapter 4

1. Niccolò Machiavelli, *The Prince*, trans. Harvey C. Mansfield (Chicago: University of Chicago Press, 1998), XV, 61 (translation slightly altered).
2. I briefly undertook such an exploration in my earlier book, with its discussion of "Machiavellianism for the People." Jeffrey Edward Green, *The Eyes of the People: Democracy in an Age of Spectatorship* (Oxford: Oxford University Press, 2010), 23–26. This chapter more fully develops the meaning of this notion, now within the idiom of "principled vulgarity."
3. Marcus Tullius Cicero, *Letters to Atticus: Volume II*, trans. D. R. Shackleton Bailey (Cambridge, MA: Harvard University Press, 1999), #126, 194–95.
4. Tacitus, *Histories: Books I–III*, trans. Clifford H. Moore (Cambridge, MA: Harvard University Press, 1925), 1.4; 3.74.
5. Ibid., 2.38; 2.91.
6. Tacitus, *Annals*, in *Histories: Books IV–V* and *Annals: Books I–III*, trans. Clifford H. Moore (Cambridge, MA: Harvard University Press, 1931), 2.77; Tacitus, *Dialogus de Oratoribus*, ed. Roland Mayer (Cambridge: Cambridge University Press, 2001), 7.16.
7. Horace, *Epistles*, in *Satires, Epistles, and Ars Poetica*, trans. H. R. Fairclough (Cambridge, MA: Harvard University Press, 1929), 1.19.36.
8. Immanuel Kant, "What Is Enlightenment?" in H. S. Reiss, ed., *Political Writings* (Cambridge: Cambridge University Press, 1991), 55–57. For Kant, this notion of maturity as thinking for oneself is political in two senses. First, it is through a free public sphere, where individuals have the right to publish, speak out, and engage in critical debate, that one can learn to become mature. This is the aspect of the relationship between politics and maturity that Kant most stresses, arguing that a free public sphere offers a forum for those who already think for themselves and, thus, are enlightened to make use of their critical rationality, gain attention, and gradually inspire the rest of society to become enlightened (ibid., 55). But second, Kant's reflections on maturity also lead him to espouse the republican ideal that is through the enlightened discourse of individuals that governments and their laws are legitimated. Such discourse is to be found not only in a parliament, which Kant takes to be a fundamental part of any viable republican regime, but ultimately in the wider public once a sufficient number of citizens make use of their critical-rational faculties. Thus Kant concludes "What Is Enlightenment?" with the expectation that, in the future, the progress of enlightenment—that is, more and more individuals coming to think for themselves—"even influences the principles of governments, which find that they can themselves profit by treating man, who is *more than a machine*, in a manner appropriate to his dignity" (ibid., 59–60). Moreover, in the same essay, Kant already gives a model of what an enlightened republic will look like, as, with regard to a state's ongoing evolution in its theological policy, he proposes free debate within congregations "until public insight into the nature of such matters . . . [would have] progressed to a point where, by general consent (if not unanimously), a proposal could be submitted to the crown" (ibid., 57).
9. See Amy Gutmann and Dennis Thompson, *Why Deliberative Democracy* (Princeton: Princeton University Press, 2004); James Bohman and William Rehg, eds., *Deliberative Democracy: Essays on Reason and Politics* (Cambridge, MA: MIT Press, 1996); Jon Elster, ed., *Deliberative Democracy* (Cambridge: Cambridge University Press, 1998).

10. Leo Strauss, *Thoughts on Machiavelli* (Glencoe, IL: The Free Press, 1958), 9.
11. Niccolò Machiavelli, *Discourses on Livy*, trans. Harvey C. Mansfield and Nathan Tarcov (Chicago: University of Chicago Press, 1996), II.2, 131.
12. Machiavelli, *The Prince*, XV, 61.
13. Quentin Skinner, *The Foundations of Modern Political Thought* (Cambridge: Cambridge University Press, 1978), Vol. 1, 118–28; Felix Gilbert, "The Humanist Concept of the Prince and the Prince of Machiavelli," *The Journal of Modern History*, 11.4 (1939): 439–83. As an example consider Francesco Patrizi who argues in his treatise from the 1470s, *The Kingdom and the Education of the King*, that the prince would have his own virtue: "The virtues of the ruler are one thing, the virtues of the people are another." In particular, Patrizi claims that ordinary citizens might possess qualities—like a "modest outlook," gratitude for benefits they receive from their monarchs, and "obedience and goodwill"—which would be inappropriate in princes (quoted in Skinner, *Foundations of Modern Political Thought*, 125).
14. Thus the same Patrizi who argues for a distinctly princely virtue (see note 13) still claims that all princely virtues will come to nothing unless they are joined with classical and Christian virtues (Skinner, *Foundations of Modern Political Thought*, 126, 131). Likewise other Italian humanists who made the case for a uniquely princely ethics—whether Oliviero Carafa's insistence that "kings . . . pursue their own advantage and are wont to put their interests before the ties of relationship and friendship" (quoted in Gilbert, "The Humanist Concept of the Prince," 469), or Bartolomeo Sacchi's argument in his 1471 *The Prince* that diplomacy is not enough and that a ruler must be able to supplement it with coercion (Skinner, *Foundations of Modern Political Thought*, 130)—did not claim that the realization of these commitments would require an active unlearning of traditional moral norms.
15. Cicero's arguments in the third book of *On Duties* about the necessary harmony of what is beneficial (*utile*) to a political community and what is honorable (*honestum*) set the stage for later humanist efforts to find in the idea of the common good a way to reconcile ostensibly transgressive acts with the demands of morality. See Cicero, *On Duties*, trans. Walter Miller (Cambridge, MA: Harvard University Press, 1913), III.36, III.64. But this utilitarianism, which would dissolve the conflict between politics and morality, is not the perspective of Machiavelli, for whom there is simply an insoluble tension between the claims of the city and the claims of the soul.
16. See, e.g., Thucydides, *History of the Peloponnesian War*, trans. C. F. Smith, 4 vols. (Cambridge, MA: Harvard University Press, 1919–1923), II.63, III.40; Kautilya, *The Arthashastra*, trans. L. N. Rangarajan (London: Penguin, 1992); Tacitus, *Annals: Books IV–VI, XI–XII*, trans. John Jackson (Cambridge, MA: Harvard University Press, 1937), 4.14.
17. Consider Machiavelli's idea of "cruelty well-used" (*The Prince*, VIII, 37–38), according to which violence should be committed all at once, rather than incrementally over time, to obtain maximum political effect with the least amount of egregiousness. In its differentiation of better and worse forms of moral wrongdoing, the idea of "cruelty well-used" might be seen as a microcosm of Machiavelli's overall contribution to political ethics.
18. As Max Weber put it, "Whoever becomes involved with politics, that is to say, with power and violence as a means has made a pact with satanic powers. . . . Anyone who does not realize this is in fact a mere child in political matters." Indeed, Weber takes it as an inescapable feature of all political action that the effective pursuit of ends necessarily requires means that will conflict with them—hence his appeal to "the tragedy in which all action is ensnared, political above all." Weber, "Politics as a Vocation," in *Vocation Lectures*, trans. Rodney Livingstone (Indianapolis: Hackett, 2004), 86, 78.
19. For example, the effective maintenance of a political machine may require morally dubious commitments, such as the occasional elevation of the leader's personality (and power and glory) over the cause he or she serves, the need at times to merely mobilize rather than genuinely persuade followers, the enforcement of strict party discipline at the expense of the intellectual independence of supporters, and the maintenance of partisan morale through rhetoric that mischaracterizes and unfairly disparages one's opponents. See Michael Walzer, "Political Action: The Problem of Dirty Hands," *Philosophy & Public Affairs* 2.2 (1973): 160–80; Weber, "Politics as a Vocation."

20. The limits of the law (i.e., the supposed need of leaders to transgress the law in times of necessity) stem from numerous factors, including the paradox of founding (no legal order can legalize its beginning) and emergency situations requiring the suspension of the law usually by illegal means. This latter dynamic arguably is figured in Abraham Lincoln's actions during the American Civil War, in which he took various steps that violated the Constitution. Three days after Union soldiers were fired upon at Fort Sumter on April 12, 1861, Lincoln ordered 75,000 troops to be raised from the states; but this was counter to the text of Article I of the Constitution which assigns to *Congress*, not the President, the power "to raise and support armies." Further, on April 27, 1861, Lincoln authorized the Chief of the Army to suspend the writ of habeas corpus whenever he found it necessary to secure transportation lines between Washington and Philadelphia; but habeas corpus was also something that, if it were to be suspended, had to be done by Congress. When Lincoln went before Congress three months later, on July 4, 1861, to justify his actions, he said, "These measures, whether strictly legal or not, were ventured upon, under what appeared to be a popular demand, and a public necessity; trusting, then as now, that Congress would readily ratify them." About the suspension of habeas corpus, he said famously, "To state the question more directly, are all the laws, but one, to go unexecuted, and the government itself go to pieces, lest that one be violated?" Congress did ratify Lincoln's actions after the fact, but they were by his own admission not strictly legal.

21. While some have thought that this alternate calculus can still be rationalized and brought into harmony with prevailing moral norms, others have pointed to it as a reason why the responsible leader sometimes will need to have his or her conscience perverted by performing deeds, such as torture, that no individual ordinarily situated would fathom. As Thompson puts it, "Because officials act for others, they assume rights and obligations that ordinary citizens do not have, or do not have to the same degree" (Dennis F. Thompson, *Political Ethics and Public Office* (Cambridge, MA: Harvard University Press, 1987), 4). Also see Walzer, who says of the purely moral politician who refuses ever to transact in dubious means, "We would not want to be governed by men who consistently adopted that position" ("The Problem of Dirty Hands," 162).

22. For example, the denial of moral dilemmas is especially pronounced in Aristotle (whose doctrine of the unity of the virtues implies that there can be no conflict among various ethical requirements), Aquinas (who held there could be no conflict in the precepts of a true moral system), Kant (who explicitly argued that "a conflict of duties and obligations is inconceivable"), and recent philosophers who have dismissed the possibility of moral conflict on either utilitarian, deontological, or other rationalist grounds (Aristotle, *Nicomachean Ethics*, trans. H. Rackham (Cambridge, MA: Harvard University Press, 1926), 1144b–1145a; Thomas Aquinas, *Summa Theologiae* (Rochester, NY: The Aquinas Institute, 2012), I-II, 6 ad 3; II-II, 62, 2; III, 64, 6 ad 3; Kant, *The Metaphysics of Morals*, trans. Mary Gregor (Cambridge: Cambridge University Press, 1996), 16). For the utilitarian rejection of the possibility of moral conflict, see Kai Nielsen, "There Is No Dilemma of Dirty Hands," in Paul Rynard and David P. Shugarman, eds., *Cruelty and Deception: The Controversy over Dirty Hands in Public Life* (Toronto: University of Toronto Press, 2000). For a deontological challenge to moral conflicts, see Christine M. Korsgaard, *Creating the Kingdom of Ends* (Cambridge: Cambridge University Press, 1996), Chapter 5. Other philosophers who have rejected or challenged the notion of moral dilemmas include R. M. Hare, "Moral Conflicts," in Christopher W. Gowans, ed., *Moral Dilemmas* (Oxford: Oxford University Press, 1986); and Alan Donagan, "Consistency in Rationalist Systems," in Gowans, ed., *Moral Dilemmas*. Utilitarianism, in particular, offers a framework for dissolving the moral dilemmas at the heart of political responsibility, since if the greatest good is unquestionably secured by what appears to be a transgressive act of a responsible leader, utilitarian morality in fact requires this act and conceives of it as fully consistent with the demands of justice. Walzer, however, persuasively calls into question this perspective ("The Problem of Dirty Hands," 168–74). Bernard Williams likewise criticizes utilitarianism for being unable to acknowledge and theorize regret (Williams, *Moral Luck* (Cambridge: Cambridge University Press, 1981), 27–30).

23. Machiavelli, *Discourses*, I.16, I.18.

24. Ibid., I.17, I.55.

25. Machiavelli, *The Prince*, IX.
26. Machiavelli, *Discourses*, I.11, 34–35.
27. Ibid., I.55, 110. The phrase "how much goodness and how much religion" is repeated a second time in the chapter (111).
28. Ibid., I.55, 110. Machiavelli concludes, "And truly, where there is not this goodness [*bontà*], nothing good can be hoped for, as it cannot be hoped for in the provinces that in these times are seen to be corrupt, as is Italy above all others" (ibid., 110).
29. Ibid, I.7, 24.
30. Machiavelli, *The Prince*, V, 21.
31. Machiavelli, *Discourses*, I.5, 18: "Without doubt, if one considers the end of the nobles and of the ignobles, one will see great desire to dominate in the former, and in the latter only desire not to be dominated; and, in consequence, a greater will to live free, being less able to hope to usurp it than are the great."
32. Ibid., I.3. For another hint of Machiavellianism deployed on the plebeian level, see the speech of the anonymous Ciompo Machiavelli constructs in his *History of Florence*, who is said to have urged fellow lower-class Florentines to persist in violence against the nobles, in part because "if we expect to be pardoned for our old transgressions, [we] must commit new ones" (Machiavelli, *The History of Florence*, in *Machiavelli: The Chief Works and Others*, trans. Alan Gilbert (Durham, NC: Duke University Press, 1965), 3.13, 1159).
33. Thucydides, *History of the Peloponnesian War*, III.42–43. Also see David Bolotin, "Thucydides," in Leo Strauss and Joseph Cropsey, eds., *History of Political Philosophy*, 3rd edition (Chicago: University of Chicago Press, 1987), 29–30. Perhaps a more democratized conception of the dirty hands tradition—in which ordinary citizens and not just elite ones face the problem of acts that are politically necessary but morally ambiguous—is suggested in Greek tragedies like Aeschylus's *Agamemnon* or Sophocles's *Antigone* in which the duty to one's polity conflicts sharply with familial obligations, but the characters are still politically elite and the idea of moral ambiguity is hardly theorized in an explicit way.
34. Roger Boesche, *The First Great Political Realist: Kautilya and His Arthashastra* (Lanham, MD: Lexington Books, 2002).
35. See Friedrich Meinecke, *Machiavellianism: The Doctrine of Raison d'État and Its Place in Modern History*, trans. Douglass Scott (New Brunswick, NJ: Transaction Publishers, 1998); Maurizio Viroli, *From Politics to Reason of State: The Acquisition and Transformation of the Language of Politics, 1250–1600* (Cambridge: Cambridge University Press, 1992).
36. For Weber, ordinary citizens are excluded from the analysis of morally fraught political ethics: their role in politics is at best occasional, marginal, and constrained by the "spiritual proletarianization" of being followers. See Weber, "Politics as a Vocation," 74–75, 90. While Thompson argues that ordinary citizens ought to be understood as consenting to and thus responsible for those ethically ambiguous acts of their leaders which are carried out with full publicity and openness—such as the use of violence to defend the polity—his analysis of the problem of dirty hands still centers on the acts leaders perform. Moreover, the specific dirty hands situation that most interests Thompson—in which leaders *in secret*, and thus without full authorization from the wider citizenry, engage in morally transgressive practices—clearly excludes ordinary citizens.. Thompson, *Political Ethics and Public Office*, 22–39.
37. See, e.g., Sanford Levinson, ed., *Torture: A Collection* (Oxford: Oxford University Press, 2004).
38. Walzer, "The Problem of Dirty Hands," 180.
39. Martin Breaugh, *The Plebeian Experience: A Discontinuous History of Political Freedom*, trans. Lazer Lederhendler (New York: Columbia University Press, 2013), 18, xv. As Breaugh elaborates, "The desire for freedom acts as a kind of invariant, to the point where it seems to be *constitutive* of plebeian political struggles" (ibid., 39). To be sure, Breaugh notes how the plebeian desire for freedom can morph into the servile submission to a leader, but there is little within his analysis regarding how the plebeian striving for freedom and dignity itself might necessarily contain a vulgar, ethically complicated element.
40. John P. McCormick, *Machiavellian Democracy* (Princeton: Princeton University Press, 2011), 147, 150. An initial critique of McCormick's account of plebeianism appeared in my essay, "Learning How Not to Be Good: A Plebeian Perspective," *The Good Society*, 20.2

(2011): 184–202. A good deal of what follows in Sections 4.2 and 4.3 draws on and elaborates the argument of that piece.

41. For Machiavelli's use of the terminology *ignobles* (*ignobili*) to refer to the plebeians, see, e.g., *Discourses*, I.5, II.30. For McCormick's parallel use of the term *ignoble*, see *Machiavellian Democracy*, 34, 46, 71, 191.

42. McCormick, *Machiavellian Democracy*, 48. McCormick cites with approval no fewer than five times in his book, including its opening epigraph, Machiavelli's line that "the desires of free peoples are rarely pernicious to freedom because they arise either from being oppressed or from suspicion that they may be oppressed"—an insistence, or overinsistence, that should give one pause (ibid., 1, 6, 24, 44, 48; quoting Machiavelli, *Discourses*, I.4, 17).

43. Ibid., 24, 44–45, 89.

44. Ibid., 24–25, 80.

45. Ibid., 5–6.

46. Ibid., 70–76.

47. Ibid., 43.

48. Ibid., 81–82.

49. Although I do not think McCormick pursues a Machiavellian moral outlook for the People, he nevertheless hints at such a perspective when he acknowledges "how difficult it is to distinguish between [popular] aggressiveness that is appropriately defensive from that which is dangerously offensive" (ibid., 87); when he argues, "neither do the people always behave so passively, nor are their desires always so invariably benign, as a superficial reading on *The Prince* and the *Discourses* might suggest" (ibid., 86–87); and when, citing Machiavelli, he seems to advocate the people "erring on the side of harshness" in its accusations and judgments in political trials (ibid., 83).

50. For instances of the equation of civility with "good citizenship," see Catriona McKinnon, "Civil Citizens," in Catriona McKinnon and Iain Hampsher-Monk, eds., *The Demands of Citizenship* (London: Continuum, 2000): 144–64, 159; Derek Heater, *Citizenship: The Civic Ideal in World History, Politics and Education* (Manchester, UK: Manchester University Press, 2004), 207.

51. The incivility of plebeian principled vulgarity occupies a middle ground between the way Strachan and Wolf construe civility and its opposite. They define civility as "rhetoric that facilitates an ongoing, functional relationship among people who disagree with one another, [in comparison to] incivility [which] includes rhetoric apt to sever relationships" (J. Cherie Strachan and Michael R. Wolf, "Political Civility—Introduction to Political Civility," *PS: Political Science and Politics* 45.3 (2012): 401–404, 402).

52. Rawls, who provides one of the most influential conceptions of civility, speaks to each of these four elements. He understands civility as the rhetorical norm that arises when we consider other citizens in undifferentiated terms (e.g., when we examine our own political commitments from the perspective of "other citizens . . . who are also free and equal"); as the norm that public appeals be made in such a fashion that "all citizens as reasonable and rational might reasonably be expected to endorse [our position along with us]"; as the related deliberative duty to exercise "a willingness to listen" and "fair-mindedness" and "to be able explain to one another on fundamental questions how the principles and policies [we] advocate and vote for can be supported by the political values of public reason"; and as the solidaristic norm that framing our public discourses in such a fashion "preserves the ties of civic friendship consistent with the duty of civility" (Rawls, *Political Liberalism* (New York: Columbia University Press, 1993), 226, 236, 217, 253). For similar accounts of these elements by other theorists of civility, see Philip D. Smith, *The Virtue of Civility in the Practice of Politics* (Lanham, MD: University Press of America, 2002); and Edward Shils, *The Virtue of Civility* (Indianapolis: Liberty Fund, 1997), 25–102, 320–55.

53. It bears repeating that plebeianism stands for the identification and regulation of *both* the most advantaged *political* class and the most advantaged *economic* class. Since my earlier work, *The Eyes of the People*, addressed the former concern, my discussion in this book focuses more heavily on the latter.

54. Rogers M. Smith, "Differentiated Citizenship and the Tasks of Reconstructing the Commercial Republic," *Journal of Social Philosophy* 41.2 (Summer 2010): 214–22, 217. To be sure,

as Smith recognizes, numerous differentiations remain, for example those based on age, sexual orientation, immigration status, and ontology (e.g., whether one is a human or a corporation). Moreover, progressive reformers, especially within the realm of racial politics, have become increasingly suspicious of color-blind politics that effectively perpetuate bias. But the ideal of undifferentiated citizenship at present garners widespread allegiance.

55. As Adam Smith describes and criticizes this phenomenon, "The disposition to admire, and almost to worship, the rich and the powerful, and to despise, or, at least, to neglect persons of poor and mean condition is the great and most universal cause of the corruption of our moral sentiments" (Smith, *The Theory of Moral Sentiments* (London: Penguin, 2010), 57). For Smith, of course, it is the excessive adulation of the rich that is vulgar and morally objectionable. His analysis nonetheless explains why plebeian efforts to impose regulatory burdens on the most advantaged class likely will offend a widespread and deeply ingrained tendency to revere the wealthy.

56. See, e.g., Jennifer L. Hochschild, *What's Fair? American Beliefs About Distributive Justice* (Cambridge, MA: Harvard University Press, 1981), 15–16.

57. See, e.g., John P. McCormick, "Contain the Wealthy and Patrol the Magistrates," *American Political Science Review* 100.2 (2006): 147–63, 147.

58. See, e.g., Benjamin I. Page and Lawrence R. Jacobs, *Class War? What Americans Really Think About Economic Inequality* (Chicago: University of Chicago Press, 2009); also see Hochschild, *What's Fair?*, 1.

59. See, e.g., Leslie McCall and Lane Kenworthy, "Americans' Social Policy Preferences in the Era of Rising Inequality," *Perspectives on Politics* 7.3 (2009): 459–84, 472.

60. It may be true that such cultural resistance to identifying and regulating the most advantaged occurs in some countries, for example the United States, more than others, but it hardly seems unique to any particular national culture. Plebeians everywhere will have to confront it. On Americans' particularly intense resistance to regulation of the most advantaged, see Robert E. Lane, "Market Justice, Political Justice," *American Political Science Review* 80.2 (1986): 383–402; Hochschild, *What's Fair?*; McCall and Kenworthy, "Americans' Social Policy Preferences in the Era of Rising Inequality"; Martin Gilens, *Why Americans Hate Welfare: Race, Media, and the Politics of Antipoverty Policies* (Chicago: University of Chicago Press, 1999).

61. McCormick, *Machiavellian Democracy*, 183.

62. John Rawls, *A Theory of Justice* (Cambridge, MA: Belknap Press of Harvard University Press, 1971), 98; also see Rawls, *A Theory of Justice: Revised Edition* (Cambridge, MA: Belknap Press of Harvard University Press, 1999), 84.

63. Both the institutional and individual-ethical elements figure prominently in recent studies that address how to design deliberation in particular real-world contexts over and against an earlier generation's more purely theoretical analysis. See David Kahane, Daniel Weinstock, Dominique Leydet, and Melissa Williams, eds., *Deliberative Democracy in Practice* (Vancouver: University of British Columbia Press, 2010); Cass R. Sunstein, *Republic 2.0* (Princeton: Princeton University Press, 2009); Mark E. Warren and Hilary Pearse, eds., *Designing Deliberative Democracy: The British Columbia Citizens' Assembly* (Cambridge: Cambridge University Press, 2008); Robert Goodin, *Innovating Democracy: Democratic Theory and Practice After the Deliberative Turn* (Oxford: Oxford University Press, 2008); James Fishkin and Bruce Ackerman, *Deliberation Day* (New Haven, CT: Yale University Press, 2005); Archon Fung, *Empowered Participation: Reinventing Urban Democracy* (Princeton: Princeton University Press, 2004); Amy Gutmann and Dennis Thompson, *Why Deliberative Democracy*.

64. The privileging of the metaphor of sphere over stage is a common trope in the voluminous literature on deliberative democracy. For explicit arguments in defense of it, see Jürgen Habermas, *Between Facts and Norms: Contributions to a Discourse Theory of Law and Democracy*, trans. William Rehg (Cambridge, MA: MIT Press, 1994), 361; Seyla Benhabib, "Models of Public Space: Hannah Arendt, the Liberal Tradition, and Jürgen Habermas," in Calhoun, ed., *Habermas and the Public Sphere*, 79, 95. On the plebeian idea of the public stage, see my earlier work: Green, *The Eyes of the People*, 7, 12, 20, 21.

65. Green, *The Eyes of the People*, especially 23–26, 137–38, 203.

66. But see the all-too-brief, poorly named article by Michael White, "A Brief History of Heckling," *The Guardian*, 28 April 2006. Also see Susan Herbst, *Rude Democracy: Civility and Incivility in American Politics* (Philadelphia: Temple University Press, 2010).

67. Max Weber, *Ancient Judaism* (New York: Free Press, 1967), 267–335.

68. For an example of heckling and related forms of disruption within the *contio*, see Sallust, *The War with Jugurtha*, in *The War with Catiline and The War with Jugurtha*, trans. J. C. Rolfe and revised by John T. Ramsey (Cambridge, MA: Harvard University Press, 2013), §34.1 On the use of the *contio* as a venue to which a leading magistrate might summon a rival magistrate and engage in a kind of cross-examination, see Morstein-Marx, *Mass Oratory and Political Power in Late Republican Rome* (Cambridge: Cambridge University Press, 2008), 170–71; also see, 4, 119, 132, 165. As Morstein-Marx observes, "The right to shout in the *contio* could even be seen as the mark of freedom itself" (ibid., 127).

69. Green, *The Eyes of the People*, 130, 162.

70. Homer, *Iliad*, trans. A. T. Murray and revised by William F. Wyatt (Cambridge, MA: Harvard University Press, 1999), II.211–14 (translation my own in part).

71. When Odysseus sets out to convince the Greeks who were considering abandoning the war that they stay and fight, he makes respectful appeals to those who are "chieftains or a person of note," but tells non-elite Greeks, like Thersites, that they should "sit still and hearken to the words of those who are your betters" (ibid., II.189–204).

72. As Odysseus admits, Thersites's speech is "reckless [*akritomuthe*]" yet he is a "clear-voiced [*ligus*] orator." Ibid., II.246.

73. For Thersites's public rant against Agamemnon, see ibid., II.224–42.

74. See ibid., II.220–24, where it is said that in addition to Agamemnon, Thersites is "most hateful [*exthistos*]" also to Achilles and Odysseus.

75. Ibid., II.245–51 (translation my own in part).

76. On the importance of deliberative assemblies to the *Iliad*, see Malcolm Schofield, "*Euboulia* in the *Iliad*," *Classical Quarterly* 36.1 (1986): 6–31.

77. Hegel, for example, defines "Thersitism" as the practice whereby a social inferior undermines the authority of a world-historical figure by exposing personal, private aspects of the individual which pertain to that individual's biological or natural status: "The Thersites of Homer who abuses the kings is a standing figure for all times. Blows—that is, beating with a solid cudgel—he does not get in every age, as in the Homeric one; but his envy, his egotism, is the thorn which he has to carry in his flesh; and the undying worm that gnaws him is the tormenting consideration that his excellent views and vituperations remain absolutely without result in the world." Yet, importantly, Hegel then adds, "But our satisfaction at the fate of Thersitism also, may have its sinister side" (Georg Wilhelm Friedrich Hegel, *The Philosophy of History*, trans. J. Sibree (New York: Dover Publications, 1956), 32).

78. Quoted in Robert Morstein-Marx, *Mass Oratory and Political Power in Late Republican Rome*, 128.

79. Recall Rawls's idea, quoted above, that a well-ordered liberal-democratic regime guided by public reason "preserves the ties of civic friendship consistent with the duty of civility." Rawls, *Political Liberalism*, 253.

80. On the latter, see, e.g., Chantal Mouffe, "Deliberative Democracy or Agonistic Pluralism?" *Social Research* 66.3 (1999): 745–58; Mouffe, *The Democratic Paradox* (London: Verso, 2000).

81. McCormick, for example, treats plebeian indignation as an ethically unambiguous phenomenon and believes that Machiavelli does as well: "Machiavelli invites us to understand popular ferocity as the righteous indignation of a normally passive people who have been violated, abused, and threatened. The people's aggressive behavior is revealed to be a legitimate and indeed necessary response to the prideful and greedy nature of elites" (*Machiavellian Democracy*, 89; also see 14). Likewise, McCormick can say of the People, "They exhibit an oppressive appetite only in response to oppression inflicted upon them; and they do so honestly, overtly, without any trace of subterfuge or guile" (ibid., 24). On the specific issue of failing to recognize plebeian unhappiness, while McCormick confronts the problem of "sociopsychological limits" imposed on plebeians, his ultimate move is to say that such concerns are exaggerated if not altogether groundless. He argues that inferior class-based designations do not "fundamentally and indefinitely debilitate the social and political agency of those

placed within such categories." And, further, McCormick points out that the class-based designations supported by plebeian theorists like himself are in no way permanent: they do not prevent social mobility between classes (ibid., 13). These are good points, but they should not be taken to mean that the problem of plebeian unhappiness—with its attendant disruption of civic friendship—is therefore illusory.

82. Machiavelli, *Discourses*, I.3, 15.

83. David Hume, "Of the Independency of Parliament," in Knud Haakonssen, ed., *Hume: Political Essays* (Cambridge: Cambridge University Press, 1994), 24.

84. Carl Schmitt, *The Concept of the Political*, trans. George Schwab (Chicago: University of Chicago Press, 1996), 61.

85. As much as McCormick celebrates the plebeianism of the Roman and certain Florentine constitutions, his work is hardly a nostalgic celebration of the past, as he is quite aware of how these regimes employed semi-naturalized class-based distinctions for oligarchic ends and engaged in discrimination grounded on gender and race. Moreover, McCormick also advocates a more restricted use of sortition and public accusation than Machiavelli proposed for the Florentine regime, on the basis that such proposals are "too unwieldy" and not suited to the "size and complexity of contemporary commercial societies" (*Machiavellian Democracy*, 172). My own account of plebeianism is even more explicitly committed to the relative moral superiority of the contemporary liberal-democratic regime.

86. For a recent critique along these lines, see, e.g., Kenneth Minogue, *The Servile Mind: How Democracy Erodes the Moral Life* (New York: Encounter Books, 2010), 271–91, 317–25.

87. On the analogy between the figure of the second-class citizen (the citizen who is being ruled rather than ruling) and the woman (who obeys the persuasive speech of her husband), see Aristotle, *Politics*, trans. H. Rackham (Cambridge, MA: Harvard University Press, 1932), 1277b22-24.

88. McCormick, *Machiavellian Democracy*, 76.

89. Machiavelli, *Discourses*, I.28. Also see I.58: "All men particularly, and especially princes, can be accused of that defect [i.e., ingratitude and inconstancy] of which the writers accuse the multitude" (116).

90. Sara Forsdyke, *Exile, Ostracism, and Democracy: The Politics of Expulsion in Ancient Greece* (Princeton: Princeton University Press, 2005), 147–48.

91. Machiavelli, *Discourses*, I.7, 23–24.

92. Ibid., I.4, I.7, I.37. Also see Machiavelli, *The Prince*, VII, where Machiavelli describes how the gruesome execution of a leading magistrate, Remirro de Orco, was a way to "purge the spirits" of citizens in the Romagna and leave them "satisfied and stupefied" (30).

93. Even if Machiavelli does not fully explain the origins of the humors, they receive insightful treatment in Anthony J. Parel, *The Machiavellian Cosmos* (New Haven, CT: Yale University Press, 1992), 101–12.

94. As Mansfield and Tarcov explain in their introduction to the *Discourses*, the ill humors are something the "people . . . harbors *toward the whole government* or toward the class of nobles," even if their venting is directed "against one individual, whose punishment satisfies the people and excuses everyone else" (xxix, emphasis added).

95. Insofar as plebeian regulation of the most advantaged is motivated by redress for the shadow of unfairness and not remediation of individual wrongdoing, it is important to restrict the penalties imposed to economic and other non-corporeal regulatory burdens—burdens which might after all be considered quasi-honors too, somewhat similar to the case of Roman aristocrats who felt compelled to pay enormous sums out of their own pockets for the commonweal, but did so for their own reputation and standing. Of course, according to a plebeian theory of liberal democracy such as I am defending in this book, *noblesse oblige* is not voluntary, but compulsory.

96. To be sure, while McCormick's plebeian theory does not explicitly recognize the idea of redress as a secondary basis for plebeian institutions, it gestures toward it. McCormick, after all, approvingly acknowledges that Machiavelli understood that public accusations and trials would "provide a regulatory benefit beyond deterrence and punishment of individual magistrates and ottimati," relating to the ability of such institutions to "provide an outlet for the ordinary venting of social 'humors' that are generated by class antagonism" (*Machiavellian*

Democracy, 116). Further, McCormick admits that to some extent the plebeian motivation to impose public burdens on elites will be engendered by historical abuses from the past: "Collective memory among the people of formal inequalities from the past seems to inspire within them a sensitivity to informal inequalities that persist in the present" (ibid., 14). Indeed, McCormick's worry about the insufficient indignation of the plebs vis-à-vis elites, and the need to actively generate it (ibid., 14), ought to be interpreted, not as an odd plebeian insensitivity to their own abuse at the hands of transgressing elites, but as a sign that it is not only actual or threatened abuse from specific individuals that motivates plebeians, but a redressive, retrospective, and partially symbolic desire to see the most powerful members of a polity forced to engage in public acts of redress—a desire which needs to be awakened and, even if justifiable on the macrolevel, no doubt will appear unfair to many of the elite individuals being publically burdened, thus contributing to the plebeian bad conscience. But in spite of all this, McCormick's theory resembles Machiavelli in only reflecting the quasi-vindictive sentiment at play in plebeian progressivism, but not acknowledging this sentiment, let alone confronting its ethical ambiguity. This is to say, McCormick leaves philosophically unexplored *why* there will be class conflict beyond that caused by the transgressions of elites as well as how the progressive channeling of this conflict might involve burdening individuals for reasons other than their concrete wrongdoing.

97. See, e.g., Andrew Rehfeld, "The Child as Democratic Citizen," *The Annals of the American Academy of Political and Social Science* 633.1 (2011): 141–66; David Owen, *Maturity and Modernity: Nietzsche, Weber, Foucault and the Ambivalence of Reason* (London: Routledge, 1994); Philip A. Michelbrach, "Democracy as Vocation: Political Maturity in Luther and Weber," *Journal of Democratic Theory* 1.4 (2011): 1–33; Tracy B. Strong, "Love, Passion, and Maturity: Nietzsche and Weber on Morality and Politics," in John P. McCormick, ed., *Confronting Mass Democracy and Industrial Technology: Political and Social Thought from Nietzsche to Habermas* (Durham, NC: Duke University Press, 2002): 15–41; Strong, "Entitlement and Legitimacy: Weber and Lenin on the Problems of Leadership," in Fred Edlin, ed., *Constitutional Government and Democracy* (New York: Westview Press, 1983).

98. On the usual assumption of democratic theorists that children should be excluded from formal politics, see Francis Schrag, "The Child's Status in the Democratic State," *Political Theory* 3.4 (1975): 441–57, 443. However, that the notion that politics is not for children is well established does not mean that it is clearly defined. Within the United States, for example, there are ongoing debates about the proper ages for various activities. The US Supreme Court ruled, in *Graham v. Florida* (2010), that it is cruel and unusual for juveniles to be sentenced to life without parole when the crime is not a homicide. However, homicide still carries the possibility of a life sentence without parole. The severity of such penalties raises questions about the consistency of age regulations. After all, if one can be incarcerated for life as a minor, why is not possible to vote, drive a car, or drink in bars? For these examples, see *The New York Times* article, "How Old Is Enough?" November 14, 2009.

99. There is reason to suspect that the oldest polities were gerontocracies, in which power was bestowed on elders—a legacy preserved in the word *senate* which comes from *senex*, the Latin word for *old*.

100. But there are exceptions, especially with regard to electoral politics. Rehfeld, for example, challenges the exclusion of minors from politics and proposes various reforms (e.g., fractional voting for older children, group representation based on age, and political spending accounts for children) meant to both promote the interests of minors and also contribute to their civic development. See Rehfeld, "The Child as Democratic Citizen." Also see Francis Schrag, "Children and Democracy: Theory and Policy," *Politics, Philosophy & Economics* 3.3 (2004): 365–79.

101. Malcolm X opposed the use of children in the civil rights movement: "Real men don't put their children on the firing line." Quoted in Andrew M. Manis, *A Fire You Can't Put Out: The Civil Rights Life of Birmingham's Reverend Fred Shuttlesworth* (Tuscaloosa: University of Alabama Press, 1999), 370.

102. On the 30-year-old age minimum for senators, see James Madison, "No. 62," in Terrence Ball, ed., *The Federalist*, (Cambridge: Cambridge University Press, 2003), 300, where Madison discusses "senatorial trust, which requiring greater extent of information and stability of

character, requires at the same time that the senator should have reached a period of life most likely to supply these advantages."

103. Henry David Thoreau, *Walden*, in *Walden* and *Civil Disobedience* (London: Penguin, 1986), 134.

104. Ibid., 133, 142, 134, 133, 382.

105. See, e.g., Jürgen Habermas, *Moral Consciousness and Communicative Action*, trans. Christian Lenhardt and Shierry Weber Nicholsen (Cambridge, MA: MIT Press, 1990), 126–27.

106. One might contest this etymology insofar as the naturalness of *naïveté* refers to the *person* (someone who is "just born yesterday")—but for the Enlightenment tradition it is nonetheless the case that what is considered immature is attributing a false naturalness to pre-existing customs, norms, and unexamined laws and policies.

107. Kant, "What Is Enlightenment?," 55–57.

108. As Weber puts it, "Anyone who wishes to engage in politics at all, and particularly anyone who wishes to practice it as a profession, must become conscious of [the] ethical paradoxes of his own responsibility for what may become of *him* under the pressure they exert. For . . . he is entering into relations with satanic powers that lurk in every act of violence" (Weber, "Politics as a Vocation," in *Vocation Lectures*, trans. Rodney Livingston (Indianapolis: Hackett, 2004), 90).

109. This conception of political maturity figures in Machiavelli's critique of Piero Soderini, the Florentine gonfalonier for life in whose administration Machiavelli served as second chancellor and ambassador and whose stewardship of the Florentine republic proved unsuccessful against the Medicis, who overthrew it in 1512. As Machiavelli quipped, "The night Piero Soderini died, his soul went to the mouth of Hell, and Pluto cried out to it: Foolish soul, why Hell? Go to Limbo with the children [*bambini*]" (Niccolò Machiavelli, *Tutte le Opere*, ed. Mario Martelli (Firenze: Sansoni, 1971), 1005). Here Machiavelli associates immaturity with the childish inability to go to hell—that is, with the inability to take the morally fraught but necessary actions of responsible political leadership.

110. Sigmund Freud, "On Narcissism," in James Strachey, ed., *Collected Papers* (New York: Basic Books, 1959), Vol. 4, 48–49. More recently, Mahoney defines emotional maturity in part as "relinquishing forever the 'infantile omnipotence' of childhood" (J. Michael Mahoney, *Schizophrenia: The Bearded Lady Disease* (Bloomington, IN: AuthorHouse, 2011), 15). Also see Eugene Pumpian-Mindlin, "Vicissitudes of Infantile Omnipotence," *Psychoanalytic Study of the Child* 24 (1969): 213–26.

111. But see Nussbaum's treatment of "an infantile demand for omnipotence" as posing a persistent threat to the integrity of a political community. Martha C. Nussbaum, *Hiding from Humanity: Disgust, Shame, and the Law* (Princeton: Princeton University Press, 2004), 15; also see 173, 182–86, 192–93. Also see Christina Tarnopolsky, *Prudes, Perverts, and Tyrants: Plato's Gorgias and the Politics of Shame* (Princeton: Princeton University Press, 2010), 186, 190.

112. Kant, for example, claims that one ought not deliberate (or argue) directly with one's employer or bureaucratic superior (Kant, "What Is Enlightenment?," 56). Contemporary deliberative democrats recognize that certain injustices may require non-deliberative responses, like marches, sit-ins, and strikes. See Amy Gutmann and Dennis Thompson, *Why Deliberative Democracy*, 51.

113. Consider the latter half of Machiavelli's famous dictum that the responsible politician must be able to learn how not to be good: "It is necessary to a prince, if he wants to maintain himself, to learn to be able not to be good, *and to use this and not use it according to necessity*" (emphasis added). Machiavelli, *The Prince*, XV, 61. A specific example of this situational logic can be seen in Machiavelli's teaching about deception. One must learn how to *appear* morally good when one is not, as it is necessary sometimes to do evil all the while maintaining one's reputation for goodness. But when deception is not needed, then one *should actually be good*: "It is [useful] to *appear* merciful, faithful, humane, honest, and religious, *and to be so*; but to remain with a spirit built so that, if you need not be those things, you are able to know how to change to contrary" (*The Prince*, XVIII, 70, emphasis added). Machiavelli's precise teaching is not to learn how not to be good in order to devolve from a state of humanity into a state of barbarism, but rather, as he says, to be like a centaur—half beast, half man—which means not relinquishing humanity, but only having the capacity to be beastly to the extent necessity requires it and, so, in all other instances to be humane (*The Prince*, XVIII, 69). Political maturity for Machiavelli is not only

being willing to dirty one's hands, but doing so as little as is necessary—and thus depends on a knowledge of the proper occasions on which moral transgressions are appropriate.

Chapter 5

1. Epicurus. *Epicurea*, ed. Hermann Usener (Cambridge: Cambridge University Press, 2010), Fragment 551, 326.
2. Ibid., Fragment 8, 94.
3. On Cicero's account of the popularity of the Epicureans at Rome, especially among the lower orders, see Marcus Tullius Cicero, *Academica*, in *De Natura Deorum* and *Academica*, trans. H. Rackham (Cambridge, MA: Harvard University Press, 1933), I.5; *Tusculan Disputations*, trans. J. E. King (Cambridge, MA: Harvard University Press, 1927), IV.6–7. For other accounts of Epicureanism as a leading, if not the most popular, philosophical school in Rome during the late Republic, see David Sedley, "Epicureanism in the Roman Republic," in James Warren, ed., *The Cambridge Companion to Epicureanism* (Cambridge: Cambridge University Press, 2009), 29–45, 44; Walter Nicgorski, "Cicero, Citizenship, and the Epicurean Temptation," in Dwight D. Allman and Michael D. Beaty, eds., *Cultivating Citizens: Soulcraft and Citizenship in Contemporary America* (Lanham, MD: Lexington Books, 2002), 7, 8, and note 43; Erlend D. MacGillivray, "The Popularity of Epicureanism in Late-Republic Roman Society," *Ancient World* 43.2 (2012): 151–72.
4. Cicero uses the phrase "plebeian philosophy" (*plebeii philosophi*) most directly to refer to those philosophies that deny the immortality of the soul, with the Epicureans clearly implicated (Cicero, *Tusculan Disputations*, I.55). Also see Cicero, *De Senectute*, 85, for the parallel notion of "lesser philosophers" (*minuti philosophi*) who think the soul is mortal (Cicero, *De Senectute*, in *De Senectute, De Amicitia, De Divinatione*, trans. W. A. Falconer (Cambridge, MA: Harvard University Press, 1923)). As Nicgorski states, for Cicero Epicureanism "is not worthy of philosophy; it is the mask of philosophy—plebeian philosophy at best" (Nicgorski, "Cicero, Citizenship, and the Epicurean Temptation," 14).
5. Nicgorski describes the "Epicurean *geist* sweeping across Rome and the Rome-dominated world," noting that Epicureanism "became the dominant philosophical school during the years Cicero lived" (see Nicgorski, "Cicero, Citizenship, and the Epicurean Temptation," 7, 8).
6. According to Clay, "More women are associated with Epicurus' Garden than are recorded for any other 'school'" (Diskin Clay, "The Athenian Garden," in James Warren, ed., *The Cambridge Companion to Epicureanism* (Cambridge: Cambridge University Press, 2009), 26). Other sources on the inclusivity of Epicureanism with regard to women and household servants include D. S. Hutchinson, "Introduction," *The Epicurus Reader: Selected Writings and Testimonia*, trans. and ed. Brad Inwood and L. P. Gerson (Indianapolis: Hackett: 1994), xi; and Pierre Boyancé, *Lucrèce et L'épicurisme* (Paris, 1963), 58.
7. MacGillivray, "The Popularity of Epicureanism in Late-Republic Roman Society," 171–72.
8. On the latter, see Epicurus, *Principal Doctrines*, in *Epicurus Reader*, #31–33.
9. Epicurus advises his followers, "They must free themselves from the prison of general education and politics" (Epicurus, *Vatican Sayings*, in *Epicurus Reader*, #58).
10. As Leslie describes the Epicurean standpoint, "Prominent participation in affairs was permissible if the necessity of self-preservation compelled, or if one were of such an inherently active disposition that only thus could he be happy" (Robert J. Leslie, *The Epicureanism of Titus Pomponius Atticus* (Philadelphia: College Offset Press, 1950), 13). According to Seneca, Epicurus taught "the wise person will not engage in public affairs except in an emergency," whereas for the Stoics it was the reverse: the "wise man will engage in politics unless something prevents him" (Lucius Annaeus Seneca, "On Leisure," in *Moral Essays: Volume II*, trans. John W. Basore (Cambridge, MA: Harvard University Press, 1932), 185).
11. Cicero, *On the Commonwealth*, in James E. G. Zetzel, ed., *On the Commonwealth* and *On the Laws* (Cambridge: Cambridge University Press, 1999), I.7–11, 5–6.

12. Cicero, *Epistulae Ad Familiares*, trans. D. R. Shackleton Bailey (Cambridge: Cambridge University Press, 1977), Vol. 2, IX.24, 218. This is a letter to his Epicurean friend L. Papirius Paetus, where after playfully affirming the seemingly Epicurean value of the company of friends as the "secret of happiness" and as an unrivaled source of "satisfaction" and a "happy life," Cicero goes on to clarify his profound commitment to politics which, implicitly, the Epicureans lack. Elsewhere, Cicero affirms service to the state as the highest virtue (see *On the Commonwealth*, I.2, I.7), as a duty (ibid., I.4), and as something good men should do to avoid the "rule of scoundrels" (ibid., I.5).

13. Montesquieu, for example, is typical when he writes, "The sect of Epicurus, which was introduced at Rome toward the end of the republic, contributed much towards tainting the heart and mind of the Romans" (Montesquieu, *Considerations on the Causes of the Greatness of the Romans and Their Decline*, trans. David Lowenthal (Indianapolis: Hackett, 1999), 97). Within the American context, according to Richard, "most of the founders . . . [were] completely persuaded by Cicero's [negative account] of Epicureanism" (Carl J. Richard, *The Founders and the Classics: Greece, Rome, and the American Enlightenment* (Cambridge, MA: Harvard University Press, 1994), 176; also see 187–94). In his polemical battles with Jefferson, Hamilton could use *Epicurean* as an epithet (see ibid., 93). Even an avowed Epicurean like Jefferson (see Letter to William Short, October 31, 1819) felt the individualism of Epicureanism needed to be supplemented by Christianity and the idea of intrinsic virtue disconnected from self-interest. See Nicgorski, "Cicero, Citizenship, and the Epicurean Temptation," 5; Jean M. Yarbrough, *American Virtues: Thomas Jefferson on the Character of a Free People* (Lawrence: University Press of Kansas, 1998), 154, 160–65.

14. Although my own extrapolitical reading of Epicureanism is distinct, in recognizing the political-philosophical dimension of Epicureanism I follow such scholars as James H. Nichols, *Epicurean Political Philosophy* (Ithaca, NY: Cornell University Press, 1976); and, more recently, John Colman, *Lucretius as Theorist of Political Life* (New York: Palgrave Macmillan, 2012). But even Nichols, who does in fact delineate and defend an Epicurean political philosophy, still recognizes that the pervasive view is that "the Epicurean teaching seems to be altogether hostile to politics as such and to urge men to avoid public life" (Nichols, *Epicurean Political Philosophy*, 14).

15. Arnaldo Momigliano, "Review of Farrington's *Science and Politics in the Ancient World*," *Journal of Roman Studies* 31 (1941): 149–57; Sedley, "Epicureanism in the Roman Republic," 43; Clay, "The Athenian Garden," 10, 16–17.

16. Cicero, *On the Laws*, in James E. G. Zetzel, ed., *On the Commonwealth and On the Laws* (Cambridge: Cambridge University Press, 1999), I.37–39, 118–119.

17. For *makaria* in its various forms of blessedness, happiness, and bliss, see Epicurus, *Principal Doctrines*, #27; *Vatican Sayings*, #17; and *Letter to Menoeceus*, in *Epicurus Reader*, §128, §134.

18. Epicurus, *Letter to Menoeceus*, §133.

19. See, e.g., Epicurus, *Principal Doctrines*, #29 (see scholiast), #30; also see *Letter to Menoeceus*, §127. As Brown summarizes Epicurus's taxonomy of desires, "Unnatural desires depend upon false opinion, and natural desires, which are free of false opinion, are necessary just in case their frustration brings pain and unnecessary otherwise" (Eric Brown, "Politics and Society," in James Warren, ed., *The Cambridge Companion to Epicureanism* (Cambridge: Cambridge University Press, 2009), 186).

20. Epicurus, *Letter to Menoeceus*, §128.

21. Epicurus, *Principal Doctrines*, #30; also see #26.

22. Epicurus, *Vatican Sayings*, #68.

23. Epicurus, *Principal Doctrines*, #10.

24. Porphyry, *To Marcella* 27, quoted in *Epicurus Reader*, 99. As Porphyry also puts it, "For a man is unhappy either because of fear or because of unlimited and groundless desire; and by reining these in he can produce for himself the reasoning [which leads to] blessedness" (*To Marcella* 29, quoted in *Hellenistic Philosophy: Introductory Readings*, trans. Brad Inwood and L. P. Gerson (Indianapolis: Hackett, 1997), 100).

25. Epicurus, *Principal Doctrines*, #21 (my translation).

26. Epicurus, *Letter to Menoeceus*, §125. Also see Epicurus, *Principal Doctrines*, #2; Lucretius, *The Nature of Things*, trans. Frank O. Copley (New York: W. W. Norton, 1977), III.830, 75: "Death, then, is nothing, concerns us not one bit." See also ibid.: III.866–69; III.921–22.

27. On the idea that we overcome the fear of death not by avoiding thinking about it but by reflecting on it, see, e.g., Epicurus's *Letter to Menoeceus*, §125, where Epicurus advises that we must "*get used to believing* that death is nothing to us" (emphasis added). Similarly, Lucretius's line "Death cannot be avoided: we must meet it" (*The Nature of Things*, III.1079, 81) can be read in a philosophical sense (the need to consider it) and not just in a biological one. Seneca, too, who imports this aspect of Epicureanism into his Stoicism, likewise states, "Nothing will help us so much as pondering mortality" (Seneca, "To Novatus on Anger," in *Moral Essays: Volume 1*, trans. John W. Basore (Cambridge, MA: Harvard University Press, 1928), 351). Horace continually calls for attunement to one's finitude, which he thinks can ultimately be a source of light-hearted joy. Horace, *Odes*, in *Odes and Epodes*, trans. C. E. Bennett (Cambridge, MA: Harvard University Press, 1995), IV.12.24–28, 332–33; *Epistles*, in *Satires, Epistles, and Ars Poetica*, trans. H. R. Fairclough (Cambridge, MA: Harvard University Press, 1929), I.4.12–16, 276–77.

28. See, e.g., Lucretius, *The Nature of Things*, III.824–1094. As Nichols summarizes, "Lucretius' argument is that excessive desire for wealth and ambition for political honors, which drive men to crimes, are nourished to no inconsiderable extent by the fear of death." Nichols goes on to explain that for Epicureans like Lucretius the fear of death is usually the motivating *but hidden* force in people's lives. Nichols, *Epicurean Political Philosophy*, 77, 88.

29. See, e.g., Epicurus, *Principal Doctrines*, #7. As Brown relates, for Epicurus, those who seek security via political power and honor are "mistaken about how best to achieve freedom from fear" (Brown, "Politics and Society," 180).

30. Lucretius, *The Nature of Things*, V.1430–35, 145.

31. Epicurus, *Principal Doctrines*, #11, #14.

32. Cicero's own political life, however much he saw it as an exemplary commitment to public service, could hardly be said to refute this aspect of the Epicurean critique: not only does Cicero uphold political commitment as a duty often discordant with the claims of private happiness, but his own political career, judging from his personal letters, was a deep and frequent source of misery. See Cicero, *Letters to Atticus: Volume II*, trans. D. R. Shackleton Bailey (Cambridge, MA: Harvard University Press, 1999), #61–63, 258–63.

33. Lucretius, *The Nature of Things*, V.1124–27. Accordingly, Lucretius rejects as foolish the hope of the powerful that they might someday reach a point of supreme prominence in which at last "their fortunes on foundations firm might rest forever and that they themselves, the opulent, might pass a quiet life" (V.1120–22). Here I follow the translation of William Ellery Leonard (New York: E. P. Dutton, 1950), 230.

34. Ibid., V.1133, 231 (Leonard translation). As Nichols elaborates the position, what the ruler takes to be his benefit in fact "is merely something he hears from others, not something real perceived by his own senses. . . . The supposed good of the most splendid and sought-after position, that of a ruler, exists only in the speech of other men; a man who seeks such an illusory good has surrendered his own independence to others and is therefore alienated from himself" (Nichols, *Epicurean Political Philosophy*, 142).

35. Horace, *Satires*, in *Satires, Epistles, and Ars Poetica*, trans. H. Rushton Fairclough (Cambridge, MA: Harvard University Press, 1929), I.6.128–31, 86–87.

36. Lucretius, *The Nature of Things*, III.994, 79; III.1058–59, 81; III.998–99, 79 (Copley translation).

37. Epicurus, *Letter to Menoeceus*, §124.

38. To be sure, if one's time horizon is sufficiently expanded, the state's deathlessness must be seen as illusory—for in the long run even the sun will burn out. However, the state's finitude, insofar as it is grounded on the inevitable disappearance of all things, both animate and inanimate, can hardly be said to be on the same level as the finitude of an individual biological life which not only will not last forever, but will end within a fairly predictable timespan. The state might end someday, but when this day will occur is by no means clear. It is the profound uncertainty regarding *when* the state will end, and not the fact *that* the state must end, that I have mind when I refer to the political community as something that is not obviously fated to die.

39. Hannah Arendt, *The Human Condition* (Chicago: University of Chicago Press, 1958), 56, 55.

40. Jean-Jacques Rousseau, *The Social Contract*, trans. Maurice Cranston (London: Penguin, 1968), III.11 ("The Death of the Body Politic"). Of course, one might find agreement with Rousseau from Christian political thinkers and, more generally, from eschatological perspectives, but the idea of a *political* duty for a popular republic to recognize its own finitude is, to my knowledge, unique to Rousseau.

41. Cicero, *On the Commonwealth*, III.23, quoted in *Augustine: Political Writings*, trans. Michael W. Tkacz and Douglas Kries (Indianapolis: Hackett, 1994), 187.

42. Thomas Hobbes, *Leviathan*, ed. Richard Tuck (Cambridge: Cambridge University Press, 1996), Chapter 30, 232.

43. It is possible, however, for rare individuals while living to have a clear sense of their future fame. See, e.g., Nietzsche, *Ecce Homo*, in *On the Genealogy of Morals* and *Ecce Homo*, trans. Walter Kaufmann (New York: Vintage, 1989), 259; Horace, *Odes*, II.20; III.30.

44. Epicurus, *Letter to Pythocles*, in *Epicurus Reader*, §86 (my translation).

45. Horace, *Odes*, I.11.9. The broader passage of the poem only further emphasizes this: "Strain the wine; and since life is brief, cut short far-reaching hopes! Even while we speak, envious Time has sped. Seize the day, putting as little trust as may be in the morrow" (Horace, *Odes*, I.11.6–9, 33, translation slightly altered). Throughout his poetry, Horace continually urges a life lived within the short-term temporality of the day, or even hour. See *Odes*, I.9.13–14; III.8.27–28; III.29.32–45.

46. Epicurus, *Vatican Sayings*, #14.

47. I am aware that for some Epicureans the withdrawal from politics was not periodic but more permanent and that Epicurean doctrines might be interpreted to support such a position. As I hope to have made clear, however, not only can a plebeian not accept this rendering of Epicureanism (since for plebeians any not caring about politics still must be balanced by an abiding care for politics), but there are ways of interpreting Epicureanism precisely as a set of teachings that enabled, for some at least, this combination of caring and not caring.

48. Lucretius, *The Nature of Things*, V.1119; also see I.42, III.938–39, and III.962. Note as well the idea of a "pacified mind [*pacata mens*]" (V.1203), which conveys a similar idea, also on the basis of a political metaphor. For Horace, see *Epistles*, I.18.112, 376.

49. Thucydides, *History of the Peloponnesian War*, trans. C. F. Smith, 4 vols. (Cambridge, MA: Harvard University Press, 1919–1923), II.39, 326. For an insightful recent treatment of *rhathumia*, or what he calls a "relaxed way of being," and the related idea of "democratic leisure," see Richard Avramenko, *Courage: The Politics of Life and Limb* (Notre Dame, IN: University of Notre Dame Press, 2011), 87–98.

50. Plato, *Republic*, trans. G. M. A. Grube and revised by C. D. C. Reeve (Indianapolis: Hackett, 1992), 561c–d, 232 (translation slightly altered).

51. I am focusing on the Epicurean tradition—as opposed to the other main philosophical school which predominated in late republican Rome, Stoicism—both because Epicureanism seems to have been especially popular among the plebeians and, even more, because its doctrines of "living unnoticed" and "avoiding politics" make it much more directly involved in the extrapolitical kind of solace I am examining in this chapter. Nonetheless, it is important to recognize that in some respects Stoic ideas and practices mirror Epicureanism in sublimating political longings in non-political directions. In regard to the present issue, for example, it is worth pointing out that Roman Stoics themselves praised equanimity, whether an *aequo animo* or *aequanimitas*, invoking it as a salutary consequence of focusing one's ethical attention on the practice of virtue, equally accessible to all, rather than on less significant aims and goals. Seneca, "On the Lesson to Be Drawn from the Burning of Lyons," in *Epistles: Volume II*, trans. Richard M. Gummere (Cambridge, MA: Harvard University Press, 1920), 91.11–12, 438; 91.18, 444. I attend to the overlap—but also the divergences—between Stoic ideas and the extrapolitical Epicurean tradition I am detailing in this chapter in notes 56, 61, 67, and 83.

52. Epicurus, *Vatican Sayings*, #31.

53. In the same vein, Horace's Epicurean-inspired poetry continually returns to the equalizing function of human mortality and also to the argument that attunement to mortality quells human striving for political and economic success: "No hall more certainly awaits the wealthy lord than greedy Orcus' destined bourne. Why strive for more and more? For all alike doth

Earth unlock her bosom—for the poor man and for princes' sons." Horace, *Odes*, II.18.29–34, 159; also see I.28.5–6, 15–16; II.3.212–28; II.14.1–28; III.1.14–16; IV.7.21–28.

54. Horace, *Odes*, I.31.17–18, 84–85.

55. Epicurus, *Vatican Sayings*, #25. Also see Lucretius, *On the Nature of Things* V.1117–19: "But if someone would govern his life with true *ratio*, great riches for a man are to live sparingly with an equal [i.e., calm] mind [*aequo animo*]; for there is never lack of a little [*penuria parvi*]" (quoted and translated in Nichols, *Epicurean Political Philosophy*, 139).

56. The Stoics, too, taught a kind of equality that went beyond the bounds of the conventional polis: such equality inheres in the ability of all human beings, no matter what their station, to lead happy lives in accordance with reason and virtue. As Seneca put it, "Virtue closes the door to no man; it is open to all, admits all, invites all, the freeborn and the freedman, the slave and the king, and the exile; neither family nor fortune determines its choice—it is satisfied with a naked human being." Seneca, "Of Benefits," in *Moral Essays: Volume III*, trans. John W. Basore (Cambridge, MA: Harvard University Press, 1935), 161. But whereas the Stoics understand virtue and rationality usually to require civic activism, with the Epicureans the focus on an already-achieved equality challenges political ideas and commitments.

57. Epicurus, *Principal Doctrines*, #27. Also see *Vatican Sayings*, #52: "Friendship dances around the world announcing to all of us that we must wake up to blessedness."

58. On the expectation in Greek philosophy that citizens in a just polis would be friends, see, e.g., Aristotle, *Nicomachean Ethics*, trans. H. Rackham (Cambridge, MA: Harvard University Press, 1926), 1155a22-3, 1161a30-33. On the Epicurean distinction between civic friendship and what they took to be a more genuine form of friendship, see, e.g., Brown who notes how "Epicurus' conception of friendship is much more demanding than the traditional ideal of 'civic friendship'" (Brown, "Politics and Society," 182).

59. Philodemus, *Philodemi Volumina Rhetorica*, ed. Siegfried Sudhaus, 2 vols. (Leipzig: Teubner, 1902–1906), II, 158.

60. See, e.g., Epicurus, *Principal Doctrines*, #28: "The same understanding which gives us confidence that nothing terrible is eternal or even long-lasting has also enabled us to realize that security amid even these limited bad things is most easily achieved through friendship" (translation slightly altered).

61. The Stoics, too, reconceive political solidarity in a way that puts pressure on the conventional polis, but in the opposite direction: rather than praise the solidarity of intimate friendship, Stoics *widen* the scope of solidarity by invoking the notion of the *cosmopolis*. Conceiving of law in the pure sense not as the statutes emanating from specific political communities, but standards of "right reason" directing human conduct, a true commonwealth according to the Stoics is defined by common allegiance of rational beings to universal standards of justice. If this alternate conception of political solidarity was for Zeno, the first Stoic, still understood in terms of a single city-state—in which "the good alone [are] citizens and friends"—for later Stoics political solidarity is reinterpreted in cosmopolitan terms: as the cosmic city of gods and human beings throughout the world insofar as they are directed by their reason to behave virtuously and work for the welfare of all persons. See Malcolm Schofield, *The Stoic Idea of the City* (Cambridge: Cambridge University Press, 1991), 3, passim. Especially to the extent they reserved the very notion of the city for the cosmopolis of virtuous individuals committed to the betterment of the world, then, Stoics reconfigured the familiar notion of political solidarity to refer to something that transcended the experiences and practices of conventional political life. However, even if Stoic cosmopolitanism disturbs the capacity of citizenship in one's home state to monopolize one's sense of solidarity, it is still consistent with working within one's local political community to make it more just and so more capable of coexisting peacefully with foreign nations. On the compatibility of Stoic cosmopolitanism with local political action—and more generally with political engagement of various forms—see Eric Brown, "The Stoic Invention of Cosmopolitan Politics," delivered at the conference, "Cosmopolitan Politics: On the History and Future of a Controversial Idea" (Frankfurt am Main, 2006). The enduring role for civic activism within the Stoic reconceptualization of solidarity makes it less extrapolitical than the Epicurean variant.

62. On this transition, see Arnaldo Momigliano, "Freedom of Speech in Antiquity," in Philip P. Wiener, ed., *Dictionary of the History of Ideas: Studies of Selected Pivotal Ideas* (New York:

Scribner, 1973), 2:260; also see David Konstan, "Friendship, Frankness and Flattery," in John T. Fitzgerald, ed., *Friendship, Flattery, and Frankness of Speech: Studies on Friendship in the New Testament World* (Leiden: Brill, 1996), 5–19.

63. See, e.g., Maximus of Tyre, "By What Criteria Should One Distinguish Flatterer from Friend?," in *The Philosophical Orations*, trans. M. B. Trapp (Oxford: Clarendon Press, 1997), 14.7, 130–32; Plutarch, "How to Tell a Flatterer from a Friend." In *Moralia: Volume I*, trans. Frank Cole Babbitt (Cambridge, MA: Harvard University Press, 1927), 261–395.

64. David Konstan et al., "Introduction," in David Konstan, Dishkin Clay, Clarence E. Glad, Johan C. Thom, and James Ware, eds. and trans., *Philodemus: On Frank Criticism* (Atlanta: Scholars Press, 1998), 5–6.

65. Philodemus, *On Frank Criticism*, Fragment 28, 45; also see Fragments 10 and 15.

66. For the Epicurean embrace of moderate wine drinking, see Diogenes Laertius, *Lives of Eminent Philosophers*, trans. R. D. Hicks (Cambridge, MA: Harvard University Press, 1925), Vol. 2, 10.11, 10.16. For the sometime Epicurean poet Horace, embrace of wine is a perpetual theme. See, e.g., Horace, *Odes* I.7, I.9, I.18, I.20, I.27, I.38, III.12, III.17, III.19, III.21, III.25, III.29, IV.11, IV.12; *Epodes*, in *Odes and Epodes*, trans. C. E. Bennett (Cambridge, MA: Harvard University Press, 1995), IX, XIII; *Epistles*, I.5, I.19.

67. Although one certainly finds instances of the Stoic conception of free speech maintaining a political focus (as in Stoic efforts to advise rulers and lead them to correct their vices), the Stoics also model a depoliticized form of *parrhesia* where the function of free speech is less to pronounce on ongoing sociopolitical matters than to bring about moral instruction for students and other onlookers. When Arrian, for example, refers to the "thought and free speech" (*dianoia kai parrhesia*) of his Stoic teacher, Epictetus, he designates not political speech but Epictetus's public moral preaching aimed at educating followers to accept the Stoic idea that happiness and freedom are fully attainable through the practice of virtue (Epictetus, *The Discourses as Reported by Arrian, The Manual, and Fragments*, trans. W. A. Oldfather, 2 vols. (Cambridge, MA: Harvard University Press, 1925–1928) I, 4). On the Stoic development of *parrhesia* to refer to moral preaching, and thus on something dedicated to the care for the self rather than only the familiar political focus on speaking truth to power, see Michel Foucault, *The Government of Self and Others: Lectures at the Collège de France, 1982–1983*, ed. Frédéric Gros and trans. Graham Burchell (New York: Picador, 2010), 345; and Foucault, *The Hermeneutics of the Subject: Lectures at the Collège de France, 1981–1982*, ed. Frédéric Gros and trans. Graham Burchell (New York: Palgrave Macmillan, 2005), 367–68. The enduring political dimension to Stoic *parrhesia*, however, once again suggests how Epicureanism represents a more radically extrapolitical philosophy.

68. Aristotle, *Politics*, trans. H. Rackham (Cambridge, MA: Harvard University Press, 1932), 1252b; 1253a; 1275b; 1326b.

69. For self-sufficiency secured through a political regime, see Aristotle, *Nicomachean Ethics*, 1134a; *Politics*, 1321b. For self-sufficiency secured through wealth and power, see Aristotle, *Politics*, 1256b; Aristotle, *Art of Rhetoric*, trans. J. H. Freese (Cambridge, MA: Harvard University Press, 1926), 1360b5-1362a16. For self-sufficiency secured through a well-ordered marketplace, see Aristotle, *Politics*, 1257a; 1321b.

70. For exceptions, see Aristotle *Nicomachean Ethics*, 1177a27-28, 613–15, where Aristotle says, "Also the activity of contemplation will be found to possess in the highest degree the quality that is termed self-sufficiency." Further, in at least one instance Aristotle puts forward the idea of a good person who is fully self-sufficing and not in need of friendship. See Aristotle, *Eudemian Ethics*, in *Athenian Constitution, Eudemian Ethics, and Virtues and Vices*, trans. H. Rackham (Cambridge, MA: Harvard University Press, 1935), 1244b. Furthermore, Aristotle also refers to the highest good as something self-sufficient (ibid., 1097b)—which repeats a Platonic theme: see, e.g., Plato, *Philebus*, in *Statesman, Philebus, Ion*, trans. Harold North Fowler and W. R. M. Lamb (Cambridge, MA: Harvard University Press, 1925), 67a.

71. As Epicurus taught, "We believe that self-sufficiency is a great good, not in order that we might make do with a few things under all circumstances, but so that if we do not have a lot we can make do with a few, being genuinely convinced that those who least need extravagance enjoy it most; and that everything natural is easy to obtain and whatever is groundless is hard to obtain; and that simple flavors provide a pleasure equal to that of an extravagant life-style

when all pain from want is removed. And barley cakes and water provide the highest pleasure when someone in want takes them in. Therefore, becoming accustomed to simple, not extravagant, ways of life makes one completely healthy, makes man unhesitant in the face of life's necessary duties, puts us in a better condition for the times of extravagance which occasionally come along, and makes us fearless in the face of chance" (Epicurus, *Letter to Menoeceus*, §130–31). Horace repeatedly returns to the importance of frugality for leading a happy life. See *Odes*, I.31.17–20; II.16.13–20; II.18.1–14; III.29.9–12; *Satires*, I.1.92–94.

72. See, e.g., Epicurus, *Vatican Sayings*, #71: "One should bring this question to bear on all one's desires: what will happen to me if what is sought by desire is achieved, and what will happen if it is not?" Or, as Horace puts the matter, in clearly Epicurean terms, "Would it not be more profitable to ask what limit nature assigns to desires, what satisfaction she will give herself, what privation will cause her pain. . . ." (*Satires*, I.1.111–13, 27).

73. Epicurus, *Vatican Sayings*, #45.

74. Ibid., #77. On the association of *eleutheria* with the negative status of not being a slave, see Mogens Herman Hansen, "Democratic Freedom and the Concept of Freedom in Plato and Aristotle," *Greek, Roman, and Byzantine Studies* 50 (2010): 1–27. Recall, too, that Lucretius argues that political rulers normally suffer from their rule because they must sacrifice some meaningful degree of independence: those involved in politics are wise "from the mouth of others" (*alieno ex ore*), since they must wage their pursuits based on other people's ideas (*The Nature of Things*, V.1133, 231). Also see Nichols, *Epicurean Political Philosophy*, 142.

75. Epicurus, *Vatican Sayings*, #64 (translation slightly altered).

76. Ibid., #81.

77. Horace, *Odes*, III.16.17–18, 232–33.

78. Ibid., III.16.42–44, 234–35.

79. Lucretius, *The Nature of Things*, V.1431.

80. See, e.g., Zeno's invocation of *autarkeia*, in Diogenes Laertius, *Lives of Eminent Philosophers*, Vol. 2, 7.30.

81. On the role *autarkeia* in Diogenes's philosophy, see George Sarton, *Ancient Science Through the Golden Age of Greece* (Mineola, NY: Dover Publications, 2011), 585.

82. See, e.g., Democritus, Fragment 246: "Life in a foreign country teaches self-sufficiency [*autarkeia*]; for bread and bed are the sweetest cures for hunger and fatigue." *Ancilla to the Pre-Socratic Philosophers: A Complete Translation of the Fragments in Diels, Fragmente Der Vorsokratiker*, trans. Kathleen Freeman (Cambridge, MA: Harvard University Press, 1983), 113.

83. The Stoics do not find active engagement in political and economic life to be antithetical to the achievement of *autarkeia*, since the Stoic practice of virtue usually involves taking part in the sociopolitical institutions of one's community. Moreover, as the Stoic teacher Epictetus recognized, Stoic indifference to one's political and economic status cannot mean an active opposition to such concerns, as this would only emphasize rather than diminish their perceived significance: "Remember that it is not only a desire for riches and power that makes you abject and subservient to others, but also a desire for quiet and leisure, and travel and learning. For the value you place on an external object, whatever it may be, makes you subservient to another. What difference does it make, then, whether you desire to be a senator or not to be a senator? Or whether you desire to hold office or not to hold office?" Of the stoic idea of *apatheia* in particular, Epictetus taught, "Not only is office external to it, but freedom from office too." Epictetus, *The Discourses*, trans. Robin Hard (London: Everyman, 1995), IV.4.i, 248; IV.4.ii, 248; IV.4.xxiii, 250.

84. Horace, *Odes*, III.8.25–28 (emphasis added): "neglegens, ne qua populus laboret, parce privatus nimium cavere et dona praesentis cape laetus horae, linque severa." Here I follow the translation of David Ferry in Horace, *The Odes of Horace*, trans. David Ferry (New York: Farrar, Straus & Giroux, 1997), 187.

85. On the idea that Epicureanism flourished in a period of decline, see A. J. Festugière, *Epicurus and His Gods* (Cambridge, MA: Harvard University Press, 1956), ix–xi; Charles Witke, *Latin Satire* (Leiden: Brill, 1970), 4; Sarton, *Ancient Science Through the Golden Age of Greece*, 591; R. W. Sharples, *Stoics, Epicureans, and Sceptics: An Introduction to Hellenestic Philosophy*

(London: Routledge, 1996), 3. Also see Malcolm Schofield, "Epicurean and Stoic Political Thought," in Christopher Rowe and Malcolm Schofield, eds., *Cambridge History of Greek and Roman Political Thought* (Cambridge: Cambridge University Press, 2006). Relatedly, Arendt associates Epicureanism with "world alienation" and a "deep mistrust of the world." See Arendt, *The Human Condition*, 310; also see 112–13.

86. See, e.g., Miriam Griffin, "Philosophy, Politics, and Politicians at Rome," in Miriam Griffin and Jonathan Barnes, eds., *Philosophia Togata: Essays on Philosophy and Roman Society* (Oxford: Oxford University Press, 1989): 1–37.

87. Allen Ginsberg, *Howl and Other Poems* (San Francisco: City Lights Pocket, 1956), 27.

88. In Constant's famous essay on the difference between the ancients and the moderns, for example, the typical ancient citizen is described as "almost always sovereign in public affairs" and having a life comprised of "the constant exercise of political rights, the daily discussion of the affairs of the state, disagreements, confabulations, the whole entourage and movement of factions, necessary agitations . . ." (Benjamin Constant, "The Liberty of the Ancients Compared with that of the Moderns," in Biancamaria Fontana, ed., *Political Writings* (Cambridge: Cambridge University Press, 1988), 311, 314). Hannah Arendt, though clearly aware of other ethics besides activism, sometimes writes as if this were not the case: e.g.: "The chief Greek concern was to measure up to and become worthy of an immortality which surrounds men but which mortals do not possess" (Arendt, *The Human Condition*, 232). For another instance of something like the false universalization of political activism in accounts of "ancient" or "classical" political ethics, see, e.g., J. G. A. Pocock, *The Machiavellian Moment: Florentine Political Thought and the Atlantic Republican Tradition* (Princeton: Princeton University Press, 1975), 56, 203.

89. Geert Roskam, *Live Unnoticed: On the Vicissitudes of an Epicurean Doctrine* (Leiden: Brill, 2007); Fritz Wehrli, *Lathe Biosas: Studien zur Ältesten Ethik bei den Greichen* (Leipzig: B. G. Teubner, 1931); L. B. Carter, *The Quiet Athenian* (Oxford: Clarendon Press, 1986).

90. For a comprehensive account, see Carter, *The Quiet Athenian*.

91. See, e.g., Pindar, dr 193: "He who meddles in many things which don't concern him / Is a fool, when he might lead a life of *apragmon* / And free of care" (quoted in Carter, *The Quiet Athenian*, 167). Also see the figure of Ion in Euripides's *Ion*, lines 595, 621–40, as well as the figure of Odysseus in Euripides's *Philoctetes*, fragments 787N, 788N, 789N (both discussed in Carter, *The Quiet Athenian*, 28, 156–62).

92. In attending to the association of an egalitarian mindset with political indifference in Homer, Plato, and Herodotus, I draw on my essay, "Apathy: The Democratic Disease," *Philosophy & Social Criticism* 30.5–6 (2004): 745–68. The final, definitive version of this paper has been published in *Philosophy & Social Criticism* 30.5–6, September, 2004 by SAGE Publications, Ltd, all rights reserved. © Jeffrey Edward Green (doi: 10.1177/0191453704045763).

93. Homer, *Iliad*, trans. A. T. Murray and revised by William F. Wyatt (Cambridge, MA: Harvard University Press, 1999), I.490–92 (emphasis added).

94. Ibid., IX.186–89. Twice in the first four lines of his re-emergence in Book 9, Achilles is described as "being delighted" (*terpomenon*)—a clear contrast to the rage and lamentation that had characterized his initial conduct in Book 1 and, indeed, that will continue to characterize him upon his return to war and politics.

95. Ibid., IX.427; XI.784.

96. Ibid., IX.318–19.

97. Today we are no less familiar with employing the language of equality to express indifference and apathy. For example, the French expression "*Ca m'est égal,*" the German "*Das ist mir egal,*" or the English "It's all the same to me" or "It makes no difference" reveal at the colloquial level the strong tendency to express indifference as a flattening of allegedly incommensurable qualities and as an equalization of supposed differences in quantification.

98. Homer, *Iliad*, IX.200–21.

99. Ibid., IX.314 (translation slightly altered).

100. The *Iliad* itself contains an alternate expression of egalitarian thinking in which the commitment to a deep and enduring equality leads, not to political indifference, but to activism. When Zeus instructs Poseidon to refrain from engagement in the Trojan War, Poseidon initially rejects this command, claiming that he has equal honor (*homotimon*) with Zeus

and that fate has decreed to each an equal share (*isomoron*) of the world's dominions (ibid., IV.186, 209). That Poseidon ultimately obeys Zeus and, like Achilles, withdraws from the struggle at Troy does nothing to change the fact that Poseidon invokes *isomoira* as that which motivates and entitles him to participate on the public stage. Recorded history is obviously replete with other examples in which the insistence on *isomoira*, and equality more generally, has inspired an impassioned and radical brand of political activism. In Athens, for example, during the archonship of Solon, leaders of a movement to redistribute land to the poor appealed to *isomoira* not simply as an eternal metaphysical truth, but as a moral principle which demanded greater economic equality within the material world. It is this materialist conception of *isomoira* that Solon has in mind when he says that he opposed land redistribution because it did not please him "to allow the equal division [*isomoira*] of our rich fatherland among the low [*kakoi*] and high [*esthloi*] alike" (Solon, W 34, in Michael Gagarin and Paul Woodruff, eds., *Early Greek Political Thought from Homer to the Sophists* (Cambridge: Cambridge University Press, 1995), 27.

101. That Plato is a critic of Homeric epic poetry, and especially its depiction of heroes like Achilles, is well-known. But in objecting to Achilles, it is not just Achilles's bellicosity and merely martial conception of civic virtue, usually emphasized by commentators, which ignite Plato's critique. In addition, it is Achilles's alleged penchant for idle lamentation (e.g., *Republic*, 386c) as well as his refusal to fight the Trojans in Book 9—or, more precisely, his refusal to fight unless properly compensated with gifts (ibid., 390e4–391a1)—that Plato finds objectionable.

102. Ibid., 561c–d, 232.

103. Pindar, however, does refer, prior to Herodotus, to the threefold distinction between the rule of the One, the Few, and the Many. Pindar, *Pythian Odes, Olympian Odes* and *Pythian Odes*, translated by William H. Race. Cambridge, MA: Harvard University Press, 1997.

104. Herodotus, *The Persian Wars* [*Histories*], trans. A. D. Godley, 4 vols. (London: William Heinemann, 1921–1925), III.83.

105. Ibid., III.80 (my translation).

106. Ibid., III.80.

107. Gregory Vlastos, "Isonomia," *American Journal of Philology* 74 (1953): 337–66.

108. Aristotle likewise suggests that the rotation of offices through sortition stems out of a democratic wish to avoid ruling and being ruled altogether. Aristotle claims that a fundamental principle of the democratic constitution is the desire to live as one likes "and from it has come the ideal of not being ruled, not by anybody at all if possible, or at least only in turn" (Aristotle, *Politics*, 1317b.14–16).

109. Thucydides, for example, notes the tendency of party leaders engaged in factional strife to rely upon the "fair-sounding name" (*onomatos euprepous*) of isonomy or aristocracy to designate what was really democracy and oligarchy (Thucydides, *History of the Peloponnesian War*, III.82, 146).

110. See, for example, Aristotle, *The Constitution of Athens*, in Stephen Everson, ed., *The Politics and The Constitution of Athens* (Cambridge: Cambridge University Press, 1996), VIII.1, XXII.5, XLIV.4, LXI.1; Thucydides, *History of the Peloponnesian War*, II.37, II.65. Gagarin and Woodruff explain that "individual merit was undoubtedly a factor in the advance screening of candidates for selection" (*Early Greek Political Thought*, 94, note 78).

111. Aristotle, *Nicomachean Ethics*, 1133a13–31. Aristotle remarks that a political or commercial association "is not formed between two physicians, but between a physician and a farmer, and generally between persons who are different, and who may be unequal, though in that case they have to be equalized." Aristotle at once recognizes the fundamental importance of equality to the political enterprise, yet also that this equality is of a limited nature, for it depends on preserving the significance of inequality outside the realm of law.

112. Friedrich Nietzsche, *The Birth of Tragedy*, in *Basic Writings*, trans. Walter Kaufmann (New York: Modern Library, 1968), 124.

113. Horace, *Odes*, I.7.30–32. Here I follow the translation by Niall Rudd in Horace, *Odes and Epodes* (Cambridge, MA: Harvard University Press, 2004), 38–39.

114. Horace, *Odes*, IV.12.24–28 (slight alteration of Bennett translation).

WORKS CITED

Ackerman, Bruce A. *Social Justice in the Liberal State*. New Haven, CT: Yale University Press, 1981.

Ackerman, Bruce A., and Anne Alstott. *The Stakeholder Society*. New Haven, CT: Yale University Press, 1999.

Ackerman, Bruce A., and James S. Fishkin. *Deliberation Day*. New Haven, CT: Yale University Press, 2004.

Adams, John. *Discourses on Davila*. In *The Works of John Adams, Second President of the United States*, Vol. 6, edited by Charles Francis Adams. Boston: Little, Brown, 1851.

Alesina, Alberto, and Eliana La Ferrara. "Who Trusts Others?" *Journal of Public Economics* 85.2 (2002): 207–34.

Amnå, Erik. "Associations, Youth, and Political Capital Formation in Sweden: Historical Legacies and Contemporary Trends." In *State and Civil Society in Northern Europe: The Swedish Model Reconsidered*, edited by Lars Trägårdh. Oxford: Berghahn, 2007.

Anderson, Christopher J., and Pablo Beramendi. "Income, Inequality, and Electoral Participation." In *Democracy, Inequality, and Representation: A Comparative Perspective*, edited by Pablo Beramendi and Christopher J. Anderson. New York: Russell Sage Foundation, 2008.

Aquinas, Thomas. *Summa Theologiae*. Rochester, NY: The Aquinas Institute, 2012.

Arendt, Hannah. *The Human Condition*. Chicago: University of Chicago Press, 1958.

Aristotle. *Art of Rhetoric*, translated by J. H. Freese. Cambridge, MA: Harvard University Press, 1926.

Aristotle. *Athenian Constitution, Eudemian Ethics*, and *Virtues and Vices*, translated by H. Rackham. Cambridge, MA: Harvard University Press, 1935.

Aristotle. *Nicomachean Ethics*, translated by H. Rackham. Cambridge, MA: Harvard University Press, 1934.

Aristotle. *Politics*, translated by H. Rackham Cambridge, MA: Harvard University Press, 1932.

Aristotle. *The Politics* and *The Constitution of Athens*, edited by Stephen Everson. Cambridge: Cambridge University Press, 1996.

Arneson, Richard J. "Luck Egalitarianism and Prioritarianism." *Ethics* 110.2 (2000): 339–49.

Augustine. *Augustine: Political Writings*, translated by Michael W. Tkacz and Douglas Kries. Indianapolis: Hackett, 1994.

Avramenko, Richard. *Courage: The Politics of Life and Limb*. Notre Dame, IN: University of Notre Dame Press, 2011.

Bachrach, Peter, and Morton S. Baratz. *Power and Poverty: Theory and Practice*. New York: Oxford University Press, 1970.

Bacon, Francis. "Of Envy." In *The Essays*, edited by John Pritcher. London: Penguin, 1985.

Badescu, Gabriel, and Katja Neller. "Explaining Associational Involvement." In *Citizenship and Involvement in European Democracies: A Comparative Analysis*, edited by Jan W. van Deth, José R. Montero, and Anders Westholm. London: Routledge, 2007.

Baecque, Antoine de. *The Body Politic: Corporeal Metaphor in Revolutionary France, 1770–1800.* Palo Alto, CA: Stanford University Press, 1997.

Baehr, Peter. *Caesar and the Fading of the Roman World: A Study in Republicanism and Caesarism.* New Brunswick, NJ: Transaction, 1997.

Baer, Douglas. "Voluntary Association Involvement in Comparative Perspective." In *State and Civil Society in Northern Europe: The Swedish Model Reconsidered,* edited by Lars Trägårdh. Oxford: Berghahn, 2007.

Bartels, Larry M. *Unequal Democracy: The Political Economy of the New Gilded Age.* Princeton: Princeton University Press, 2008.

Bauman, Richard A. *Political Trials in Ancient Greece.* London: Routledge, 1990.

Bederman, David J. *The Classical Foundations of the American Constitution: Prevailing Wisdom.* Cambridge: Cambridge University Press, 2008.

Benhabib, Seyla. "Models of Public Space: Hannah Arendt, the Liberal Tradition, and Jurgen Habermas." In *Habermas and the Public Sphere,* edited by Craig J. Calhoun. Cambridge, MA: MIT Press, 1992.

Bennett, Stephen Earl, and David Resnick. "The Implications of Nonvoting for Democracy in the United States." *American Journal of Political Science* 34.3 (1990): 771–802.

Beramendi, Pablo, and Christopher J. Anderson. "Inequality and Democratic Representation: The Road Traveled and the Path Ahead." In *Democracy, Inequality, and Representation: A Comparative Perspective,* edited by Pablo Beramendi and Christopher J. Anderson. New York: Russell Sage Foundation, 2008.

Beramendi, Pablo, and David Rueda. "Social Democracy Constrained: Indirect Taxation in Industrialized Democracies." *British Journal of Political Science* 37.4 (2007): 619–41.

Bickford, Susan. *The Dissonance of Democracy: Listening, Conflict, and Citizenship.* Ithaca, NY: Cornell University Press, 1996.

Blaug, Ricardo. *Democracy: A Reader.* New York: Columbia University Press, 2001.

Blom, Raimo, Harri Melin, and Eero Tanskanen. "Social Inequality IV: Finnish Data." FSD 2514 International Social Survey Program, 2009. Available online: http://www.fsd.uta.fi/english/data/catalogue/FSD2514/.

Bloom, Allan. *The Closing of the American Mind: How Higher Education Has Failed Democracy and Impoverished the Souls of Today's Students.* Chicago: University of Chicago Press, 1987.

Boeckmann, Robert J., and Tom R. Tyler. "Trust, Respect, and the Psychology of Political Engagement." *Journal of Applied Social Psychology* 32.10 (2002): 2067–88.

Boesche, Roger. *The First Great Political Realist: Kautilya and His Arthashastra.* Lanham, MD: Lexington Books, 2002.

Boisvert, Raymond D. *John Dewey: Rethinking Our Time.* Albany: State University of New York Press, 1998.

Boix, Carles. *Democracy and Redistribution.* Cambridge: Cambridge University Press, 2003.

Bolotin, David. "Thucydides." In *History of Political Philosophy,* 3rd edition, edited by Leo Strauss and Joseph Cropsey. Chicago: University of Chicago Press, 1987.

Bowles, Samuel, Herbert Gintis, and Melissa Osborne Groves, eds. *Unequal Chances: Family Background and Economic Success.* Princeton: Princeton University Press, 2005.

Boyancé, Pierre. *Lucrèce et L'épicurisme.* Paris: Presses Universitaires de France, 1963.

Brady, Henry E. "An Analytic Perspective on Participatory Inequality and Income Inequality." In *Social Inequality,* edited by Kathryn M. Neckerman. New York: Russell Sage Foundation, 2004.

Brady, Henry E., Kay Lehman Schlozman, and Sidney Verba. "Prospecting for Participants: Rational Expectations and the Recruitment of Political Activists." *The American Political Science Review* 93.1 (1999): 153–68.

Breaugh, Martin. *The Plebeian Experience: A Discontinuous History of Political Freedom,* translated by Lazer Lederhendler. New York: Columbia University Press, 2013.

Broome, John. *Weighing Goods: Equality, Uncertainty, and Time.* Cambridge, MA: Basil Blackwell, 1995.

Brown, Eric. "Politics and Society." In *The Cambridge Companion to Epicureanism,* edited by James Warren. Cambridge: Cambridge University Press, 2009.

Brown, Eric. "The Stoic Invention of Cosmopolitan Politics." Delivered at the conference "Cosmopolitan Politics: On the History and Future of a Controversial Idea." Frankfurt am Main, 2006.

Brown, Gillian. *The Consent of the Governed: The Lockean Legacy in Early American Culture.* Cambridge, MA: Harvard University Press, 2001.

Burstein, Paul. "Public Opinion, Public Policy, and Democracy." In *Handbook of Politics: State and Society in Global Perspective,* edited by Kevin T. Leicht and J. Craig Jenkins. New York: Springer, 2011.

Caesar, Julius. *Civil Wars,* translated by A. G. Peskett. Cambridge, MA: Harvard University Press, 1914.

Campbell, David E. *Why We Vote: How Schools and Communities Shape Our Civic Life.* Princeton: Princeton University Press, 2006.

Carter, L. B. *The Quiet Athenian.* Oxford: Clarendon, 1986.

Censer, Jack R., and Lynn Hunt. *Liberty, Equality, Fraternity: Exploring the French Revolution.* University Park, PA: Pennsylvania State University Press, 2001.

Chandola, T., A. Britton, E. Brunner, H. Hemingway, M. Malik, M. Kumari, E. Badrick, and M. Kiyimaki. "Work Stress and Coronary Heart Disease: What Are the Mechanisms?" *European Heart Journal* 29.5 (2008): 640–48.

Christ, Matthew R. "Liturgy Avoidance and Antidosis in Classical Athens." *Transactions of the American Philological Association* 120 (1990): 147–69.

Cicero, Marcus Tullius. *Academica,* in *De Natura Deorum* and *Academica,* translated by H. Rackham. Cambridge, MA: Harvard University Press, 1933.

Cicero, Marcus Tullius. *On the Commonwealth* and *On the Laws,* edited and translated by James E. G. Zetzel. Cambridge: Cambridge University Press, 1999.

Cicero, Marcus Tullius. *On Duties,* translated by Walter Miller. Cambridge, MA: Harvard University Press, 1913.

Cicero, Marcus Tullius. *Epistulae Ad Familiares,* Vol. 2, translated by D. R. Shackleton Bailey. Cambridge: Cambridge University Press, 1977.

Cicero, Marcus Tullius. *Letters to Atticus: Volume I,* translated by D. R. Shackleton Bailey. Cambridge, MA: Harvard University Press, 1999.

Cicero, Marcus Tullius. *Letters to Atticus: Volume II,* translated by D. R. Shackleton Bailey. Cambridge, MA: Harvard University Press, 1999.

Cicero, Marcus Tullius. *The Orations of Marcus Tullius Cicero,* translated by C. D. Yonge. London: George Bell and Sons, 1875.

Cicero, Marcus Tullius. *Rhetorici Libri Duo Qui Vocantur De Inventione,* edited by Eduard Ströbel. Leipzig: Teubner, 1915.

Cicero, Marcus Tullius. *De Senectute, De Amicitia, De Divinatione,* translated by W. A. Falconer. Cambridge, MA: Harvard University Press, 1923.

Cicero, Marcus Tullius. *Tusculan Disputations,* translated by J. E. King. Cambridge, MA: Harvard University Press, 1927.

Clay, Diskin. "The Athenian Garden." In *The Cambridge Companion to Epicureanism,* edited by James Warren. Cambridge: Cambridge University Press, 2009.

Cohen, G. A. *Rescuing Justice and Equality.* Cambridge, MA: Harvard University Press, 2008.

Cohen, Joshua. *The Arc of the Moral Universe and Other Essays.* Cambridge, MA: Harvard University Press, 2010.

Cohen, Joshua. *Rousseau: A Free Community of Equals.* Oxford: Oxford University Press, 2010.

Colman, John. *Lucretius as Theorist of Political Life.* New York: Palgrave Macmillan, 2012.

Connolly, William E. *The Ethos of Pluralization.* Minneapolis: University of Minnesota, 1995.

Constant, Benjamin. "The Liberty of the Ancients Compared with that of the Moderns." In *Political Writings,* edited and translated by Biancamaria Fontana. Cambridge: Cambridge University Press, 1988.

Conway, Margaret. *Political Participation in the United States.* Washington, DC: Congressional Quarterly Press, 1986.

Cooper, David E. "Equality and Envy." *Journal of Philosophy of Education* 16.1 (1982): 35–47.

Crawford, M. H., ed. *Roman Statutes*, Vol. 1. London: Institute of Classical Studies, University of London, 1996.

Cropsey, Joseph. "Thucydides." In *History of Political Philosophy*, edited by Leo Strauss and Joseph Cropsey. Chicago: University of Chicago Press, 1987.

Crowell, Steven Galt. "Who Is the Political Actor? An Existential Phenomenological Approach." In *Phenomenology of the Political*, edited by Kevin Thompson and Lester E. Embree. Dordrecht: Kluwer, 2000.

Cusack, Thomas R., and Pablo Beramendi. "Taxing Work." *European Journal of Political Research* 45.1 (2006): 43–73.

Davies, James B., Susanna Sandström, Anthony Shorrocks, and Edward N. Wolff. "The World Distribution of Household Wealth." In *Personal Wealth from a Global Perspective*, edited by James B. Davies. Oxford: Oxford University Press, 2008.

Dewey, John. "Creative Democracy—The Task Before Us." In *The Later Works, 1925–1953*, Vol. 14, edited by Jo Ann Boydston. Carbondale: South Illinois Press, 1988.

Diogenes Laertius. *Lives of Eminent Philosophers*, Vol. 2, translated by R. D. Hicks. Cambridge, MA: Harvard University Press, 1925.

Dobson, Andrew. *Listening for Democracy: Recognition, Representation, Reconciliation.* Oxford: Oxford University Press, 2014.

Domeij, David, and Paul Klein. "Public Pensions: To What Extent Do They Account for Swedish Wealth Inequality?" *Review of Economic Dynamics* 5.3 (2002): 503–34.

Donagan, Alan. "Consistency in Rationalist Systems." In *Moral Dilemmas*, edited by Christopher W. Gowans. New York: Oxford University Press, 1986.

Doyle, William. *The Oxford History of the French Revolution.* Oxford: Clarendon Press, 1989.

Duff, David. "Abolition of Wealth Transfer Taxes: Lessons from Canada, Australia, and New Zealand." *Pittsburgh Tax Review* 3 (2005): 71–120.

Dworkin, Ronald. *Is Democracy Possible Here? Principles for a New Political Debate.* Princeton: Princeton University Press, 2006.

Dworkin, Ronald. *Justice for Hedgehogs.* Cambridge, MA: Belknap Press of Harvard University Press, 2011.

Dworkin, Ronald. "A New Map of Censorship." *Index on Censorship* 35.1 (2006). 130–33.

Dworkin, Ronald. *Sovereign Virtue: The Theory and Practice of Equality.* Cambridge, MA: Harvard University Press, 2000.

Dworkin, Ronald. *Taking Rights Seriously.* Cambridge, MA: Harvard University Press, 1977.

The Economist. "Democracy Index 2014: Democracy and Its Discontents," *The Economist* Intelligence Unit, 2015.

Edlund, Jonas, and Stefan Svallfors, "ISSP 2009—Social Inequality IV: Sweden." Umeå University, Department of Sociology, 2009. Gothenburg, Sweden: Swedish National Data Service (SND). Available online: http://snd.gu.se/en/catalogue/study/577.

Eliot, T. S. *Four Quartets.* Orlando, FL: Harcourt, 1971.

Emerson, Ralph Waldo. *Self-Reliance and Other Essays.* Mineola, NY: Dover Publications, 1993.

Enns, Peter K., and Christopher Wlezien, eds. *Who Gets Represented?* New York: Russell Sage Foundation, 2011.

Epictetus. *The Discourses*, translated by Robin Hard. London: Everyman, 1995.

Epictetus. *The Discourses as Reported by Arrian, The Manual, and Fragments*, 2 vols., translated by W. A. Oldfather. Cambridge, MA: Harvard University Press, 1925–1928.

Epicurus. *Epicurea*, edited by Hermann Usener. Cambridge: Cambridge University Press, 2010.

Epicurus, *The Epicurus Reader: Selected Writings and Testimonia*, translated and edited by Brad Inwood and L. P. Gerson. Indianapolis: Hackett, 1994.

Epstein, Joseph. *Envy.* New York: New York Public Library, 2003.

Ericson, Bengt. *Den Nya Överklassen: En Bok Om Sveriges Ekonomiska Elit.* Stockholm: Fischer & Co., 2010.

Faulks, Keith. *Political Sociology: A Critical Introduction.* New York: New York University Press, 2000.

Fearon, James. "Deliberation as Discussion." In *Deliberative Democracy*, edited by Jon Elster. Cambridge: Cambridge University Press, 1998.

Ferree, Myra Marx. *Shaping Abortion Discourse: Democracy and the Public Sphere in Germany and the United States*. Cambridge: Cambridge University Press, 2002.

Festugière, A. J. *Epicurus and His Gods*. Cambridge, MA: Harvard University Press, 1956.

Forsdyke, Sara. *Exile, Ostracism, and Democracy: The Politics of Expulsion in Ancient Greece*. Princeton: Princeton University Press, 2005.

Foucault, Michel. *The Government of Self and Others: Lectures at the Collège de France, 1982–1983*, edited by Frédéric Gros and translated by Graham Burchell. New York: Picador, 2010.

Foucault, Michel. *The Hermeneutics of the Subject: Lectures at the Collège de France, 1981–1982*, edited by Frédéric Gros and translated by Graham Burchell. New York: Palgrave Macmillan, 2005.

Frank, Jill. "Citizens, Slaves, and Foreigners: Aristotle on Human Nature." *American Political Science Review* 98.1 (2004): 91–104.

Franzese, Robert J. *Macroeconomic Policies of Developed Democracies*. Cambridge: Cambridge University Press, 2002.

Franzese, Robert J., and Jude C. Hays. "Inequality and Unemployment, Redistribution and Social Insurance, and Participation: A Theoretical Model and an Empirical System of Endogenous Equations." In *Democracy, Inequality, and Representation: A Comparative Perspective*, edited by Pablo Beramendi and Christopher J. Anderson. New York: Russell Sage Foundation, 2008.

Fraser, Steve, and Gary Gerstle, eds. *Ruling America: A History of Wealth and Power in a Democracy*. Cambridge, MA: Harvard University Press, 2005.

Freeman, Kathleen, trans. *Ancilla to the Pre-Socratic Philosophers: A Complete Translation of the Fragments in Diels, Fragmente Der Vorsokratiker*. Cambridge, MA: Harvard University Press, 1983.

Freeman, Samuel. *Justice and the Social Contract: Essays on Rawlsian Political Philosophy*. Oxford: Oxford University Press, 2007.

Freeman, Samuel. *Rawls*. London: Routledge, 2007.

Freud, Sigmund. *Group Psychology and the Analysis of the Ego*, translated by J. Strachey. New York: Liverwright, 1949.

Freud, Sigmund. *On Narcissism*. In *Collected Papers*, Vol. 4, edited by James Strachey and translated by Joan Riviere. New York: Basic Books, 1959.

Fung, Archon. *Empowered Participation: Reinventing Urban Democracy*. Princeton: Princeton University Press, 2004.

Galston, William. "Realism in Political Theory." *European Journal of Political Theory* 9.4 (2010): 385–411.

Gant, Michael M., and William Lyons. "Democratic Theory, Nonvoting, and Public Policy: The 1972–1988 Presidential Elections." *American Politics Quarterly* 21.2 (1993): 185–204.

Gagarin, Michael, and Paul Woodruff, eds. *Early Greek Political Thought from Homer to the Sophists*. Cambridge: Cambridge University Press, 1995.

Gaventa, John. *Power and Powerlessness: Quiescence and Rebellion in an Appalachian Valley*. Urbana: University of Illinois Press, 1980.

Gelzer, Matthias. *The Roman Nobility*, translated by Robin Seager. Oxford: Blackwell, 1969.

Geuss, Raymond. *Philosophy and Real Politics*. Princeton: Princeton University Press, 2008.

Geuss, Raymond. "The Politics of Managing Decline." *Theoria* 52.108 (2005): 1–12.

Gewirth, Alan. *Self-Fulfillment*. Princeton: Princeton University Press, 2009.

Gilbert, Felix. "The Humanist Concept of the Prince and the Prince of Machiavelli." *The Journal of Modern History* 11.4 (1939): 439–83.

Gilens, Martin. *Why Americans Hate Welfare: Race, Media, and the Politics of Antipoverty Policy*. Chicago: University of Chicago Press, 1999.

Gilens, Martin. *Affluence and Influence: Economic Inequality and Political Power in America*. Princeton: Princeton University Press, 2012.

Gilens, Martin, and Benjamin I. Page. "Testing Theories of American Politics: Elites, Interest Groups, and Average Citizens." *Perspectives on Politics* 12.3 (2014): 564–81.

Ginsberg, Allen. *Howl and Other Poems*. San Francisco: City Lights Pocket, 1956.

Goodin, Robert E. *Innovating Democracy: Democratic Theory and Practice After the Deliberative Turn*. Oxford: Oxford University Press, 2008.

Goodin, Robert, and John Dryzek. "Rational Participation: The Politics of Relative Power." *British Journal of Political Science* 10.3 (1980): 273–92.

Graetz, Michael J., and Ian Shapiro. *Death by a Thousand Cuts: The Fight Over Taxing Inherited Wealth*. Princeton: Princeton University Press, 2005.

Gray, John. *Isaiah Berlin*. London: Fontana Press, 1995.

Gray, John. *Two Faces of Liberalism*. New York: The New Press, 2000.

Green, Jeffrey Edward. "Apathy: The Democratic Disease." *Philosophy & Social Criticism* 30.5–6 (2004): 745–68.

Green, Jeffrey Edward. *The Eyes of the People: Democracy in an Age of Spectatorship*. Oxford: Oxford University Press, 2010.

Green, Jeffrey Edward. "Learning How Not to Be Good: A Plebeian Perspective." *The Good Society* 20.2 (2011): 184–202.

Green, Jeffrey Edward. "On the Difference Between a Pupil and a Historian of Ideas." *Journal of the Philosophy of History* 6.1 (2012): 86–112.

Green, Jeffrey Edward. "Political Theory as Both Philosophy and History: A Defense Against Methodological Militancy." *Annual Review of Political Science* 18 (2015): 425–41.

Green, Jeffrey Edward. "Three Theses on Schumpeter: Response to Mackie." *Political Theory* 38.2 (2010): 268–75.

Griffin, Miriam. "Philosophy, Politics, and Politicians at Rome." In *Philosophia Togata: Essays on Philosophy and Roman Society*, edited by Miriam Griffin and Jonathan Barnes. Oxford: Oxford University Press, 1989.

Guicciardini, Francesco. "Considerations of the *Discourses* of Niccolò Machiavelli." In *The Sweetness of Power: Machiavelli's Discourses & Guicciardini's Considerations*, edited and translated by James B. Atkinson and David Sices. Dekalb, IL: Northern Illinois University Press, 2002.

Guicciardini, Francesco. *Discorso di Logrogno*. In *Republican Realism in Renaissance Florence: Francesco Guicciardini's Discorso di Logrogno*, edited and translated by Athanasios Moulakis. Lanham, MD: Rowman & Littlefield, 1998.

Gutmann, Amy, and Dennis F. Thompson. *Why Deliberative Democracy?* Princeton: Princeton University Press, 2004.

Habermas, Jürgen. *Between Facts and Norms: Contributions to a Discourse Theory of Law and Democracy*, translated by William Rehg. Cambridge, MA: MIT Press, 1998.

Habermas, Jürgen. *Moral Consciousness and Communicative Action*, translated by Christian Lenhardt and Shierry Weber Nicholsen. Cambridge, MA: MIT Press, 1990.

Hacker, Jacob S., and Paul Pierson. *Winner-Take-All Politics: How Washington Made the Rich Richer—and Turned Its Back on the Middle Class*. New York: Simon & Schuster, 2010.

Hamilton, Alexander, James Madison, and John Jay. *The Federalist*, edited by Terrence Ball. Cambridge: Cambridge University Press, 2003.

Hansen, Mogens Herman. *The Athenian Democracy in the Age of Demosthenes: Structure, Principles, and Ideology*, translated by J. A. Cook. Oxford: Blackwell, 1991.

Hansen, Mogens Herman. "Democratic Freedom and the Concept of Freedom in Plato and Aristotle." *Greek, Roman, and Byzantine Studies* 50 (2010): 1–27.

Hare, R. M. "Moral Conflicts." In *Moral Dilemmas*, edited by Christopher W. Gowans. New York: Oxford University Press, 1986.

Harrington, James. *The Commonwealth of Oceana* and *A System of Politics*, edited by J. G. A. Pocock. Cambridge: Cambridge University Press, 1992.

Harrop, Martin, and William L. Miller. *Elections and Voters: A Comparative Introduction*. New York: New Amsterdam Books, 1987.

Hart, H. L. A. *The Concept of Law*. Oxford: Clarendon Press, 1961.

Hayek, F. A. *The Constitution of Liberty*. Chicago: University of Chicago Press, 1960.

Heater, Derek. *Citizenship: The Civic Ideal in World History, Politics and Education*. Manchester, UK: Manchester University Press, 2004.

Hedges, Chris. "Why I Am a Socialist." *Truthdig*. 29 December 2008. Available online: http://www.truthdig.com/report/item/20081229_why_i_am_a_socialist.

Hegel, Georg Wilhelm Friedrich. *The Philosophy of History*, translated by J. Sibree. New York: Dover Publications, 1956.

Heidegger, Martin. *Being and Time*, translated by John Macquarrie and Edward Robinson. New York: Harper Perennial, 2008.

Held, David. *Models of Democracy*, 3rd edition. Cambridge: Polity, 2006.

Hendricks, Frank. *Vital Democracy: A Theory of Democracy in Action*. Oxford: Oxford University Press, 2010.

Herbst, Susan. *Rude Democracy: Civility and Incivility in American Politics*. Philadelphia: Temple University Press, 2010.

Herodotus, *The Persian Wars*, 4 vols., translated by A. D. Godley. London: William Heinemann, 1921–1925.

Hesiod. *Theogony, Works and Days, Testimonia*, translated by Glenn W. Most. Cambridge, MA: Harvard University Press, 2006.

Hindness, Barry. "Citizenship and Empire." In *Sovereign Bodies: Citizens, Migrants, and States in the Postcolonial World*, edited by Thomas Blom Hansen and Finn Stepputat. Princeton: Princeton University Press, 2005.

Hobbes, Thomas. *Leviathan*, edited by Richard Tuck. Cambridge: Cambridge University Press, 1996.

Hochschild, Jennifer L. *What's Fair? American Beliefs about Distributive Justice*. Cambridge, MA: Harvard University Press, 1981.

Hölkeskamp, Karl-J. "Conquest, Competition and Consensus: Roman Expansion in Italy and the Rise of the 'Nobilitas.'" *Historia: Zeitschrift Für Alte Geschichte* 42.1 (1993): 12–39.

Homer. *Iliad*, translated by A. T. Murray and revised by William F. Wyatt. Cambridge, MA: Harvard University Press, 1999.

Horace. *Odes and Epodes*, translated by Charles E. Bennett. Cambridge, MA: Harvard University Press, 1995.

Horace. *Odes and Epodes*, translated by Niall Rudd. Cambridge, MA: Harvard University Press, 2004.

Horace. *The Odes of Horace*, translated by David Ferry. New York: Farrar, Straus & Giroux, 1997.

Horace. *Satires, Epistles, and Ars Poetica*, translated by H. R. Fairclough. Cambridge, MA: Harvard University Press, 1929.

Huckfeldt, Robert, Jeanette Morehouse Mendez, and Tracy Osborn. "Disagreement, Ambivalence, and Engagement: The Political Consequences of Heterogeneous Networks." *Political Psychology* 25.1 (2004): 65–95.

Huckfeldt, Robert, and John Sprague. "Political Parties and Electoral Mobilization: Political Structure, Social Structure, and the Party Canvass." *American Political Science Review* 86.1 (1992): 70–86.

Hume, David. "Of the Independency of Parliament." In *Hume: Political Essays*, edited by Knud Haakonssen. Cambridge: Cambridge University Press, 1994.

Huntington, Samuel P. *The Third Wave: Democratization in the Late Twentieth Century*. Norman: University of Oklahoma Press, 1991.

Husserl, Edmund. *Ideas: General Introduction to Pure Phenomenology*, translated by W. R. Boyce Gibson. New York: Collier, 1931.

Husserl, Edmund. *Logical Investigations*, translated by J. N. Findlay and revised by Dermot Moran. London: Routledge, 2001.

Hutchinson, D. S. "Introduction." In *The Epicurus Reader: Selected Writings and Testimonia*, edited and translated by Brad Inwood and L. P. Gerson. Indianapolis: Hackett, 1994.

Inwood, Brad, and L. P. Gerson, trans. *Hellenistic Philosophy: Introductory Readings*. Indianapolis: Hackett, 1997.

Jacobs, Lawrence, and Theda Skocpol, eds. *Inequality and American Democracy: What We Know and What We Need to Learn.* New York: Russell Sage Foundation, 2005.

Jefferson, Thomas. *Writings,* edited by Merrill D. Peterson. New York: Library of America, 1984.

Jones, A. H. M. *The Criminal Courts of the Roman Republic and Principate.* Oxford: Blackwell, 1992.

Jung, Hwa Hol. *Rethinking Political Theory: Essays in Phenomenology and the Study of Politics.* Athens, OH: Ohio University Press, 1993.

Juvenal, *Satires.* In *Juvenal and Persius,* translated by Susanna Morton. Cambridge, MA: Harvard University Press, 2004.

Kahane, David, Daniel Weinstock, Dominique Leydet, and Melissa Williams, eds. *Deliberative Democracy in Practice.* Vancouver: University of British Columbia Press, 2010.

Kant, Immanuel. *Grounding for the Metaphysics of Morals,* translated by James W. Ellington. Indianapolis: Hackett, 1993.

Kant, Immanuel. *The Metaphysics of Morals,* translated by Mary Gregor. Cambridge: Cambridge University Press, 1996.

Kant, Immanuel. "What Is Enlightenment?" In *Political Writings,* edited by H. S. Reiss. Cambridge: Cambridge University Press, 1991.

Karhunen, Jussi, and Matti Keloharju. "Shareowning Wealth in Finland 2000." *Liiketaloudellinen Aikakauskirja / The Finnish Journal of Business Economics* 2.1 (2001): 188–226.

Kateb, George. *Human Dignity.* Cambridge, MA: Belknap Press of Harvard University Press, 2011.

Katz, Richard S. *Democracy and Elections.* Oxford: Oxford University Press, 1997.

Kautilya, *The Arthashastra,* translated by L. N. Rangarajan. London: Penguin, 1992.

Keller, Bill, ed. *Class Matters.* New York: Times Books, 2005.

Kenworthy, Lane. "Tax Myths." *Contexts* 8.3 (2009): 28–32.

Kluegel, James R., and Eliot R. Smith. *Beliefs about Inequality: Americans' Views of What Is and What Ought to Be.* New York: A. De Gruyter, 1986.

Konstan, David. "Friendship, Frankness and Flattery." In *Friendship, Flattery, and Frankness of Speech: Studies on Friendship in the New Testament World,* edited by John T. Fitzgerald. Leiden: Brill, 1996.

Konstan, David, Diskin Clay, Clarence E. Glad, Johan C. Thom, and James Ware. "Introduction." In Philodemus, *On Frank Criticism,* edited and translated by David Konstan, Dishkin Clay, Clarence E. Glad, Johan C. Thom, and James Ware. Atlanta: Scholars Press, 1998.

Korsgaard, Christine M. *Creating the Kingdom of Ends.* Cambridge: Cambridge University Press, 1996.

Kramer, Peter D. *Listening to Prozac.* New York: Penguin, 1993.

Krugman, Paul. *The Great Unraveling: Losing Our Way in the New Century.* New York: W. W. Norton, 2003.

Kuper, H., and M. Marmot. "Job Strain, Job Demands, Decision Latitude, and Risk of Coronary Heart Disease Within the Whitehall II Study." *Journal of Epidemiology and Community Health* 57.2 (2003): 147–53.

Lane, Robert E. "Market Justice, Political Justice." *American Political Science Review* 80.2 (1986): 383–402.

Lehning, Percy B. *John Rawls: An Introduction.* Cambridge: Cambridge University Press, 2009.

Leiter, Brian. "Classical Realism." *Philosophical Issues* 24 (2001): 244–67.

Leslie, Robert J. *The Epicureanism of Titus Pomponius Atticus.* Philadelphia: College Offset Press, 1950.

Levinson, Sanford, ed. *Torture: A Collection.* Oxford: Oxford University Press, 2004.

Lijphart, Arend. "Unequal Participation: Democracy's Unresolved Dilemma." *American Political Science Review* 91.1 (1997): 1–14.

Lintott, Andrew. *The Constitution of the Roman Republic.* Oxford: Oxford University Press, 1999.

Locke, John. *Two Treatises of Government,* edited by Peter Laslett. Cambridge: Cambridge University Press, 2000.

Lucas, J. R. *The Principles of Politics.* Oxford: Clarendon Press, 1966.

Lucretius. *On the Nature of Things,* translated by William Ellery Leonard. New York: E. P. Dutton, 1916.

Lucretius. *The Nature of Things*, translated by Frank O. Copley. New York: W. W. Norton, 1977.

Lupu, Noam, and Jonas Pontusson. "The Structure of Inequality and the Politics of Redistribution." *American Political Science Review* 105.2 (2011): 316–36.

MacDowell, Douglas M. *The Law in Classical Athens*. Ithaca, NY: Cornell University Press, 1978.

MacGillivray, Erlend D. "The Popularity of Epicureanism in Late-Republic Roman Society." *Ancient World* 43.2 (2012): 151–72.

Machiavelli, Niccolò. *Discourses on Livy*, translated by Harvey C. Mansfield and Nathan Tarcov. Chicago: University of Chicago Press, 1996.

Machiavelli, Niccolò. *The Prince*, translated by Harvey C. Mansfield. Chicago: University of Chicago Press, 1998.

Machiavelli, Niccolò. *Il Principe*. Milan: Mondadori, 1986.

Machiavelli, Niccolò. *Machiavelli: The Chief Works and Others*, 3 vols., translated by Alan Gilbert. Durham, NC: Duke University Press, 1965.

Machiavelli, Niccolò. *Tutte le Opere*, edited by Mario Martelli. Firenze: Sansoni, 1971.

MacKendrick, Paul. *The Athenian Aristocracy: 399 to 31 B. C.* Cambridge, MA: Harvard University Press, 1969.

Madison, James. "Note to His Speech on the Right of Suffrage (1821)." In *The Founders' Constitution*, Vol. 1, edited by Philip B. Kurland and Ralph Lerner. Chicago: University of Chicago Press, 1987.

Maffettone, Sebastiano. *Rawls: An Introduction*. Cambridge: Polity, 2011.

Mahoney, J. Michael. *Schizophrenia: The Bearded Lady Disease*. Bloomington, IN: Author House, 2011.

Mandle, Jon. *Rawls's A Theory of Justice: An Introduction*. Cambridge: Cambridge University Press, 2009.

Manin, Bernard. *The Principles of Representative Government*. Cambridge: Cambridge University Press, 1997.

Manis, Andrew M. *A Fire You Can't Put Out: The Civil Rights Life of Birmingham's Reverend Fred Shuttlesworth*. Tuscaloosa: University of Alabama Press, 1999.

Manning, William. *The Key of Liberty: The Life and Democratic Writings of William Manning, "A Laborer," 1747–1814*, edited by Michael Merrill and Sean Wilentz. Cambridge, MA: Harvard University Press, 1993.

Manow, Philip. *In the King's Shadow: The Political Anatomy of Democratic Representation*. Cambridge: Polity, 2010.

Mantena, Karuna. "Another Realism: The Politics of Gandhian Nonviolence." *American Political Science Review* 106.2 (2012): 455–70.

Marmot, M. G., G. Rose, M. Shipley, and P. J. Hamilton. "Employment Grade and Coronary Heart Disease in British Civil Servants." *Journal of Epidemiology and Community Health* 32.4 (1978): 244–49.

Marshall, Monty G., and Benjamin R. Cole. *Global Report 2011: Conflict, Governance, and State Fragility*. Vienna, VA: Center for Systemic Peace, 2011.

Marshall, Monty G., and Benjamin R. Cole. *Global Report 2014: Conflict, Governance, and State Fragility*. Vienna, VA: Center for Systemic Peace, 2014.

Martin, Bill, and Judy Wajcman. "Understanding Class Inequality in Australia." In *Social Inequalities in Comparative Perspective*, edited by Fiona Devine and Mary Waters. Malden, MA: Blackwell, 2004.

Martines, Lauro. *Power and Imagination: City-States in Renaissance Italy*. New York: Knopf, 1979.

Maximus of Tyre. "By What Criteria Should One Distinguish Flatterer from Friend?" In *The Philosophical Orations*, translated by M. B. Trapp. Oxford: Clarendon Press, 1997.

Mayhew, David R. "Political Science and Political Philosophy: Ontological Not Normative." *PS: Political Science and Politics* 33.2 (2000): 192–93.

McCall, Leslie, and Lane Kenworthy. "Americans' Social Policy Preferences in the Era of Rising Inequality." *Perspectives on Politics* 7.3 (2009): 459–84.

McClelland, J. S. *The Crowd and the Mob: From Plato to Canetti*. London: Routledge, 2011.

McCormick, John P. "Contain the Wealthy and Patrol the Magistrates: Restoring Elite Accountability to Popular Government." *American Political Science Review* 100.2 (2006): 147–63.

McCormick, John P. *Machiavellian Democracy*. Cambridge: Cambridge University Press, 2011.

McKinnon, Catriona. "Civil Citizens." In *The Demands of Citizenship*, edited by Catriona McKinnon and Iain Hampsher-Monk. London: Continuum, 2000.

Meinecke, Friedrich. *Machiavellianism: The Doctrine of Raison d'État and Its Place in Modern History*, translated by Douglass Scott. New Brunswick, NJ: Transaction Publishers, 1998.

Michelbrach, Philip A. "Democracy as Vocation: Political Maturity in Luther and Weber." *Journal of Democratic Theory* 1.4 (2011): 1–33.

Milbrath, Lester W., and Madan Lal Goel. *Political Participation: How and Why Do People Get Involved in Politics?*, 2nd edition. Chicago: Rand McNally, 1977.

Mill, John Stuart. *On Liberty and Other Essays*, edited by John Gray. Oxford: Oxford University Press, 1998.

Millar, Fergus. *The Crowd in Rome in the Late Republic*. Ann Arbor: University of Michigan Press, 2002.

Millar, Fergus. "The Political Character of the Classical Roman Republic, 200–151 B.C." *Journal of Roman Studies* 74 (1984): 1–19.

Millar, Fergus. *The Roman Republic in Political Thought*. Hanover, NH: University Press of New England, 2002.

Minogue, Kenneth. *The Servile Mind: How Democracy Erodes the Moral Life*. New York: Encounter, 2010.

Molho, Anthony, Kurt A. Raaflaub, and Julia Emlen, eds. *City States in Classical Antiquity and Medieval Italy*. Ann Arbor: University of Michigan Press, 1991.

Momigliano, Arnaldo. "Freedom of Speech in Antiquity." In *Dictionary of the History of Ideas: Studies of Selected Pivotal Ideas*, edited by Philip P. Wiener. New York: Scribner, 1973.

Momigliano, Arnaldo. "Review of Farrington's *Science and Politics in the Ancient World*." *Journal of Roman Studies* 31 (1941): 149–57.

Montesquieu. *Considerations on the Causes of the Greatness of the Romans and Their Decline*, translated by David Lowenthal. Indianapolis: Hackett, 1999.

Montesquieu. *The Spirit of the Laws*, translated by Anne M. Cohler, Basia Carolyn Miller, and Harold Samuel Stone. Cambridge: Cambridge University Press, 1989.

Mora, Gonzalo Fernández de la, and Antonio de Nicolas. *Egalitarian Envy: The Political Foundations of Social Justice*. Oxford: Oxford University Press, 1987.

More, Thomas. In *The Complete Works of St. Thomas More*, edited by Edward Surtz and J. H. Hexter. New Haven, CT: Yale University Press, 1965.

Morstein-Marx, Robert. *Mass Oratory and Political Power in the Late Roman Republic*. Cambridge: Cambridge University Press, 2004.

Mouffe, Chantal. "Deliberative Democracy or Agonistic Pluralism?" *Social Research* 66.3 (1999): 745–58.

Mouffe, Chantal. *The Democratic Paradox*. London: Verso, 2000.

Mouritsen, Henrik. *Plebs and Politics in the Late Roman Republic*. Cambridge: Cambridge University Press, 2001.

Mueller, Nora, Sandra Buchholz, and Hans-Peter Blossfeld. "Wealth Inequality in Europe and the Delusive Egalitarianism of Scandinavian Countries," MPRA Paper 35307. University Library of Munich, Germany, 2011.

Nelson, Eric. *The Greek Tradition in Republican Thought*. Cambridge: Cambridge University Press, 2004.

Nicgorski, Walter. "Cicero, Citizenship, and the Epicurean Temptation." In *Cultivating Citizens: Soulcraft and Citizenship in Contemporary America*, edited by Dwight D. Allman and Michael D. Beaty. Lanham: Lexington Books, 2002.

Nichols, James H. *Epicurean Political Philosophy: The De Rerum Natura of Lucretius*. Ithaca, NY: Cornell University Press, 1976.

Nicolet, Claude. "Le cens sénatorial sous la République et sous Auguste." *Journal of Roman Studies* 66 (1976): 20–38.

Nicolet, Claude. *The World of the Citizen in Republican Rome*, translated by P. S. Falla. Berkeley: University of California, 1980.

Niebuhr, Reinhold. *Moral Man and Immoral Society: A Study in Ethics and Politics*. Louisville, KY: Westminster John Knox Press, 2013.

Nielsen, Kai. "There Is No Dilemma of Dirty Hands." In *Cruelty and Deception: The Controversy over Dirty Hands in Public Life*, edited by Paul Rynard and David P. Shugarman. Toronto: University of Toronto Press, 2000.

Nietzsche, Friedrich. *Beyond Good and Evil: Prelude to a Philosophy of the Future*, translated by Walter Kaufmann. New York: Vintage, 1966.

Nietzsche, Friedrich. *The Birth of Tragedy*. In *Basic Writings of Nietzsche*, translated by Walter Kaufmann. New York: Modern Library, 1968.

Nietzsche, Friedrich. *On the Genealogy of Morals* and *Ecce Homo*, translated by Walter Kaufmann. New York: Vintage, 1969.

Nietzsche. Friedrich. *On the Advantage and Disadvantage of History for Life*, translated by Peter Preuss. Indianapolis: Hackettt, 1980.

Nietzsche, Friedrich. *Twilight of the Idols*, in *Twilight of the Idols/The Anti-Christ*, translated by R. J. Hollingdale. London: Penguin, 1990.

Norman, Richard. "Equality, Envy, and the Sense of Justice." *Journal of Applied Philosophy* 19.1 (2002): 43–53.

Norris, Pippa. *Democratic Phoenix: Reinventing Political Activism*. Cambridge: Cambridge University Press, 2002.

Nozick, Robert. *Anarchy, State, and Utopia*. New York: Basic Books, 1974.

Nussbaum, Martha C. *Frontiers of Justice: Disability, Nationality, Species Membership*. Cambridge, MA: Harvard University Press, 2006.

Nussbaum, Martha C. *Hiding from Humanity: Disgust, Shame, and the Law*. Princeton: Princeton University Press, 2004.

Nussbaum, Martha C. *Sex and Social Justice*. New York: Oxford University Press, 1999.

Ober, Josiah. *The Athenian Revolution: Essays on Ancient Greek Democracy and Political Theory*. Princeton: Princeton University Press, 1996.

Ober, Josiah. *Mass and Elite in Democratic Athens: Rhetoric, Ideology, and the Power of the People*. Princeton: Princeton University Press, 1989.

Oliver, Eric J. *Democracy in Suburbia*. Princeton: Princeton University Press, 2001.

O'Neill, Peter. "Going Round in Circles: Popular Speech in Ancient Rome." *Classical Antiquity* 22.1 (2003): 135–76.

O'Neill, Martin, and Thad Williamson, eds. *Property-Owning Democracy: Rawls and Beyond*. Hoboken, NJ: Wiley-Blackwell, 2014.

Oppenhuis, Erik. *Voting Behavior in Europe: A Comparative Analysis of Electoral Participation and Party Choice*. Amsterdam: Het Spinhuis, 1995.

Owen, David. *Maturity and Modernity: Nietzsche, Weber, Foucault and the Ambivalence of Reason*. London: Routledge, 1994.

Page, Benjamin I., and Lawrence R. Jacobs. *Class War?: What Americans Really Think About Economic Inequality*. Chicago: University of Chicago Press, 2009.

Palma, Giuseppe Di. *To Craft Democracies: An Essay on Democratic Transitions*. Berkeley: University of California Press, 1990.

Parel, Anthony J. *The Machiavellian Cosmos*. New Haven, CT: Yale University Press, 1992.

Parijs, Philippe Van. "Difference Principles." In *The Cambridge Companion to Rawls*, edited by Samuel Freeman. Cambridge: Cambridge University Press, 2003.

Pettit, Philip. *Republicanism: A Theory of Freedom and Government*. Oxford: Oxford University Press, 1997.

Pettit, Philip. *On the People's Terms: A Republican Theory and Model of Democracy*. Cambridge: Cambridge University Press, 2013.

Phillips, Kevin. *Wealth and Democracy: A Political History of the American Rich*. New York: Broadway Books, 2002.

Philodemus, *On Frank Criticism*, edited and translated by David Konstan, Dishkin Clay, Clarence E. Glad, Johan C. Thom, and James Ware. Atlanta: Scholars Press, 1998.

Philodemus. *Philodemi Volumina Rhetorica*, 2 vols., edited by Siegfried Sudhaus. Leipzig: Teubner, 1902–1906.

Philp, Mark. *Political Conduct*. Cambridge, MA: Harvard University Press, 2007.

Pindar. *Pythian Odes*. In *Olympian Odes* and *Pythian Odes*, translated by William H. Race. Cambridge, MA: Harvard University Press, 1997.

Plato. *The Collected Dialogues of Plato*, edited by Edith Hamilton and Huntington Cairns. Princeton: Princeton University Press, 1996.

Plato. *Philebus*. In *Statesman, Philebus, Ion*, translated by Harold North Fowler and W. R. M. Lamb. Cambridge, MA: Harvard University Press, 1925.

Plato. *Republic*, translated by G. M. A. Grube and revised by C. D. C. Reeve. Indianapolis: Hackett, 1992.

Plutarch, "How to Tell a Flatterer from a Friend." In *Moralia: Volume I*, translated by Frank Cole Babbitt. Cambridge, MA: Harvard University Press, 1927.

Pocock, J. G. A. "The Ideal of Citizenship Since Classical Times." In *Theorizing Citizenship*, edited by Ronald Beiner. Albany: State University of New York Press, 1995.

Pocock, J. G. A. *The Machiavellian Moment: Florentine Political Thought and the Atlantic Republican Tradition*. Princeton: Princeton University Press, 1975.

Pogge, Thomas. *John Rawls: His Life and Theory of Justice*. Oxford: Oxford University Press, 2007.

Popkin, Jeremy D. *A History of Modern France*. Upper Saddle River, NJ: Pearson, 2006.

Posner, Richard A. *Law, Pragmatism, and Democracy*. Cambridge, MA: Harvard University Press, 2003.

Przeworski, Adam. "A Minimalist Conception of Democracy: A Defense." In *Democracy's Value*, edited by Ian Shapiro and Casiano Hacker-Cordón. Cambridge: Cambridge University Press, 1999.

Pumpian-Mindlin, Eugene. "Vicissitudes of Infantile Omnipotence." *Psychoanalytic Study of the Child* (1969): 213–26.

Rampell, Catherine. "How Old Is Enough?" *The New York Times*, 14 November, 2009.

Rancière, Jacques. *Disagreement: Politics and Philosophy*, translated by Julie Rose. Minneapolis: University of Minnesota, 1999.

Rawls, John. "Constitutional Liberty and the Concept of Justice." In *John Rawls: Collected Papers*, edited by Samuel Freeman. Cambridge, MA: Harvard University Press, 2001.

Rawls, John. "Distributive Justice." In *John Rawls: Collected Papers*, edited by Samuel Freeman. Cambridge, MA: Harvard University Press, 2001.

Rawls, John. "Distributive Justice: Some Addenda." In *John Rawls: Collected Papers*, edited by Samuel Freeman. Cambridge, MA: Harvard University Press, 2001.

Rawls, John. "Justice as Fairness." In *John Rawls: Collected Papers*, edited by Samuel Freeman. Cambridge, MA: Harvard University Press, 2001.

Rawls, John. *Justice as Fairness: A Restatement*, edited by Erin Kelly. Cambridge, MA: Belknap Press of Harvard University Press, 2001.

Rawls, John. "Justice as Reciprocity." In *John Rawls: Collected Papers*, edited by Samuel Freeman. Cambridge, MA: Harvard University Press, 2001.

Rawls, John. "The Justification of Civil Disobedience." In *John Rawls: Collected Papers*, edited by Samuel Freeman. Cambridge, MA: Harvard University Press, 2001.

Rawls, John. "A Kantian Conception of Equality." In *John Rawls: Collected Papers*, edited by Samuel Freeman. Cambridge, MA: Harvard University Press, 2001.

Rawls, John. *Lectures on the History of Moral Philosophy*, edited by Barbara Herman. Cambridge, MA: Harvard University Press, 2000.

Rawls, John. *Political Liberalism*. New York: Columbia University Press, 1993.

Rawls, John. "The Sense of Justice." In *John Rawls: Collected Papers*, edited by Samuel Freeman. Cambridge, MA: Harvard University Press, 2001.

Rawls, John. *A Theory of Justice.* Cambridge, MA: Belknap Press of Harvard University Press, 1971.

Rawls, John. *A Theory of Justice: Revised Edition.* Cambridge, MA: Belknap Press of Harvard University Press, 1999.

Rehfeld, Andrew. "The Child as Democratic Citizen." *The Annals of the American Academy of Political and Social Science* 633.1 (2011): 141–66.

Richard, Carl J. *The Founders and the Classics: Greece, Rome, and the American Enlightenment.* Cambridge, MA: Harvard University Press, 1994.

Roberts, Jennifer Tolbert. *Athens on Trial: The Antidemocratic Tradition in Western Thought.* Princeton: Princeton University Press, 1994.

Roller, Edeltraud, and Tatjana Rudi. "Explaining Level and Equality of Political Participation: The Role of Social Capital, Socioeconomic Modernity, and Political Institutions." In *Social Capital in Europe: Similarity of Countries and Diversity of People? Multi-Level Analyses of the European Social Survey 2002,* edited by Heiner Meulemann. Leiden: Brill, 2008.

Rosen, Michael. *Dignity: Its History and Meaning.* Cambridge, MA: Harvard University Press, 2012.

Rosenstone, Steven J., and John Mark Hansen. *Mobilization, Participation, and Democracy in America.* New York: Longman, 1993.

Roskam, Geert. *Live Unnoticed: On the Vicissitudes of an Epicurean Doctrine.* Leiden: Brill, 2007.

Rousseau, Jean-Jacques. *The Social Contract,* translated by Maurice Cranston. London: Penguin, 1968.

Sacks, Peter. *Tearing Down the Gates: Confronting the Class Divide in American Education.* Berkeley: University of California Press, 2007.

Saez, Emmanuel, and Gabriel Zucman. "Wealth Inequality in the United States since 1913: Evidence from Capitalized Income Tax Data." National Bureau of Economic Research, Working Paper 20625 (2014). Available online: http://gabriel-zucman.eu/files/SaezZucman2014.pdf.

Salkever, Stephen G. *Finding the Mean: Theory and Practice in Aristotelian Political Philosophy.* Princeton: Princeton University Press, 1990.

Sallust. *The War with Catiline* and *The War with Jugurtha,* translated by J. C. Rolfe and revised by John T. Ramsey. Cambridge, MA: Harvard University Press, 2013.

Salmon, Felix. "Swedish Inequality Datapoint of the Day." *Reuters Analysis & Opinion.* 25 March 2011. Full link available at: http://blogs.reuters.com/felix-salmon/2011/03/25/swedish-inequality-datapoint-of-the-day/.

Sandel, Michael J. *What Money Can't Buy: The Moral Limits of Markets.* New York: Farrar, Straus and Giroux, 2012.

Sarton, George. *Ancient Science Through the Golden Age of Greece.* Mineola, NY: Dover Publications, 2011.

Schattschneider, E. E. *The Semisovereign People: A Realist's View of Democracy in America.* New York: Holt, Rinehart and Winston, 1960.

Schattschneider, E. E. *Two Hundred Million People in Search of a Government.* New York: Holt, Rinehart and Winston, 1969.

Scheffler, Samuel. "What Is Egalitarianism?" *Philosophy & Public Affairs* 31.1 (2003): 5–39.

Scherer, Matthew. "Saint John: The Miracle of Secular Reason." In *Political Theologies: Public Religions in a Post-Secular World,* edited by Hent de Vries and Lawrence E. Sullivan. New York: Fordham University Press, 2006.

Scheuerman, William E. *The Realist Case for Global Reform.* Cambridge: Polity, 2011.

Scheve, Kenneth, and David Stasavage. "Democracy, War, and Wealth: Lessons from Two Centuries of Inheritance Taxation." *American Political Science Review* 106.1 (2012): 81–102.

Schlozman, Kay Lehman, Benjamin I. Page, Sidney Verba, and Morris P. Fiorina. "Inequalities of Political Voice." In *Inequality and American Democracy: What We Know and What We Need to Learn,* edited by Lawrence R. Jacobs and Theda Skocpol. New York: Russell Sage Foundation, 2005.

Schlozman, Kay Lehman, Sidney Verba, and Henry E. Brady. *The Unheavenly Chorus: Unequal Political Voice and the Broken Promise of American Democracy.* Princeton: Princeton University Press, 2012.

Schmitt, Carl. *The Concept of the Political*, translated by George Schwab. Chicago: University of Chicago Press, 1996.

Schmitt, Richard. "Phenomenology." In *The Encyclopedia of Philosophy*, edited by Paul Edwards. New York: Macmillan, 1967.

Schoeck, Helmut. *Envy: A Theory of Social Behavior*. New York: Harcourt, Brace & World, 1969.

Schofield, Malcolm. "Epicurean and Stoic Political Thought." In *The Cambridge History of Greek and Roman Political Thought*, edited by Christopher Rowe and Malcolm Schofield. Cambridge: Cambridge University Press, 2006.

Schofield, Malcolm. "*Euboulia* in the *Iliad*." *Classical Quarterly* 36.01 (1986): 6–31.

Schofield, Malcolm. *The Stoic Idea of the City*. Cambridge: Cambridge University Press, 1991.

Schrag, Francis. "Children and Democracy: Theory and Policy." *Politics, Philosophy & Economics* 3.3 (2004): 365–79.

Schrag, Francis. "The Child's Status in the Democratic State." *Political Theory* 3.4 (1975): 441–57.

Sedley, David. "Epicureanism in the Roman Republic." In *The Cambridge Companion to Epicureanism*, edited by James Warren. Cambridge: Cambridge University Press, 2009.

Sen, Amartya. *The Idea of Justice*. Cambridge, MA: Belknap Press of Harvard University Press, 2009.

Seneca, Lucius Annaeus. *Epistles: Volume II*, translated by Richard M. Gummere. Cambridge, MA: Harvard University Press, 1920.

Seneca, Lucius Annaeus. *Moral Essays*, 3 vols., translated by John W. Basore. Cambridge, MA: Harvard University Press, 1928–1935.

Shaffer, Stephen D. "Policy Differences Between Voters and Non-Voters in American Elections." *The Western Political Quarterly* 35.4 (1982): 496–510.

Shapiro, Ian. *The Real World of Democratic Theory*. Princeton: Princeton University Press, 2011.

Sharples, R. W. *Stoics, Epicureans, and Sceptics: An Introduction to Hellenistic Philosophy*. London: Routledge, 1996.

Shils, Edward. *The Virtue of Civility*. Indianapolis: Liberty Fund, 1997.

Simmons, A. John. "Ideal and Nonideal Theory." *Philosophy & Public Affairs* 38.1 (2010): 5–36.

Skinner, Quentin. *The Foundations of Modern Political Thought*. Cambridge: Cambridge University Press, 1978.

Smith, Adam. *The Theory of Moral Sentiments*. London: Penguin, 2010.

Smith, Philip D. *The Virtue of Civility in the Practice of Politics*. Lanham, MD: University Press of America, 2002.

Smith, Rogers M. "Differentiated Citizenship and the Tasks of Reconstructing the Commercial Republic." *Journal of Social Philosophy* 41.2 (2010): 214–22.

Smith, William. "Tribunus." In *Dictionary of Greek and Roman Antiquities*. Boston: Longwood Press, 1977.

Solt, Frederick. "Civics or Structure? Revisiting the Origins of Democratic Quality in the Italian Regions." *British Journal of Political Science* 34.1 (2004): 123–35.

Solt, Frederick. "Economic Inequality and Democratic Political Engagement." *American Journal of Political Science* 52.1 (2008): 48–60.

Spragens, Thomas A. *Civic Liberalism: Reflections on Our Democratic Ideals*. Lanham, MD: Rowman & Littlefield, 1999.

Stimson, James. "Perspectives on Representation: Asking the Right Questions and Getting the Right Answers." In *The Oxford Handbook of Political Behavior*, edited by Russell J. Dalton and Hans-Dieter Klingemann. New York: Oxford University Press, 2007.

Stimson, James A., Michael B. MacKuen, and Robert S. Erikson, "Dynamic Representation." *American Political Science Review* 89.3 (1995): 543–65.

Strachan, J. Cherie, and Michael R. Wolf. "Political Civility—Introduction to Political Civility." *PS: Political Science and Politics* 45.3 (2012): 401–404.

Strauss, Leo. *Thoughts on Machiavelli*. Glencoe, IL: The Free Press, 1958.

Strauss, Leo. *What Is Political Philosophy? And Other Studies*. Chicago: University of Chicago Press, 1959.

Strong, Tracy B. "Entitlement and Legitimacy: Weber and Lenin on the Problems of Leadership." In *Constitutional Government and Democracy*, edited by Fred Edlin. New York: Westview Press, 1983.

Strong, Tracy B. "Love, Passion, and Maturity: Nietzsche and Weber on Morality and Politics." In *Confronting Mass Democracy and Industrial Technology: Political and Social Theory from Nietzsche to Habermas*, edited by John P. McCormick. Durham, NC: Duke University Press, 2002.

Suetonius. *Life of Vespasian*. In *The Lives of the Caesars*, Vol. 2, translated by J. C. Rolfe. Cambridge, MA: Harvard University Press, 1914.

Sunstein, Cass R. *Republic 2.0*. Princeton: Princeton University Press, 2009.

Tacitus. *Dialogus de Oratoribus*, edited by Roland Mayer. Cambridge: Cambridge University Press, 2001.

Tacitus. *Histories: Books I–III*, translated by Clifford H. Moore. Cambridge, MA: Harvard University Press, 1925.

Tacitus. *Annals: Books IV–VI, XI–XII*, translated by John Jackson. Cambridge, MA: Harvard University Press, 1937.

Tacitus. *Histories: Books IV–V* and *Annals: Books I–III*, translated by Clifford H. Moore. Cambridge, MA: Harvard University Press, 1931.

Tacon, Judith. "Ecclesiastic *Thorubos*: Interventions, Interruptions, and Popular Involvement in the Athenian Assembly." *Greece & Rome* 48.2 (2001): 173–92.

Tan, Kok-Chor. *Justice, Institutions, and Luck: The Site, Ground, and Scope of Equality*. Oxford: Oxford University Press, 2012.

Tarnopolsky, Christina. *Prudes, Perverts, and Tyrants: Plato's Gorgias and the Politics of Shame*. Princeton: Princeton University Press, 2010.

Taylor, Lily Ross. *Roman Voting Assemblies from the Hannibalic War to the Dictatorship of Caesar*. Ann Arbor: University of Michigan Press, 1966.

Taylor, Robert S. *Reconstructing Rawls: The Kantian Foundations of Justice as Fairness*. University Park: Pennsylvania State University Press, 2011.

Temkin, Larry S. "Egalitarianism Defended." *Ethics* 113.4 (2003): 764–82.

Teorell, Jan, Mariano Torcal, and José Ramón Montero. "Political Participation: Mapping the Terrain." In *Citizenship and Involvement in European Democracies: A Comparative Analysis*, edited by Jan W. van Deth, José Ramón Montero, and Anders Westholm. London: Routledge, 2007.

Teorell, Jan, Paul Sum, and Mette Tobiasen. "Participation and Political Equality: An Assessment of Large-Scale Democracy." In *Citizenship and Involvement in European Democracies: A Comparative Analysis*, edited by Jan W. van Deth, José Ramón Montero, and Anders Westholm. London: Routledge, 2007.

Thompson, Dennis F. *Political Ethics and Public Office*. Cambridge, MA: Harvard University Press, 1987.

Thoreau, Henry David. *Walden* and *Civil Disobedience*. London: Penguin, 1986.

Thucydides, *History of the Peloponnesian War*, 4 vols., translated by C. F. Smith. Cambridge, MA: Harvard University Press, 1919–1923.

Tillich, Paul. *The Religious Situation*. New York: Meridian Books, 1967.

Tocqueville, Alexis de. *Democracy in America*, translated by Harvey C. Mansfield and Delba Winthrop. Chicago: University of Chicago Press, 2000.

Tomasi, John. *Free Market Fairness*. Princeton: Princeton University Press, 2012.

Tomlin, Patrick. "Envy, Facts and Justice: A Critique of the Treatment of Envy in Justice as Fairness." *Res Publica* 14.2 (2008): 101–16.

Trask, H. A. Scott. "William Graham Sumner: Against Democracy, Plutocracy, and Imperialism." *Journal of Libertarian Studies* 18.4 (2004): 1–27.

Unger, Roberto Mangabeira. *False Necessity: Anti-Necessitarian Social Theory in the Service of Radical Democracy*. Cambridge: Cambridge University Press, 1987.

Uslaner, Eric M., and Mitchell Brown. "Inequality, Trust, and Civic Engagement." *American Politics Research* 33.6 (2005): 868–94.

Väänänen, Ari, Aki Koskinen, Matti Joensuu, Mika Kivimäki, Jussi Vahtera, Anne Kouvonen, and Paavo Jäppinen. "Lack of Predictability at Work and Risk of Acute Myocardial Infarction: An 18-Year Prospective Study of Industrial Employees." *American Journal of Public Health* 98.12 (2008): 2264–71.

Verba, Sidney, et al. *Elites and the Idea of Equality: A Comparison of Japan, Sweden, and the United States.* Cambridge, MA: Harvard University Press, 1987.

Verba, Sidney. "Would the Dream of Political Equality Turn Out to Be a Nightmare?" *Perspectives on Politics* 1.4 (2003): 663–77.

Verba, Sidney, Kay Lehman Schlozman, and Henry E. Brady. *Voice and Equality: Civic Voluntarism in American Politics.* Cambridge, MA: Harvard University Press, 1995.

Verba, Sidney, Norman H. Nie, and Jae-on Kim. *Participation and Political Equality: A Seven-Nation Comparison.* Cambridge: Cambridge University Press, 1978.

Verkes, Robbert J., Michiel W. Hengeveld, Rose C. Van der Mast, Durk Fekkes, and Godfried M. J. Van Kempen. "Mood Correlates with Blood Serotonin, but Not with Glucose Measures in Patients with Recurrent Suicidal Behavior." *Psychiatry Research* 80.3 (1998): 239–48.

Veyne, Paul. *Bread and Circuses: Historical Sociology and Political Pluralism,* edited by Oswyn Murray and translated by Brian Pearce. London: Penguin, 1990.

Viroli, Maurizio. *From Politics to Reason of State: The Acquisition and Transformation of the Language of Politics, 1250–1600.* Cambridge: Cambridge University Press, 1992.

Vlastos, Gregory. "Isonomia." *American Journal of Philology* 74.4 (1953): 337–66.

Voice, Paul. *Rawls Explained: From Fairness to Utopia.* Chicago: Open Court, 2011.

Walcot, Peter. *Envy and the Greeks: A Study of Human Behaviour.* Warminster, UK: Aris & Phillips, 1978.

Walsh, Katherine Cramer, M. Kent Jennings, and Laura Stoker. "The Effects of Social Class Identification on Participatory Orientations Towards Government." *British Journal of Political Science* 34.3 (1999): 469–95.

Walzer, Michael. "Political Action: The Problem of Dirty Hands." *Philosophy & Public Affairs* 2.2 (1973): 160–80.

Warren, Mark E., and Hilary Pearse, eds. *Designing Deliberative Democracy: The British Columbia Citizens' Assembly.* Cambridge: Cambridge University Press, 2008.

Wasson, Ellis. *Aristocracy and the Modern World.* New York: Palgrave Macmillan, 2006.

Weber, Max. *Ancient Judaism.* New York: Free Press, 1967.

Weber, Max. "Politics as a Vocation." In *The Vocation Lectures,* translated by Rodney Livingstone. Indianapolis: Hackett, 2004.

Wehrli, Fritz. *Lathe Biosas: Studien zur Ältesten Ethik bei den Greichen.* Leipzig: Teubner, 1931.

White, Michael. "A Brief History of Heckling." *The Guardian,* 28 April, 2006.

Wilkinson, Richard. *The Impact of Inequality: How to Make Sick Societies Healthier.* New York: The New Press, 2006.

Wilkinson, Richard, and Kate Pickett. *The Spirit Level: Why More Equal Societies Almost Always Do Better.* London: Penguin, 2010.

Williams, Bernard. *In the Beginning Was the Deed: Realism and Moralism in Political Argument.* Princeton: Princeton University Press, 2005.

Williams, Bernard. *Moral Luck.* Cambridge: Cambridge University Press, 1981.

Winters, Jeffrey A. *Oligarchy.* Cambridge: Cambridge University Press, 2011.

Winters, Jeffrey A., and Benjamin I. Page. "Oligarchy in the United States?" *Perspectives on Politics* 7.4 (2009): 731–51.

Witke, Charles. *Latin Satire: The Structure of Persuasion.* Leiden: Brill, 1970.

Wolff, Jonathan. "Social Justice and Public Policy: A View from Political Philosophy." In *Social Justice and Public Policy: Seeking Fairness in Diverse Societies,* edited by Gary Craig, Tania Burchardt, and David Gordon. Bristol, UK: Policy Press, 2008.

Wolfinger, Raymond E., and Steven J. Rosenstone. *Who Votes?* New Haven, CT: Yale University Press, 1980.

Wolin, Sheldon S. "Political Theory as a Vocation." *American Political Science Review* 63.4 (1969): 1062–82.

Wright, Erik Olin. *Envisioning Real Utopias*. London: Verso, 2010.

Wyatt, Chris. *The Difference Principle Beyond Rawls*. New York: Continuum, 2012.

Yarbrough, Jean M. *American Virtues: Thomas Jefferson on the Character of a Free People*. Lawrence: University Press of Kansas, 1998.

Yavetz, Zvi. *Plebs and Princeps*. London: Oxford University Press, 1969.

Young, Robert. "Egalitarianism and Envy." *Philosophical Studies* 52.2 (1987): 261–76.

Žižek, Slavoj. *Welcome to the Desert of the Real: Five Essays on September 11 and Related Dates*. New York: Verso, 2002.

Zolo, Danilo. *Democracy and Complexity: A Realist Approach*. Cambridge: Polity, 1992.

INDEX